PSALMS FOR LIVING

PSALMS FOR LIVING

Daily Prayers, Wisdom, and Guidance

REVISED EDITION

Mark Lanier

BIG BEAR BOOKS

The hardcover first edition has been cataloged by the Library of Congress
under the ISBN 978-1-4813-0683-6.

The ISBN for the hardcover revised edition is 978-1-4813-0805-2.

The ISBN for the paperback revised edition is 978-1-4813-0806-9.

Printed in the United States of America on acid-free paper.

To Will, Nora, Ebba, Gracie, JT, Rachel, Rebecca, and Sarah

INTRODUCTION

This book is a creation from my own devotional life written to share with my children, extended family, and close friends. I dedicate it to Will, Nora, Ebba, Gracie, JT, Rachel, Rebecca, and Sarah.

For others who do not know me who may stumble across this book, I am a trial lawyer by trade, but have my training in biblical languages (Greek and Hebrew). I have spent my life translating and trying to understand and teach matters of the Bible. I am a Christian by faith for, at this point, almost forty five years

Through these decades of walking with the Lord, my private devotional time in the Psalms has pulled me deeper into faith, obedience, wisdom, and understanding. This makes many of these devotionals very personal, something which I readily confess. My prayer is that God would use my thoughts in these pages to bless others in the same way.

May our Lord pour his blessings upon your head each day!

Special Thanks

My special thanks to the godly people at Crossway, who have graciously allowed me free rights to use the English Standard Version for this project. Dane Ortlund, Lane Dennis, Nicole Gosling, Randy Jahns, and Al Fisher have been most kind in giving and securing this permission. Most every verse utilizes this marvelous translation except for a few where I dare give my own translation.

Of course I have to thank my friend of four decades, Charles Mickey, for his eagle-eye editing, his incredible grammar edits, and overall assistance and encouragement.

My final thanks go to my godly family. My spectacular wife, Becky, who is my heartbeat and best friend, served as my sounding board in this project. My children, Will, Gracie, Rachel, Rebecca, and Sarah, along with my granddaughter Ebba were my motivation for this. My parents (Mom–Carolyn; Dad–Bill, and now with the Lord) reared me to love God and seek life's answers in his word. My marvelous sisters, Kathryn and Hollie, and their husbands, Randy and Kevin, are constant encouragers. I hope that all these people will be able to identify ways they have directly or indirectly influenced the meditations on these pages.

Carey Newman and the folks at Baylor University came through in the clutch to publish this. I am deeply in their debt.

Warnings

Each day has a passage from a psalm, a narrative of reflective thought, and a short prayer. Many of the narratives are based on my own life. I don't mean to be narcissistic, but the personalization goes with the idea behind this book, which was to write my children a set of devotionals from their dad.

It is easy for me to write these as my devotional thoughts reflecting my concerns at this stage of life. I have tried, however, to reflect thoughts from earlier stages and ages as well, looking to be most fruitful to a wider range of ages. My hope is that regardless of your place in life, you will find some nourishing devotionals here. If that works, then you can pick this up as a teenager, and then pick it up again in middle age, finding something new and fresh.

Not only are these devotional thoughts, but I have also worked to make some instructive. Some of the passages mean a lot more when we understand the Hebrew poetry form in which they are written as well as the Hebrew vocabulary. So mixed into the devotionals are some times of teaching as well.

One of the drawbacks to a book like this is I have used small passages from the Psalms, and rarely use the entire psalm. To some degree that can take the Psalms out of their immediate context. I have tried to remedy that by keeping the devotional true to the context, even though that context is not given in each daily reading.

JANUARY 1

Blessed is the man who walks not in the counsel of the wicked, nor stands in the way of sinners, nor sits in the seat of scoffers; but his delight is in the law of the LORD, and on his law he meditates day and night. He is like a tree planted by streams of water that yields its fruit in its season, and its leaf does not wither. In all that he does, he prospers. The wicked are not so, but are like chaff that the wind drives away. (Ps. 1:1-4)

I love the two vivid pictures drawn in this, the very first of the Psalms. These two images set the course for the whole Psalter. First is an image of a tree full of life, placed in a thriving, vibrant location healthy, growing, and providing nourishment to others. Contrasted with the tree is the second image—chaff blown away by the wind. Chaff is the dry, scaly husk that surrounds wheat and other grains. Humans can't digest it. It is a waste product left to the wind, animals, or decay.

Which one do I want to be? Useless or useful? Giving nourishment or decaying? Treasured or ignored? That is simple. I want to be the tree!

The rest of the psalm tells me how to be the tree in very easy, simple to follow instructions:

1. Don't follow the steps of the wicked.
2. Say no to peer pressure.
3. Don't look to the ungodly to learn how to walk in this life.
4. Don't do as the ungodly do; they are not your examples. Don't talk as they talk. Don't value what they value. Don't mock what they mock.
5. Instead, delight in what God has to say. Let God's word be your inspiration, your model, your guide.

This is not a Sunday exercise at church. This is a day-in, day-out practice. It is not a chore, it is a joy! We get to receive insight into God's instructions through his word.

I am excited that God promises to train me and make me like a healthy tree, blessing others with the fruit from my life.

Lord, please instill in me the practice of communing with you through your word. Teach me, guide me, train me, and then use me to nourish others. For Jesus' sake, Amen!

JANUARY 2

Why do the nations rage and the peoples plot in vain? The kings of the earth set themselves, and the rulers take counsel together, against the LORD *and against his Anointed, saying, "Let us burst their bonds apart and cast away their cords from us." He who sits in the heavens laughs; the Lord holds them in derision.* (Ps. 2:1-4)

There are people who set themselves against God. They generally don't do it intentionally. In fact, many of them do not even acknowledge God. They find the God of the Bible too restrictive, too out-of-date, too culturally irrelevant, and too hard to believe. There are those who think it more intellectual and profound to rid themselves of this "old concept people call God," opting rather for the intellectually liberated freedom of skepticism or outright disbelief.

I have mixed responses to these people. Many of them are dear to me, and I care for them and pray for their souls. I want so badly to inform them of who God is, to meet their arguments head on, to "be the lawyer" who presents the compelling case in court for God such that everyone stops and says, "Yes, now I see! There is such a God!" Even in that, however, I recognize that these "mere people" do not change the God who is there. Their ignorance of him, even under the illusion of it being true intellectual wisdom, is not altering God one iota.

God is. This is true whether or not we acknowledge him, believe in him, or follow him. Our beliefs, or lack thereof, speak about us, not about him.

I am not saying God is not up to intellectual challenge or rigor. But I am saying he is God. We are not. Even the best of our minds are flawed, and I do not ever want my own arrogance to get in the way of a humble faith. The psalm ends, "Serve the LORD with fear, and rejoice with trembling. Kiss the Son, lest he be angry, and you perish in the way. . . . Blessed are all who take refuge in him."

Lord, may I, and may those in my realm of influence and care, always seek you for who you are, and not for who we think you should or should not be. Please remove haughty pride and any concept that we have a better grasp on truth than that revealed by you and accepted through faith. For Jesus' sake, Amen!

JANUARY 3

O LORD, how many are my foes! Many are rising against me; many are saying of my soul, there is no salvation for him in God. But you, O LORD, are a shield about me, my glory, and the lifter of my head. I cried aloud to the LORD, and he answered me from his holy hill. (Ps. 3:1-4)

Some days are filled with bright sunshine. The wind is gentle, and life is good! Other days, dark clouds fill the horizon; I am battling a war, and it is not always going well. In fact, sometimes it feels like everything and everyone are stacked against me!

I often experience a struggle between my heart and my mind. Even with my mind knowing God, my feelings can infuse me with dread that doom is around the corner. This is magnified when there are others who want me to fail (or worse). I remember one particular lawyer under whom I worked, who tried to destroy my legal career. I think he was jealous to some degree, but not so much about my legal skills. This fellow did not believe there was a God, and he found my faith particularly galling. I think he felt that if he could destroy me, he could destroy my faith, and in a sense validate and prove his own unbelief.

This psalm ministered to me then, and it is no less ministering decades later. In fact, as I now look back on it, I find its truth borne out not only in my head, but also in my heart. I can testify from the other end of time, Yes! The Lord IS a shield about me. The Lord IS my glory, I neither need nor want any other! The Lord DOES lift my head! He DOES hear my cries for help, and he DOES rescue me!

The psalmist had peace in the midst of his mess. He proclaimed, "I lay down and slept; I woke again, for the LORD sustained me" (Ps. 3:5). The dark clouds of today stand no more chance against the Lord than the dark clouds of yesterday. My God made the clouds. He is over them, and they are nothing but tools in his hands. I can confidently proclaim with the psalmist, "I will not be afraid of many thousands of people who have set themselves against me all around" (Ps. 3:6).

Lord, may you use all things today, use the good and use the bad, use those who follow you, use those who are set against you, use the easy path, and use the struggles to make me what I need to be for you and your kingdom. Shape me, Lord. Protect me in such a way that I am molded into exactly the person you call me to be to fulfill the good works you have laid out for me. For Jesus' sake, Amen!

JANUARY 4

Answer me when I call, O God of my righteousness! You have given me relief when I was in distress. Be gracious to me and hear my prayer! (Ps. 4:1)

I like to pray. I need to pray, especially in the midst of distress. Distress comes from many causes. I get distressed because of my own shortcomings. I am not who I need to be nor who I want to be. Sin is a nasty habit, and it sneaks into corners of my life I didn't even know were there! My attitudes, my self-discipline, my actions—they all betray my shortcomings and sin. Yet there is a God who relieves the distress of sin. This God is *my righteousness.* This God is not mine because I am righteous. He is the God who grants me righteousness in Jesus Christ. He makes me righteous both in a true legal sense of full forgiveness, but also in a practical sense of changing who I am daily, transforming me into the likeness of his Son (2 Cor. 3:18).

Distress also visits me because of the actions of others. It seems that many, even those with the best motives, can bring distress into my life. Turmoil is not hard to find when we live among sinful folks! Yet again with this distress, we have a God who gives relief. We have a gracious God who hears our prayers and sustains us.

Of course, distress also comes about through the world. Hurricanes destroy cities. Fires ravage homes. Economics can turn south fast. Good health is tenuous for everyone, regardless of age. Even there we can find God. He doesn't always save us from being in the fire, but he does promise to walk through the fire and bring us out the other side (Dan. 3:19-29).

God is gracious and hears our prayers of distress. This teaches me something simple: in times of distress, PRAY TO GOD! Paul taught the Philippians this same thing (I like the way *The Message* translates it): "Don't fret or worry. Instead of worrying, pray. Let petitions and praises shape your worries into prayers, letting God know your concerns. Before you know it, a sense of God's wholeness, everything coming together for good, will come and settle you down. It's wonderful what happens when Christ displaces worry at the center of your life" (Phil. 4:6-7).

Lord, I set my distresses before you. I can name them, and place them before you and your all-knowing will, your all-powerful strength, and your all-loving heart. My prayer is not that you will remove distress from me, but that you will teach me faith as you walk with me through those distresses. May I learn in real time to trust you for the end of all things, large and small. For Jesus' sake, Amen!

JANUARY 5

For you are not a God who delights in wickedness; evil may not dwell with you. The boastful shall not stand before your eyes; you hate all evildoers. You destroy those who speak lies; the Lord *abhors the bloodthirsty and deceitful man.* (Ps 5:4-6)

It should be obvious. But we get so caught up in time, so caught up in our own stories and our own feelings that sometimes we need a good reminder: sin is not a good thing. It does not breed good things. One cannot practice vice virtuously.

God didn't instruct us in his ways because no devised some arbitrary set of rules that he felt should be followed. Nor are his instructions simply what he inherited from his culture, from his parents, or from his friends.

God is a moral being. He has a morality and ethics to him, and this is what he has used to instruct us. He has hardwired his morality into us, so we inherently know some things are right and wrong. Now the heart is deceitful above all things (Jer. 17:9), so we aren't always the best barometers of right and wrong, but we are moral beings who recoil at injustice, who feel betrayed by dishonesty, who appropriately label someone crossing boundaries as an abuser.

Psalms like this serve as an important reminder that God is moral, and that morality matters. It matters to God, but it matters also to us. God's morality is what we call "good," and it produces good things in our lives. That which is anti-God, that which God is NOT, we call "evil." It includes the "big sins"—we are not to murder—but it also includes boasting and lying (in other words, all of us have a long way to go), and it produces bad things in our lives. Let us commit to living right!

Lord, I confess myself unrighteous before you. I know the difference between right and wrong, and all too often I choose the wrong rather than the right. I confess that as sin, and I seek the forgiveness that is rooted in the substitutionary sacrifice of Christ. I thank you for making my sin "right," not by some unjust mercy, but by a mercy rooted in justice and reality. Strengthen and guide me in growing more in your goodness. Through my Lord Jesus, Amen!

JANUARY 6

Be gracious to me, O Lord, for I am languishing; heal me, O Lord, for my bones are troubled. My soul also is greatly troubled. But you, O Lord—how long? (Ps. 6:2-3)

Some days these verses seem more personal than other days. The Hebrew for "languishing" is an adjective with a semantic range including "feeble" or "weak." This psalm is a cry out of weakness. It is a cry from one who is "terrified" and "disturbed" (the Hebrew that is translated "troubled").

In the dark nights of life, when fears grow, when answers seem far away, and when we are weak in heart and body, we should seek the graciousness or favor of God. I wish that when I cry to God for his gracious favor, it came immediately, like the light shining after I flip the wall switch on. However, that doesn't seem to be the case, at least not usually.

Similarly, the psalmist had to ask, "How long?" How long will God allow the circumstances that have produced the foreboding fear? How long will God allow the oppression that destroys peace and contentment? How long does trouble continue?

The palmist pushes this question with great detail to God. The psalm continues, "I am weary with my moaning; every night I flood my bed with tears; I drench my couch with my weeping" (Ps. 6:6). This was not an easy time for the writer.

By the end of the psalm, the answers have not come with changes in life's circumstances. The answers are there, but they are answers of faith. They are expressions of confidence in what God *will* do. The writer knows, "The Lord has heard my plea; the Lord accepts my prayer" (Ps. 6:9), even though it's not evident. This is our confidence in the Lord.

The young and immature part of me doesn't want this kind of life. I don't want struggles. I don't want pain. I don't want to lie awake at night worried sick. I want a nice, kind, gentle walk with God, where the weather is fine, my job works well, my family never gets sick, and utopia exists on earth. Of course, that is not reality. This is *not heaven*. This is a war zone. I am not on the other side of the Jordan. I am in the wilderness. Heaven forbid I forget that or grimace over the necessary learning pains.

Lord, I seek you in times of pain. I lay my troubled soul before you for healing and protection. I do so in faith, knowing I face nothing alone, and no trouble can separate me from the love you have for me. Give me confidence in your love and trust in your timing. May I live for you, not for an easy life. In Jesus' name, Amen!

❧ ❧ ❧

JANUARY 7

I will give to the LORD the thanks due to his righteousness, and I will sing praise to the name of the LORD, the Most High. (Ps. 7:17)

This is a marvelous proclamation: I will give thanks to the Lord. This is a choice. I can choose an attitude of gratitude or I can callously live life, disregarding the giver of all good things.

I remember the church service when I was in college and our minister Don Finto stood up in the middle of a song, stopping us mid-verse. He took the microphone from the song leader and said to us congregants, "This is a praise song. You are singing praise to God. The melody is beautiful, the words are smooth and touching, but what really counts is that you are *singing it to God.* You make a decision to praise him. You close your eyes if necessary, lift your hands if helpful, stand, sit. Heavens, you can kneel if you need to. Take whatever posture, do whatever is necessary to allow you to approach God's throne and sing this as praise to him." Don then told the song leader to start over, and I found a new layer of worship in my life.

God is called "Most High." There is no one higher. None higher in power. None higher in wisdom. None higher in patience. None higher in truth. None higher in love. None higher in caring. None higher in holiness. None higher in righteousness. God is Most High and, therefore, worthy of all praise.

So this choice I have is really a no-brainer. Why wouldn't I praise this God and give thanks to him? For as high as he is, he has stooped all the way down to my level, picking me up, and bringing me into his presence. I have a place before the Most High God, opened and secured by the sacrifice of Jesus, his Son (Heb. 10:19). That is a good thing, because when I am before the Holy God, I quickly recognize my sin. For as high as he is, I am just as low. As exalted as he is, I am debased. Yet in Christ, I am forgiven and made new. Amazing, really!

Lord, I do give thanks to you as not only the Righteous One, but the one who has made me righteous. I give praise to you and proclaim you to all as the God Most High. May this praise and worship be not only words from my lips, but the devotion of my heart that is also seen by the world in the choices and actions of my life. Through Jesus Christ crucified, Amen!

JANUARY 8

Lift up the light of your face upon us, O LORD! *You have put more joy in my heart than they have when their grain and wine abound.* (Ps. 4:6-7)

What makes you happy? Not simply in a good mood, but a deep down happiness and contentment that changes your disposition in life—what we call "joy." Many people chase it, but few find it. Some think it comes with money, and money can bring a certain level of joy (burden too, but that is another devotional!). Some think it comes from popularity, and they are willing to sacrifice a lot to gain acceptance with their peers. Some find their joy in what they consume, comfort food and drink. Some think joy comes from success, and the drive for success pushes them by the second.

But there is another joy. One that far exceeds anything offered by the world or its goods. This is a deep down happiness and contentment that comes from the "face of God" shining upon us.

This psalm echoes back from a core Old Testament blessing found in Leviticus 6:24-26: "The LORD bless you and keep you; the LORD make his face to shine upon you and be gracious to you; the LORD lift up his countenance upon you and give you peace."

When we seek God's face to shine upon us, or the light of God's face being lifted upon us, we are calling forth his blessings, his protection, and his peace. This produces in the believer great joy. The joy is unlike the enjoyment one might find from great food and drink. It's not based on anything as physical or temporary. It's not a joy that comes and goes with popularity or something else mercurial. It is not dependent on anyone, on any success, or on any condition. The blessings of God are blessings that touch deep to the heart.

When God's face is shining on us, we experience his presence. This joy of God's presence trumps everything else. To the extent joy is found in security, there could be no greater joy than being secure in the arms of Almighty God. If joy can be found in what we have or what we do, there could be no greater joy than having what we need to do what God calls us to do. God supplies all we need to do his will. This joy of God's blessings supersedes. Thank you, Lord!

Lord, lift up the light of your face upon us. In Jesus' name, Amen!

JANUARY 9

In peace I will both lie down and sleep; for you alone, O LORD, make me dwell in safety.
(Ps. 4:8)

Early in my devotional walk, I would do my devotionals at night before going to bed. I think it might have been a vestige from bedtime prayers taught me as a child. There are a number of psalms that seem to fit the bedtime prayer and devotional best. (Many fit the morning best!) This is one of those for bedtime.

I recall many times finding this psalm when procedures at work loomed large. One time I had a boss that was really hard to work for. He seemed to want me to fail rather than succeed. I think he wanted me to quit. I remember going to bed on those nights, dreading the next day. I knew I couldn't easily find a new job. I knew that each month I needed to make the mortgage payments and put food on the table for my family. If I thought about it much at all, I feared what might happen if things didn't improve.

This psalm often came up at a perfect time in my reading rotation. I loved the fact that before going to sleep, or before *trying* to go to sleep, I could deliver all of my cares and concerns to the Lord. He was bigger than my boss, bigger than my job, bigger than my responsibilities. God was not only more powerful than all I had going on; he was also *interested* in what I had happening. He was interested in me! He cared about what I cared about. He was ready and waiting for me to take my cares to him.

God had the power, and God had the interest. That was all I needed to know. Once I delivered control over to God, I could lie down and go to sleep. God was going to keep me safe, regardless of how my work was maligned. God would watch over me in the night irrespective of how I had to interact with anyone the next day. God was already prepared for the next day. The "worry" generator in my mind had no place in a walk of faith. Try as I might, I couldn't conceive of anything to worry about that would be bigger than my God could and would handle.

Now work didn't get easier overnight, but I grew in faith as I watched the awesome strong arm of my God, protect and direct me through really tough times. I write this thirty years later, and still remember the salve of prayer and trust. Of course, even with thirty years more, I still sleep at night *because God is awake and keeping me safe.*

Lord, I trust in you, 24/7, 365 days a year. I need you to protect me by day and night. Without you, I am left to the whims of others or the futility of myself as director. Please take your rightful position as Lord and God of my life. I entrust it to you. In Jesus' name, Amen!

JANUARY 10

But let all who take refuge in you rejoice; let them ever sing for joy, and spread your protection over them, that those who love your name may exult in you. For you bless the righteous, O LORD; you cover him with favor as with a shield. (Ps. 5:11-12)

I like to think about the times of the psalmist. We live in a very secure country in a very secure age. Yes, we have tragedies like 9/11 and the Oklahoma City bombing, but those pale in comparison to the days of raiding marauders, of armies performing military raids, of no police force to keep the peace, of no alarm systems or burglary patrols. It was sketchy enough that I would need a 24-hour security guard on alert just to feel safe enough to sleep at night.

There was such a service available. God was the 24-hour protector. All who took refuge in God could rejoice. They sang a song of joy, not fear. God "spread" his protection over his people the way we spread butter from one end of the toast to the other. That same God is a protector today.

In our modern age, we may seem less vulnerable, but of course that is an illusion. We still have susceptibility to disease, to the elements, to destabilized families, to difficulties at work, difficulties in social relationships, even difficulties at church! But God still protects. He spreads his protection over those who take refuge in him, bringing forth songs of joy.

Now the psalmist adds in this context that God blesses "the righteous." If we read that as a "works-based" blessing, then many of us will have to bail out because of an acute realization of our unworthiness. But I think this is something else. This is a simple fact that God teaches us righteousness because that is where we find many of his blessings. God made this world cause-and-effect. Certain sins can produce certain consequences that otherwise don't happen. I was asked by a college class where I was speaking, "If there is a God, why does he let children be born in the slums to unwed mothers strung out on drugs?" That was an easy one to answer! I explained, "Unwed mothers strung out on drugs can have sex with men and, if it occurs at the right time, the mother's egg can be fertilized and she will have a baby nine months later." God doesn't set himself as a cosmic contraceptive device limiting childbirth to those who are worthy. This is a cause-and-effect world.

So I want to take refuge in God. I want his protection. I want to sing for joy. So I will seek to live righteously before him!

Lord, please help me walk in your ways, growing in your blessings, and singing for joy. For Jesus' sake, Amen!

🌿 🌿 🌿

JANUARY 11

O LORD, our Lord, how majestic is your name in all the earth! You have set your glory above the heavens. . . . When I look at your heavens, the work of your fingers, the moon and the stars, which you have set in place, what is man that you are mindful of him, and the son of man that you care for him? Yet you have made him a little lower than the heavenly beings and crowned him with glory and honor. You have given him dominion over the works of your hands; you have put all things under his feet, all sheep and oxen, and also the beasts of the field, the birds of the heavens, and the fish of the sea, whatever passes along the paths of the seas. O LORD, our Lord, how majestic is your name in all the earth! (Ps. 8)

I met this psalm as a young boy. I became intimate with it later in college when I was translating the Psalms out of Hebrew about the same time that Christian musician Keith Green put the psalm to a moving melody, releasing it on an album I bought. I listened to (and sang!) it over and over, bringing deep into my devotional thoughts the fact that God's "name" is majestic in all the earth.

Today one's name is a label, but the Hebrew idea of "name" meant much more. One's name was their reputation. It stood for who they were and what they had done. Accordingly, the "name" of God spoke to who he was and what he had done. It was not simply an identifying label. So the psalm speaks of God's majestic name showing his glory above the heavens. The moon, the stars, and all of the heavens declare the greatness of God, as his handiwork. Therefore glorious as the heavens are, God's glory is above them.

In this sense, how little is humanity. A singular human being is small, compared to the vastness of space, something we know far better than anyone 3,000 years ago. Yet people are *not* insignificant. For the same God who fashioned the stars, made us. He tasked us with important roles over all his other creations in the animal world. We people, in our God-given roles and responsibilities also reflect the handiwork of God. For God made us, just as he made the stars, but unlike the stars, God charged us with real responsibilities. The key is that we see our abilities not as our greatness, but as the greatness of God.

Lord, as I reflect on the grandeur of the world, let it wash over me as a reflection of something far less than your true grandeur, even as it demonstrates how great you are. Lord, as I reflect on my own frailties and inadequacies, let me also see your role in making me and transforming me. In that, may I join in the psalmist's voice in proclaiming you as the majestic, great, glorious Lord. In your <u>name</u>, Amen!

❧ ❧ ❧

JANUARY 12

I will give thanks to the LORD with my whole heart; I will recount all of your wonderful deeds. I will be glad and exult in you; I will sing praise to your name, O Most High. (Ps. 9:1-2)

I'm not sure whether this psalm challenges me more during good times or bad.

During good times it is easy to give thanks to the Lord, but there is also a difficulty paying as much attention to him when times are great. It is when things are going poorly, that my focus on God becomes more focused. So, during rough times I am quicker to seek the Lord, but frequently I am pouring out my woes rather than giving thanks!

The apostle Paul seemed to have found the secret to both. He was quick to praise God and give prayers of thankfulness for things going well. In Philippians 1:3-6 he recounted to that church his frequent prayers of joyful thanks for the partnership he shared with the church in ministry. Yet in the same letter, he found reason to encourage those in the church who were worried, to lay their anxieties before the Lord in prayers of "supplication with thanksgiving" (Phil. 4:6).

So this psalm for me serves as a great reminder. Anytime I see it, regardless of how life is going at that particular moment, it is a marvelous thing to stop and be thankful to God. A genuine gratitude is called forth, not in a generic fashion of "Oh God, thank you for life's blessings," but in a very specific recounting of those blessings. I want to call out his blessings one by one.

When I was young, we sang a song in church that had a chorus calling us to "count your blessings; name them one by one. Count your blessings; see what God has done." That is an assignment worth taking up today!

Lord, thank you. Thank you for many blessings. For the comforts of home, the love of a great family, the fellowship of a devoted church, the beauty of life, the good health of today, the freedom of this country, the joys of hard fruitful labor, the protection of living under your wings, and so many more blessings. Create in me a thankful spirit and appreciative heart. Thank you for salvation in Jesus, in whom I pray, Amen!

JANUARY 13

But the LORD *sits enthroned forever; he has established his throne for justice, and he judges the world with righteousness; he judges the peoples with uprightness.* (Ps. 9:7-8)

This psalm intrigues me, scares me, humbles me, and encourages me, all in these short two verses.

The lawyer in me is intrigued. God has "established his throne for justice." Justice is consistency. It means that a crime or violation is met with the consistent or just consequence. While we no longer demand an eye for an eye, we still extract an "eye full" of Justice when the crime warrants that It is for justice, for consistency in right and wrong, that God has established his throne.

This is also what scares me. God judges the world justly. He judges the world with consistency. This is a death-producer! I have not led the kind of life that wants a just punishment from God. I have rebelled against him in my heart and deeds. At times I find myself greedy, selfish, envious, and more. I don't love my neighbor as myself. I don't seek first the kingdom of God. To quote my friend Tim Wilson who, in coming to Christ, was reading Matthew and called me upset saying, "I just read this stuff. I'm going to hell!" God judges with righteousness and uprightness. I can find that quite scary.

This is then what humbles me. I know of God's justice, so I know I need his mercy. I am unworthy of anything but a just punishment, so I do not approach him on any of my own merit. I am not so foolish to think I could ever stand before the throne for justice and survive. So I am humbled, but also encouraged.

This passage encourages me because it pushes me to my knees to cry out for God's mercy. The message of the cross is one of perfect justice and perfect mercy. God's throne demands justice, and that justice is met by the substitution of Christ on my behalf. He willingly paid the penalty of my sins so that justice is met. He did it on my behalf as an act of mercy. So in Christ Jesus, I have all the righteousness of God imputed to me. I have full and total forgiveness, not simply because God looked the other way from my sin, but because he embraced and paid the price for my sin. Justice was fully dispensed and met. I can be judged right with God by his mercy and justice combined.

Lord, thank you for the justice of Christ. Thank you for holding firm my forgiveness in Jesus. I claim his death through faith, and live to walk in your righteousness given mercifully and freely. In the name of Jesus, thank you and amen!

❧ ❧ ❧

JANUARY 14

The LORD *is a stronghold for the oppressed, a stronghold in times of trouble. And those who know your name put their trust in you, for you, O* LORD, *have not forsaken those who seek you.* (Ps. 9:9-10)

Dr. Harvey Floyd taught me to love this passage. He used it to teach a very important concept that is lost to many in our age. In the twenty-first century, names are used very much as labels. We put our names on forms, name tags, signatures attesting to letters or emails, verifying the authenticity of our agreements on contracts and more.

But 2,000 years ago a "name" meant much more. Your name was your reputation. It was an accounting of who you were and what you'd done. If your name didn't fit who you were, your name was changed. Oftentimes, mothers would name their children after events significant in the child's life (or conception or birth).

In this psalm, the claim is made that those who know God's name would put their trust in him. God's name, as expressed to Moses, was the four Hebrew consonants YHWH (Exod. 3:13-14). In most English Bibles, these four letters are translated by the word "LORD," written in all capitals but with a smaller font size for the last three letters. It is used twice in the verses by the psalmist. "*The* LORD *is a stronghold for the oppressed*" and "*you, O* LORD, *have not forsaken those who seek you.*" Sandwiched between those two usages is the claim, "*those who know your name put their trust in you.*"

The psalmist is not claiming that those who could say (or who knew) that God's name was YHWH would trust God. Rather the claim is made that those who know who God is, what he has done, his faithfulness and abiding love, will put their trust in him. This unlocks many biblical passages otherwise a bit insignificant to us. For example, the first of the Ten Commandments is not to take the Lord's "name" in vain. That is not simply an instruction against using "God" lightly in speech. It is an admonition against taking lightly *who God is and what he has done!* It is the sin committed by Israel when they grumbled against him in the desert, as if he had misled them. It is the sin I make when I worry that things are beyond his care or control. It is my sin when I think that God is not hearing my prayers or has left me high and dry.

I should know better. So should we all. As we remember and recount the deeds of the Lord, let us realize we are praising his "name," what he has done and who he is. Then as we know him for who he is, we *will*, as the psalm says, put our trust in him.

Lord, you are the name above all names, as you have done what no other could do. I worship you as God and trust you with all I have and all I am. In Jesus' name, Amen!

❧ ❧ ❧

JANUARY 15

The wicked shall return to Sheol, all the nations that forget God. For the needy shall not always be forgotten, and the hope of the poor shall not perish forever. (Ps. 9:17-18)

This is a bit of a tricky passage that is unfolded and best understood as Hebrew poetry. Hebrew poetry was not based on rhyming. Instead, the hallmark of Hebrew poetry was using phrases in some related or parallel fashion. Sometimes there are couplets with a second phrase repeating the theme of the first phrase, but in a way that highlights a further meaning. Sometimes the second phrase gives further meaning or definition by being an opposite, contrasting the first phrase.

These verses are made of four phrases (two couplets) that fold in against each other in a pattern that gives encouragement as well as exhortation in how to live. Look at the four phrases as:

1. The wicked shall return to Sheol (or the "grave")
2. All the nations that forget God
3. For the needy shall not always be forgotten
4. And the hope of the poor shall not perish forever.

There is intricate poetry at work in these four phrases. Phrase 2 modifies and explains phrase 1. Phrase 4 modifies and explains phrase 3. Yet the two couplets (phrases 1 and 2 being one couplet and phrases 3 and 4 being the second couplet) also fold into each other, so that phrases 1 and 4 relate together for meaning and phrases 2 and 3 do also.

Phrase 1 sets out the "wicked" (or "evil people") as ones destined to die. Phrase 2 gives a definition of "wicked" as those that forget God. In other words, wicked people are those who live without regard to God and what God has instructed people. Phrase 3 folds back into phrase 2 as a contrast. Phrase 2 speaks of the nations that forget God, while phrase 3 says the needy will not always be forgotten. The word "forgot" is the key that links these two phrases. It tells us that one way the wicked (phrase 1) forget God (phrase 2) is by not remembering and helping the needy (phrase 3). And while the wicked go to the grave (phrase 1), the poor's hope will not perish (phrase 4).

This artfully sets out the importance of helping those in need in a way that causes one to think through the importance and implications.

Lord, I am surrounded by those in need—physical need as well as those poor in spirit. May I be alert and seek to be godly by being your vessel to meet those needs, in Jesus' name, Amen!

❧ ❧ ❧

JANUARY 16

Arise, O LORD; O God, lift up your hand; forget not the afflicted . . . to you the helpless commits himself; you have been the helper of the fatherless. (Ps. 10:12, 14)

There was an obscure Christian band in the late 70s–early 80s named DeGarmo & Key. They had a lyric in a song entitled "Only the Meek Survive," where they said, "You say that God is a God of goodness. He only helps those who help themselves. You see I found God, he helps the helpless. And leaves all the rest to help themselves."

The song made an impression on me because I had often heard the opposite, that "God helps those who help themselves." We hear the admonition of pulling oneself up by one's bootstraps. The song lyric, however, nails a different truth that is found in the psalm: God commits himself to helping the helpless. This reveals·not only a great resource for us, but it also reveals the character of our God and his traits we need to cultivate in ourselves.

We rightly see that God wants to meet our needs. He runs to the hurt and afflicted and stands ready to be salve for their pains. We should never be bashful about taking our hurts, needs, and problems to God. God is a problem-solving God. He is in the business of helping his children. Jesus asked what father would give a stone to a child asking for bread (Matt. 7:9). Of course, if God is a problem-solving, need-meeting God, then we as his children are to put ourselves to the Father's business. In other words, we are to seek to meet the needs of the needy and be fathers to the fatherless.

Now there is also a subtle line that we find as we read through Scripture. While God helps the helpless, God does expect for people to work toward success and accomplishment. Paul relates the ideas similarly when he encouraged the Philippians to work out their salvation because God is working in us (Phil. 2:12-13). That God helps the helpless should never be a crutch for laziness or irresponsibility. It is a charge for us to work not only for what God has set before us in our own lives, but also to work to meet the needs of others. Sometimes those needs are met by pushing others to be responsible. Other times it is met by filling needs directly. We need sensitive hearts to know how to meet others' needs without enabling them in the process.

Lord, this is a struggle on several levels. First, we are a needy people who rely upon you for meeting our needs. Also, we see others in need and we want your heart to reach out and meet their needs. In the process of all this, Lord, please give us your heart to know how to truly live. Help us know when to give someone a fish and when to teach someone how to fish. Help us to find the line between enabling one to be irresponsible and giving them the help needed to live responsibly. In Jesus' name, Amen!

❧ ❧ ❧

JANUARY 17

The LORD *is king forever and ever; the nations perish from his land. O* LORD, *you hear the desire of the afflicted; you will strengthen their heart; you will incline your ear to do justice to the fatherless and the oppressed, so that man who is of the earth may strike terror no more.* (Ps. 10:16-18)

Read this passage twice. It is not an ordinary passage one might use in a devotional book, but it certainly belongs. First of all, how many kings reign forever? None but God. No earthly king lives forever, much less reigns forever. Kingdoms come and go. Nations come and go, but God God still sits enthroned. He has not gone anywhere, nor will he be gone tomorrow.

God not only is king "forever and ever," but he is an active king. He is not a king who lives to be waited on. The psalm does not tell us God as king sits around to be courted by the powerful or rich. To the contrary, God is a servant king!

God listens and hears from the afflicted. God gives audience to those in need. He hears the cries of the weak in heart and strengthens their hearts. This echoes the beatitude of Jesus, "Blessed are the poor in spirit, for theirs is the kingdom of heaven" (Matt. 5:3). Those who are afflicted belong to the kingdom of heaven where the reigning king (God) listens to them and comes to their rescue.

There are classes of people that are taken advantage of and are often defenseless in the kingdoms of earth. Classic examples are the orphans and the economically or socially oppressed. While earthly kingdoms shun, ignore, or even abuse such, not so the kingdom of heaven. God the king forever inclines his ears to give justice to those. He rescues them from the attacks of abusers.

For me this psalm is ageless. As more time moves into history, the truth of this psalm just grows. Two thousand, five hundred years after it was written, God still reigns as king. We still know of his kingdom that is not of this world (John 18:36), but has far outlasted the nations of biblical times or since. This is the king we serve. The challenge for us is to see his will done on earth as it is in his heavenly kingdom (Matt. 6:10).

Lord God our king, may your name be held holy on earth as it is in heaven. May your kingdom unfold on earth, reflecting its presence in heaven. May your will be done on earth, as your will is done in heaven. May your people rise up, may I rise up, with a heart for the fatherless, the oppressed, the afflicted. And may we be your kingdom ministering in the name of Jesus to these unfortunate people. Amen.

❧ ❧ ❧

JANUARY 18

In the Lord *I take refuge; how can you say to my soul, "Flee like a bird to your mountain, for behold, the wicked bend the bow; they have fitted their arrow to the string to shoot in the dark at the upright in heart; if the foundations are destroyed, what can the righteous do?" The* Lord *is in his holy temple; the* Lord's *throne is in heaven; his eyes see . . . .* (Ps. 11:1-4)

In life, there are always waves of trouble—troubles at school, at work, at home, and most any other place. The question is not, "Will you face trouble?" Rather, the question is, "*How* will you face trouble?"

The unbeliever can approach trouble only through personal resources. Those resources might allow one to stand and fight through the difficulty. Or if the difficulty is too great, they may cause one to flee. That was the counsel being given the psalmist in his/her day of trouble. "Flee! The wicked are about to get you!" was the message. This was no small problem. It was life or death. It was equated to wicked people loading up to shoot killing arrows at the persecuted. It was seen as life's foundations being destroyed.

I have been there. I have hit the wall at work where there seemed no way out. I have been at my wits' end trying to match expenses to income only to come up short. I have struggled to find peace in relationships that seem to foster as much peace as the Middle East. The temptation is always easy, "Flee!" But the psalmist offers something different.

The psalmist urges the reader to reason carefully with faith. Is there a crisis? Yes. Are the foundations being destroyed? It may seem that way. But we know by faith that there is a God. And that Lord is not absent or off location. He is in his heavenly temple where his eyes see. He is watching. Nothing escapes his notice. He knows and is on point. Knowing that is the first big faith step for any crisis.

A crisis should never push us to do anything less than walk in godliness before our Lord and Maker. Once we do that, we find God in the midst of the crisis or difficulty. The psalmist ended with the assurance that, "the upright shall behold his face" (Ps. 11:7). That is enough!

Lord God Almighty, we acknowledge you reigning over all that troubles our soul. We know you are bigger than any of our problems, and we know you have answers for all of them. So we seek your face in uprightness, for Jesus' sake, Amen!

❧ ❧ ❧

JANUARY 19

Save, O LORD, for the godly one is gone; for the faithful have vanished from among the children of man. Everyone utters lies to his neighbor; with flattering lips and a double heart they speak. May the LORD cut off all flattering lips, the tongue that makes great boasts, those who say, "With our tongue we will prevail, our lips are with us; who is master over us?" (Ps. 12:1-4)

This psalm scares me. I am a trial lawyer, after all. I make my living with words, and the psalm holds rebuke for those who are not very careful with their words.

Words are immensely powerful. Words can stir people to actions they might not otherwise take. Words can influence opinions and create beliefs. We use words to build up and words to bring down.

Scripture gives great power to words ("And God *said*, 'Let there be light,' and there was light"; Gen. 1:3). James compared the small tongue to the small rudder of a ship, warning, "the tongue is a small member, yet it boasts of great things. How great a forest is set ablaze by such a small fire! And the tongue is a fire, a world of unrighteousness. The tongue is set among our members, staining the whole body, setting on fire the entire course of life, and set on fire by hell" (Jas. 3:5-6). With the same tongue we can bless God and curse those made in his image. James warns the believer that, "If anyone thinks he is religious and does not bridle his tongue but deceives his heart, this person's religion is worthless" (Jas. 1:26).

So I have this tongue, and God takes what I say very seriously. Lies have no place coming from my mouth. Big lies, little lies, misrepresentations, mispainted pictures, none of these belong to me. Even flattering people to get what I want is wrong. Flattering is not the same as complimenting. Flattering is a lie for effect. A compliment is an encouraging word to build up.

I want to be meticulous. James challenges the believer to be "quick to hear," but "slow to speak" (Jas. 1:19). That is hard for me. But I am going to work on it!

Lord, give me a heart for using my tongue right before you. May I speak carefully and truthfully. May I never tear down with my words, but may I build up with genuine sincerity. Keep me from gossip, from slander, from speaking ill of others, and from using words to manipulate. Let my words be seasoned with your grace and bring your love and truth to the world around me. Through Jesus, the True Word, Amen!

❧ ❧ ❧

JANUARY 20

"Because the poor are plundered, because the needy groan, I will now arise," says the LORD; *"I will place him in the safety for which he longs." (*Ps. 12:5)

I was writing these devotionals thinking about the Lord's concern for the poor, the fatherless, the oppressed and needy. Those verses always trigger a reaction in me, I think in part because I have been blessed with super parents, blessed with resources, blessed with a committed wife and children that hold our family as dear as I do. It concerns me because God gave me these blessings not for me, but for me to use.

So it was interesting to me to have finished writing one of these devotionals on this subject when my sweet Becky came to me and told me about someone in deep need. This person wasn't asking for help, but she needed it. Badly. Becky wanted to know what I thought we should do.

I would love to say I immediately said, "Oh, no question, we help! We help as much as she needs!" knowing that this fine woman would not be taking advantage of anyone or anything we could do. In fact, taking help from us would likely be her last resort. But I wasn't so holy. Not even after writing the devotionals! There was a hesitancy in my mind that I can only describe as sinful. I thought, "Ugh!" No sooner was that thought in my mind, however, before the Scripture devotion I had just written jumped immediately into my mind and trumped the sinful hesitancy.

So with the help of these devotionals, with the encouragement of Scripture, good sense managed to trump my selfishness so I was able to give the right answer to my wife, "Of course we help however we can."

These devotionals I am writing out for others (primarily my children and family), are not a waste of time. The Psalms are important in my Christian walk, and have been for decades. In Scripture, I find the morsels that nourish me on my walk. I never cease to be amazed at the words that I have read and considered prayerfully are the very ones I need shortly thereafter. God is good.

Lord, thank you for your Word. Thank you for explaining in so many ways how we are to behave and think. Please continue to bless us with understanding. May your Spirit make the words of Scripture more than simple statements. May we absorb them as the words of life. May we act on what we read. In Jesus' name, Amen!

❧ ❧ ❧

JANUARY 21

How long, O Lord? Will you forget me forever? How long will you hide your face from me? How long must I take counsel in my soul and have sorrow in my heart all the day? How long shall my enemy be exalted over me? (Ps. 13:1-2)

There are times, even after walking with the Lord for over four decades, when I feel as if God is not answering my prayers. It's as if he is absent. My prayers seem a vain muttering of words that bounce off the ceiling. The operative word there is "feel." This feeling is not of faith, it is a doubting that must be challenged head-on by faith.

I am not alone. The psalmist wondered where his prayers were going. He wondered why it seemed the Almighty ignored him. His feelings were involved, expressed by the "sorrow" he held in his heart all day.

The psalm continues with the psalmist calling out to God. "Consider and answer me, O Lord my God; light up my eyes, lest I sleep the sleep of death" (Ps. 13:3). Feelings must be trumped by continued prayers of faith. Just because I feel my prayers are unanswered, does not mean they are in vain.

The psalmist concluded this short psalm with a proclamation of faith that trumped his feelings. "But I have trusted in your steadfast love; my heart shall rejoice in your salvation. I will sing to the Lord, because he has dealt bountifully with me" (Ps. 13:5-6).

I like this process, and have been quick to adapt it in my life. I pray to God; I lay my problems before him. When my heart is down, and I *feel* no presence of the Lord, I don't quit and I don't despair. I call out honestly to God. I ask him for his presence and answers. I ask him to trump my feelings with his reality. I then proceed to live in faith (aka "trust"). I *know* of his steadfast love, whether I *feel* it or not. I need look no further than my crucified Savior. So in faith, I can be confident, feelings will pass away, and I *will sing* to the Lord again. He has dealt bountifully with me, whether I feel it or not!

Lord, I set before you the cares and concerns of my heart. Some of my prayers have been on my list before you for years. I do not quit, Lord. I seek your answers. I need you to come to the rescue, for no one else has the ability. These are God issues I have Lord. I trust you in your steadfast love to bring answers in your timing, and I thank you for the assurance of your presence, in spite of any of my perceptions or feelings. Through my crucified Lord I pray, Amen!

❧ ❧ ❧

JANUARY 22

The fool says in his heart, "There is no God." They are corrupt, they do abominable deeds, there is none who does good. The LORD looks down from heaven on the children of man, to see if there are any who understand, who seek after God. They have all turned aside; together they have become corrupt; there is none who does good, not even one. (Ps. 14:1-3)

Most people who say, "There is no God," would be insulted at the idea of being labeled a "fool." They would argue that they are the "smart ones" for figuring out there is no God. God does not debate with these, but this psalm seems to indicate that the denial of God is not always an academic enterprise. Somewhere it surfaces from the heart. Many who deny God actually feel betrayed by him. Often you hear the refrain, "If there was a God then *ABC* would not happen."

This psalm also indicates that a disbelief in God does not end there. The disbelief affects one's behavior. Without God, there is a serious question about who or what defines morality. Is moral behavior defined by the whims and desires of the person? Does 51 percent of society get to decide what is "right" and "wrong"? Maybe the strong or the powerful, or maybe the intellectuals get to decide "right" and "wrong" for the rest of us?

To one who believes in God, "right" and "wrong" are defined by God's nature. As we grow with God, we learn right and wrong from that relationship. Not so the fool.

A "fool" in a biblical sense is not someone who is intellectually deficient or immature. There is a strong moral element in the Hebrew idea of a "fool." A fool is someone who lives in disobedience to God. In that sense, it is hard to look at humanity and find anyone who isn't a fool to some degree! Paul saw as much and used this psalm in Romans 3:10-12 to discuss the need everyone has for salvation in Christ.

As I muse on this passage, I am left with a strong reaction of wanting to seek God, know God, understand God, and faithfully obey God. I want to walk in wisdom, not foolishness, able to discern his will and obey it.

Lord, give me eyes to see you clearly. Let me rejoice in knowing you, gladly seeking obedience in all things, large and small. May I never take for granted your constant love and concern, and may I share it with others while on this journey. In Jesus' name, Amen.

❧ ❧ ❧

JANUARY 23

Oh, that salvation for Israel would come out of Zion! When the LORD restores the fortunes of his people, let Jacob rejoice, let Israel be glad. (Ps. 14:7)

For centuries, Israel expected a Messiah. God had promised through Eve to bring forth one who would make right those things corrupted in the Garden of Eden (Gen. 3:15). This promise was further defined in God's assurance that through Abraham, all the nations of the earth would be blessed (Gen. 12:3). From Abraham, the promise of lineage passed to Isaac (Gen. 17:9), Jacob, and on through Judah (Gen. 28:14), and David (2 Sam 7:12-14).

By the time of Jesus, the Jews had endured much heartache. Israel's northern tribes had been taken away and dissimulated. Those of the tribe of Judah (from which we get the term "Jews") had been conquered by the Babylonians who destroyed Jerusalem, and deported most Jews to Babylon where they stayed for generations. But this was the branch of Israel from which would come the promised Messiah. Many Jews kept their identity during this period, returning to populate the Promised Land. The temple was rebuilt, the priests resumed their roles, and the people continued to await the Messiah, even as they suffered conquests from many others.

It was while under Roman occupation that the people began to hope that a miracle-working Galilean, a carpenter by trade, might actually be the Messiah. One Sunday, Jesus came riding into Jerusalem on a donkey, a sign of conquest, and the people laid palm branches in his path shouting "Hosanna!" This Aramaic phrase means, "We pray for you to save us!" The people wanted Jesus to be their savior. They wanted him to be Judah's king. They wanted an overthrow of Roman occupation. They wanted an earthly Messiah. As the psalmist wrote, they wanted the Lord to restore their fortunes, rejoicing in being a world power rather than a subjugated people.

This happened as Jesus came into Zion (Jerusalem). The people had the right Messiah, but the wrong idea! Salvation came *out of Zion*. It came out as Jesus drug his cross to Golgotha, where he died for all. He restored the fortunes of his people, not only the Jews, but all nations. He restored the fortunes of Eden. He brought back peace between God and sinners. He redeemed Adam and Eve's offspring. Now that is a reason to rejoice and be glad! We live in the post-Christ era of the psalm. Are we not rejoicing at the salvation of our God?

Lord, we do rejoice in the victory over sin brought by the death of Jesus. We thank you for restoring the fellowship with you that was lost in Eden. In Jesus, Amen!

JANUARY 24

O LORD, who shall sojourn in your tent? Who shall dwell on your holy hill? (Ps. 15:1)

Whenever I read this opening verse to Psalm 15, I always shout inside, "Me! Me!!! I want to sojourn in the tent of God!!! I want to live on his holy hill!!!" Then I read the next verses that tell me who the people are:

He who walks blamelessly and does what is right and speaks truth in his heart; who does not slander with his tongue and does no evil to his neighbor, nor takes up a reproach against his friend; in whose eyes a vile person is despised, but who honors those who fear the LORD; who swears to his own hurt and does not change; who does not put out his money at interest and does not take a bribe against the innocent. He who does these things shall never be moved (Ps. 15:2-5).

As a "list" type of person, I immediately enumerate these lines to make sure I am dwelling with God on his holy hill. Number 1—Walk blamelessly. Well, that one is impossible, but I know that in Jesus, God has ascribed to me the perfection of Christ. So I have the ultimate blamelessness. Beyond that though, I need to set my own personal goal to walk "blamelessly." What does the psalmist mean by that?

Hebrew is known for making a bold statement, and then giving the explanation of that statement. For example, in Deuteronomy 19:2, God told Moses and the Israelites, "Be holy, for I am holy," and then spends the rest of the chapter explaining what people need to do to be holy. That is much the same with this psalm. Verse 2 says, "walk blamelessly," and then the remaining verses explain what is meant by that. The remaining verses really start the list:

1. Do right.
2. Be honest.
3. Don't speak ill of others or do ill to others (or encourage anyone else to do so).
4. Honor those faithful to God, and not those rebellious to him.
5. Keep my word, even when it hurts me.
6. Help people in need without regard to it helping me.
7. Protect those needing protection.

If I work on these specific things in my life, I live a life closer to my Lord. That is a worthy thing I want to pursue.

Lord, I want to be closer to you. Help me to walk in your ways, In Jesus' name, Amen!

❧ ❧ ❧

JANUARY 25

Preserve me, O God, for in you I take refuge. I say to the LORD, "You are my Lord; I have no good apart from you." (Ps. 16:1)

When I was a young man, I heard a Christian comedian who made an impression on me with several lines I have remembered for over forty years now. One of them went roughly as follows: A man came up to me and said, "Hey Mike, for you, Jesus is just a crutch." And I said, "Yeah, man, but when you're crippled, you need one."

I liked Mike's openness. Jesus/God is a crutch for many. He is a crutch for me. I am a needy person when it comes to God. Recently I was interviewed by a psychologist lawyer who had never expressed to me any affirmative faith in God. I wasn't sure she had ever really talked much to a devout Christian about such things. She was a very successful lawyer, had tried many lawsuits to victory, and had a wide national reputation. My interview was for her article in a national trial magazine. She wanted to know a lot about how I did things in trial, but perhaps her greatest curiosity was what made me tick. She asked how I handled the pressure. I gave a polite and not too heavy answer, but she pressed deeper. "How do you handle the pressure of millions of dollars at stake, of holding an entire family's future and fate in your hands, of knowing the world is watching, and knowing so many hope you succeed while so many also hope you fail?" She was particularly inquisitive about how I managed to do it with a smile and joy.

I finally decided she deserved a forthright answer, and she could decide what she printed and what she didn't. I said, "Lisa, I don't know how familiar you are with such things, but I *really* do believe there is a God. I *really* believe he knows me, loves me, and has set into motion certain definite tasks he wants me to do in helping bring human history to its right conclusions. This is why I don't panic or sweat from the pressure of what I do. My pressure is really simple, I am to do my best before God and with prayer, trust him with the consequences." My goal in life is not to write the script. My goal is to live the life of another's script. I have accepted his script. I know when things are tough, when pressures are tight, that I take refuge in the Lord God. I have no good apart from the Lord, nor do I want any. He is my Lord, and I am at peace with that. More than at peace, I find joy and rejoice in that.

Lord, thank you for your care and concern. Thank you for your love. Thank you for taking care of the script, and giving me the tasks you have given me. May I do what I do to your glory, never doubting, and always knowing you are God. In Jesus' name, Amen!

❧ ❧ ❧

JANUARY 26

As for the saints in the land, they are the excellent ones, in whom is all my delight. The sorrows of those who run after another god shall multiply; their drink offerings of blood I will not pour out or take their names on my lips. (Ps. 16:3-4)

We live in a hero-driven world. We see major sports figures that accomplish incredible feats of physical skill, and it impresses us. When I was ten and eleven, my best friend was from Manchester, England, and we would play soccer, taking turns at who "got to be" Bobby Charlton (a famous Manchester United soccer star). How often do we see young people with posters of music or movie stars on their rooms? I am always a bit stunned about the near encyclopedic knowledge some people have of their heroes.

As people age, the heroes (idols?) change a bit. People begin to admire the social elite, in awe when they get to talk to or be close to them. In a recent trial, a juror answered a questionnaire that her greatest life moment was meeting Henry Winkler—the "Fonz" from the 1970's Happy Days television show! I have seen men and women who seem to think that the most important thing in life is money. Those with it are special—worth knowing and pursuing. Those without it are simply normal. People pay thousands of dollars at "fundraisers" to have their picture taken with presidents and others in power. It is as if being in touch with one of power will cause part of the power to rub off.

This psalm puts a very special focus on whom we are to admire and emulate. The psalmist wants to "delight in" or take pleasure in those who are "saints" or "holy." These are people who walk right before the Lord. "Holy" and "saint" aren't mystic words when written of people in the Old Testament; they are words of behavior and character. The psalmist wants to be around and be like those who are walking right before the Lord. The writer knew that those who chase other priorities, those who "run after another god," are dead ends. They do not share the destiny of the redeemed. Their road does not end in a pleasant place. Their road is not one worth walking.

How different would this world be if we, whether young or old, found our heroes in those who truly loved the Lord, living for him in devotion and care? How different if we pursued encyclopedic knowledge of those who are holy ones of God? I want that.

Lord, give me eyes to see what has value in this world and beyond. Give me a heart for holiness, in me and in others. Guide me into the lives of those who are holy, and may my life be a light of your holy care by the way I live. As our Lord Jesus so lived, Amen!

❊ ❊ ❊

JANUARY 27

The LORD is my chosen portion and my cup; you hold my lot. The lines have fallen for me in pleasant places; indeed, I have a beautiful inheritance. (Ps. 16:5-6)

The "lines" that are spoken of in this passage are the lines that were drawn around land to designate the boundaries of the land. When the psalmist writes, *"the lines have fallen for me in pleasant places,"* it is a poetic expression of appreciation for the provisions of the Lord in this life. It is a prayer of thanks and praise to God.

Many reading the psalm can likely identify with the writer as to the blessings of this life. Most in America, for example, live with food to eat, an opportunity for education, freedom to worship, freedom to vote, the joys of friendships, the blessings of family, clean water and air, safety from foreign invaders, a secure economy, and more. There are likely many who read the psalm, however, even in America, whose lives are not as easy. Poor health, difficult times or families, and more would cloud many from thinking that the "lines have fallen for me in pleasant places." The key for all, however, lies in the phrase before.

The excerpted passage begins with the affirmation, *"The LORD is my chosen portion and my cup."* This is the core that defines who we are, what we have, and in what we delight. God is at work in a great cosmic plan, putting right the things that humanity has messed up. God doesn't dictate what humans do. He hasn't made computers that he preprogrammed. He has made beings that have their own moral choices. But somehow in the midst of humanity's free choices, God has made a plan that will ultimately culminate in the triumph of Christ and his kingdom. As a part of that, God has assigned out certain "lots" in this life. He has also given clear instructions on how to live.

Our goal in this life needs to be to follow his instructions, trusting in his plan for the triumphant Christ. Part and parcel with this is the acceptance of the role that the Lord has for us in his plans. What God has planned is what we choose. Anything else is not our blessing, but an error needing correction. So we can rightly say with the psalmist, *"The LORD is my chosen portion."* He does hold our "lot." This makes our inheritance "beautiful," regardless of how the world or anyone else sees it. The beauty is being in line with the will and plan of Almighty God to bring the kingdom of Christ to fruition.

Lord, your ways are not always our ways. Your plans are not always the plans we would devise. But there is a grace in that, knowing you are God and we are your children. May we see and understand the many blessings you have given us, even when we are in need or trouble. In Jesus' holy name, Amen!

❧ ❧ ❧

JANUARY 28

I bless the LORD who gives me counsel; in the night also my heart instructs me. I have set the LORD always before me; because he is at my right hand, I shall not be shaken. Therefore my heart is glad, and my whole being rejoices; my flesh also dwells secure. (Ps. 16:7-9)

Advice for life is everywhere. Radio call-in shows will give you answers to your questions about life. Of course, you can also find palm readers, tarot readers, seers, and others who will gladly take your money to tell you about your future and which choices to make. Did I mention fortune cookies and horoscopes for living instructions?

No, thank you. I really don't want to know what the cards say about how I should live. I'm not giving money to those who assure me they have the secret mystic knowledge. I'm not even slightly interested in my horoscope for today or tomorrow. I have a better source.

I want to get my counsel from the Lord on High. I am interested in how the Creator wants me to live. I want to know his will for me. I look at it this way. First, I can see the actions of Christ and know that the Creator God cares for me beyond measure. He has my best interests at heart, and has demonstrated it to the extreme. Second, God has vision beyond my vision. He is not guessing at what tomorrow brings. To him, tomorrow is the same as yesterday. It is not speculation; it is foreknowledge. Third, I entered God's kingdom. That is akin to joining a team in the sense that my concerns are what is best for the kingdom. My life is not my own. It belongs to him for his will.

I like the idea of getting counsel from someone who knows what is going to happen, who has a purpose, who has called me to work toward his goals, and has prepared me to fulfill certain important tasks toward those goals. With that in mind, I will seek the Lord's counsel. I will do so while setting him before me as my instructor and my goal. In this a confidence arises noted by the psalm. I will not be shaken. God will achieve his goals through me as I willingly surrender to him. I can be secure in that with no fear.

Lord, I bless you as an indescribable God. I praise you for your plans, and I am honored that you have sought me out to help achieve those plans. I pray my heart will be a willing heart, my focus will be on you, and you will use me as best befits your kingdom. I place all my self-interest on the altar, and proclaim myself at your disposal. May Jesus be praised as I pray this through him, Amen!

❦ ❦ ❦

JANUARY 29

You make known to me the path of life; in your presence there is fullness of joy; at your right hand are pleasures forevermore. (Ps. 16:11)

Everyone likes "fullness of joy" and "pleasures evermore." This psalm offers joy and pleasures, explaining they are found on God's path for our life and in his presence.

God offers life in a way that humanity hasn't known since the tree of life was forbidden after the fall. It takes a redemption from the curse of sin to restore people to the tree of life. But in the redemption that comes through Jesus, we have a restoration of life. We might even say, Jesus is "the path of life." So as I meditate on this psalm's revelation, I center my thoughts on how I bring my life into alignment with that of my Savior Jesus.

Before his crucifixion, Jesus said he was going to prepare a place for us, that where he is, we might be also (John 14:2-3). Jesus was speaking of the cross. By dying in our stead, he brings us forgiveness of sins. By affiliating with him in his death, we also affiliate with him in his resurrected life. Jesus and the cross become the path of life that takes us into the presence of God. There we experience "fullness of joy" and "pleasures forevermore."

The joy in the presence of God is nothing so superficial as the joy of a good meal, a good job, or a good vacation. The joy of the presence of God is a deep-seated joy that produces inner contentment. There is a deep peace and satisfaction that combines with awestruck wonder and amazement. It is not temporary, but emanates consistently from God's throne.

Likewise, the pleasures of God's right hand are not as temporary as pleasures of the senses or intellectual pursuits. These are deeper and more lasting. The pleasures from God's right hand (where, not coincidently we are told Jesus resides; 1 Pet. 3:22) are the pleasures of walking with Christ, in good times and bad. The pleasures of knowing intimately the one who gave everything in love to save your soul. This is the path of life!

Lord, thank you for Jesus. Thank you for his death and resurrection on our accord. Thank you for his eternal presence at your right hand. Thank you for the intimacy he has brought in our walk with you. We bless you for making known to us the path of life, and for the joys and pleasures that come from fellowship with you. Through Jesus our Lord, Amen!

❧ ❧ ❧

JANUARY 30

I call upon you, for you will answer me, O God; incline your ear to me; hear my words. Wondrously show your steadfast love, O Savior of those who seek refuge from their adversaries at your right hand. Keep me as the apple of your eye; hide me in the shadow of your wings. (Ps. 17:6-8)

My friend Bob and I travel together a lot. Many times I have heard him call his wife on the cell phone while on the road. On the rare occasion she doesn't answer, Bob frequently leaves a message to the effect of, "Why did we buy you a cell phone, and why do we pay the monthly fee, if you aren't going to answer it?" Bob is joking, but it rings true that we can be frustrated when we have something important to say, and we are unable to get the right person's attention to hear us.

Not so with God. We can call upon him any time, night or day, and he will always hear and answer us. Sometimes the answer might be, "No," and sometimes it might be, "Not yet," but God does answer. It is really remarkable to think about. The God of the universe hears our specific requests and prayers.

He does so because we are his children and his children are precious in his sight. He holds an intense love and devotion to us as we walk in relationship with him. Think of Jesus' relationship with his followers. They were not servants of Jesus; Jesus served them, even as he regarded them as his friends.

The psalmist knew of this love of God. The psalmist wrote of God who would, "*keep me as the apple of your eye.*" God listens to us, answers us in his wondrous steadfast love, rescues us from trouble, and hides us from the enemies that would do us wrong. God hears and answers our prayers. He is never busy or away from his phone. Praise the Lord!

Lord, thank you for hearing our prayers. Thank you for your love and your care. Help us to share that love with those who don't know it. May we not be bashful about telling them of your love, especially how you expressed it at Calvary. Your love for us stirs up responsive love within us. Praise you in Jesus' name, Amen!

JANUARY 31

As for me, I shall behold your face in righteousness. (Ps. 17:15)

In the summer between my sixth and seventh grade years, I lived in Rochester, New York, and listened to AM pop radio a good bit. One of the hit songs that summer came from the recent play *Godspell.* The song was "Day by Day," based upon a medieval prayer. In it, the lyric asks, "Day by day, Oh dear Lord, three things I pray: To see thee more clearly; Love thee more dearly; Follow thee more clearly; Day by day." The song still echoes in my head forty-four years later, especially when reading this passage from Psalm 17.

In the passage, the psalmist contrasts the fate of the wicked to that of the writer. The wicked love their abundance in this life. They have no pity for the unfortunate. They are arrogant and self-seeking, without regard to those who are hurt or destroyed in the process. Not so the writer. The writer is more concerned upon being found in relationship with God. The writer wants to be the apple of God's "eye" (v. 8), while also "seeing" God's face (translated "beholding").

I want to see God's face. I want to see and experience life intimately with the divine countenance of God.

The key is where the writer knows God's face will be seen. If I were to be able to travel somewhere and find God's presence, I would most certainly go. I would climb the highest mountain, traverse the widest ocean, endure extreme heat or cold to be in the divine presence and to see God better. The writer tells us where God's face is seen: "*I shall behold your face in righteousness.*"

So I don't have to travel to a location to see God's face, I need to be holy and obedient, and I will see God's ever-present face where I am. Jesus said it this way, "Blessed are the pure in heart, for they shall see God" (Matt. 5:8). The writer of Hebrews echoed, "Strive for the holiness without which no one will see the Lord" (Heb. 12:14). It is curious that I will travel anywhere to see God. Yet while it is so much cheaper and more convenient to see God *here*, it is so much more difficult. For it is not simply packing and going, it is changing the way I live, and to some degree who I am. This is the journey of life I want to take.

Dear Lord, three things I pray, to see you more clearly, love you more dearly, and follow you more nearly. For in loving you, I will follow you in righteousness. And in following you, I will see you more clearly. In Jesus' name, Amen!

❧ ❧ ❧

FEBRUARY 1

I love you, O LORD, my strength. The LORD is my rock and my fortress and my deliverer, my God, my rock, in whom I take refuge, my shield, and the horn of my salvation, my stronghold. (Ps. 18:1-2)

I know people who have grown up in households where it is uncommon to express love verbally. There are those who are uncomfortable saying, "I love you," even to those they love the most. Not so in the Lanier house. We Laniers grew up hearing it daily from our parents, and it is a phrase we unhesitatingly tell our own children (and others we love).

Here David tells the Lord, "I love you." It is not complicated or wrapped in fashionable language. It is expressed as commonly and bluntly as a spouse might say to a spouse, or a parent to a child.

David's expression of love quickly moves to his considering the relationship history with God, expressing the many ways God had taken care of David. This is not to say that David's love was selfish, but appreciative. David recognized the many ways God had shown his love to David, even before David was expressing his love for God. It is similar to how Jesus showed his love first ("Greater love has no one than this, that someone lay down his life for his friends"; John 15:13), which then moves us to love him ("We love because he first loved us"; 1 John 4:19)

David had experienced the LORD being his rock—his solid ground, the reliable and steady one, the secure foundation. He knew the LORD as his fortress—his protection, the wall that kept enemies at bay. His life had proven the LORD would deliver him, not from hardship, but through the hardships of life. The LORD was not simply God, but David's God in a personal sense. David could rest in that, confident that whatever the day might bring, in God was a refuge, a shield of protection, and ultimate salvation.

I like that. I need that. Don't we want a life where the troubles that come do not cause us to question God, but bring us into a reliance upon him that fosters later testimony, "My God saved me from . . ."? It naturally stirs up great responsive love.

Lord, you have saved me, over and over, from so many problems and pains in this world. You have never left or forsaken me, and I know the magnificence of reliance on you. Thank you, my God, for your ever-present love. I love you. In Jesus' name, Amen!

❧ ❧ ❧

FEBRUARY 2

I call upon the LORD, *who is worthy to be praised, and I am saved from my enemies.* (Ps. 18:3)

This was the beginning of a song we sang in youth group when I was in high school. The song was short and contained this passage plus the refrain, "The Lord liveth, and blessed be my rock and may the God of my salvation be exalted," which comes from verse 46 of this psalm, a good link to the verse given above.

There are three segments in the psalmist's claim. The decision to call upon the Lord, the justification for calling on him, and the faith in the result. The decision to call is not based on some blind leap of faith. It is not a shot in the dark, when human efforts have failed. It is not a new and sudden turn to God. It is based on what God has done before. It is based on an intimate and experiential knowledge of God. He is "worthy to be praised," meaning he is doing and has done things that merit praise. The psalmist *knew* God and *knew* what he could do and what he would do. This instilled in the psalmist the faith and confidence that God was not going to allow things to go awry. Nothing would happen that was beyond God's sovereign interest and control.

There are many other things we might do before turning to God. Part of this stems from the recognition that God does expect us to act as well as pray. We don't simply sit by and watch God "do." God "does" in part *through* us. But in our own efforts, we must never place our efforts above (or apart) from the direction and provision that comes from prayer to the Almighty. We don't "Do!" then pray when our efforts fail. We pray and do together.

I like this psalm's deliberate decision to call upon the Lord in full reliance of his rescue. There were many times in my life where circumstances looked bleak. When we worry about making ends meet, try to cobble together relationships that seem permanently splintered, face health crises, or turmoil at work, we should take courage in the psalmist's declaration, "I *will* call upon the Lord. So *shall* I be saved from my enemies!"

Lord, there are times and seasons of dark clouds and storms in this life. As we experience those, may we do so with the confidence and courage that come from calling upon you, trusting that you will save us for Jesus' sake, Amen!

FEBRUARY 3

In my distress I called upon the Lord; *to my God I cried for help. From his temple he heard my voice, and my cry to him reached his ears. Then the earth reeled and rocked; the foundations also of the mountains trembled and quaked, because he was angry.* (Ps. 18:6-7)

Now this is a ferocious passage! God is no trifling God!

The psalmist cries out to God in distress. The Hebrew idea in the word "distress" means "bound" or "tied up." This is someone who is unable to do what is needed. There is no way to rescue oneself. It is the person tied up who can only shout out for help. I have been there. There have been those times where I not only didn't see a way out of my predicament or crisis, but if there was a way, it was beyond my ability to do it. Now this should never be the only time we cry out to God, but these times come in everyone's life. So when they do, we can and should cry out to God for help.

God heard the cry of the psalmist. God also hears our cry. He is a listening God. Even though God is eternal and outside time, he is also alert and tuned in to what is happening in our present.

God has a reaction to the distress of the psalmist. It is not a "namby-pamby all is fine" reaction. It is fierce! God takes umbrage at the abuse of his children. And when God is "angry," then nothing can stand in the way. The earth itself reels and rocks. Mountain foundations shake. The psalm continues that God "came down" from his throne using images of a terrible thunderstorm to illustrate the power of engaging God in times of crisis and emergency. The psalmist declares that God lifted him from the pit, rescuing him from those too mighty for him to handle on his own.

I know there are things that seem to be under my control. I can choose how to behave and handle many situations that arise. But sometimes, there are things with devastating potential that are out of my control. I am bound and tied up, completely unable to affect the outcome. In those situations, I take particular confidence in knowing the listening, all-powerful God is a cry away from making sure all is right.

Lord, please inspire us to turn to you first, in any and every problem. Bring your might to make things right. We gladly suffer for the good of your kingdom, but Lord, when that is not the point, please protect your children who live to serve you. For Jesus' sake, Amen!

FEBRUARY 4

The LORD dealt with me according to my righteousness; according to the cleanness of my hands he rewarded me. For I have kept the ways of the LORD, and have not wickedly departed from my God . . . I was blameless before him, and I kept myself from my guilt. So the LORD has rewarded me according to my righteousness, according to the cleanness of my hands in his sight. (Ps. 18:20-21, 23-24)

I struggle with this passage and many similar ones in the Psalms. I know there is truth to the maxim that Paul explained as "you reap what you sow" (Gal. 6:7). I know that things we do have consequences in this world. This is a truth, as certain as if you put your finger in fire, you will get burned.

Yet my struggle lies not in the concept, but in the absolute language of the psalm. I usually try to put myself in the position of the psalmist and try to read and pray the words as if they are my own. I can't get there with this psalm.

If the Lord were to deal with me based on *my own* righteousness that comes from the cleanness of *my hands*, I am as good as dead. My deeds just aren't that good. Not even close. I haven't kept his ways, but have violated more than I can count, certainly more than I care to remember! I haven't kept myself from guilt; I will more likely plunge headlong into guilt. I am not only in trouble for my bad deeds, but I am in deep trouble simply for things I fail to do!

So this psalm troubles me. It leaves me feeling very inadequate and unworthy of God's love. But as much as the psalm troubles me, it also brings me great joy. Yes, I have found a way—and only one way—that I can pray this psalm. I can pray this psalm through the mercies of Jesus Christ and his atoning death for my sins. I understand that as he has taken on the punishment my sin justly incurs, he has also imparted to me his own righteousness. In Christ, I have a righteousness not based on my own deeds, but based on his purity and obedience. Now I truly can pray with clean hands, but not hands clean from my proud production of my own good deeds. My prayer stems from the mercies afforded me by the loving Christ.

Lord, I confess myself a full-out sinner, incapable of righteousness in little ways or big. I do not do the things I need or want to do. The things I don't want or need to do are the ones I do. Lord, as I confess that, and repent of it, I also acknowledge and accept the forgiveness of Jesus, who is my Lord in this life and beyond. Thank you for his righteousness and for the assurance you will deal with me through him, Amen!

❦ ❦ ❦

FEBRUARY 5

With the merciful you show yourself merciful; with the blameless man you show yourself blameless; with the purified you show yourself pure; and with the crooked you make yourself seem tortuous. For you save a humble people, but the haughty eyes you bring down. (Ps. 18:25-27)

I find a great truth about human nature here. We see and understand God, in terms related to what kind of people we are. If we live God's love for others, we grow in understanding our loving God. As we work to be holy as God is holy, we understand his holiness more than ever before, which then spurs us to grow even more. As we work to be pure before our pure God, purity becomes a priority that shines brighter in our understanding of God's nature, guiding into greater purity ourselves.

But there is another principle at work here. Even though Genesis teaches that God made people in his (God's) image, for all of history, people have been constantly trying to remake God in *our* human image. We want a God who is basically what we think a God should be. If God meets that expectation, then we will worship and "live with" that God. If God doesn't meet our expectation, then we remake him, or outright reject him.

There is a danger here. We may not readily come to God and try to learn of him for who he is. In this sense, God is no longer the real God, but becomes a little "g" god who is really some reflection of who we are. This is a god we may think we can worship, but are we worshipping the God who is, or the god we make? Here the psalmist makes the point that to crooked people, God becomes a crooked god who is, rather than being as we are, letting god be what we make him to be. The lesson is also a bit deeper. God does reveal himself, but his revelation is only as useful as the eyes of those who are looking. If our eyes are dulled by pride, arrogance, haughtiness, even "brilliant insight and intelligence," we are not ready to see the God who is there. We will see the god who is the product of our sin.

More than ever, I want to be humble before God, seeing God as God, rather than anything less.

Lord, please open my eyes to see you in mercy, love, purity, righteousness, strength, compassion and justice. Let my life reflect these godly qualities in humility. Your revelation is nowhere more apparent than in the life (and death/resurrection) of Jesus my Lord, and in him I pray, Amen!

❧ ❧ ❧

FEBRUARY 6

It is you who light my lamp; the LORD *my God lightens my darkness. For by you I can run against a troop, and by my God I can leap over a wall. This God—his way is perfect; the word of the* LORD *proves true; he is a shield for all those who take refuge in him.* (Ps. 18:28-30)

Darkness and light have a strange relationship. Darkness exists where no light is found. Once light comes into darkness, the darkness retreats. I have seen darkness in the world, but also darkness in myself. I need light to dispel the darkness, and this psalm makes it clear where that light comes from. The Lord God lights my lamp and dispels the darkness. That is a total game changer.

The psalm gives the difference God's light makes in almost Superman terms. I can run against a troop! I can leap over a wall! The psalmist is taking his dark/light analogy into the realm of everyday problems. Light doesn't just help us see, it gives us direction in real life problems that result in real life actions that overcome real life obstacles. Darkness has no chance when God lights the lamp.

So the natural question is, "How does God light my lamp?" We get the answer in the next sentences. God lights our lamp by teaching us "his way." We learn that through his word. God's way is perfect and we get to it through his word which is true.

All of these phrases are echoed by John in his gospel speaking of Jesus. Jesus is the Word (John 1:14). Jesus is the perfect "Way" of the Lord (John 14:6). Jesus is the light who overcomes the darkness (John 8:12). In Jesus, we have God giving us direction. In Jesus, we have God explaining and revealing who he is and what his will is. In Jesus, we are able to be more than conquerors. We leap over walls and run against entire troops.

We can also take John's understanding back into the psalm and see in it a significance to the final phrase, "he is a shield for all those who take refuge in him." Jesus is that shield. In Jesus, we see and have God's protection and devotion. That doesn't mean that we live cushioned lives. To the contrary, we pick up our crosses (figuratively) to follow Christ (Matt. 16:24). Yet in so following him, we are in his will and under his wing. Nothing that happens can or will separate us from his love for us (Rom. 8:35-39). Jesus is the ultimate game changer.

Lord, thank you for Jesus. Thank you for his light. Thank you for dispelling our darkness and that of the world around us. May we live in humble obedience to your will following Christ, the Way, through whom we pray, Amen!

※ ※ ※

FEBRUARY 7

For who is God, but the LORD? *And who is a rock, except our God?—the God who equipped me with strength and made my way blameless. He made my feet like the feet of a deer and set me secure on the heights. He trains my hands for war, so that my arms can bend a bow of bronze. You have given me the shield of your salvation, and your right hand supported me, and your gentleness made me great. You gave a wide place for my steps under me, and my feet did not slip. I pursued my enemies and overtook them.* (Ps. 18:32-36)

We have a God who equips us for battle! I may forget there is a war going on, but never for long. I know battles. I battle in my mind. I am called to follow Christ in sacrificial love, yet find myself too often thinking about my wants and needs. I battle in my body. Even something as small as controlling appetite can be a battle, much less handling the tongue, or battling disease and sickness. I battle with my pride. God loves humility and lifts up the poor in spirit, but I like it when people know and appreciate me. I battle with temptation. I know the right things to do, but often fail to do them (or I do the things I know I shouldn't). I battle with the world. It is rarely easy at work; hence it is spelled "W-O-R-K" instead of "F-U-N." I battle with others. Relationships take work and sacrifice, and do not grow by themselves.

I need to be equipped for battles. I need a God who teaches and provides me as necessary to win these confrontations. He will give me "strength," which I desperately need as I grow weary in the struggle. He makes my way straight, something I tend to miss as I meander about the battleground.

We find this concept echoed by Paul in Ephesians 6:11ff. where he speaks of God equipping us for the spiritual wars against Satan. *My* feet are secure (Ps. 18) because they are shod with the gospel (Eph. 6:15). I stand on the firm foundation of Jesus. The "shield of salvation" (Ps. 18) is the shield of faith (Eph. 6:16). Through faith in Jesus we are saved from Satan's fiery darts. My hands are trained for war (Ps. 18) as they handle the sword of the Spirit, which is the word of God (Eph. 6:17). God has given me what I need for the battles I face.

Lord, may I walk in the armor you have provided. Give me the ability by your mercy and strength to overcome the battles I face, and thank you for the forgiveness in Jesus when I fail. In his name, Amen!

❧ ❧ ❧

FEBRUARY 8

The L*ORD* *lives, and blessed be my rock, and exalted be the God of my salvation.* (Ps. 18:46)

There is a long song (over nine minutes) by Hillsong called "Closer Than You Know." That song blesses me often. The song has two parts. It begins with God singing to his children about all he has done and does for us. God's request in the song is, "Don't turn your eyes from me; for my love won't be undone. Don't hide your face from me; for my light has surely come." The communication from God ends with the plea, "Lift up your eyes and see heaven is closer than you know . . . My love won't let you go!" At a midpoint in the song, the instrumentation, tempo and melody change as the speaker changes from God to the believer.

The believer answers God, "Lord, I hear you; I know you're there . . . You're always with me." The song crescendos with the proclamation, "You are here! You are here! And my soul will praise you; my soul will praise you!"

I love the song. It speaks to me as this psalm passage does. The Lord lives. God is no fiction. God is not simply a "nice code to live by" or a "marvelous way to raise a family." There is a God. He is the "L*ORD*," the name God gave Moses (Exod. 3:13-15). There is a real God who lives and takes an interest in me. He is unshakable. He is my rock. He is my salvation.

This is an amazing reality upon which we constantly need to focus. Distractions of the world will try to convince us God is nothing but a convenient legend or idea. We can too easily lose sight of the kind and loving God who stepped into history and saved humanity.

Regardless of how we "feel," the truth never changes. God lives. God saves. God loves, even as he hates evil. He is worthy of our praise. We rightly lift him up to others. We exalt the living God who is active in our lives today!

Lord, you have reached out to us. You have reached out to me. You have been a rock, securing for me salvation. You save eternally, but also in the here and now. You save me from the snares of the wicked one. I thank you and exalt you. Give me vision to show you alive and caring in this blinded and wounded world. May I shine your light so brightly that people see you and respond to your love. Even as Jesus prayed, Amen!

FEBRUARY 9

The heavens declare the glory of God, and the sky above proclaims his handiwork. Day to day pours out speech, and night to night reveals knowledge. (Ps. 19:1-2)

I was playing outside late on July 20, 1969, when my mom made me come in the house. It was nighttime, and before I went to bed, mom wanted me to watch something on the television. She said, "Remember this, it is a very important moment in history." I watched as Neil Armstrong stepped on the moon.

It was such an amazing thing that a number of people believed it was faked. Yet it was real. It was made possible by something staggering that we call "laws of nature." The universe exists, not as a magical world of fantasyland, but as a cause-and-effect world of very consistent and unchanging rules or laws of nature. We know from these laws where the moon will be tomorrow. We know the sun rises from the east every day, not just most days. This consistency is a hallmark of our God.

Scripture is distinct from other ancient religions in that God is not found in the elements of nature. God is not the sun, the thundering storms, or the ocean depths. God is responsible for such things, but they are not God. We see in them what Paul calls God's "invisible attributes" and "divine nature" (Rom. 1:20). God is a God of laws and consistency. God is a God of reliability, not a capricious and changing God. God is the same yesterday, today and tomorrow (Heb. 13:8). We can rely on that as certainly as we can know the placement of the stars.

No one should be shocked by this. Psalm 19 goes on to explain that everyone hears the "voice" of the heavens declaring the wonders of God. When the sun rises and sets, we see the handiwork of God (Ps. 19:3-6). This is the divine nature expressed in the handiwork of nature's designer.

The psalm then explains that as the heavens declare God's glory, so we see in the law God's perfection. "The law of the LORD is perfect, reviving the soul" (Ps. 19:7). God did not simply set his glory in nature; he gave practical words that fit the Hebrews in their culture with a perfect expression of what God intended for them. We are beneficiaries of this God who leaves a trail of revelation for his children to follow. We have it in the heavens, and we have it in the Scriptures. God is not silent. We just need to listen.

Lord, may we hear your voice in the things you have made, and in the ways you have revealed to us your will. May we take delight in following your will, bringing your glory to greater brightness on earth, in Jesus' name, Amen!

✺ ✺ ✺

FEBRUARY 10

More to be desired are they than gold, even much fine gold; sweeter also than honey and drippings of the honeycomb. (Ps. 19:10)

If one were to take Psalm 19:10 entirely by itself, without any context or any knowledge of what came before or after, one would jump at whatever "they" are. If "they" are more to be desired than a lot of pure 24-karat gold, if "they" are sweeter than honey, then "they" are something worth getting, if possible. Some might even think there is no chance of getting whatever "they" are because few are able to get "much fine gold," much less something more valuable.

Yet the "they" are not hard to find. As difficult as they are to "do," they are quite available for the doing! The "they" in Psalm 19:10 are God's testimony, precepts, commandments, or rules (those are different English words for much the same thing). God's testimony turns a simple person into a wise one (Ps. 19:7). God's precepts bring joy to the heart as one experiences doing the will of God (Ps. 19:8). This might seem odd to some who think that sin is more "fun," but they are quite wrong! God's commandments enlighten our eyes and help us see the world and life much better with greater understanding (Ps. 19:8). God's rules are true, not false. They bestow righteousness, not corruption (Ps. 19:9).

These are things that are very precious because they have a greater effect on our state of mind, our state of being, and our future, than any effect of lots of even the purest gold or the greatest monetary sums. These are the things that produce great reward in this life. They produce love, security, peace of mind and heart. The consequences from God's living under God's instructions lead to a greater manifestation of his will, and what is right for his children.

This calls us to respond. If we believe what we are reading, then wouldn't we want to get such a valuable thing? Wouldn't we want the "they" that are most valuable? We need to invest in finding God's will and doing it. We should not only in life's steps and choices but also in our personal prayers and meditations. So our prayer today is from the last verse of Psalm 19 (v. 14).

Lord, let the words of my mouth and the meditation of my heart be acceptable in your sight, O LORD, my rock and my redeemer. Amen!

FEBRUARY 11

May the LORD answer you in the day of trouble! (Ps. 20:1)

Occasionally there a psalm that vocalizes prayers of my heart. Psalm 20 is one such psalm. I can remember countless times praying this psalm over my children at various ages and stages of life. Similarly, I have prayed it over my wife, and other family and friends.

When I read this psalm, I often pick out someone and pray the psalm in a very personal way for that person. This is the core of my devotional for today. I will reproduce the psalm in italics below, adjusting the language to reflect a prayer, adding personalized thoughts in standard font, with the encouragement to you to read it prayerfully, filling in the blank with the name of someone dear to you.

LORD, please answer _____ in the day of trouble!

By your name (who you are and what you've done) *God of Jacob protect _____! Send _____ help from the sanctuary and give _____ support from Zion!*

Please remember (take action because of) *all _____'s offerings and regard with favor _____'s burnt sacrifices!* (_____'s best efforts)

Please grant _____ _____'s heart's desire and fulfill all _____'s plans!

LORD, may we shout for joy over _____'s salvation, and in your name our God may set up our banners! (proclamations to the world of who we live for and belong to)

LORD, please fulfill all _____'s petitions!

This is a prayer we can pray with confidence. The psalmist knew it. The psalm ends with the faithful confirmation.

Now I know that the LORD saves his anointed; he will answer him from his holy heaven with the saving might of his right hand. Some trust in chariots and some in horses, but we trust in the name of the LORD our God.

So he does, and so may we.

Lord, give us prayerful hearts to pray for those in our lives, watching you act responsively in accordance with your will in Jesus' name, Amen!

FEBRUARY 12

O LORD, in your strength the king rejoices, and in your salvation how greatly he exults! (Ps. 21:1)

Our two oldest daughters loved *The Wizard of Oz* movie when they were young. Unfamiliar with some of the words, they called the movie "The Lizard of Oz." Most know the movie. A tornado takes Dorothy to a foreign land and she needs the help of the famous wizard of Oz to help her get home. The wizard is sought out also by the scarecrow who wants a brain, a tinman who wishes for a heart, and a cowardly lion who needs courage. All of them think the wizard is the key to getting their desires.

Oz is the Hebrew word for "strength." In this passage the psalmist recounts the king rejoicing in the Lord's "strength." Here we have the Hebrew word "*Oz*." Unlike the movie, where the wizard didn't really have any supernatural powers, God really does have all power and strength. The wizard brought illumination to Dorothy and crew. God brings illumination, but so much more. God is no mere wizard telling us to tap into what we already have. He is no illusion that, once we remove the smoke and mirrors becomes just a mirage or reflection of ourselves. God is the Almighty One who truly has almighty strength.

The righteous king rejoices not in his own strength or that of his army. The righteous and wise king sees that true strength resides in the Lord. It is the Lord who brings "salvation." Reading this psalm as a Christian adds to the import of the second phrase, "in your salvation how greatly he exults." The Hebrew for "salvation" is *yeshua*, also the name for Jesus. Jesus is the ultimate salvation of God for his people, not only from the travails of this world, but eternally, as Jesus sets his people in right standing with God.

In this way, we not only see Jesus as salvation, but we see Jesus as the strength of God made manifest. Jesus is God's strength to save over the powerful grip of sin. Jesus is God's strength to save over the devastating effects of sin. Jesus is God's strength to save from the despair of sin. In Jesus, we have forgiveness, purpose, hope, and destiny. Those are things no wizard of Oz or any other place could ever provide.

Lord God, we praise you as the God of strength. We praise you as the God of salvation. We thank you for Yeshua/Jesus and ask that his salvation be real in our lives. Not only in providing us our eternal route home to you, but also in giving us purpose and power to live today to your glory and in victory over sin. May we bring praise to your name through Jesus, Amen!

❧ ❧ ❧

FEBRUARY 13

My God, my God, why have you forsaken me? Why are you so far from saving me, from the words of my groaning? . . . It shall be told of the Lord to the coming generation; they shall come and proclaim his righteousness to a people yet unborn, that he has done it. (Ps. 22:1, 30-31)

Too often we live in snapshot moments. We are concerned about what is happening right now. We see things in the immediate, and we often need to be challenged to look at things from a larger perspective. This even influences how we read the Bible. For example, many know that while on the cross, Jesus uttered words found in the opening of this psalm. "My God, my God, why have you forsaken me?" (Matt. 27:46; Mark 15:34), and they assume Jesus was lost in the moment. However, this is not fair.

Clearly, the Lord was so well versed in Scripture, that in his hour of deepest darkness, he didn't have to pull a Bible from the shelf to find some reassurance. He didn't email someone and ask for a Bible verse. He cried out from the psalms, a passage that not only expressed his moment, but also expressed his faith *beyond the moment*. If we read that in snapshot mode, we might think of the loneliness Jesus might have felt on the cross at the moment of the cry. Then we would miss that Jesus was quoting a psalm that takes a distinct turn in its verses. Jesus wasn't caught in the moment, he was proclaiming his faith.

This psalm starts out in the despair of isolation, but it transforms into praise for God's faithfulness. Verse 26 sets out the confidence of faith that God will rescue those in despair, *"The afflicted shall eat and be satisfied; those who seek him shall praise the LORD!"* We should not see Jesus quoting the psalm as a snapshot of despair, but see the larger picture of Jesus knowing and proclaiming a psalm of despair turned to praise. Jesus is recounting in his time of need, that God reaches the needy.

The psalm ends in a way that also gives meaning to Jesus' last words on the cross. The last verse tells of the *"coming generation"* that *"shall come and proclaim his righteousness to a people yet unborn, that he has done it."* This gives added substance to Jesus' dying statement, *"It is finished"* (John 19:30). As the psalmist wrote, *"God has done it!"* Righteousness will come even *"to a people yet unborn."* That includes ME!

Lord, thank you for the amazing love and faithfulness of Jesus on the cross. Thank you for the righteousness made at that moment in history, and that it reaches me today. I thank you in Jesus' name, Amen!

❧ ❧ ❧

FEBRUARY 14

The L*ORD* *is my shepherd; I shall not want. He makes me lie down in green pastures. He leads me beside still waters. He restores my soul. He leads me in paths of righteousness for his name's sake.* (Ps. 23:1-3)

The 23rd Psalm may be the most quoted of all the Psalms. It is loaded with powerful and memorable lines. The above particularly speak to me.

First, I love the idea of being a sheep in the flock of the Lord. Good shepherds spend their time and energy on their sheep. They are there when the sheep are born, and know the sheep well from then on. The sheep thrive in the protection and provision of the shepherd. This aspect of the selected verses brings me comfort.

The psalmist says that the Lord "*makes me lie down in green pastures.*" It is only one Hebrew word that is translated here as "makes me lie down." The verb is "lie down," but here it is written in a special Hebrew construction (called the "*hiphil*") that makes the verb "causative." That is why it is translated "*makes*" me lie down. God *causes* me to lie down in green pastures. It is not something I would or even could do on my own!

Left to my own devices, I would lie down amidst the thorns and thistles, convinced that was going to be the fun spot. I have seen many beguiled by the sinful traps of this world, walking into them willingly, even eagerly, seduced by the promises of this world. Without fail, those sins turn out to be the very opposite of where any right-thinking person would want to be. Yet that is where I would be without a Lord who shepherds me, *making me lie down in green pastures.*

This is the God who restores my soul. This is the God of righteousness who leads me in those paths of his righteousness. This is my Good Shepherd.

Not surprisingly, Jesus owned the analogy of the Good Shepherd (John 10:11ff.). Jesus reinforced not only knowing his sheep, but his sheep knowing him. John places a pun in this teaching with Jesus, as Good Shepherd, "laying down" his life for his sheep. Our God, not only makes us lie down in green pastures, but he also lays himself down sacrificially for us, thereby enabling our green pastures eternally!

Lord, thank you for your great provision. May we live in awe and wonder at your rescuing love and provision, this day and each one to come, in Jesus' name, Amen!

FEBRUARY 15

The earth is the LORD's and the fullness thereof, the world and those who dwell therein, for he has founded it upon the seas and established it upon the rivers. (Ps. 24:1-2)

As a youth, I often saw copies of a small book entitled *Your God Is Too Small*, written by J. B. Phillips, an Anglican clergyman. The book was written to a generation that thought of God as some quaint idea from childhood, totally unfit to cope with the problems of a nuclear age, and of a world trying to sort out the implications of a cold war. I read the book, found it a blessing, and wished the book's audience would read Psalm 24.

The psalm begins with the truth: everything is God's. The entire earth belongs to the Lord, everyone and everything. That means God is not only bigger than the problems of our planet and its people, he claims ownership of our planet and its people. The last verses of the psalm call for the "gates to be lifted up" so "the King of Glory may come in." God is so great, the big city gates aren't tall enough for him! Neither is our mind.

I am amazed at those who don't understand how "big" or great God is, but I have to be careful with that judgment, because I often fall into the same trap. Every time I claim ownership of any portion of this earth, I am failing to recognize the greatness of God. When I act as if I have the ownership of my life, of my income, of my car, home, or body, I am diminishing God in my mind. Of course, I don't diminish him in reality, for God could never truly be diminished. But I often fail to recognize his greatness.

God founded the earth. God established this world. God is responsible for all good things. Our usurpation of God's ownership correlates well with the many problems of this earth. When we take control, when we act as if we have ownership, we see the root of many evils. This has produced greed and avarice of many types. It lies at the root of envy, jealousy, and bitterness. Suddenly, our agenda trumps God's agenda. At its core, it is a form of idolatry, as we set ourselves up as God, claiming ownership of things that rightfully belong to him.

I need to be more careful about this. It's not just a matter of tithing to God. I don't want to surrender only a tenth. I want to surrender fully to him, and handle what he has entrusted to me as he desires. After all, it is his, and so am I.

Lord, please remind me daily that all I have is yours. Let me have the wisdom to live as you wish me to, giving and using my time, resources, talents, health, and energy for you and your kingdom. In Jesus' name, and by his strength, Amen!

❋ ❋ ❋

FEBRUARY 16

Who shall ascend the hill of the LORD*? And who shall stand in his holy place? He who has clean hands and a pure heart, who does not lift up his soul to what is false and does not swear deceitfully. He will receive blessing from the* LORD *and righteousness from the God of his salvation.* (Ps. 24:2-5)

This is one of those passages where I hold up the hand of my heart and shout, "ME, ME, ME!!! I want to go there! I want to ascend the hill of the Lord!" I know that in God's presence is strength, and I need that strength to make it through the day. I know that in God's hand is mercy, and I need his mercy for my yesterdays as well as my today and tomorrows. I know that God is the one who will make my paths straight, and I need that help, for I tend to walk very aimlessly at times. I know that from God's priorities come the priorities I need. I know that from God's efficiencies comes the time I need to do my tasks. I know that from God's planning come the good works he has assigned me to do. So I want to ascend his hill. No, I NEED to ascend his hill. I desperately need to be in his holy place and presence.

So I raise my hand and say, "ME!" but what next? The psalmist gives some very practical instructions. I need clean hands. What I do with each moment of my day needs to be what is right before the Lord. Not only what I do but how I do it. I need a pure heart. My life needs to be about truth, deep in its core. It needs to be true in the way I deal with others and the way I deal with myself. People need to see and rightly trust in my integrity. I can't be led astray by thinking anything less is better for the moment or the task.

The psalmist assures me that these are the people who receive the blessings from the Lord, the righteous God. These are the people who experience God's salvation in the here and now. Who find God working in their moments and days, bringing his fruit and all the blessings that proceed from his hands. I want and need those. I am going to live in such a way that they pour forth!!

Lord, I give my day to you. I give my life to you. As you give me strength in your Spirit, I want to serve you rightly. I want my energies today to be put to the tasks you have at hand for me, and to nothing else. I want to live truthfully in your mercy. I need you each hour and minute. Thank you, Lord, for your faithful love, and for meeting me today. In Jesus, my righteousness, Amen!

❊ ❊ ❊

FEBRUARY 17

To you, O LORD, I lift up my soul. O my God, in you I trust; let me not be put to shame; let not my enemies exult over me. Indeed, none who wait for you shall be put to shame. (Ps. 25:1-3)

This psalm contains a simple truth, but one wrapped in some very difficult directions. The simple truth is that none who wait for the Lord will be put to shame. It is important we view this truth from a time perspective. Many people who "wait" on the Lord do experience shaming at the hands of enemies, the world, or even life's circumstances—when we are viewing the circumstances in the moment. But that is not what the psalmist is saying. To see the real truth, we need to look at the larger passage.

The psalmist is first lifting up his soul to the Lord. The psalmist is trusting God. This means that the psalmist does not live in the feelings or even experiences of the moment. The psalmist is taking the long view of God and eternity. The psalmist doesn't get caught up in seeing things as ends in themselves, but knows that events happen within the context of one's entire life before God. The psalmist lives for something beyond himself or herself. Therefore, the psalmist finds God's reasons as the reasons that matter.

Here is where there is no shame for the person: when we put our lives in God's hands, and when we are living for God and trusting in God, then whatever may come, it is enveloped into a life that is part of God's will and plan.

Can shameful or disappointing things happen? (The Hebrew word for "shaming" can also signify "disappointing.") Of course they can, in a worldly sense. But not at all in the eternal scheme of God, his kingdom, this world, and eternity.

I am frequently asked how I can handle losing lawsuits, especially when the publicity is there and the lawyers who win taunt and make a big deal out of the victory. My reply is fairly simple, and I learned it from psalms like this. My goal in this life should always be to lift up my soul to the Lord. To dedicate what I do, and do it as best I can, for him. Once I do that, he takes care of the results. If they turn out great, great! If they turn out terrible, great! God is in control. I need not be ashamed. If I am ashamed, I need to check and make sure that I am giving my life to the Lord and trusting him.

Lord, I give my soul and life to you. Use me, mold me, make me your vessel for your plans. I trust you in my life to do with it as is best for your kingdom. In that I find joy, regardless of the circumstances! As with my Lord Jesus, Amen!

※ ※ ※

FEBRUARY 18

Make me to know your ways, O LORD; teach me your paths. Lead me in your truth and teach me, for you are the God of my salvation; for you I wait all the day long. (Ps. 24:4-5)

I know a lot of people with common sense. I think to some degree I have common sense. One might say, "I know the right way to live." It seems that right and wrong are fairly ingrained in our minds and hearts. Yet the psalmist is asking God to "make me to know your ways." The request is that the Lord would "teach me your paths" and "lead me in your truth." What shall we make of this?

A young lawyer wrote me after hearing me speak at a seminar. He emailed me seven questions including: What do you attribute your success to? What is the difference between those who are good and those who are great? If your books were destroyed, your verdicts erased, your practice gone, your collection and church destroyed in a natural disaster, and all you had was a legal pad and a pen, what three (or more) truths in life would you write down to give to your kids? What advice would you give your 30-year-old self? I gave him my answers, and then asked him to answer the same questions. His were good and well thought out, but there was something distinctly missing.

His answers to the three truths in life he would write down and give to his kids are commonsense good! He said, "My three truths: (a) the only thing you can control in life is your effort; (b) there is never a good reason to tell a lie; (c) cliché, but, you miss 100 percent of the shots you don't take." My answers to that question were quite different. I said, "(1) There is an infinite, personal, and moral God. (2) He cares and wants a relationship with you. (3) He has made that possible by atoning for your inadequacies (sins) and you can trust him to make good on that."

I think that God's ways and his paths are beyond the common sense of daily life. His ways and paths are those that draw one deeper into relationship with him. We need to see that God is not simply the God of good instructions. He is the God of *my* salvation. He has chosen *me* as the recipient of his love. His paths are ones where we walk *with him*. This is huge, and more than commonsense living. This is a God worth waiting on for direction, purpose, and meaning.

Lord, I want to know your ways. I want to walk closely with you. I want you to be my purpose, my path, my companion and my goal. Lord, lead me closer to you through my Lord Jesus, Amen!

※ ※ ※

FEBRUARY 19

Remember your mercy, O Lord, and your steadfast love, for they have been from of old. Remember not the sins of my youth or my transgressions; according to your steadfast love remember me, for the sake of your goodness, O Lord! (Ps. 25:6-7)

Sometimes English can get in the way of a good understanding of a Hebrew psalm! Here is a classic example. In English, the psalmist is asking God to remember his mercy. It seems as if the psalmist is worried God might forget! What kind of God do we have if he cannot even remember something that important? Then the psalmist seems to be asking God to *forget* the sins of youth. So do we have a God who needs to be told what to remember and what to forget?

The Hebrew word for "remember" is not fairly translated simply by the English word "remember." The Hebrew (*zacar*) includes the idea of taking action based on a memory. This is the same word used in the Noah flood account where we read that "God remembered Noah" and made the waters recede (Gen. 8:1). Our God had not forgotten Noah!!! God took an action (receding the waters) based on his earlier commitment to Noah that was present in his mind.

This then is what the psalmist seeks. The psalmist asks God to act out of God's mercy, rather than out of recompense for the sins of the psalmist. God is asked to act out of his steadfast commitment to love that proceeds from the very character of God and his goodness. We can take from the psalm a personal plea of confession and repentance. This psalmist is giving an Old Testament example of a New Testament practice. The psalmist comes before God confessing sins, and asking God to have mercy and forgive those sins. This is a cry of faith and trust in the Lord as a forgiving God. It is an Old Testament "sinner's prayer." We should never fail to pray the same.

Lord, I am also a sinner. I have sinned more times than I can count, in things I have done and in things I have failed to do. Even some of my best deeds have been sinful in ways of the heart and mind. Lord, please forgive me of those sins. May I turn from them as an adult turns from childhood. I ask you to come into my life and reign as Lord and king through the forgiveness and sacrifice of Christ, Amen!

FEBRUARY 20

Good and upright is the LORD; *therefore he instructs sinners in the way. He leads the humble in what is right, and teaches the humble his way. All the paths of the* LORD *are steadfast love and faithfulness.* (Ps. 25:8-10)

We all know the expression, "You can lead a horse to water, but you can't make him drink." There is a real truth to that. I have seen times where my stubbornness has kept me from accepting and learning something very important. I confess that sometimes I have purposely turned my head from directions I needed, thinking I already knew which way I should go. (I am speaking metaphorically beyond simple driving directions!)

I think this is a key with God and this psalm. The psalmist notes that God instructs "sinners" in the way and teaches or leads the "humble." The proud, the self-righteous, the arrogant or haughty are not looking to God and see no need to learn from him or follow his way. God could offer them insight and direction, but they would no more follow it than the horse refusing to drink the water.

These psalms scare me a bit. I get scared because I don't want to be haughty. I don't want to miss the Lord's instructions because I think I am smart enough to figure out life on my own. (Which actually would be pretty dumb of me!) I don't want to fail to learn his ways because I am satisfied enough with my own righteousness and I don't see myself for the sinner I really am. I see these problems breed among the intellectuals who think they have figured out life and God (or explained God away), and it scares me because I like the intellectual aspect of faith. The folks who are behaviorally good by the world's standards tend not to fall on their knees, head bowed, and tongue confessing sinfulness. The catch on this is that God is truth, and intellectual pursuit of him is a good thing. Similarly, God is righteous, and righteous living before him is a good thing. The answer must lie in humility.

I think the key to humility for almost anyone, certainly for me, stems first and foremost from real encounters with God in his glory. It's why I get so absorbed in songs like "Closer Than You Know" by Hillsong. When I experience in worship, in quiet time, in song, in prayer, or other quiet moments, an encounter with the Almighty God, it places me in my place, and there is nothing but humility available. It illuminates my sin as brightly as the sun. It brings me to my knees. Then I am ready to learn.

Lord, you are a great and awesome God, perfect in love and purity. I am not. I am not perfect, or even close. I am not pure. I do a poor job seeking you and a poor job walking with you. I need your touch in Jesus' name. Please teach and lead me. Amen.

❧❧ ❧❧ ❧❧

FEBRUARY 21

The friendship of the Lord *is for those who fear him, and he makes known to them his covenant.* (Ps. 25:14)

I stay awed at the idea of a God who is over the vastness of the universe, especially knowing he knows it on a subatomic level. That is a God beyond any comprehension in some ways, yet he has revealed himself to make himself known by us. I like the way God revealed himself. God has used human terms to help us understand him and to relate to him.

God reveals himself as the Almighty God, Creator of heaven and earth, the Highest Lord of Hosts, King of kings, Lord of lords, holy and dwelling in unapproachable light. There are times where I especially need that God, and where knowing him as such helps me survive through difficulties in life that would otherwise bring me to despair.

God also reveals himself as Father. Jesus showed us God as Father, calling him "Abba," an Aramaic equivalent to today's "Papa" or "Daddy" (Mark 14:36). Paul used this term as well, calling us God's children (Rom. 8:15; Gal. 4:6). I was blessed to have a marvelous earthly father, so the idea of God as Father is a beautiful thing to me. There are times where I need the Father who is in my corner, who cares about nurturing and training me, who wants to help me develop and grow into a mature child of faith.

There is another way God chose to reveal himself to us. God relates to us not simply as awesome God or Father God; he relates to us as a friend. Jesus, God the Son, came to earth and didn't simply head to the cross. He walked for years as a friend, mentoring, loving, meeting needs, laughing, challenging, modeling godliness, and more. Jesus laid down his life, and in doing so pointed out that he was doing it for his friends! (John 15:13ff.).

This psalm points to God as friend, but puts the friendship into perspective. It is not a true revelation and relationship with the Lord if we do not recognize that even as our friend, he is our Lord. We hold him in reverence (Hebrew idea translated "fear") even as we have him as friend. This is sometimes just what I need. On those days when Almighty God is a bit too removed, when Father God seems too paternal, my heart cries out for a friend. There, waiting for me, is God.

Lord, thank you for the many ways you relate to me. Thank you for seeing fit to reach into all corners of my life and existence. May I be friend to you, even as I worship you and hold you in awe as God Almighty and my Father in heaven, through Jesus I pray, Amen!

❧ ❧ ❧

FEBRUARY 22

Turn to me and be gracious to me, for I am lonely and afflicted. The troubles of my heart are enlarged; bring me out of my distresses. Consider my affliction and my trouble, and forgive all my sins. (Ps. 25:16-18)

The Beatles sang, "Help! I need somebody. Help! Not just anybody. Help! You know I need someone. HELP!" I have been there, more times than I can count. I have been there when work seems to be crushing me under the weight of too many things to do with too little time. I have been there when financial pressures seem insurmountable. I have been there when relationships that should be solid and foundational were being destroyed before my eyes.

One thing I have learned in the midst of all these crises of need: I can turn to God and he is there. He answers my loneliness. He addresses my crisis and affliction. He takes the troubles of my heart that keep me awake, that keep me worried, that seem to chain my mind and emotions captive, and he releases those chains. He instills confidence, not in me, not in luck, but in his control and ability to walk on the roughest waters with me, holding me aloft, even when my own faith is flagging.

This is not because I am worthy, for surely I am not. I have to have my sins forgiven, just as anyone else does. In fact, it is often sin that gets us into our problems. But in confidence I can turn to the Lord, knowing he will hear me, knowing he cares. I can confess sin, confident in his forgiveness. I can recognize his presence, knowing I never face my problems alone even though I may feel isolated. There is no burden that I need carry alone, for he stands ready to help carry each one. I worship the Lord who was clear, "Take **my** yoke upon you, and learn from me, for I am gentle and lowly in heart, and you will find rest for your souls. For **my** yoke is easy, and my burden is light" (Matt. 11:29-30).

God solves both the crisis and the loneliness. He trades my troubles and stresses for a walk with him that, in faith, I can know will work out for the best. That moves me to rejoice, even as I walk through the circumstances, whatever they are.

Lord, I testify to your goodness and mercy. I have seen it in your forgiveness and steadfast love. I have experienced it in your companionship. I bless your name, even as I cry out to you for continued mercy and presence. I pray through Jesus my Lord, Amen!

❧ ❧ ❧

FEBRUARY 23

O LORD, I love the habitation of your house and the place where your glory dwells. (Ps. 26:8)

Of course, God has never been "confined" to a house or geographical location. God is at every location in every moment of time. In the Old Testament era, when Israel's neighbors all believed in territorial gods, the God of Israel never revealed himself as a regional God. He was the God over all creation who called Israel into a special relationship. Still, God set out a physical location to manifest his glory. There was a tabernacle coming out of the exodus experience, with its Ark of the Covenant. Then Solomon built a temple where God's glory was on full display as the home for the sacrifices and corporate worship of the nation. Once that temple was destroyed, the Jews returned from captivity and rebuilt a second temple, again as a "home" for God. But those temples, with their designated altars and the spaces set aside as the holiest of holies, were never the only places to find or encounter God.

So with a God who is everywhere, why did he recognize certain locations as his "house" or home? Undoubtedly God had many reasons. One reason that makes good sense is God used those opportunities to teach us that there is a calling on the people to come seek out God. We do not simply live accepting what is before us; we are to affirmatively seek out God in places and times of worship.

This is not because we have a God who *needs* our worship. He is not an empty God needing us to fill him up, nor is he an egotistic God needing to feast on the praises of people. We worship God because *we* need to do so. We are creatures who are not the end unto ourselves, we are hard-wired to worship. Our struggle is to worship God, rather than money, popularity, power, looks, heroes, or other substitutes.

As we understand the need to seek God out and worship him, it becomes something more than a chore. It becomes a marvelous experience. We find God and his glory and we transition into more of what we should be. Our eyes are taken off of the idols of this life, and we get transfixed on the King of Glory! This becomes something we love—worshipping and encountering God in his glory.

Lord, may we seek you in your holy righteousness. Help us become a people who love you and want to be in your presence, seeing your glory, and trumpeting it in worship. We love you and thank you in Jesus' name, Amen.

❧ ❧ ❧

FEBRUARY 24

The LORD is my light and my salvation; whom shall I fear? The LORD is the stronghold of my life; of whom shall I be afraid? . . . Though an army encamp against me, my heart shall not fear; though war arise against me, yet I will be confident. (Ps. 27:1, 3)

When I was four years old we lived in Abilene, Texas. I found myself in the backseat of the car while Dad drove through a torrential rainstorm, complete with booming thunder and crackling lightning. Mom told me there were tornados nearby and that they could cause a lot of damage. I was unfamiliar with the word "tornado" and my brain turned the word into the closest thing I knew. I thought there were monstrous big *tomatoes* coming and causing damage. Mom soon explained the difference in greater detail, and I knew what I really needed to fear.

Some people seem to have no fear. Then there are the rest of us. Some fear more than others, but to many of us, there is a lot to fear. We fear health issues, ours and others. I rarely hear of a disease that I don't worry I might have. We fear relationship problems, even when there is no cause for concern. We fear economic circumstances that might rage beyond our control. We fear life and death, and most everything in between.

Sometimes our fear makes sense. It is an objective fear that any sane person would have. Other times the fears may not make sense, but simply grow out of a troubled heart or mind. Our fear is often rooted in our lack of control. Where the unknown lurks, and where events spiral beyond our ability to predict or change, it stirs up fear.

We should face our fears with our faith in the Lord. Faith is rooted in knowing that God is in control. There is nothing that can sneak in without his watchful eye. With God as our stronghold and light, what should we fear? There isn't an army too strong for him.

When Paul was arrested in Jerusalem, the Roman tribune was going to have him scourged, a Roman torture devised to wrangle confessions. It often resulted in death and maiming. The crowds and Jewish hierarchy wanted Paul's head as well. God appeared to Paul and said, "Take courage, for as you have testified to the facts about me in Jerusalem, so you must testify also in Rome" (Acts 23:11). That was enough. Paul's fears were allayed, and he was protected by the unseen hand of God Almighty. Paul made it to Rome to testify, in spite of shipwreck, poisonous snakebites, unruly locals, unfair accusations, trials, and more. Such is our God.

Lord, please put my fears to rest. In Jesus' name, Amen!

❧ ❧ ❧

FEBRUARY 25

One thing have I asked of the LORD, that will I seek after: that I may dwell in the house of the LORD all the days of my life, to gaze upon the beauty of the LORD and to inquire in his temple. (Ps. 27:4)

If you could ask God for one thing, one personal request, as opposed to requests for those you love, what would it be? I like the psalmist's request. It might be mine.

To dwell in the house of the Lord each and every day of life would be incredible! The dwelling place of the Lord is a place of safety. No one can break into the house of God and do damage! God's dwelling is a place of provision. He has unlimited stores of all good things ready to provide. With God in the house, all the answers of life are there as well. After all, God knows all, so we have the perfect place to ask our questions. No wonder the psalmist seeks to *dwell* in the house of the Lord, not simply drop in for a visit! Gazing upon God in his beauty, inquiring and learning what is needed, these are great blessings.

For the psalmist, this idea was centered in the temple in Jerusalem. That was the house of God or dwelling of God. It is there the psalmist would "inquire" of the Lord. Times are different in these latter days (i.e., the days since the resurrection of Christ). We no longer have an earthly temple where the Lord symbolically dwells. God dwells within each believer! We are the temple of God, corporately as the "church" as well as individually as his Spirit dwells within us (1 Cor. 3:16; 6:19). This brings a whole new perspective to the psalm.

Now I can commune with God directly through the intermediary of Jesus my Savior. Now I can seek and inquire of the Lord without ceasing. Now I need not go somewhere to find God; he is at the door of my heart knocking and wanting to enter. God comes to dwell with me, not me with him. What could bring about this reversal? An intense desire by God to be with his children! We serve a God who seeks us out, calls us by name, and cares for us immensely.

Lord, how marvelous is the dwelling of your Spirit within us. May we seek to fellowship in that Spirit, may we live a life of unceasing prayer, may we walk in your light that you shine within us, and may your beauty transform our marred lives into something more closely resembling your Son our Savior through whom we pray, Amen!

❧ ❧ ❧

FEBRUARY 26

For he will hide me in his shelter in the day of trouble; he will conceal me under the cover of his tent; he will lift me high upon a rock. And now my head shall be lifted up above my enemies all around me, and I will offer in his tent sacrifices with shouts of joy. (Ps. 27:5-6)

When I was a young man, I listened to Amy Grant sing "Mountain Top," a song about how she would love to live on a mountaintop fellowshipping with the Lord as opposed to the valleys where toils and tribulations lie. Her heart was for the soaring fellowship of divine encounters, but she knew that part of life was going out into the valleys of the world to reach others so they could experience mountaintops with God.

I think of this often, but in a slightly different vein with this psalm. There is a world where problems lie. There is also a refuge from that world in the strong arms of our loving God. Like a mountaintop experience, in times of trouble we can flee to God and his protection. Through prayer and quiet times, we can set our concerns before God and find his peace and provision. He will "conceal" us from danger and rescue us.

But we no more live under the cover of his tent or in his shelter, than we live on the mountaintop. God doesn't shelter us so that we stay sheltered for the duration of life. God shelters us to prepare us to go back into the troubles and problems armed with his strength and direction. He empowers us and goes forth with us into troubles so we can live in victory over them, rather than simply run from them. He charges us to tell others of his role as a shelter in life's storms.

We see this as the psalmist writes that God will not only shelter and conceal but will also "lift me high upon a rock." That God will lift "my head above my enemies all around me" shows us that God doesn't just hide us. He shelters as we need it, but with a goal toward bringing us forth in victory! This is our mighty God at work growing us up in his love and power to do the things he has prepared for us. We love to live on the mountaintop, but those experiences are really just retreats that allow us to advance against the troubles of the world.

Lord, I come to you with the troubles of this life. Please rescue me. Be my rock and shelter in the storms of life. Hide and conceal me from my enemies until I can go forth built up in you, strong by your Spirit, ready to do battle on your behalf and on behalf of your kingdom. I thank you for your presence and your commitment to growing me up as your child. In the name of my Blessed Savior Jesus, Amen!

FEBRUARY 27

I believe that I shall look upon the goodness of the LORD *in the land of the living! Wait for the* LORD; *be strong, and let your heart take courage; wait for the* LORD! *(Ps. 27:13-14)*

I confess, I hate going to the dentist. Having someone put her hands in my mouth is not fun. Having shots in my mouth, drilling in my mouth, or heaven forbid, a root canal, is miserable. Yet I can endure these things because they are for a better tomorrow, and I usually tell myself, I can handle most things for an hour or two.

Going to the dentist pales in comparison to some of the tragedies of life. Loss of a loved one, destruction of a relationship, seeing someone dear abandon faith or get ensnared in darkness, these are ordeals that are not over in an hour. Travails at work or in a career, chronic health issues are not short-term events. I have seen people dear to me living with clinical depression or other mental problems. These are things that are a daily weight crying out for solutions when not one is in sight.

I wish at times we had a genie God who would resolve all our problems with the rubbing of a lamp and presentation of our wish. But God is not a bellhop who takes our luggage where we want at the snap of our fingers. We live in a fallen world where bad things happen, even to good people. We live in a world remade by sin, with all of the junk that goes with sin. God doesn't snap his fingers and remove our issues. He walks with us through the long journey. Resolution often takes time. The psalmist calls that "waiting upon the Lord."

It is something we do by faith. We put one step in front of the other in the midst of the world's garbage, believing that we will see God's goodness in this life. We take strength in faith, knowing who the Lord is. We know what he has done in history, ancient and our own, and we encourage our hearts with that knowledge. God is not absent, but he has his own timing. We wait for him, knowing that we are not alone in the process. He is with us, and will bring the deliverance in his timing. Until then, we wait faithfully, trusting our God with our lives.

Lord, I give you today. I have worries and concerns, some of which have long been here and look likely to continue for a long time. Father, I confess the difficulties of waiting, but do so asking for your grace and mercy in teaching me patience in your timing. So today is yours, Lord, with all that I struggle through. Be my strength as I wait for you. Through Jesus my Lord, Amen!

❧ ❧ ❧

FEBRUARY 28

To you, O LORD, *I call; my rock, be not deaf to me, lest, if you be silent to me, I become like those who go down to the pit. Hear the voice of my pleas for mercy, when I cry to you for help, when I lift up my hands toward your most holy sanctuary.* (Ps. 28:1-2)

I tend to live life on two levels. I work to make sure the levels merge. Let me explain.

On one level, life is constantly throwing curve balls where the unexpected or the difficult happens. These are times where I must make decisions. I have to prevent problems from getting out of hand, or have to fix them if they are out of hand. How to live responsibly, how to use time wisely, how to be productive in relationships and life, on one level, I address these things by how I choose to live.

On a second level, I seek and need divine assistance. Often this is because there are things that I can't control, fears that can paralyze; difficulties with no apparent way out drive me to my knees (or the knees of my heart), seeking the Lord.

These two levels need to merge. When I was a child, our preacher once said, "Live like it's all up to you. Pray like it's all up to God." I've chewed on that one for forty-five years. I'm still not sure about the details on that, but I like the way it merges the two levels. I have friends who were unemployed and decided not to look for a job, instead simply praying and trusting that God would bring the job to their door. They didn't merge the two levels (and didn't get a job until months later when they started looking!).

God made us as decision makers. We are made in the image of the Creator God. We can create. We can make opportunities. We should do so. Yet we should never live only on the level of our actions. Without level two, without seeking God in even the small details, we rush headlong into disaster; it's just a matter of time. Here is the psalmist cry, "God, hear our prayers! Listen and answer! If you don't, all is hopeless."

The key is to make that a daily prayer. Pray even when the skies are *not* gray and dismal. Pray even when the storms don't enter conscious thought because the sun is out and the wind is nice. Let the prayerful cry of our heart constantly merge with the actions of our lives.

Lord, hear our prayer and attend to our cries. We need you in each minute of our day. We need you just as much when the day is pretty as when the storms of life rage. Be our vision, be our strength, be our direction, even as you are our hope through Jesus, Amen!

❧ ❧ ❧

FEBRUARY 29

For by you I can run against a troop, and by my God I can leap over a wall. (Ps. 18:29)

February 29! Leap day in leap year! A great year and a great day to remember, by God's help, we can *leap* over a wall, or run against a troop!

There is no obstacle that stands in the way of God working in his children. As we bring willing hearts, faithful lives, and trusting commitment into concert with the will of God, anything can happen.

Jesus understood this, teaching his disciples, "Truly, I say to you, if you have faith like a grain of mustard seed, you will say to this mountain, 'Move from here to there,' and it will move, and nothing will be impossible for you" (Matt. 17:20). When I was a young teenager, I figured that I might never have enough faith to move a mountain, but maybe if I worked at it hard enough, I might be able to move a pencil! It seemed to me that faith might be like weights at the school gym. The more I exercised it, the more it would grow. So I might want to start moving something really small!

As I grew older, and as I grew in faith, I learned where I had gone wrong. Jesus spent his life teaching others the importance of serving God, modeling his love, and in humility, growing in holiness. This means that we need to learn God's will, and apply ourselves to it. That is the given, before we ever get to the passage about moving mountains by faith. With that understanding, I grew to realize that the only mountain I would seek to move in faith, is the one that God declares should be moved! (The same is true for moving pencils.) I don't want to move any other mountain, and no one acting and living in faith would either.

This same idea is behind Paul's teaching to the Philippians that, "I can do all things through him who strengthens me" (Phil. 4:13). Paul said that not in the sense that he brought great and marvelous things into his life. He said it in the context of learning to be at peace when he was impoverished.

When we walk in alignment with God's will, there is no wall we can't climb. There is no troop we cannot charge. As I look at my life in leap year, or any year, on February 29 or any day, I can look at the walls and adversaries, and know that all I need to do is find God's will. Then I can be at peace.

Lord, in the midst of all that is in this world and my life, teach me to find your will, and empower me to pursue your will. In Jesus' holy name, Amen!

❧ ❧ ❧

MARCH 1

Do not drag me off with the wicked, with the workers of evil, who speak peace with their neighbors while evil is in their hearts. . . . Because they do not regard the works of the LORD or the work of his hands, he will tear them down and build them up no more. (Ps. 28:3, 5)

Who are you hanging around? Who are your close friends and companions? When I started work after law school, I was at a large firm where the few people I first worked with did not seem to be people of faith. Several seemed quite far from it! I thought several of them might even be "wicked" in the sense of this psalm. They "spoke peace" with their co-workers while "evil was in their hearts." They acted nice, but were bent on beating their co-workers on the road to partnership. Of the fifty-six lawyers hired in my year, the rumor was that only five would eventually get to be a partner.

This made these people tough to be around. I knew we often become like those with whom we spend time, and I sure didn't want to become like them. In prayer, I began asking God to send a Christian brother into the firm to be a friend and companion. He honored that prayer almost immediately and Chip became my bud. He still is over thirty years later. God also showed me a number of other really good people working there.

Because of our tendency to be like the people with whom we associate, we need to choose carefully who become our intimate friends. They need to be people who regard the Lord and the works of his hands. Those friends will enhance our lives, and vice versa.

The wicked really will be "dragged off," as the psalmist notes. They will be torn down. This is the way the world is set up. This should not make us think that God is mean. It is true because sin is destructive. God has told us as much. It is not God's fault if he tells us, "If you put your hand on a hot stove, you will get burned" and then we do it. He warned us about the world and its consequences. So it is with sin. Sin breeds destruction and death. It may take a while. It may not be obvious. But it does.

So take care in making your friends. Of course this does not mean that as believers we should withdraw from the world. We are called to be salt and light (Matt. 5:13ff.). We are to aid the work of Jesus and "seek" to save the lost (Luke 19:10). But as we do so, we do so in a community of believers, built up and secured in relationships rooted in the truth of God. We don't want to go down with the evildoers!

Lord, place in our lives other believers who can encourage, uplift, and help us focus on a life of service to you. Let our counselors be godly friends who know you. May we likewise be available to be such friends to other believers, even as we reach out to the lost in Jesus' name, Amen!

MARCH 2

Blessed be the LORD! For he has heard the voice of my pleas for mercy. The LORD is my strength and my shield; in him my heart trusts, and I am helped; my heart exults, and with my song I give thanks to him. (Ps. 28:6-7)

The Hebrew of this psalm is classic Hebrew poetry. One line especially stands out to me, both for the beauty of its poetic structure and the meaning that structure imparts.

The premise of the line is set forth in the first half of the verses above. In blessing the Lord, the psalmist declares God as "my strength and my shield." This is the God who has heard the cries for mercy. Then comes "the line": "in him my heart trusts, and I am helped; my heart exults, and with my song I give thanks to him." In the Hebrew this is just eight words, though it takes twenty-one English words to translate it.

A hallmark of Hebrew poetry is the way it mirrors itself in parallel structures. It will say one line, and then say the same basic thing using other words. The poetry is found in discerning the variation in the two parallel statements and finding the nuanced difference in meanings. (Sometimes the parallel statement conveys the opposite of the first statement, or even other times the next logical step in a sequence of thought.) Here we have simple parallel structures of thought to help us get nuanced meaning.

Setting out a literal translation, I will put brackets around the many English words it takes to make up some of the single Hebrew words, and bold font the key repeated word: Phrase 1's four words: [In him] trusts [**my heart**] [and I am helped]. Phrase 2's four words: exults [**my heart**] [and with my song] [I give thanks to him]. Now the nuance and point of this meditation: As I trust in God with my heart, or as I give my emotions and thoughts up to him, I get his help. Going hand in hand with trusting God with my heart is exulting or praising him with my heart. I do so with songs of thanksgiving. This is a beautiful poetic idea that we come before God with trust and thanksgiving, knowing he will hear our cries for mercy and come to our rescue. Paul put it less poetically, but more bluntly when he told the church at Philippi, "*do not be anxious about anything, but in everything by prayer and supplication with thanksgiving let your requests be made known to God. And the peace of God, which surpasses all understanding, will guard your hearts and your minds in Christ Jesus*" (Phil. 4:6-7).

Lord, we take all that we have before us today and set it before you. Embolden us, empower us, direct us, strengthen us, move us, teach us, use us. We trust you to do with our day what is in the very best interests of your kingdom we seek to serve. Thank you for hearing our prayer and for answering our cries for mercy. In Jesus' name, Amen!

✻ ✻ ✻

MARCH 3

Teach me to do your will, for you are my God! Let your good Spirit lead me on level ground! (Ps. 143:10)

In the United States, as in most developed countries, education is mandatory. By the age of five, children are in kindergarten, and many children start preschool before that. Of course, all learning is not done at school, much happens at home. I was blessed with an older sister who would come home from school each day and find me waiting to play. One of my sister's favorite games to play with me was "school." She would teach me what she learned that day. Needless to say, it gave me a great jump on school when I finally started.

Today's passage is a call for God to teach us. We are not asking for his help with reading, writing, or arithmetic, rather we want him to teach us his will. This is a most valuable thing well worth learning. Knowing the will of God, we can make the best choices. It will affect everything from the practical (where we live, what we do, who we marry, etc.) to the moral (how we live, right and wrong, etc.). Knowing the will of God is called "wisdom" in the Bible (Col. 1:9).

Paul wrote of two kinds of wisdom, common wisdom of the world, which he explained could often be foolish, and wisdom of God, which is insight into God's will and ways (1 Cor. 1:17-2:7). James told the believers to pray for wisdom with the assurance God would answer that prayer (Jas. 1:5). Paul prayer for the Ephesians to have a spirit of wisdom in the knowledge of God (Eph. 1:17).

How does God teach wisdom? He uses a variety of ways. A very basic one is found in the words of Scripture. Paul explained to Timothy that the Bible, though he was speaking of the Old Testament it applies equally to the New Testament, contained inspired words from God that are useful for teaching, training and the like (2 Tim. 3:16). By reading the words of God, we better understand his ways. We also learn wisdom from God by studying the life of Christ. Jesus was "filled with wisdom" (Luke 2:40), and as we read of him, we can learn. Of course, God also teaches us wisdom through life itself. This is not always easy. Sometimes it is the "school of hard knocks," but God uses discipline, good and bad events, to teach us his wisdom, just as a parent does a child (Heb. 12:5-6).

Wisdom draws us nearer to God, gives us insight for living, and puts our feet on the right paths for a joyful and successful life. I want this wisdom of God. I want to know his ways and will. James says if I ask, God will teach it to me. The psalmist modeled such a prayer.

Lord, please teach me to do your will. Give me wisdom and insight for living. Lead me in the ways I should go. In Jesus' name and for his sake, I pray amen!

❧ ❧ ❧

MARCH 4

The voice of the LORD is over the waters; the God of glory thunders, the LORD, over many waters. The voice of the LORD is powerful; the voice of the LORD is full of majesty. The voice of the LORD breaks the cedars; the LORD breaks the cedars of Lebanon. He makes Lebanon to skip like a calf. . . . The voice of the LORD flashes forth flames of fire. The voice of the LORD shakes the wilderness. . . . The voice of the LORD makes the deer give birth and strips the forests bare, and in his temple all cry, "Glory!" (Ps. 29:3-9)

This psalm uses amazing pictures of a terrifying and life-threatening thunderstorm to help the readers "hear" the voice of the Lord! God speaks into our lives and world, and he does so loudly, yet many of us do not recognize his voice.

God's voice is powerful. What God has to say matters. It confronts our reality and reveals truth. The power of God's voice stems from who God is. God is the majestic, all-knowing God who speaks out of wisdom and holiness. When we hear his voice, we are hearing something that changes the world. God speaks and things change on a personal level, a national level and an international level. God is not relegated to some small aspect of life; his voice can be heard everywhere, over many waters.

The power of God's voice is like the roar of thunder. It is like the flash of lightning. These are things over which no one can exercise control. No one dictates when thunder or lightning happens. They proceed independently of you or me. They *are*. So with the voice of God. He is not a stereo we turn on when we are in the mood for music. We do not select the song he sings. God issues forth his voice, and our choice is fairly limited. We can understand it is the voice of God and let his praise be heard in our responsive voice ("and all cry 'Glory!' "), or we can write his voice off as a thunderstorm and live on in ignorance.

I know the voice of God through his word and Word. Through the Scriptures, we have God giving us his words to help us understand him, understand ourselves, and understand our lives. These words also help us "hear" the Word with a capital W. Jesus as the Word of God thunders forth into this world and into our lives as a real historical event. In the life of Jesus, we hear God's powerful voice speaking to us of his love, his desire to be with us, and his power over the grave. God is speaking to us loudly. Am I listening?

Lord, I confess I do not always hear you speaking. Sometimes I shut myself off. Sometimes I am distracted. Sometimes I don't want to hear and am rebellious. I confess that, and ask not only for your forgiveness, but pray for you to speak into my life, opening my ears and moving my heart to acknowledge your voice and ascribe you all glory! In Jesus, your voice, Amen!

❊ ❊ ❊

MARCH 5

I will extol you, O LORD, for you have drawn me up and have not let my foes rejoice over me. O LORD my God, I cried to you for help, and you have healed me. (Ps. 30:1-2)

Today we still have the expression of being "down." We speak of being "down in the dumps." James Taylor and Carole King sing of being "down and troubled" when you need the helping hand of a friend. Simon and Garfunkel's "Bridge over Troubled Water" speaks to one who is "down and out," "weary, feeling small." Eric Clapton hit the charts with his version of the 1923 blues song written by Jimmie Cox, "Nobody Knows You When You're Down and Out," complaining that when you're broke, you have no friends.

The idea of being "down" is not a late idea in civilization. It was back in the Psalms. This psalm uses the idea as it credits God for being there when one is down and in need. God doesn't simply meet the one who is down and sit in the dumps with that person. God "draws up" the psalmist who was down. The ones responsible for the psalmist's problems are not greater than the God who meets the psalmist in need.

The psalmist let out a cry to God for help, and the help came. The psalmist continues testifying that "weeping may tarry for the night, but rejoicing comes in the morning" (Ps. 30:5). That is real consolation, but we need to be careful to understand it. Weeping can "tarry for the night." That means that sorrow, and down times might not be resolved in the instant we pray. It is also unfair to put a twelve-hour limit on any of our sad emotions. When we are sad, when we are down, we constantly seek the presence of God and he comes to us. We can rest assured he will stay with us, and we can be sure that the sadness will eventually pass, as certainly as night passes into morning.

Too many times we live in the moment, letting the struggles of our current emotional state dictate our reality. Yet that is not how we should live. Our struggles of the moment are simply that: struggles of the moment. God transcends time and struggles and promises to lift us out of the dumps! He will come to our rescue. He will hear our cries. He will be merciful and he will heal us.

Lord, when our emotions rock us back and forth, when sadness captures our present reality, please turn our hearts and minds to you. Hear our cries for mercy. Help us in our crises, and help us live in faith, trusting your love and power over our circumstances and feelings. May we bask in the confidence of our Savior who set down his own emotions before you, trusting in your deliverance from the grave. By his grace and in his name, Amen!

❧ ❧ ❧

MARCH 6

You are my rock and my fortress; and for your name's sake you lead me and guide me. . . . Into your hand I commit my spirit; you have redeemed me, O Lord, faithful God. (Ps. 31:3, 5)

It is hard for someone familiar with the crucifixion story to read this passage without immediately thinking of Jesus uttering his last words on the cross, "Father, into your hands I commit my spirit!" (Luke 23:46). In reading it with Jesus in mind, sometimes I forget how the psalm is also written to admonish and lead me in life. I need to live a life of total surrender to God.

If we carefully think through our conscious thoughts, we find that we often live directed out of what we want, what we think best, where we wish to be, and how we believe things should be. That is all well and good, but only if the superior thought that governs our actions as well as thinking is one of submitting to God.

It helps me to take each day, although sometimes I need to break it down further than a day, and consciously surrender myself to God. Prayerfully acknowledging God and submitting to his specific will can be as simple as adding a line to the Lord's Prayer, saying, "Thy will be done, on earth as it is in heaven, and in my life, as it is in heaven!" It can also be more directed to, "Lord, today I am doing *ABC*. In doing those things, I submit myself to you. Use me, work through me, express your will in how and what I do."

This type of surrender is powerful and right, but it is also *smart!* After all, as the psalmist assures us, God can be our rock and fortress. God leads and guides us, not letting us wander around lost or searching for something. We are smart in surrendering to such a God because we know that we will be exactly where we need to be, doing exactly what we need to be doing. God is not a removed supervisor who periodically checks in on us. He is hands-on, caring about the smallest details, and wanting to engage with us in ways that grow us and his kingdom.

So we see in Jesus on Calvary, an absolute and total surrender to the faithful God that brought him forth from the grave. We may never come close to Jesus' surrender to God, but it shouldn't stop us from coming as close as we can. God is no less faithful to us, as evidenced by the fact of Jesus' death. It is evidence of his love and care for us.

Lord, I surrender myself to you. Fully and without question, Lord, today belongs to you in my life. Each moment, each challenge, each opportunity, each responsibility, I lay before you and commit to your hand. Use me as you see fit. In the name of Jesus, my role model, Amen!

❄ ❄ ❄

MARCH 7

Be gracious to me, O LORD, for I am in distress; my eye is wasted from grief; my soul and my body also. For my life is spent with sorrow, and my years with sighing; my strength fails because of my iniquity, and my bones waste away. . . . But I trust in you, O LORD; I say, "You are my God." My times are in your hand. (Ps. 31:9-10, 14-15)

Earlier on the day I'm writing this, I had brunch with a high school friend (and her husband) I hadn't seen in thirty-eight years. We worked to catch up on nearly four decades in one hour. A good bit of our time was spent talking about their autistic daughter. My friends amazed me. They spoke with love and concern about the difficulties. How their daughter went almost one year in high school without uttering a single syllable. This daughter is now twenty-five, and they still have to help her brush her teeth, they rinse the shampoo from her hair, and more. This is more than a lifetime challenge, assuming the daughter outlives my friends.

Sometimes our struggles are fairly short term. We have a problem, but the problem then passes. It may be days, weeks, or even months. But sometimes our challenges and difficulties last much longer. The psalmist writes of "years with sighing" and a "life spent with sorrow." This was not a short-term problem. This was long term!

When faced with events that change life, we have choices. We can run, living in denial or irresponsibility. We can grandstand our misery calling out a pity party from anyone who will listen. Or we can trust in God, placing our lives in his hands in confidence that come what may, God is at work. Regardless of how we feel, we can know there is a God who loves tenderly, overflowing with mercy. So even in the midst of great and constant difficulty, God is reaching out to take care of his children.

This is where my friends are. They told me that God has taught them so much over the twenty-five years they've faced this challenge. My friends are working on what will happen to their daughter once they pass on. They will make plans, but they know that ultimately it is in God's hands. They are at peace with that.

I need more faith. I don't have problems like my friends do. My worst challenges are relatively mild compared to theirs. Yet my need to trust in God is no less. I need to learn from the psalmist and my friends.

Lord, rewire my mind to better understand this life. Help me to see your hand at work, even in this fallen world where things aren't fair, where people aren't always healthy, where suffering and distress are common. Let me find trust in you. You are my God. My times are in your hands. In Jesus' name, Amen!

❧ ❧ ❧

MARCH 8

Blessed is the one whose transgression is forgiven, whose sin is covered. Blessed is the man against whom the Lord counts no iniquity, and in whose spirit there is no deceit. (Ps. 32:1-2)

This passage means a lot to me on several levels. It attests to a forgiveness that I desperately need in my life. God's forgiveness of my sins marks the difference between a life worth living and a dead life just waiting to expire. If my sins were tied to me, and there was no forgiveness, then I am uncertain how I would function in any even remotely constructive way. The impending doom would be too great.

This passage also helps me understand my sin. In it are several Hebrew words used for sin, noted by a range of words used in translation: "transgression," "sin," "iniquity," and "deceit." The forgiveness of God also compels several Hebrew words: "forgiven," "covered," "counts no . . . ," and "there is no." Each has a level of nuance.

The word "transgression" indicates a rebellion or breaking loose from God. It is me tearing away from God. This is paired with the word translated "forgiven," indicating a "lifting up." So, I tore away from God, and he lifted me back up. Thank you, God.

"Sin" conveys the idea of deviating from that which is pleasing to God. Those sins are mine. It is paired with the word for "cover" or "conceal," because God has taken my sins and concealed them. He has made them invisible as if I never did them, and he sees them no more. Thank you, God.

"Iniquity" conveys the idea of "perversion" or "distortion." I have surely perverted the will and instructions of God. I have distorted his righteous morality, yet he doesn't "count" or "number" such horrors of my behavior. Thank you, God.

"Deceit" refers to my desire to hide, deny, or excuse my sins. I am not to do that, under the instruction of this psalm. God will forgive, lift up, cover, not count, my many sins, but I better not make excuses or try to hide them on my own. I can't hide my sin from God; I can only confess it and seek his forgiveness. When I do so, he forgives and I am "blessed." Thank you, God!

Lord, I do confess myself a rebellious sinner who has done wrong over and over in my life, both in my actions and in what I fail to do. Even when I have done "right" by you, I have too often done so with poor or inadequate motives. Lord, may I walk in your forgiveness and the joy of your blessings rather than some misplaced latent guilt. May the forgiveness rooted in Jesus free me to smile as I serve you today. In him, Amen!

❦ ❦ ❦

MARCH 9

I will instruct you and teach you in the way you should go; I will counsel you with my eye upon you. Be not like a horse or a mule, without understanding, which must be curbed with bit and bridle, or it will not stay near you. (Ps. 32:8-9)

Education is expensive. Public school education may seem free, but it isn't. It has a high cost that is paid by tax dollars. Private schools thrive because parents are willing to pay large sums to see their children get the best education possible. It is never the money, however, that ensures the quality of the education. Educational quality is determined by the quality of the teacher and the willingness of the student. An outstanding teacher *has* the knowledge to impart and knows how to best impart it. A good student has a desire to learn and the ability to do so.

The psalmist wrote of education in how to live. In living, one may learn from a "School of Wisdom," or one may learn from the "School of Hard Knocks," whose colors are black and blue. We can learn the importance of honesty by listening to one teach it, or we can learn by being burned from being dishonest. We can learn the importance of sobriety by listening to teaching, or we can experience the messes in life that come from drunkenness. We can learn the importance of _____—fill in the blank with most any sin—by listening to the Lord's instructions, or we can experience the devastation of sin, and with regret say, "If only I'd listened."

This psalm delivers this message as a good teacher. The psalmist explains that wisdom and Scripture will instruct people in how to live. From God's word, we get important and simple guidelines that help us in our homes, business, social relationships, and in our individual efforts to grow. We can find the importance of morality which Jesus summed up in two commandments: loving God fully, and loving our neighbors as we love ourselves (Matt. 22:37-40). Our choice as students is simple. Do we choose to learn from these instructions, or do we, thinking we know better, set ourselves upon our own course, choosing our own way based on our own hearts and minds.

Should we take the latter approach, we are warned, the truth will still enter our lives, albeit the hard way. Like a horse needing tight reins and a bit/bridle, we wind up with life controlling us, rather than us seizing the reins and living life controlled by God. The instructions we have, are not to make us miserable. They set us where we need to be, to become who we should become. That is what I want, so I need to listen and learn!

Lord, teach me. I want to listen and learn. Give me a willing and submissive heart. In Jesus' name, Amen!

MARCH 10

Many are the sorrows of the wicked, but steadfast love surrounds the one who trusts in the LORD. *Be glad in the* LORD, *and rejoice, O righteous, and shout for joy, all you upright in heart!* (Ps. 32:10-11)

I didn't grow up in a church that was outwardly expressive. The church taught us to love and worship the Lord, and there were marvelous and holy people in the church who worshipped the Lord devoutly. But it was rather unanimated. Then I went off to college, and began worshipping at a church that was almost the opposite. It was a place where people were quite expressive in their worship. It was not uncommon during certain songs to see some standing while others sat and a few even knelt. Some had their palms lifted upward, some had arms held high, and some kept their arms at their sides. Some gazed heavenward, others straightforward, and some bowed their heads. I found it unusual, and it was difficult for me to understand those heavily expressive in a physical sense—until one night at a Bruce Springsteen concert where things changed for me.

I had no issues with the response of the concert crowd, who sang as urged by Bruce, swayed as urged by Bruce, pumped their fist with shouts or were hushed into silence. The thought hit me like a downbound train: I understood being more fully involved in singing at a concert than being so involved in singing to God. I knew I needed an attitude change.

Lots of people have lots of problems. But those people who know God, and are in a relationship with him, find a joy in the midst of problems. This joy stems from God's faithful and constant love for us. Problems? Yes! But we need not fear. We have a Lord who surrounds us. This makes us glad. We appropriately respond to God in worship, but not simply "singing." As the psalmist instructs, we praise with "shouts of joy." In church, we are with others who live in fellowship with the protecting and loving God.

This is the unbridled worship and joy being called for in this psalm: not to the distraction of others, but not self-conscious limitation either. This purely comes from a heart in tune with the praiseworthy God. Here we find shouting to the Lord not just allowable, but encouraged! To modify Bruce, "Baby we were born to worship!"

Lord, with a loud voice, let me proclaim to the nations, to the powers and principalities your magnificence as the God who saves us in love and compassion. You have reached into our lives to bring us deeply into a walk with you, fulfilling your purposes for us during our days on earth. What an honor and blessing! THANK YOU LORD! *In Jesus, Amen!*

❧ ❧ ❧

MARCH 11

Shout for joy in the LORD, *O you righteous! Praise befits the upright. Give thanks to the* LORD *with the lyre; make melody to him with the harp of ten strings! Sing to him a new song; play skillfully on the strings, with loud shouts.* (Ps. 33:1-3)

Praising God is right! It is what the righteous should be doing. God has done great things. He is a great God. He has cared for us beyond what we deserve because he has the character of a loving and kind God. He is patient, and will go as far as possible to restore our relationship with him. He seeks to destroy evil with its horrid implications for us. He teaches us how to behave so we best avoid the traps of sin's seductions. He restores us when we fall, he redeems us from sin, and he sets us into the path of eternity. He uses us for his good works, empowering us to achieve things we'd otherwise never do.

Praise is rightly due our God, and so we are right when we praise him. This praise includes our thanks to him. We are to recognize him as the source of every good thing (Jas. 1:17). This includes life, family, friends, freedoms, jobs, food, clothing, opportunities, our relationship with him, our insights into his nature and character, the answers to our prayers, the protection from evil's natural ends, the strength to endure life's hardships, the wisdom to be productive, the forgiveness of sins, the indwelling of the Holy Spirit, and more. Our gratitude and appreciation toward God should be proclaimed on our lips.

This praise is not because God is a despot in need of adoration from his little creatures. It is right and proper because he *deserves* praise. It is the honor due his name. We also praise him because of what it does *for us*. Praising God removes us from the throne as we recognize him there. We need to worship him for our own sakes! It gives us a grip on reality! We can't be god if we are truly worshipping the real God!

So let's follow the psalm and worship the Lord. Let's do so, not subconsciously or halfheartedly. Let's do so deliberately and with purpose. We can use our talents (instruments) to bear on our praise. Let's do so skillfully because he is worthy of our best efforts. We dare not praise with anything less than the best we have. Let's sing and write new songs, after all, his work in our lives is new every morning. Praise the Lord!

Father and God, we lift your name high, singing to you the praises due your name. You alone are God. You alone are worthy of our praise. You are worthy of all glory and honor. We are yours, and we have grateful hearts for your many blessings. Forgive our ingratitude, even as we continue to walk in your blessings, most notably in Jesus, through whom we pray, Amen!

MARCH 12

*Our soul waits for the L*ORD*; he is our help and our shield. For our heart is glad in him, because we trust in his holy name. Let your steadfast love, O L*ORD*, be upon us, even as we hope in you.* (Ps. 33:20-22)

Read this passage from the middle out! The middle sentence informs the sentence before and the sentence after. The middle sentence says our joy in the Lord—a deep-seated joy in the heart—comes from trusting in God's name. Trusting in his name means we trust in his power and character. Who he is and what he's done gives us the confidence to rely on him for our today and tomorrow. Our fears subside in the strength of our God. Our worries melt away in the bright burning love of the almighty God.

Now see how the middle sentence drives the meaning of the first sentence. Our soul waits for the Lord *because* of our confidence in him. We know he will be where we need, when we need, and how we need him. He is our help. He protects and defends. We do not live an isolated life when we are God's. We live an active life with him at our side.

This makes sense in light of the resources of God our helper. He comes to our aid knowing us fully, the events of our lives, our strengths and weaknesses. He knows our situation in life, the challenges, the pitfalls, the dangers, the trouble spots. God also comes to bear on our lives with all the power needed to render aid. He has power to resurrect the dead. He has all of nature at his disposal. After all, he made it.

Of course, all the knowledge, and all the power would be meaningless if God didn't also have the desire to help. Here is the significance of God's name. We have a God who not only numbers the hairs on our heads (Matt. 10:30), but who has shown repeatedly in history he wants to walk with us in our lives. He desires our fellowship. In Christ, we see not only redemption but fellowship.

This naturally leads to the prayer of the final sentence. We pray for God's steadfast love, even as we wait for it to be manifest. He doesn't leave us alone. He doesn't periodically visit us with an ambivalent or nonchalant manner. He is a zealous and caring Father who comes upon our lives in love. He is looking out for us. We can wait confidently assured of this because it is rooted in who he is, not in who we are!

Lord, we gladly wait for you, with open eyes and trusting hearts. We pray for you to come rescue us, touch us, direct us, infuse us with your love and heart for others. Let us take up your kingdom and will as reasons for living. Empower us to fulfill your plans for us. In this we have great joy, through Jesus our Lord, Amen!

❦ ❦ ❦

MARCH 13

The king is not saved by his great army; a warrior is not delivered by his great strength. The war horse is a false hope for salvation, and by its great might it cannot rescue. Behold, the eye of the LORD is on those who fear him, on those who hope in his steadfast love, that he may deliver their soul from death. (Ps. 33:16-19)

We must be careful with verses like these. They correctly teach that a king's army is not what keeps the king or the people safe. No matter how strong or talented a warrior, that skill set is not what will win the day. One can have the best equipment and support (a "warhorse" in ancient terminology), but that is an illusory protection. The verses also correctly teach that deliverance comes from the Lord. God watches over his people and protects them as part of his steadfast unfailing love.

So how must we be careful with these verses? The verses do *not* teach that a king shouldn't have an army, that a warrior should not work on his strength, or that a warhorse is not a valuable item in battle. All of those are valuable! But they are only as valuable as the Lord who works in and through them. The earthly view sees the army/warrior/horse as the key. The spiritual view sees the God behind those things, both providing them and bringing them success. They are God's tools!

This equates well with the story of Nehemiah, the Jew who worked to rebuild the fallen walls of Jerusalem. The enemies who were set against the reconstruction were determined to stop the progress, with violence and battle if need be. Nehemiah prayed to God for protection of the workers. Nehemiah was a holy and faithful fellow who, in seeking God's protection was doing the right thing. After praying, Nehemiah, still a holy and faithful fellow, then put soldiers up on the wall to provide protection! "And we prayed to our God and set a guard as a protection against them day and night" (Neh. 4:9).

Here we see the full story. Our lives are to be lived in prayer to the Lord for right consequences in his will. We are to set our needs before him in prayer. We are also to act in confirmation of the prayer knowing God frequently chooses to work through us. He is at work in teaching us, renewing our minds, making us more insightful in wisdom as well as holiness. With faith, we see the effects of our labors working as driven by God. We are not sitting in the back seat leaving the driving to God. We are driving as he directs us and as he empowers us.

Lord, we give you our lives. Give us wisdom and insight to be whom you want us to be, to access the tools you wish us to use, and to do the tasks you set before us. In Jesus' name, Amen!

❧ ❧ ❧

MARCH 14

I will bless the L<small>ORD</small> *at all times; his praise shall continually be in my mouth. My soul makes its boast in the* L<small>ORD</small>; *let the humble hear and be glad. Oh, magnify the* L<small>ORD</small> *with me, and let us exalt his name together!* (Ps. 34:1-3)

Notice the transition in today's psalm. It begins with "me" and moves to "we."

The psalm starts with "I will bless the Lord." Not right now, not on Sundays, but "at all times." It is something I will do when I am happy, and something I will do when I am sad. I will bless him when things are marvelous and when times are bad. I will bless him at all times, and others will hear it! They will hear because his praise is continually coming from my mouth. I will let others know the greatness of the Lord, even when my skies are gray and sorrows are on my doorstep. I will tell of his wonderful love regardless of where my struggle is in life.

The psalmist words his praise a second way. *"My soul makes its boast in the* L<small>ORD</small>." Boasting and pride should never be in one's own actions or achievements. If we are honest, as believers we know our success is directly linked to the Lord. Nothing we can do would prosper without him and the blessings he has placed in our lives. So as we find victory, and as the world sees us walk in victory, we need to readily say, "God is good!" For me as a trial lawyer, when that jury returns a successful verdict, and all the crowd of well-wishers surround me to congratulate me, the right thing to say is simple, "God is good." When the trial turns out against my client and me, the reaction must still be the same, "God is good." I will boast in the Lord at all times.

At this point the psalm turns in transition. As I proclaim the Lord and praise him, making him my boast, then those who are humble will hear *and* be glad. It takes a humble heart to truly hear the work of the Lord. When we are proud, we associate victory with human strength. That, after all, is what makes us proud—what we have done and how we have done it. But those who are humble in heart, more readily understand the truth behind the praise to God, and they join in that praise also being glad at the work of the Lord.

The psalm then calls upon the readers to join in and "magnify the L<small>ORD</small> *with* me." Together we will exalt his name. This is the progression, as we proclaim God continually, it becomes infectious. It has an effect on others who are moved to praise also. I like this.

Lord, I lift your name and praise you as a marvelous, caring, compassionate God. You have been patient with me, you have taught me, you have disciplined me when needed. You put encouragement in my heart; you bring peace amidst turmoil. You are worthy of all praise. In Jesus' name, Amen!

MARCH 15

Those who look to him are radiant, and their faces shall never be ashamed. (Ps. 34:5)

This is a short verse, but one worth our focus. Looking to God will change our appearance. When we look to God, the psalm says we become "radiant" (or we "shine"). The Hebrew idea behind "look" includes looking upon someone, but also the idea of "paying attention to" or "showing regard to." This can and does show on us. Why?

We know that Moses was told he could not look upon the face of God and live (Exod. 33:20). However, Moses glimpsed the back of God in his glory and that alone caused Moses' face to reflect God's glory with his face shining so much that he wore a veil (Exod. 33:23, 30-33)

There is a tremendous thing that happens when we regard the Lord. As we look to him, we turn away from the ideas and thoughts of the world. Our focus leaves the shadows and is brought into the light. It changes our mood, it changes our countenance, it changes how we behave, it changes our perspective, it changes beliefs, it changes our priorities, it changes *how* we think, it instills confidence, faith, hope, love, it trains us, it provides direction, it empowers us and comforts us, it removes fear of this life and our adversaries, it melts away worries and stress, and much, much more. Of course as these things happen, it is reflected in our appearance.

We have all seen the effect stress has on people. We see people truly weighed down with worry. I suspect that concerns in this life alone are partly responsible for at least fifteen of the extra pounds I carry! It is called "comfort food" for a reason!

I need to learn to turn to the Lord. I need to pay attention to him and give him due regard. Early each morning, I need to turn to him in prayer. Before I go to sleep at night, I need to speak with him in prayer. During the day, I need to readily and rapidly come to him in prayer, in the midst of daily life. My mind needs to stay in constant dialogue with the God who made it all possible through the intermediary Jesus Christ.

Some days the change will be drastic; other days it may not be so visible. But no one can be in the presence of the Lord and remain unchanged. He will change us on the inside, and as whole people made of body and spirit, such changes will reflect on the outside. This also gives us a chance to praise God before those of the world who say, "What is it about you that is so different?" That is a marvelous conversation starter about looking to the Lord!

Lord, we look to you. Let us see you in ways that bring about your will in our lives. We want to be like you and reflect your glory to the world through Jesus, Amen!

MARCH 16

Oh, taste and see that the Lord *is good! Blessed is the man who takes refuge in him! Oh, fear the* Lord, *you his saints, for those who fear him have no lack! The young lions suffer want and hunger; but those who seek the* Lord *lack no good thing.* (Ps. 34:8-10)

Experiencing God can be rich! We might be tempted to think of our interaction with God involving only our minds. After all, we read Scripture with our minds, we pray in our minds, we contemplate God in our minds, and we seek him in our thoughts. But the psalmist in these verses makes a bold metaphor that moves the experience of God beyond the mind.

"Taste and see" presents two physical senses. We taste with our mouths and see with our eyes. We know that this is only an expression, for surely the psalmist is not recommending a literal taste and see, but in choosing this metaphor, the psalmist is calling us to something beyond a mental realm of experiencing God. We are physical people and our interaction with God is based on our physical life.

To think of anything less is to be a bit schizophrenic with our humanity. We are both body and thought, physical flesh and spirit. We are not one to the exclusion of the other. So the psalmist thinks of experiencing God as based in what we do with our lives, not simply our thoughts.

It is interesting that the psalmist placed "taste" before "see." Tasting is rooted in a physical experience while seeing denotes not just physical sight, but perception and knowledge. The knowledge we have of God is informed by our experiences with God. This makes it real important that we grow with God and experience God on a daily basis.

I have met many people who accept God's reality, but live with little to no experience of it. Then later in life when crisis hits, they wonder why they do not understand God, do not experience his presence, and find him unavailable in prayer. In truth, these people have so little experience with God, they know little of him, hardly recognize him, and are in no position to find his presence when finally needed.

I don't want to be that way. I want to taste God in the sense of food. I eat at least three times a day! I know tasting. It is very routine and integral to my life. Similarly, I want to taste God. I want to experience him more frequently than food. This will lead me to take refuge in him in times of trouble. I will not suffer lack. He will supply me with all good things needed in my life (though he may teach me to redefine "good things" from what I might otherwise think)

Lord, be a part of my life today. With each meal I take, remind me to taste and experience you. I want to grow in my walk with you every day. Through Jesus my Lord, Amen!

❀ ❀ ❀

MARCH 17

Come, O children, listen to me; I will teach you the fear of the LORD. What man is there who desires life and loves many days, that he may see good? Keep your tongue from evil and your lips from speaking deceit. Turn away from evil and do good; seek peace and pursue it. (Ps. 34:11-14)

Some use the word "karma" to describe the effect that actions have on the actor. One's deeds influence one's future, good for good or bad for bad. While the origin of the word is from eastern religion (Hinduism and Buddhism both teach it), the concept is more universal. The Bible doesn't teach the eastern view of karma as controlling one's destiny from one human life through reincarnation to another, but the Bible does teach karma of sorts. Paul bluntly told the Galatians, "Do not be deceived: God is not mocked, for whatever one sows, that will he also reap" (Gal. 6:7). This is a type of karma, and it is real. The biblical key is that the mercy of God in Jesus *trumps* karma. The substance of Christianity is that in an eternal sense, Jesus reaped what we have sown. Apart from that eternal view, however, the principle is still alive and well in this life.

Paul's teaching is found in psalms like this one. The psalmist offers to teach the children (physically or spiritually) the "fear of the Lord." The Lord, of course, is the designer of this universe where cause and effect reign in the physical as well as immaterial world. If I put my finger in fire, it will burn. Not because we have a mean God who is going to burn my hand for that deed, but because in this cause-and-effect world God made, fire has a burning effect on flesh. We should recognize this and fear fire! Similarly, there are cause and effects that are just as reliable in the unseen world. God has explained those rules for us, and we should fear him and follow his instructions.

So if we wish to fear God in this way, and reap the benefits of his instructions, then we have some cause-and-effect rules set out in this psalm. First, if we want a happy life filled with good days, we need to be careful with our words. We should be honest and reliable in what we say. We should use our words to build up and encourage. We should avoid gossip and idle chatter. In sum, we should "keep our tongues from evil and our lips from speaking deceit." I have seen the positives and negatives in this in business and law. Lying lips have brought down many a company. We should do good, not evil. This is not simply to woo God's favor, it is a fact of nature that doing good is going to lead to better consequences than evil, regardless of how it might seem at some particular moment. We need to learn this psalm and teach it to others!

Lord, teach us how to follow your will. May we walk in your blessings and protection as we seek to do good with our hearts, minds, words, deeds, and lives. We want to live to your glory and see the fruits that come accordingly. In Jesus, Amen!

❧ ❧ ❧

MARCH 18

The eyes of the Lord *are toward the righteous and his ears toward their cry. The face of the* Lord *is against those who do evil, to cut off the memory of them from the earth.* (Ps. 34:15-16)

There is a contrast in what happens with the face of God when it addresses those who truly seek him as opposed to those who have no regard for him. Those who truly seek God are the righteous who care so much about God that it affects the choices they make in life and how they live. Those who are evil are those who live by their own passions, without regard to what the Lord says.

With the righteous, God turns his face toward them. His eyes look out for them. His ears respond to their cries. Now this is not to say God has the physical features of a person, but this anthropomorphism ("projecting human qualities onto one not a human") is to make the point that God responds positively to his children. The face of God is not turned toward the evil, but against them. In Hebrew, this is just the change of a few letters. The letters *"al"* go before the words "the righteous" to teach that God turns *toward* them. The letter *"b"* is before "evil" to show God turns *inward on* them, rather than in favor to them (also in Lev. 20:3, 5, 6, 17, etc.).

This is a confidence builder for me as I try to live right before God. If I were not caring about God, I would likely not even be reading this psalm, so the message would not seem to matter. But the psalmist wants the righteous to know God hears their cries and *"delivers them out of all their troubles"* (v. 17). When we are hurting, God is nearby ministering to us and healing us (v. 18). Even though the godly will still experience many problems in this life, they do so with God at hand to bring them through those problems safely (v. 19). This is not the case with the wicked.

I can testify to the truth of this psalm. God has rescued me and redeemed me more times than I can count. He has saved me from myself, from bad judgments, from dangerous situations. He has done this even when I was too blind to see it at the moment. His mercies and care are real. I am eternally grateful.

A Keith Green prayer song fits this well:

Lord, you're beautiful. Your face is all I seek. For when your eyes are on this child, your grace abounds to me. I want to take your word and shine it all around, but first help me just to live it, Lord. And when I'm doing well, help me to never seek a crown. For my reward is giving glory to you. Oh Lord, you're beautiful. Your face is all I seek. In Jesus, Amen!

❧ ❧ ❧

MARCH 19

Contend, O LORD, with those who contend with me; fight against those who fight against me! Take hold of shield and buckler and rise for my help! Draw the spear and javelin against my pursuers! Say to my soul, "I am your salvation!" (Ps. 35:1-3)

In our twenty-first century, we have reached a point in civilization where physical life and death confrontations are rare. We don't generally live with fear that someone may take a sword and shield and challenge us to battle. At least not physically.

But we still face adversaries. We face them at work (or school), in the world at large, and sometimes even in the intimate places of church and family. Everyone knows what it is like to be under attack, even if not with a metal sword: the stinging words of one who is envious; the manipulations of one who is greedy; the personal affronts that come from the callous. The burdens of guilt heaped up by those who wish to control another. There are attacks that are no less vicious than a sword and shield.

The psalmist seeks the aid of God in these attacks. He calls God into action, asking for God's intervention and defense. God is not physically taking up a shield or spear, but he is no less at work.

In God we find our value. In him we get assurance that we are loved, accepted, and equipped. We know that we have a place in his plan, and that saves us from words of attack and gossip. He is going to guide us in his way to empower us to do the good works he has already prepared for us (Eph. 2:10), such that the manipulations of the greedy come to naught. With God we have the assurance that he can hedge us in and protect us from the onslaughts of the callous, even as he works to break into their hard hearts.

The greatest battle we face, and the greatest victory God has won on our behalf, is the victory over sin. There is a power of sin that not only sets us on the road to eternal condemnation but enslaves us to a grip too powerful for us to overcome. This power of sin is brought to nothing through the atoning work of Jesus. Jesus defeated death, he bested the powers and principalities of darkness, and he released us from the death spiral of sin. In Jesus, we have access to a power greater than all our adversaries combined. The Spirit of God indwells the believer and brings forth a life of victory not otherwise possible. Our God is a saving God!

Lord, we thank you for the salvation in Jesus. We ask you to protect us, teach us, deliver us from the darkness of this present age in all its manifestations. Be with us, Lord, in Jesus, Amen!

❦ ❦ ❦

MARCH 20

Let them be put to shame and dishonor who seek after my life! Let them be turned back and disappointed who devise evil against me! Let them be like chaff before the wind, with the angel of the LORD driving them away! Let their way be dark and slippery, with the angel of the LORD pursuing them! (Ps. 35:4-6)

Is it wrong to pray against our enemies? This psalm clearly prays that God would come against the psalmist's enemies, bring them shame, dishonor, and fruitless disappointment. The prayer is for God to drive them away and stay in pursuit all while making the enemies' getaway path dark and slippery.

I have had my share of enemies. The world is full of people who seek to take what is not theirs, who are envious, and who have an unhealthy wish for the failure or pain of others. There are gossips and people who maliciously spread rumors. There are people who take credit for your accomplishments, rather than theirs. Some people are just downright mean.

There are a number of psalms like Psalm 35 that pray for God's judgment on enemies, calling down all sorts of calamities. Scholars call these "imprecatory psalms" from the verb "imprecate," which means "to utter a curse" or "invoke evil" against someone. When I read these imprecatory psalms, I always think about the admonition of Jesus in his Sermon on the Mount, *"You have heard that it was said, 'You shall love your neighbor and hate your enemy.' But I say to you, Love your enemies and pray for those who persecute you"* (Matt. 5:43-44).

Which shall it be? The imprecations of the psalms or the blessings of the Sermon on the Mount? I take both! I do pray against my enemies. I pray the imprecations of the verses above, but I do so within the guidelines of Jesus' admonition. I want the enemies to be broken, shamed, dishonored, whatever it takes for God's light to break through and capture their hearts! Abraham Lincoln is credited with saying, "The best way to destroy an enemy is to make him a friend." I see this as the goal behind the imprecations and the Sermon on the Mount. Paul told the Romans, "if your enemy is hungry, feed him; if he is thirsty, give him something to drink; for by so doing you will heap burning coals on his head" (Rom. 12:20). This ancient language teaches us to love our enemies to repentance (the impact of carrying coals on one's head is to find repentance).

Lord, may my life and actions be protected from evil. Please chase evil away, and bring it to a fruitless conclusion. Visit the evildoers with harsh judgment that moves them to repentance. May I not glory in their fall, but be there to lovingly pick up the pieces in Jesus' name, Amen!

MARCH 21

Your steadfast love, O LORD, *extends to the heavens, your faithfulness to the clouds. Your righteousness is like the mountains of God; your judgments are like the great deep; man and beast you save, O* LORD. (Ps. 36:5-6)

There are days where I want—where I need—to bask in the love of the Lord. It helps put everything into perspective, and it dissolves away worry, stress, and more. It is a spa day for the soul! Today's devotional is a lingering time of luxuriating in the love of the Lord.

The Lord has steadfast love. It does not waver when we are faithless. It does not wax and wane with our performance. It is constant and patient. He pursues us in love when we are running. He disciplines us in love when we need it to grow. He holds us in love when we hurt. He protects us in love when evil is plotting and working against us. He speaks to us in love when we need to hear his voice. He died for us in love when our sins needed atonement. Truly his steadfast love extends beyond our ability to see—to the ends of the heavens.

Hand in hand with his steadfast love is his faithfulness. He does not work for our good some days, while getting sidetracked with different projects on other days. He is not a 50 percent, or even a 99 percent faithful God. He is 100 percent faithful. We need not worry about God's agenda. We *are* God's agenda!

God's character is loving and faithful. He is also *righteous*. He doesn't do things that are wrong. We never have to worry that we might find God on a bad day when harshness might trump his righteousness. He is always going to do what is right and good. It is why he could never accept us with unwashed sins. We need righteousness to fellowship with him. In his righteousness, he supplies our righteousness in Jesus. Of course, this is a supreme example of his love and faithfulness.

The psalm also recounts the great judgments of God. God must be judge. It is uniquely his role, his ability, and his responsibility. God sits as God. Again, this is wrapped up in the same phrases of God given in the earlier part of the psalm, all of which find the ultimate expression in Jesus. The God of steadfast love and faithfulness, who is righteous and who judges in righteousness, reaches each of us in that loving, faithful, righteous judgment in Jesus Christ, through whom we walk hand in hand with God, basking in his love!

Lord, thank you for your steadfast love, your faithfulness, righteousness, and judgment in our Lord Jesus through whom we pray to you. Amen!

❧ ❧ ❧

MARCH 22

How precious is your steadfast love, O God! The children of mankind take refuge in the shadow of your wings. They feast on the abundance of your house, and you give them drink from the river of your delights. For with you is the fountain of life; in your light do we see light. (Ps. 36:7-9)

None of us see well in a dark room. We need light to see. How strong that light is, relates closely to how well we see. How do I see life? By what light do we perceive the things around us? I want it to be by the light of God.

The poet writes that by the light of God we see light, and so it should be. I want to understand things, seeing them as God sees them. I want to know his ways, have his heart, share his concerns, seek his ministries, work on his agenda, and follow his plans. His light and plans grow out of his steadfast love. It provides his children places of refuge. His love provides the blessings of life. His love provides his light.

The Gospel of John takes this idea of the light of God being our light and explains it in the most graphic showing of God's love for us. John explains that Jesus Christ was the "true light" that came into the world (John 1:9). He is the light that shines in the darkness, which darkness cannot and will not conquer (John 1:4-5). Matthew quotes Isaiah 42:7 as reflecting on Jesus' Galilean ministry as a time where "the people in darkness have seen a great light" (Matt. 4:16).

The life of Jesus as God's light to humanity fits hand in glove with this psalm. Jesus manifests the steadfast love of God. In Jesus we have one who came to save a lost people from their sins. He never waited on us to get cleaned up for his coming. He came and saved us while we were yet sinners.

If we see life by God's light, we see it entirely differently than much of the world. In Christ, we find a true and abundant life, promised by the psalm. The life in Christ might not be what the world wants, as the world seeks to live by the feelings and passions of the moment. But in Jesus we live a life settled in God's hands. We are at peace with the maker, in a loving relationship and there can be no greater place or blessing.

Lord, we embrace the light of this world, your light in Jesus Christ our Lord. We pray through him, we live through him, in the peace that he has made and the grace he has established by his own death and resurrection. We love you Lord, in Him, Amen!

MARCH 23

Fret not yourself because of evildoers; be not envious of wrongdoers! For they will soon fade like the grass and wither like the green herb. Trust in the LORD, and do good; dwell in the land and befriend faithfulness. Delight yourself in the LORD, and he will give you the desires of your heart. (Ps. 37:1-4)

Do you ever find yourself looking at ungodly people who, for all intents and purposes, seem happy and successful? I can remember when I was younger looking at several lawyers who were very successful in the world's eyes. They had a string of victories, fame and fortune. When they walked into the courtroom, all eyes noticed and hushed whispers were barely audible pointing out the presence of the lawyers. One in particular stands out in my mind. It was years later when I was hired to represent that lawyer who was at risk of losing it all. His inability to handle things sent him into deep addiction. His life fell apart, and he died without a lot of joy.

I don't want that, at least not when I am at my best! Fame feels good to the ego, but that is not the part of my life I want fed. Money can do a lot of good, but it is a trap and a harsh master if left to its own devices. I don't want to live for this life and the pleasures it offers. They are illusions of happiness.

At my best, I want to trust in the Lord and his goodness. I want what he has planned for me, be it plenty or be it scarce. I want to live the life he has made me to live. I want to model God in my behavior. I want his faithfulness to mean so much to me that I try to have that same faithfulness to him, to his mission, to my loved ones, and to the world. I want people who see me to see some semblance of the Lord I serve.

I want God to be my delight. I want serving him to be my joy. I want his will to be my will. I want his cares to be my cares. I want his heart to be my heart. I want to walk with him, converse with him, cry with him, laugh with him, seek his counsel, live in his strength, share his priorities, and trust in his care.

Walking with God in his truth and plans means so much more than anything experienced by those who do not know him or live in rebellion to him. This is the best.

Lord, I give my life to you again. Today, each moment, and each activity, I dedicate to you. Take who I am and make me who I can be. Take my will and mold it to yours. Take my plans and align them with yours. Take my hopes and meet them in Jesus. Take my desires and purify them before meeting them.

Thank you, Lord, for all this and more. Your faithfulness has sustained me and is my hope in Jesus' name, Amen!

MARCH 24

Be still before the LORD and wait patiently for him. (Ps. 37:7)

This passage has always bothered me. It is very soothing and full of emotion for me. Yet at the same time, it is hard for me to express why. It is a verse that calls me to contemplative silence, even as I try hard to figure it out!

Stillness is foreign to me. I have a tendency to wake up with the "go, go, goes" and generally don't stop until my body forces sleep. I think that ships have rudders that only work if the ship is moving. I have heard—though I don't think it's true—that sharks must always be moving or they die. I know that God calls me to do things (Eph. 2:10), so I am always trying to be about his business. I am a hard person to vacation with because I am trying to fill each day with activities. There is very little "relaxation" for me on vacation, at least as most people think of it.

I know some for whom life is the opposite. Stillness is their default mode. They have trouble doing much, and would rather do nothing. I don't mean they sit on the sofa and spend their time watching television; I mean they are truly content sitting and thinking. I have to work on that.

This passage makes sense to me intellectually; it is in experience that I find it difficult. I know that God is in charge. He certainly knows best, and has a plan for this world and my life. His plan is built on his timing, and I understand that, too. It is very sensible that there will be times where I am ready and wanting to move, but the timing is not right yet. He may be delaying for his purposes I don't see, or he may be delaying until I am right to do the work. I may be needing to learn some patience or some other trait before I am on task again. But making intellectual sense and being real in my life sometimes are different things.

The psalm itself explains a bit of this for me. Part of being still is given in the later verses: "Refrain from anger, and forsake wrath! Fret not yourself; it tends only to evil" (Ps. 37:8). Even "waiting" involves something! That helps! Some of waiting before the Lord is not responding to people in anger, but letting him calm me before I react. I should not let wrath govern my behavior, but only the Lord. Worry is not to be my driver; faith is. In this sense, then, I can wait! When I am tempted to act in anger, wrath, or from worry, I need to bite my tongue, hold back my hand, and wait for God's reactions. This makes sense. This is good.

Lord, please teach me to be still before you when I am tempted to act out of anger, wrath, worry or some other emotion. Let me wait on you and your direction, in Jesus' name, Amen!

❦ ❦ ❦

MARCH 25

The meek shall inherit the land and delight themselves in abundant peace. (Ps. 37:11)

Many immediately recognize this passage as one Jesus quoted in his beatitudes in the Sermon on the Mount ("Blessed are the meek, for they shall inherit the earth"; Matt. 5:5). It always raises the question to me, what exactly is "meekness"?

The Hebrew word translated "meek" has a full semantic range of meaning that sees the translation in English as "meek," but also "humble" and "poor." The meek person is one who in humility regards others as more important. That runs very contrary to much of today's society. Some immediately scoff at the idea of regarding others as more important. Yet it is that characteristic that Paul urged on the Philippians, "Do nothing from selfish ambition or conceit, but in humility count others more significant than yourselves" (Phil. 2:3).

We tend to associate meekness with weakness, but that would be wrong! Moses was called "meek" in Numbers 12:3, and he was anything but "meek" in the sense of weak or ineffectual. Moses was a very strong leader who took on pharaoh, who reacted in anger to the sins of the people, who managed to lead an entire nation through years of wilderness wanderings. How was Moses meek? Moses was always seeking the good of the people over that of his own. Moses interceded with God for the people, urging God to take his wrath out on Moses rather than the Israelites. In Deuteronomy 9, Moses recounted many of the times he had to intercede for the Israelites. Moses' concern for the people trumped his own need for advancement.

Jesus was also termed "meek," although he had little problem confronting the rulers of his day, throwing moneychangers out of the temple, standing before the High Priest and the Roman ruler Pilate without capitulating. Jesus' care for God's mission and his people trumped his personal comfort or safety.

We have a choice in how we live. We can live for ourselves or others. Our church taught this to our children at church camp with the "JOY award." They received it for putting "Jesus" first, then "Others" second, and "Yourself" last, spelling JOY. This is meekness. And God says we do not have to worry about what we get out of this for ourselves. God takes care of us, and we inherit the earth!

Lord, I want to put others first. Help me to place my own ambitions and concerns out of the way, placing Jesus first and others second. Let me model the humility of Christ and his saints. Father, I pray this in Jesus' name, Amen!

❦ ❦ ❦

MARCH 26

The wicked borrows but does not pay back, but the righteous is generous and gives; for those blessed by the LORD *shall inherit the land, but those cursed by him shall be cut off.* (Ps. 37:21-22)

This passage has four clauses and they fold in the middle like a piece of paper! The Hebrew poetic structure is called a "chiasm" from the Greek letter *chi*, which looks like a big X. The letter X can be folded over at the midpoint and the top will match the bottom while the middle parts also match. So with a chiasm. These four clauses fold over in the sense that the first clause matches the last clause and the two center clauses also go together. Look at the clauses this way, and we get further meaning in the poem.

Clauses one and four tell us "The wicked borrow, but does not pay back" and "those cursed by the Lord shall be cut off." The behavior of borrowing and not paying back is cursed behavior! Why? At its root, such behavior is really no more than lying (saying you will return or pay back when you don't) and stealing (taking something that isn't yours under a false pretext you will return it). We tend not to see it so, but at its core, that's what it is.

Clauses two and three also match up. They tell us "the righteous is generous and gives" and "those blessed by the Lord shall inherit the land." God's blessings, rather than curses, fall on those who are generous and giving. This contrasts with those who wrongfully take, who are cursed. When we are generous and give, we match the behavior of our God, who is most generous and gives more than we can imagine. God gave us this earth. He gave us insight into how it works and how we work. He gave us his presence and love. He gave us himself in Jesus, at the price of great humiliation and pain. He gives us the opportunity to live with him in intimate fellowship in this life and beyond.

When we are generous and giving, we not only model the behavior of God, we also recognize God as our supplier. We do not live in fear of want. We know that God will meet our needs. The giver should be seeing herself or himself as a vessel who has charge of God's supplies. Our possessions are not our own, they belong to him. We are stewards who are responsible to him for what we do with *his* things. Reflecting his giving nature with his things is the responsible thing to do!

Lord, we thank you for being so giving to us. From the breath we take, the food we eat, the company we enjoy, the forgiveness and fellowship in Jesus, all these things and more you have graciously given us. Make our hearts like yours. May we be generous and giving, responsibly handling your possessions you have placed in our care. In Jesus' name, Amen!

MARCH 27

The steps of a man are established by the LORD, when he delights in his way; though he fall, he shall not be cast headlong, for the LORD upholds his hand. (Ps. 37:23-24)

Very few steps of life are directed by God in GPS fashion. This took me a while to figure out. Of course, the believer wants to walk in God's will. Who would not be thrilled to walk precisely the way God wants? I want to live in the house God wants, in the city God wants, working in the job God wants. Heavens, I want to eat the lunch God wants me to eat! All I need are those perfect GPS instructions. "Go 300 feet and turn right!" Even though we are told to seek and follow God's will, it rarely works like GPS.

When I was young, I wanted writing on the wall. I wanted God to tell me with clarity and precision what decisions to make. I tried listening for an audible voice. I tried to sense an internal voice. Sometimes I thought I was discerning something; other times it was blank.

It took awhile, but the answers I needed for making decisions were generally clear in Scripture. Could God write on a wall? Certainly. Could he speak audibly? No doubt. Was that the normal fare for life? Absolutely not. Those are incredibly rare, almost singular moments. But that doesn't mean God is silent in directing our paths. To the contrary, he is quite vocal.

First, Scripture gives us principles and rules to live by. We know not to lie. We know to be giving. We know to love others. I have found these instructions govern 90 percent of my life's decisions. Other decisions are often determined by God's opening and closing of doors. He hedges me in at times to help direct my decisions. Still there are other times where God seems to give no direction at all. Where multiple choices are all aligned with Scripture and where multiple doors are open.

Those circumstances and choices are ones where Scriptures like this psalm come into play. The assurance of Scripture is that we make those choices in faith knowing God will establish our steps. It is as if God is saying, "This is your choice to make. You decide, and I will bless you either way!" God did not make us puppets. He made us with the ability to make decisions and choices. He wants us to do so. He blesses us as we do so. These choices need to be godly, but as they are, he will establish our steps. This is part of Paul's explanation that God is at work renewing our minds to discern his will (Rom. 12:2).

Father, teach me your ways. Help me to follow them. May I seek your will in my life. As you renew my mind, may I use it to make godly decisions, seeking your will and your kingdom first. Establish my steps in your ways, for the sake of Jesus, Amen!

❧ ❧ ❧

MARCH 28

Turn away from evil and do good; so shall you dwell forever. For the LORD loves justice; he will not forsake his saints. (Ps. 37:27-28)

This passage falls into the category of "Of course! That's a gimme!" I suspect such was true when it was written as well. Yet the psalmist saw fit to write it, and the Holy Spirit has seen fit to include it in the Holy Writings. Why?

I believe this is a good reminder, one that we all need. It is good to stop and remember the things set out in these few verses. First, there is evil and there is good. These aren't just fuzzy ideas. They aren't generalized directions on a moral compass, one sort of going one way and the other another way. There really is a good and there really is an evil.

The biblical teaching is that God himself is a moral being. There is a morality inherent in God and God's moral character is what we call "good." That morality that is ungodly we call "evil." God didn't make evil; evil exists as that which God isn't. God is truth; therefore, we can call truth "good." God didn't make "untruth" or lies. They simply exist as that which is ungodly. Therefore, we call lies "evil." God is a giving and selfless love; therefore, we call giving love "good." Selfishness and self-love at the expense of another is ungodly and we understand that as evil. The Bible uses other metaphors to talk of God's morality and good and evil. A common metaphor is light and darkness. God is light (or good) and in him is no darkness (or evil).

We are to turn from evil and do good because we are made in God's image. His moral code is hard-wired into our being. We instinctively know there is good and evil, and we generally can tell the difference. We learn more as God works in our lives to repair the marring of his image that has occurred as part of our rebellious nature and our sin. So we are admonished to live by what is good and right, and turn from any tendency to follow what is ungodly or evil.

The psalm teaches that there are consequences to our actions. This is also hard-wired into the universe. It is a part of God's "justice." We can think of justice as "consistency." God is unchanging, and his goodness is too. Of course as circumstances change, the true good might have a different face. For example, faced with one who is hungry, we offer food. Faced with someone full, we don't. The true good is unchanging as we meet needs. It is right we should be reminded, turn from evil and do good!

Lord, we confess that we do not always do good. The intent of our heart is not always pure, nor are the deeds of our flesh. Please help us do good, even as you forgive us in Jesus. Amen!

❧ ❧ ❧

MARCH 29

The mouth of the righteous utters wisdom, and his tongue speaks justice. The law of his God is in his heart; his steps do not slip. (Ps. 37:30-31)

Wisdom has always held an allure to me. There is something majestic and powerful in wisdom. It has the power to help one walk a road that benefits both the world and one's self. As a young man, I hung onto the promise of God in James 1:5 that "If any of you lacks wisdom, let him ask God, who gives generously to all without reproach, and it will be given him." I would constantly ask God for wisdom. Soon after beginning that prayer, I learned that an entire section of the Old Testament was called "wisdom literature" because of its content. That section included the Psalms and Proverbs, so I commenced trying to read through them each month. With one hundred and fifty psalms, I made it through reading five a day. With thirty-one chapters of Proverbs, I could read them in a month pacing it one chapter daily.

Over years of reading through these books monthly, I began to find other instructions about wisdom, including this passage. These two verses have a parallel structure, a common feature of Hebrew poetry. There are four clauses, two in each sentence. In this case, all four basically say the same thing, but with a different emphasis to give a fuller meaning to the concept. The instruction about wisdom is in clause one, but it really finds its fullest meaning by considering each clause. The first clause affirms: "*The mouth of the righteous utters wisdom.*" If I want to utter wisdom, there is a real link set out that I need *to be* righteous. Wisdom does not come from the mouth of one who is a "fool" (the Hebrew equivalent of one unrighteous.) Wisdom is rooted in knowing God and letting knowledge of him affect us. Such a one will be righteous.

The second clause fleshes out the idea of righteousness as well as wisdom. It equates it to speaking justice. The righteous person has control of the tongue, rather than letting the tongue run rogue. Wisdom is found in justice—where right trumps favoritism.

The third clause adds even more. We understand from it the importance of having God's law in one's heart. This means not simply reading the Bible, but knowing it intimately. It is where our words and thoughts immediately convert into the language of Scripture. This means that to get and utter wisdom, I need to be deep in God's word.

The final clause assures me that being wise, speaking honestly and justly, nourished on the word of God, will ensure my steps. I will walk with God and not slip. All of this started from a young boy seeking wisdom from God. God continues to answer this prayer.

Lord, please give us wisdom. Teach us your word. Use it to change our lives in ways that bring you glory. In Jesus' name, Amen.

❧ ❧ ❧

MARCH 30

O LORD, rebuke me not in your anger, nor discipline me in your wrath! For your arrows have sunk into me, and your hand has come down on me. There is no soundness in my flesh because of your indignation; there is no health in my bones because of my sin. For my iniquities have gone over my head; like a heavy burden, they are too heavy for me. (Ps. 38:1-4)

Oh, I wish I was perfect! I wish I'd never known sin. There are big pages in my life's story where an eraser would be nice. Better yet, I'd like scissors that would cut any lingering trace of the events away.

God doesn't like sin. No wonder—sin is destructive. It is not a good thing and it doesn't lead to good results. It might be fun for the moment. It might satisfy an itch, albeit briefly. It sure seems enticing, but cannot live up to its billing. There is a good reason God doesn't like sin.

All of us sin. Sometimes we quickly move into repentance, and the effects of sin are minimal. Other times, the sin digs deeply into the soul, gashing wounds that aren't so readily healed or covered over.

Even in these times of deep sin and devastating consequences, God is at work. He is not simply bringing anger down for anger's sake. God is not a trivial God. He is at work trying to get our attention, trying to bring us to repentance and a true change in behavior. The psalmist felt it. The description is pungent: "My wounds stink and fester because of my foolishness, I am utterly bowed down and prostrate . . . I am feeble and crushed" (Ps. 38:5-8).

In the midst of this condition, the psalmist knew what to do. Repent! The psalm continues, "I confess my iniquity; I am sorry for my sin" (Ps. 38:18). This is right, as God is steadfast in his love, and in Jesus has forgiveness for the most callous sin. In repentance and a turning, something happens, even when the consequences of sin have been severe. God works on sin's wounds. He begins to heal. There comes a time where the scar from the sin may still be visible in memory or consequences, but the scar serves as a testimony to the healing God, and is no longer a site of pain. Sin is real, but so is God's love.

Lord, I confess myself a sinner in need of the redemptive work of Jesus. I thank you for that redemption and the forgiveness found on the cross of Christ. Please treat me in your love and mercy. Without that, I could never stand or function. Standing in Jesus, I pray, Amen!

MARCH 31

O LORD, make me know my end and what is the measure of my days; let me know how fleeting I am! Behold, you have made my days a few handbreadths, and my lifetime is as nothing before you. Surely all mankind stands as a mere breath. (Ps. 39:4-5)

Working through the Psalms I pray this prayer more times than I can count. I think it is a good thing, but it is certainly sobering, because God has answered the prayers.

Death is a very real part of everyone's life. We will all die. It isn't something many think about at a young age (absent praying this psalm over and over!), but it is no less real when young than old. Every day we are one step closer to the end of our time on this earth. We have no rewind buttons to life. We have no ability to put life on pause.

One of our daughters was born on March 31. Like the rest of us, she was born with a number of days that God held in his mind, even though we are not privy to that. Each day comes with its own joys and grief, and then it passes. Days can be long, but the years are short. They fly by, faster and faster as we age.

In the midst of this is a prayer, "God, make me aware of this. Make me conscious of the fact of what is happening as my life's pages flip by in rapid succession." As we learn and consider it, it should change the way we live. Knowing I will not have today again makes me want to treat today with a special care. Even when experiencing grief that I want to get over, I am careful not to be too eager. I don't get today back.

This ties me to a desire to embrace the Lord's hand tightly. I want to see things through his eyes. I want to spend my days productively doing the things he wants me to do. I like the assurance that the things I do for God have eternal value, while everything else is a waste. Paul used the metaphor of building, contrasting those who build with wood, hay and stubble (our own activities) with those building with gold, silver, and precious stones (doing the works of God). Paul explained that a day of fire comes with the end of life, where our works will stand or be consumed (1 Cor. 3:12-15). I want to build with things that will withstand eternity. I want to spend my limited days trying to do what God wants done. Days are fleeting, and they pass by too rapidly. I want to use them rightly!

Lord, teach us to number our days in ways that bring us into a serious realization of what we do each day. I want my days to be in alignment with your purposes, Lord, and need your help to see that through. Please strengthen me, give me vision, and bring me to success for the sake of your kingdom and our Lord Jesus, through whom I pray, Amen!

❧ ❧ ❧

APRIL 1

I waited patiently for the LORD; he inclined to me and heard my cry. He drew me up from the pit of destruction, out of the miry bog, and set my feet upon a rock, making my steps secure. He put a new song in my mouth, a song of praise to our God. Many will see and fear, and put their trust in the LORD. (Ps. 40:1-3)

In 1982 I began liking the Irish upstart band called U2. At the time, I didn't realize they were my age, nor did I realize that most of them were committed Christians. I just liked their music. It didn't take long, however, for me to find their beliefs. Their lyrics revealed an underlying faith. On their 1983 album, they put a song entitled "Forty," a song they used repeatedly to close their live shows. A couple of years later, I was in dialogue with some other U2 fans who told me the song was entitled "Forty" because it was written, recorded, and mixed in forty minutes. I told them that may have happened, but I suspected it wasn't the source for the song's title. They asked, "Then what was?" I told them the lyrics are straight from Psalm 40:1-3. They were dumbfounded, but I found a Bible and verified it.

U2's verses are, "I waited patiently for the Lord. He inclined and heard my cry. He brought me up out of the pit. Out of the miry clay. He set my feet upon a rock. And made my footsteps firm. Many will see. Many will see and hear." The chorus proclaims, "I will sing, sing a new song."

The Psalms were songs. U2 found a marvelous way to take an ancient lyric that proclaimed God put a new song into the psalmist's mouth, and to make that lyric itself a new song over 2,500 years later.

God is still at work. We can continue to wait patiently for him, because in his time, and in his way, he still pulls us out of the pits of despair, of frustration, of sin, of emotional stress and pain, of worry about tomorrow, of poor health, of brokenness, and more. He sets us on a rock. Jesus explained that if we listen to his teaching and respond appropriately, it is akin to building our entire house on a rock (Matt. 7:24-25). Our steps are secure.

As we live securely in God's word, shining the life and words of Christ to the world, we have a new song of joy. The world sees and hears God through our lives. This is one way that God reaches others through us.

Lord, may we walk in your will. Please lift us from the miry muck, making more of our lives than we might on our own. May we sing your glory over your victory in ways that bring others to you. Through Jesus our teacher, Amen!

APRIL 2

Blessed is the man who makes the LORD *his trust, who does not turn to the proud, to those who go astray after a lie! You have multiplied, O* LORD *my God, your wondrous deeds and your thoughts toward us; none can compare with you! I will proclaim and tell of them, yet they are more than can be told.* (Ps. 40:4-5)

When I was *very* young, there was a television show called *Let's Make a Deal!* The show would frequently give the contestant a choice among three curtained areas of the stage. ("Do you want door number 1, door number 3, or door number 3?") Behind some doors would be a joke like a box of popsicles. Occasionally behind a door would be a new car! Sometimes people would be asked if they'd like to trade a box for a big area with a "door." Some made great deals; others made deals that were sour.

This psalm informs us we are often choosing "deals," even though we may not realize it. We have choices about where to put our trust: door number 1—trust in those who are self-sufficient (aka the "proud" who believe they get there on their own); door number 2—trust in those who pursue a will independent of God's (i.e., pursue a lie, rather than the God of truth); or door number 3—trust in the Lord.

Of course, the choice never seems so graphic, or only a fool would say, "I am trusting someone other than God." Yet we need to heed the psalm's admonition. The ways of the world are not the ways of God. While God can use the things of this world, including the people of this world, to achieve his purposes, our primary focus always needs to be on following God in trust that he securely leads us. As we do so, we can follow assured that he will bless our path.

God will "multiply" his wonderful deeds toward us. They are not haphazard, nor are they accidental. God "thinks" (to use a human term for a non-human God) about us. In other words, he is deliberate about blessing us as we seek him and follow him. As God dispenses his blessings to us, we need to follow the psalmist's direction and give him credit. To do any less would be to become proud on our own, believing the lies of our own achievements. But instead, as we are blessed by the Lord, we need to proclaim the blessings as his wondrous deeds that proceed from a kind, loving, and attentive God who cares immensely.

Lord, we do trust in you to give us direction and instruction. We want our lives to be at your disposal for the good of your kingdom and your purposes. We pledge ourselves to you for that, trusting you to use us as you see fit, and being at peace with that. In the name of our Lord Jesus, Amen!

❧ ❧ ❧

APRIL 3

In sacrifice and offering you have not delighted, but you have given me an open ear. Burnt offering and sin offering you have not required. Then I said, "Behold, I have come; in the scroll of the book it is written of me: I delight to do your will, O my God; your law is within my heart." (Ps. 40:6-8)

The killing of a goat, sheep, or dove never satisfied the justice requirement for removing anyone's sin. No rebellion against God, against right or truth (terms of God) has ever justly been alleviated by killing an innocent animal. To think otherwise is silly. Of course, we are more likely to think that justice is requited by saying, "I'm sorry." Any who have seen sentencing hearings in court know that apologies are great but aren't "just" punishments.

Fair justice on human sin requires something greater than the death of an animal; it requires the death of a human. Sin calls forth death. Sin is a corruption of good, and the corruption is properly disposed of or eliminated (i.e., put to death). Of course, if the human is sinful, the death is appropriate for that human's own sin. So we have the death of Christ, an innocent human, as a substitution for the penalty of our own sin.

Where does that leave us today? Where did that leave the psalmist? Both in the same place, albeit with some slight distinctions. The psalmist lived before the incarnation and death of Christ, and so he is left trusting God for a redemption yet to come. Under the law of Moses, sacrifices were put in place as a foreshadowing of the meaningful sacrifice of Christ, as well as a way to feed and supply the priestly caste. But the ultimate call of God was for obedience. True obedience begins with a heart that is right before God. As one was obedient under the Law of Moses, sacrifices would be made and lessons learned. But a dead animal would never be seen as an adequate answer to sin.

Today we have the sacrifice of Christ. We know how God can forgive sin with full justice met in the mercy of Christ. Our calling to trust in this way is not a license to sin. We who are redeemed by so costly a price should know the value of living right before God. It should be our delight to live holy. We want our lives to demonstrate that God's morality makes a difference, that sin is real, that sin's consequences are devastating, and that the grace we have cost more than all humans could ever accumulate. It cost the innocent life of Jesus the Savior.

Lord, we thank you for Jesus. We thank you for the only sacrifice that could atone justly for our sins. We confess ourselves sinners in need of that sacrifice, and we proclaim ourselves trusting in it, resting in your forgiveness as we try to live lives right before you. Through Jesus we pray, Amen!

❧ ❧ ❧

APRIL 4

I have told the glad news of deliverance in the great congregation; behold, I have not restrained my lips, as you know, O LORD. *I have not hidden your deliverance within my heart; I have spoken of your faithfulness and your salvation; I have not concealed your steadfast love and your faithfulness from the great congregation.* (Ps. 40:9-10)

Some people are much more natural at speaking about God than others. Many times earlier in my life, I have been reticent. I am not sure why. It certainly is not God's failure to work deliverance for me. He has wrought deliverance from sin through the mighty work in Christ. Of that I am not in doubt, and I am eternally grateful. He has also brought me deliverance from times of trouble, from the snare of sin, from personal crises and more. In my heart, I readily give him glory for constant involvement in my walk. I have never held back because of a fear that I don't know what to say. The words and ideas haven't escaped me.

Yet for some reason, there were times in my younger years when I was hesitant to tell others, most specifically nonbelievers, about the great and mighty works of the Lord. Things changed for me when I began praying for a list of people who need to know the Lord or draw closer to him. As I prayed through that list, I found myself praying that God would send someone to share appropriately with each person. For some of those people, I realized that I was the most appropriate person to share with them, yet for some reason I had not done so. This needed to change.

The psalmist is my example. The Greek translation of the Hebrew psalm that was used by the earliest church employs the Greek word "gospel" in speaking of "glad news" of deliverance. The gospel of Jesus dying for my sins is a deliverance story that I should share. It is right and fitting for me to tell the world what God has done for me and what he continues to do for me. Two thousand years ago, he conquered sin, the powers of darkness, and the grave on my behalf. He continues daily to work deliverance to me from all sorts of obstacles and traps in life.

I need to commit to sharing his greatness to the world today and every day. I need to commit to proclaiming his direct involvement on my behalf. He is worthy of my praise, and I intend to give it!

Lord, thank you for your great deeds of deliverance on my behalf. Thank you for the victory wrought by Jesus over sin and death. Thank you for giving that victory to me through faith. May I unabashedly tell the world what you have done and what you continue to do in Jesus' name. Amen!

❧ ❧ ❧

APRIL 5

Blessed is the one who considers the poor! In the day of trouble the LORD delivers him; the LORD protects him and keeps him alive; he is called blessed in the land; you do not give him up to the will of his enemies. The LORD sustains him on his sickbed; in his illness you restore him to full health. (Ps. 41:1-2)

"Poor" is a Hebrew concept that doesn't mean only "impoverished." The word has a range of semantic meaning that includes people who are sick in body or mind, who are weak or frail, and who are in need of support. The psalm pronounces God's blessings on those people who are attentive to these people in need. The reader is instructed to live with thoughtful consideration giving help to those needing it.

This is an Old Testament equivalent that finds a counterpart in Jesus' story of the Good Samaritan. Jesus told that story in response to the question, "Who is my neighbor?" Jesus showed the importance of coming to the aid of one in need, even if such a person wasn't in the same social circle (a Samaritan rather than a Jew). The psalm doesn't limit which poor people we are to help. We are called to consider simply, "the poor," regardless of who they are. God then ministers to us as we minister to others.

God is calling us to do the very thing God himself does. If we view ourselves accurately, we are all poor and in need before God. We are weak, frail, and in need of support. God himself comes to the rescue of the frail. He comes to our rescue. Our God is a God in service of those in need, even as Almighty God. It is rather stunning to contemplate that the God behind the universe seeks to serve a lost humanity in need. We see it clearest in Jesus. Jesus made it plain in stating his purpose, "For the Son of Man came to seek and to save the lost" (Luke 19:10). While we should be serving the King of Kings, in reality, he has come to our aid, seeking to serve in love. When the apostles were arguing over who was the greatest, on the eve of Jesus' crucifixion, Jesus explained, "let the greatest among you become as the youngest, and the leader as one who serves. . . . I am among you as the one who serves" (Luke 22:26-27).

As God himself comes to our aid, considering us impoverished, and serving us fully, so we should have the same attitude of Jesus. We should regard others as more important, seeking to bless them in their impoverished state, whether economical, emotional, or otherwise. We are to be blessing people with our lives, resources, and abilities, as opportunity permits.

Lord, open my eyes to see the poor. Let me see people not for what they can do for me, but for what I can do for them. May I love and serve them in the name of Jesus, bringing your love into their lives. For Jesus' sake, Amen!

❧ ❧ ❧

APRIL 6

Blessed be the LORD, the God of Israel, from everlasting to everlasting! Amen and Amen.
(Ps. 41:13)

There are passages in the Bible that pronounce praise to God. This psalm calls forth a proclamation of God as blessed from before all time to time everlasting. This is a right and good call.

It is right for us to praise God because God alone is worthy of our praise. He is purity beyond all purity. He is righteous beyond our conceptions of right. He is non-laughing, though all others in in their He loves selflessly even the most selfish among us. He seeks the lost who do not want to be found. He holds the wounded and brings healing. He is a father to the fatherless and a husband to the widow. He is a friend to the friendless. He heals the sick in body and heart. He shows compassion to the hurting. He lifts up the humble. He rescues the perishing. He shows mercy to those in need.

He also humbles the proud. He disciplines the sinner. He brings the mighty to their knees. He finds those ignoring him and drives their attention to him.

There are a number of places where holy writers proclaim God in his majesty, setting forth his praises in marvelous language. Paul blessed God as "the blessed and only Sovereign, the King of kings and Lord of lords, who alone has immortality, who dwells in unapproachable light, whom no one has ever seen or can see. To him be honor and eternal dominion. Amen" (1 Tim. 6:15-16). Jude, the brother of Jesus, blessed him writing, "Now to him who is able to keep you from stumbling and to present you blameless before the presence of his glory with great joy, to the only God, our Savior, through Jesus Christ our Lord, be glory, majesty, dominion, and authority, before all time and now and forever. Amen" (Jude 24-25). Ephesians 3:20-21 proclaims the personal and powerful blessing, "Now to him who is able to do far more abundantly than all that we ask or think, according to the power at work within us, to him be glory in the church and in Christ Jesus throughout all generations, forever and ever. Amen."

These are just a few of the many blessings of God in Scripture. We are called to write and proclaim our own blessings as well. In the prayer below, I start the blessing, but I urge you to add your own proclamation of a way God is great!

Lord, you are our God, our Provider, and Sustainer. Thank you for your constant and steadfast love, your overflowing mercies, and so much more in Jesus' name, Amen!

❧ ❧ ❧

APRIL 7

As a deer pants for flowing streams, so pants my soul for you, O God. . . . My tears have been my food day and night, while they say to me all the day long, "Where is your God?" These things I remember, as I pour out my soul: how I would go with the throng and lead them in procession to the house of God with glad shouts and songs of praise, a multitude keeping festival. Why are you cast down, O my soul, and why are you in turmoil within me? Hope in God; for I shall again praise him, my salvation and my God. (Ps. 42:1, 3-6)

One day in college, a classmate asked our Greek professor, "Dr. Floyd, how do you feel about your salvation?" Dr. Floyd looked almost put out as he responded, "How do I *feel*? What does it matter how I *feel* about my salvation? Let me tell you what I *think* about my salvation." He then went on to explain the importance of the faith he had placed in God to save him, while at the same time telling the class how unreliable feelings were. He used this psalm to illustrate his point that thoughts often need to trump the heart in such matters.

This 42nd Psalm separates into three streams of thought. In Hebrew it is joined to Psalm 43 to make one whole. Each verse begins with a successive letter of the alphabet and it takes the two psalms to make it through the Hebrew alphabet. The psalms also fit together thematically. Both have the three streams of thought. I set out a sample of the three streams in the verses above.

The first thought is the emotional longing of the writer. The psalmist does not feel connected to God, and complains of the isolation felt. "My tears have been my food while they say, 'Where is your God?' " The second thought is the mental response that over rules the emotional. "These things I remember. . . ." The psalmist doesn't let feelings win the day. Instead, the mind recalls the blessings and joys that have flowed from the earlier walk with the Lord. This leads to the third thought. "Hope in God; for I shall again praise him, my salvation and my God." The psalmist in faith recognizes that the feelings of isolation are temporary. God will restore joy.

If the psalm ended there, that would be enough. Reading the rest of Psalm 42 and Psalm 43 adds to the picture, however. The psalm goes right back to "My soul is cast down within me," the first stream of thought, and the cycle begins again. In other words, in spite of faith, the bad feelings do not go away. Not the second time, and not the third time. So it is sometimes. But we must still remember it is not what we feel that rules the day. Feelings come and go. Our faith is steady in the Lord who is steadfast in love. We should never let our feelings dictate our reality.

Lord, hold us in your love. Renew our minds to govern our hearts in Jesus, Amen!

APRIL 8

O God, we have heard with our ears, our fathers have told us, what deeds you performed in their days, in the days of old. (Ps. 44:1)

A very important task Moses assigned to parents involved telling the next generation about the amazing works of God. In Deuteronomy 4:9 Moses told the Israelites that they should "take care" and "keep" their "soul diligently" so they wouldn't forget the works of the Lord. They should "Make them known to your children and your children's children."

It is very easy to forget what God has done, especially if we feel aggrieved by him, abandoned by him, or if we begin walking in deliberate sin. It may be a full forgetfulness, where we let his marvelous deeds pass from our minds. Or it may be a subtle forgetfulness, where we don't tie the deeds to God. We begin thinking things were chance or came from personal effort. (Personal pride can be a big source of forgetting God.) We write God off and walk ignorant to his presence. Moses warned the Israelites to be diligent to remember the works of the Lord, and then tells them to pass that memory to the next generation.

The psalmist was in a generation who had received this "pass on" of God's goodness. The psalmist remembered what the fathers had related about the works of God. This is a good thing. It reminds us how important it is to first, register and recognize the hand of the Lord in your life; second, remember what God has done; and, third, pass that story with appropriate credit on to the next generation.

This is, in part, a drive behind these devotionals. These are written out of a desire to share with my children a sample of how God has worked in my devotional life through the Psalms. I want my children to know how critical God has been to helping me through crisis, to steering me through faith, to teaching me the joys of worship, to giving me wisdom for life, to providing meaning and love, to forgiving me and training me in righteousness. I want my children to hear of God's faithfulness even in the midst of my failings. They need to know that God has rescued me from depths of despair, has walked with me through trials of fire, and has sustained me through emotional turmoil. He has strengthened me when weakness abounded, has wiped away my tears, given faith in my fears, and never, never, NEVER abandoned me. God is good. I want, I need, to realize that truth and pass it on!

Lord, thank you for your constant love. Thank you for working in my life. Thank you for my faithful parents who told me of your love as I grew up. Help me to tell your faithfulness to the next generation and the one after that. For Jesus' sake, Amen!

❧ ❧ ❧

APRIL 9

You are my King, O God; ordain salvation for Jacob! Through you we push down our foes; through your name we tread down those who rise up against us. For not in my bow do I trust, nor can my sword save me. But you have saved us from our foes and have put to shame those who hate us. In God we have boasted continually, and we will give thanks to your name forever. (Ps. 44:4-8)

The theme song to the detective show *Monk* begins, "It's a jungle out there!" While the show was a bemused look at life and death, there are seasons of life where we do battle against foes and problems. For Israel, that was often a physical battle against warring neighbors who might come in to maraud the fields as the crops ripen. For us, more often the battle is one Paul described as not against flesh and blood, but against "the rulers, against the authorities, against the cosmic powers over this present darkness, against the spiritual forces of evil in the heavenly places" (Eph. 6:12). Paul spent a good bit of the letter explaining that these are the battles we face in trying to be good husbands, wives, children, and workers. These are battles of holiness in a world that encourages sin.

This psalm passage gives a marvelous explanation of how to conduct these battles in faith. First, we properly see the battle as one where God is involved. We do not win against these struggles on our own. I am not strong enough in my own power to be the husband, father, or believer I would like to be. Through God I will achieve! As the psalm indicates, we do not have the tools to win the fights in this life on our own. My willpower is not great enough. My wisdom is not sufficient. My skill set will only go so far, and it certainly is not far enough. If left on my own, I will never be what I want and need to be.

But with God, the story is entirely different! Now I have the weapons of war that Paul described also in Ephesians 6. I have a helmet of salvation that tops everything off, knowing I am secure in God's gracious victory over sin, regardless of my own merit. I have a shield of faith that allows me to trust in God, knowing he will protect and defend me. I can seek his deliverance from evil. I have the sword of the Spirit, the word of God in Scripture. It gives me insight, encouragement, and direction.

Now I can walk in God's victory, and as I am doing well in this life over the enemies, I can follow the psalm's example, giving praise to God who arms me for war. I boast in God!

Lord, I am in need of you 24 hours a day, 7 days a week. I need your help in being who I can and should be, to your glory, and for the sake of your kingdom. I pray for you to infuse me with your faith and your Spirit, to the purposes of your will. In Jesus I pray, Amen!

❧ ❧ ❧

APRIL 10

You have rejected us and disgraced us. . . . You have made us like sheep for slaughter. . . .
You have made us the taunt of our neighbors, the derision and scorn of those around
us. . . . All day long my disgrace is before me, and shame has covered my face. . . . All this
has come upon us, though we have not forgotten you, and we have not been false to your
covenant. Our heart has not turned back, nor have our steps departed from your way;
yet you have broken us . . . for your sake we are killed all the day long; we are regarded as
sheep to be slaughtered. (Ps. 44:9, 11, 13, 15, 17-19, 22)

Psalm 44 has some very difficult verses, including these. These are
the kind of passages that we wish weren't there. There is a part of us that
wants God to run the world like a well-run kindergarten class, where good
things immediately are recognized, praised and rewarded, while bad things
are called out and dealt with appropriately and immediately. Yet God is not
a kindergarten teacher, and this world is not a kindergarten class. So we
have real psalms like this one that disturb us. For this psalm points out
that there is suffering that not only is unjustified but can even be because
of our faithfulness to God.

This psalm points out a time where disgrace, rejection, scorn, derision,
harm, and more have come upon the writer even though the writer was
living holy before God, trusting upon God, and specifically living *for* God.
In spite of this holy walk, the psalmist writes of being "broken" by God,
"killed," and "regarded as sheep to be slaughtered."

What shall we make of this? I can't explain it away. I can't skip over
it. I read it and it registers. It tells me that there is unjustified suffering in
this world. This is not Utopia or Eden, and there are times and ways that
people suffer unfairly. It might be me suffering, it might be my neighbor, it
might be someone in a far-off land. This should not really surprise us. Jesus
himself suffered unjustly, and he warned us we would too.

Paul quoted from this psalm in Romans, where he assured his readers
that no suffering, regardless of how great, should ever be seen as anything
that would separate the believer from God's love. Unjust suffering is not a
removal of God's love. It is a time where the assurance of God's love helps
us through. After quoting from Psalm 44, Paul wrote the famous words,
"No, in all these things we are more than conquerors through him who
loved us. For I am sure that neither death nor life, nor angels nor rulers,
nor things present nor things to come, nor powers, nor height nor depth,
nor anything else in all creation, will be able to separate us from the love
of God in Christ Jesus our Lord" (Rom. 8:37-39).

Lord, thank you for your love. Hold us tenderly, please. We need you. In Jesus, Amen!

❧ ❧ ❧

APRIL 11

Your throne, O God, is forever and ever. The scepter of your kingdom is a scepter of uprightness; you have loved righteousness and hated wickedness. (Ps. 45:6-7)

Growing up in the churches of my youth, we learned the Lord's Prayer, but saying it ritually was not common. We didn't say it each Sunday or even each month. It was said but not as part of any routine. I was surprised in reading church history that one of the earliest church instruction manuals outside of Scripture, the *Didache*, taught the early church to say the Lord's Prayer three times a day. I began to try that in my prayer life and found it changing the way I prayed. The challenge, as it often is with prayer, was and is to say it each time with meaning, rather than simply a rote repetition.

One of the phrases of the Lord's Prayer that stands out is "Your kingdom come." In praying this often, we begin sensing the personal responsibility to live lives working toward this goal of God's kingdom coming. In other words, I am not simply seeking to pray, "Your kingdom come"; I am seeking to live it. I want my actions to be in furtherance of the coming kingdom of God.

In this sense, this psalm teaches me something about life. The throne of God, from which he reigns over his kingdom, is not temporary. Nor is it changing or evolving. God's throne, as it was, shall ever be. It is forever and ever, constant and unchanging. The throne is one where God's scepter is "uprightness." God does not reign as an amoeba, shifting shapes and forms from righteous to unrighteous and back again. God doesn't have a throne where wickedness finds a home. Evil does not reside at the side of God.

This idea has affected me and continues to change my life. I see from this psalm a need to be cleansed from my own wickedness and sin. I have impurities that must be washed clean if I wish to find my home at the throne of God. Of course, I have no ability to wash myself clean of wickedness but by the gift of God in Christ on Calvary. That cleansing is available through faith and trust. This change in my status made me right before God and able to be in his kingdom of righteousness.

This recognition continues to affect me in that I am now looking to bring God's kingdom into greater expression on earth. It means that my life today needs to be characterized by the same righteousness and uprightness that are hallmarks of God's throne. I am to love righteousness. I am to hate wickedness. It starts with me and my life, but extends out to how I live and perceive the world.

Lord, may your kingdom come and your will be done on earth, and particularly in my life, as it is in heaven. Through Jesus, Amen!

❧ ❧ ❧

APRIL 12

God is our refuge and strength, a very present help in trouble. Therefore we will not fear though the earth gives way. (Ps. 46:1-2)

One of my father's favorite movies was the musical *The Music Man*. The movie came out in 1962, so my dad would have been thirty years old. I think Dad had memorized every word to each song. I am reasonably certain if my father were alive and reading this psalm passage, he would immediately start singing, "We've got troubles, my friends, right here in River City. With a capital T and that rhymes with P and that stands for pool." Yes, there was trouble in River City, but not the cataclysmic problems contemplated by the psalmist.

We do find problems somewhere along the scale of the musical to the psalm. For some our troubles arise from work. I remember when I was having to work for bosses who seemed ungodly and uncaring, if not downright mean and malicious. I would read this psalm and take strength. For here the psalmist, in the midst of severe problems, declares God as "refuge," "strength," and a very "present help." I like to read this psalm in the Hebrew because each of these words stands out in ways that help dispel fear.

The word for refuge is a "tent" or "shelter" that would protect one from the sun or rain. It become a figurative image in a number of the Psalms to describe a place of protection. The prophet Isaiah used the word figuratively to describe the ungodly, who use lies as their refuge (Isa. 28:15). I will take protection from the God of truth in the face of trouble. I know better than to lie my way out of problems!

The word for strength conveys the idea of power. For the faithful, they find God as the power that infuses them in ways to let them face any problem. I like to think of it in weight-lifting terms. A power lifter's problem is a bar with heavy weights. The challenge is to find the strength or power to lift it. As we face our problems, our strength is not from our own muscles, our own wisdom, our own talents or resources. Our power for lifting our problems comes from God. We have his power! There is no reason to fear any problem we face when we have God's strength.

The final phrase is "very present." "Very" functions in Hebrew just like English. It means "intense." The word for present conveys the idea of "found." God is "very present" or "easily found!" We do not have to hunt for him. There is no need to awaken him or worry he might be on vacation, ignoring us, or anything else. He is readily found, very present. Now with a God who is our shelter, our power, and readily found, what shall we fear?

Lord, in you we take refuge. Please walk us through our problems with your strength, In Jesus' name, Amen!

❦ ❦ ❦

APRIL 13

There is a river whose streams make glad the city of God, the holy habitation of the Most High. God is in the midst of her; she shall not be moved; God will help her when morning dawns. The nations rage, the kingdoms totter; he utters his voice, the earth melts. The LORD *of hosts is with us; the God of Jacob is our fortress.* (Ps. 46:4-7)

Any Old Testament reader of this psalm would know there is no river in Jerusalem, the "city of God." Jerusalem is on a hill/mountain. The river in this psalm represents the presence of God. Isaiah 33:20-21 uses a similar metaphor for God's presence in Jerusalem. (In Jerusalem "the LORD in majesty will be for us a place of broad rivers and streams.")

Rivers were important aids to life in the Old Testament era, as they are to many around the world today. Rivers were a ready source of water to drink, water to feed animals, water for crops, water to wash, a source of fish for food. They served as a place where animals and wildlife would gather to drink and therefore provided good hunting grounds. In a real sense, rivers were a source of life. This context makes the metaphor stronger for God's presence as a river making the city glad. The river as life brings joy to the inhabitants of the city.

Psalm 36:8 speaks of the "river of [God's] delights." God's presence comes with God's supplies. As rivers met so many diverse needs, so does the presence of God. His delights and gifts flow to those in his presence, just as the blessings of a river flow forth.

The presence of God renders any place of his faithful a glad place. The unfaithful and wicked will rue the presence of God, but his people rejoice over God's presence. Where God is, there is stability. Where God is, there is help for the faithful. I want to live in the presence of God. I need to receive the nourishment of God. Knowing the turmoil of those without God enhances my realization of my desire for and need for him. I want to live in the presence of God. I need to receive the nourishment of God. Knowing the turmoil of those without God enhances my realization of my desire for and need for him.

The Christian group White Heart sang "The River Will Flow." In the song, a tired and thirsty Christian hears God say, "I am the river full of power and truth. You've been looking outside yourself, when it's there inside of you." The song's chorus explains, "The river is love. The river is peace. And the river will flow through the hearts of those who believe."

Lord, I want to go down to the river of your presence, and let the sacred stream wash me clean. As I kneel before you, may your river of love and peace direct my life in Jesus, Amen!

❧ ❧ ❧

APRIL 14

"Be still, and know that I am God. I will be exalted among the nations, I will be exalted in the earth!" The LORD of hosts is with us; the God of Jacob is our fortress. (Ps. 46:10-11)

Stillness is hard to find. It is hard for me to be still in my body. I am a fidgeter. My eyes are constantly taking in what is around me. My hands want to be busy. My feet tap to songs playing in my head. I go on vacation and look for things to do.

It is even harder to be still in my mind and spirit. To stop the whirring of thoughts and constant ideas. To be quiet and still inside is harder than it is outside.

The call of this psalm to me is one of the most difficult in Scripture. To be quiet and dwell on knowing God is not easy. I can last a few minutes on a good day, and then my mind wanders. Maybe that is why these devotionals are so important to my walk. Certainly while my fingers are flying on the keyboard, I am not being still. Yet, in preparation for my typing, I have time to pause and contemplate who God is, what he is saying, and what he is doing.

In this way, I grow to know God better. This is no small matter. John 17:3 proclaims, "And this is eternal life, that they know you the only true God, and Jesus Christ whom you have sent." Knowing God is also knowing Christ. After all, Jesus is "the way, the truth, and the life" (John 14:6), and as we know the "truth," the truth sets us free! (John 8:32). I learn of God, I grow to know God, as I grow to know Jesus.

This opened up a whole new aspect of this psalm for me. I have sought to read the gospels and learn of Jesus. I want to know him better and better. There is a marvelous blessing from reading through the gospels and pausing after each story to absorb it, from being still and thinking about what is revealed about Jesus and God in the story. As I am still and learn of him, as I grow in knowing him, I begin to see my life transform. God is exalted in my life before a watching world. God moves around my priorities. He shifts my reliance on others and feeds my soul as he bathes me in peace.

"Be still, and know that I am God" is a difficult instruction, but one that I am coming to appreciate more and more as I spend time with the Lord Jesus in quiet contemplation and prayer.

Lord, help me find quiet places. Give me time to think about you, grow closer to you, and become more like you. I want people to see Jesus in me, and I need your work for that to happen. I pray to you and live for you through Jesus, my Lord, Amen!

❧ ❧ ❧

APRIL 15

Clap your hands, all peoples! Shout to God with loud songs of joy! For the LORD, *the Most High, is to be feared, a great king over all the earth. . . . God has gone up with a shout, the* LORD *with the sound of a trumpet. Sing praises to God, sing praises! Sing praises to our King, sing praises! (Ps. 47:1-2, 5-6)*

Sing! Clap! Shout! CELEBRATE!!!! Celebrate God! Celebrate his victories! Celebrate his strength. Celebrate his wisdom. Celebrate who he is and what he's done. Praise him! Lift him up! Hear your own voice proclaim his greatness. Let the world hear your voice proclaim his greatness. Praise him with your deeds, and not just your words. Let your actions show that you value God. Show you value his priorities. Show you value his teachings. Show your faith that he knows best. Show your faith that he loves you.

This psalm is not asking us to worship the Lord. It is telling us to! It is giving us concrete language about how to do it. It says for us to shout *to* God. We are to sing praises *to* God. We sing praises *to* our king. Our worship is first and foremost not an exercise at singing *about* God, it is singing *to* God.

I love the worship songs that are prayers directed *to* God. Songs that place us before his throne in praise bear fruit in my life, giving me strength and insight that come from being in God's presence. These songs to God are not only those giving him honor in the sense that we normally think of it. In Matthew 21 we read of the people shouting "Hosanna" to Jesus as he entered Jerusalem. When the priests expressed indignation, Jesus replied that praise would come out of the mouths even of infants and nursing children (Matt. 21:15-16). This is instructive for praise.

"Hosanna" was an Aramaic cry for Jesus to save the people. We could easily translate into modern English as, "Save us, please!" In other words, to Jesus, calling upon him to save and rescue us *is* praise! We praise God when we ascribe to him his rightful place in things. So the psalmist praises him, calling him "a great king over all the earth," something he certainly is. So also we praise him when we call upon him to save us. For that is a proclamation that God is a saving God and we are a people in need of him. There is no more truthful assignment of God to his rightful place than calling him Savior!

I need worship songs n my life, and not just on Sunday morning! Find some! Find ones that are *to* God, not simply about him. Then sing those songs. Sing loudly. Don't be ashamed! Lift up the Lord in praise!

Great and amazing Lord. You make a vast universe with billions of people, and yet know our name, the hairs on our heads, and you love us. What a God! In Jesus, Amen!

APRIL 16

Great is the LORD *and greatly to be praised in the city of our God! . . . We have thought on your steadfast love, O God, in the midst of your temple. As your name, O God, so your praise reaches to the ends of the earth. Your right hand is filled with righteousness.*
(Ps. 48:1, 9-10)

If we think about God's steadfast love, we will also join the chorus proclaiming him great! For many, love is like the moon, it comes and goes in cycles, sometimes in full form, other times barely recognizable. Not so the love of God. It is steadfast and constant. We do not worship a God who is fickle in his affections. He does not have bad days where he chooses to avoid us or treat us poorly.

If God disciplines us, it is for our own growth. If God sees pain and sickness come upon us, he promises to work it for the best, both for us and for his kingdom. These are signs of God's steadfast love, not indicators of anything less.

I know a man, a very typical man actually, who has decided to have nothing to do with God. God failed the man, so the man thinks. The man's sister died when she was just 18. Now, fifty years later, the man still has nothing to do with God, blaming God for the loss. I wish I could change the man's understanding. I wish he were able to see that his sister did not die without God. She died with God. The death was tragic, and Jesus shows us tears in the face of death, even as he was about to call forth a resurrection, because God knows death is tragic (John 11:35). God didn't make people to die. He made us for eternal fellowship with him. Yet death is part of this fallen world. All people die. Some young, some old, but all die. Even if we see this life as merely the prelude to eternity, the age of death will dissolve somewhat, but it is still painful, and God knows this.

So our minds need to dwell on these things, but dwell on them "in the midst of the temple" or the presence of God. We do not need to take our counsel from the doubters and skeptics on the streets of despair. We need to come before the Lord and in that place utter our thoughts of despair, isolation, fear, etc. For there we will meet the God of steadfast love. As we think of him, as we contemplate who he is, as we think about the incarnation, death, and resurrection of Jesus, we will better understand life. It may not answer all our questions at once, but it will take hold of who we are. In worship, we will find God.

Lord, you are truly great. You have steadfast love. You have shown it to us. You have lived it before us. Surely there is no greater love than that you showed in Christ. So many doubt your love, Father, help us to show it to them by our lives. May we reflect Jesus, in whom we pray, Amen!

❧ ❧ ❧

APRIL 17

Tell the next generation that this is God, our God forever and ever. He will guide us forever. (Ps. 48:13-14)

There are many places in the world where people wonder about where they will get their next meal. I must confess, not so much me. I have never gone hungry because I cannot access food. I tend to take food for granted. It is available to me, and I can get it when I want it. I may not like the choices, but I don't wonder if there is food. On this, I suspect I am not alone.

I fear we often take God for granted in much the same way. God is always there. We figure if we pray, he hears us. We don't need to get on his calendar or find when he has an opening to talk to us. When we sin, we figure he will forgive us. That's just what he does. He is God, and he is always there, he wants to hear from us, and he wants to forgive us.

The apostles chased away kids because the apostles were trying to value Jesus' time, but Jesus scolded the apostles, and said he wanted the kids to come to him. He laid hands on the children and blessed them (Matt. 19:13-15). We know these stories, and they tend to feed our taking God for granted. We know he wants us to come, and we trust he is there when we "need" him. (As if there's a time we don't need God!)

But we should never take God for granted. Not because he isn't going to be there for us, for surely he is, but because it isn't right! We need to recognize God as God Most High, and be appreciative for who he is. We need to see him active in our world and in our lives. We need to engage with him in the big and the little. As we do so, we are in place to fulfill the instructions of this psalm.

We are to tell the next generation about God! If we take him for granted, so will the next generation (if they take him at all). So we tell the next generation about what God has done in our lives. We explain how he was there when times were rough. How he gave us joy in the midst of difficulty. We proclaim his answering prayers that came through fear in the darkest nights of life. This ever-present, ever-loving, full-of-grace God will change us and has changed us, and we need to be bold and upfront about telling others. This is the way faith grows. It is also the way the next generation will grow. They will see that God "guides us forever" and will better follow his lead.

Lord, you have been faithful God to me. I thank you for forgiving my sins, the wrongs I have done, as well as the good things I have failed to do. I thank you for leading me in paths of righteousness for your name's sake. I thank you for Jesus in whom I pray, Amen!

❧ ❧ ❧

APRIL 18

Hear this, all peoples! Give ear, all inhabitants of the world, both low and high, rich and poor together! My mouth shall speak wisdom; the meditation of my heart shall be understanding. (Ps. 49:1-3)

God's wisdom is universal. We should never think it is only for some people. His instructions do not work only some of the time or in certain circumstances.

God has made this world and imbued it with a thumbprint of his own ꟷꟷꟷ ꟷꟷꟷ ꟷꟷꟷ. Paul said it this way, "[God's] invisible attributes, namely, his eternal power and divine nature, have been clearly perceived, ever since the creation of the world, in the things that have been made" (Rom. 1:20). As maker of the universe, he knows humanity. He knows who we are and how we work. He would know, above all others, what is good and useful for people, what will lead to the best in people's lives. These are the instructions he has delivered to us for our understanding and application.

This does not mean that we are not often faced with perplexing problems where we need to seek God's wisdom. Many of his instructions are tools that we bring to bear in unique circumstances where a ready answer is not apparent. But we have the tools of Scripture. Among those tools, is the ability to pray to God. We are told that when we pray and ask for wisdom, he is faithful to give it to us. (Jas. 1:5: "If any of you lacks wisdom, let him ask God, who gives generously to all without reproach, and it will be given him.") God will honor that prayer for wisdom. Another tool Scripture teaches us we have is to seek counsel from godly counselors. (Prov. 11:14: "Where there is no guidance, a people falls, but in an abundance of counselors there is safety.") That is where this psalm lies. This psalm gives us counsel to listen to others who are godly.

I have always been amazed at believers who are stuck in a moral problem, and seek their counsel from people of the world. If the problem is not really moral or spiritual, then a nonbeliever may have the best advice. If I need medical attention, I seek the best doctor, not a lesser one who happens to be a believer. But in like manner, if I am addressing a problem with spiritual or moral overlays, I want my counsel from someone who understands the Lord and his ways. That is the counselor who will best understand the Lord's wisdom. This is an important reason to ensure your best friends are solid Christians. They will give the best counsel and wisdom in such matters.

Lord, do give me wisdom for this life. Let me know your ways. And may I be a resource to other believers, sharing the wisdom you've given me, as others seek it out. Thank you Lord, in Jesus, Amen.

❧ ❧ ❧

APRIL 19

Truly no man can ransom another, or give to God the price of his life, for the ransom of their life is costly and can never suffice, that he should live on forever and never see the pit. (Ps. 49:7-9)

The need for something miraculous to ransom the lives of sinners is not a New Testament novelty. It was never a concoction of some new theological idea put forward by a group of Galilean fishermen to give meaning to the death of their carpenter friend, Jesus. The idea is deeply embedded in the Old Testament truths and wisdom.

This passage makes a thought provoking point. How can anyone give to God the price or ransom for their life? What do I have that I can supply to God that is sufficient for the life my life? I could give him all my money, but that doesn't buy me life. God doesn't need my money. I could give him my house. But what is God going to do with my house? I old give God my family, but God is the reason they exist, not me. I could give God my heart, but even my heart is impure, and giving God something impure hardly seems adequate or appropriate.

I don't have anything to give God of such value that God would hold me into eternity as a sinful and troubled man. Paul explained the predicament to the Romans. By God's justice, deeds receive their just reward. If I do right, I will get God's righteousness. But if I sin, I get the condemnation of sin. Romans 2:6-9 says, "He will render to each one according to his works: to those who by patience in well-doing seek for glory and honor and immortality, he will give eternal life; but for those who are self-seeking and do not obey the truth, but obey unrighteousness, there will be wrath and fury. There will be tribulation and distress for every human being who does evil." I know where I am, and where everyone is in Paul's equation. I have been self-seeking and disobedient to the truth. This does not bode well.

Yet thankfully it doesn't end there. This is the good news! The psalm promised the "God will ransom my soul" (Ps. 49:13). There is one who was no ordinary man whose life was sufficient to ransom me and all others. Jesus Christ was not just a carpenter, he built a way for humanity to find God. Through the death of the righteous one, the price for sin is paid. Paul gives this alternative to our own deeds in Romans 3:21-22, "But now the righteousness of God has been manifested apart from the law, although the Law and the Prophets bear witness to it—the righteousness of God through faith in Jesus Christ for all who believe."

Lord, thank you for the deliverance in Jesus. I do not deserve it. I am not adequately appreciative of it. But I embrace it. I need it. I am sinful and desperately in need of a Savior beyond myself. I live and pray through Jesus, Amen!

❧ ❧ ❧

APRIL 20

For he sees that even the wise die; the fool and the stupid alike must perish and leave their wealth to others. Their graves are their homes forever, their dwelling places to all generations, though they called lands by their own names. Man in his pomp will not remain; he is like the beasts that perish. This is the path of those who have foolish confidence. . . . But God will ransom my soul. (Ps. 49:10-13, 15)

I watch people for a living. It is part of the life of a trial lawyer. I need to know how people tick, what they value, and how they think. It amazes me that some think themselves too smart for God or too smart for faith. So many of these think themselves smart because they believe the physical things they see (physically or through what their minds can conceive) are the limit to what is there. This seems really foolish and sad. It is rooted in pride, as if we have understanding of all the grand things that are or could be.

If all we have and all we are is this physical world, then eat, drink, and be merry! For once this life is over, then there is blackness. Nothing you have will follow you to the grave. It doesn't matter how smart you are or how rich you are, there is no getting away from death.

If there is no God, then life is really just a time where the chemicals in the Jello we call our "brains" is merely an electronic firing of neurons in some order made possible by our genetics and our exposure to outside influences (i.e., the "environment"). If there is no God, then "love" is really just part of this chemical soup that follows laws of nature and is not something "special"; personality is simply a function of brain, and choice is an illusion.

Yet everything in me shouts, "No!" There is something more to this life than living and dying. There is something more than gathering up toys or green pieces of paper we call "money" to leave behind for people I love. There has to be more to life!

Augustine wrote of a God-shaped hole we have that is filled with a relationship with God. People sense the hole, and try to fill it with things: money, sex, alcohol, drugs, knowledge, work, etc. Nothing satisfies the vacuum we have, except a relationship with God. The God-shaped hole cannot be filled except with God. That is the cry of the saved, of those who find that longing met. There is an answer and we can join with the psalmist. Our life is not over with the grave. It is not spent in vain. God will ransom our souls from the grave. We are more than a sack of chemicals. We are his children, made in his image, to spend eternity with him!

Lord, thank you for making us. Thank you for redeeming us. Thank you for giving this life purpose. Thank you for Jesus. In him, we live and say, Amen!

APRIL 21

Man in his pomp yet without understanding is like the beasts that perish. (Ps. 49:20)

This passage concludes Psalm 49. It follows verses that speak of the power and influence of rich people and how that power and riches mean nothing in the grand scheme of life. Neither the riches nor that power can follow someone into the grave, a place where everyone is headed.

Yet so many people believe that money, power, or other worldly things are worth pursuing as if they have an intrinsic value in themselves. They don't. Money is a marvelous tool and can be used for good or evil (or can be wasted), but it is still only a tool. The value will be seen only in how the tool is used. It is the usage of the tool that has value. People lose sight on this when they love the money, rather than valuing the good the money can do.

Power is a tool. Influence is one like it. Power and influence give one abilities one would not have otherwise. One can use those abilities to make the world a better place, to enrich the lives of others, to bring glory to God, or one can use power to self-enrich, self-aggrandize, abuse others, or worse. People lose sight of this when they seek power for power's sake, or because of how that power makes the possessor feel. Then the power is not about the good it can do but becomes an end to itself.

Do we see a pattern here? There are other riches people possess that are open to the same logical patterns. Some people possess a rich mind. They are able to think carefully and rapidly. They are creative in their thoughts and are able to find solutions to problems others find daunting. This "rich mind" is a tool, and a very dangerous one at that. It can be used for good, bringing glory to God and the work of his kingdom. One can read the writings of rabbi Paul and see how brilliant he was. He was clearly fluent in Greek, Hebrew, Aramaic, and likely Latin. He knew poetry, was a top law student, understood the rules and practices of rhetoric, and could relate to all sorts of diverse people. In his own life, he used the tool of his rich mind both to persecute the church and to propagate the church. With his mind he blessed the Lord and God's work, after having used the same mind to try and destroy God's work.

So the mind can be a tool for good or evil. It can also be a dangerous tool, for some love the knowledge more than what it can do. Then those people are ensnared by their own thoughts, so proud in what their mind can do, they become confident in the mind as an end to itself. Thoughts and knowledge supplant God. The psalm tells us to find understanding to go with our riches. Riches without understanding are a trap!

Lord, enrich our minds and hearts with godly wisdom and understanding, in Jesus, Amen!

APRIL 22

Our God comes; he does not keep silence; before him is a devouring fire, around him a mighty tempest. He calls to the heavens above and to the earth, that he may judge his people: "Gather to me my faithful ones, who made a covenant with me by sacrifice!" (Ps. 50:3-5)

Do you hear God? If you don't, either you do not recognize him or you are not listening.

I was corresponding by email with an atheist who read my book *Christianity on Trial*. He received my email address through Internet research and wrote me, challenging some of my conclusions of faith. During the email exchange, which has now been ongoing over a year, the man told me that one of the reasons he knows there is no God is because he has never seen any evidence of God. He has never heard God. I wrote him back and asked him what he thought our email chain was? I was only spending time discussing these things with him *because* God loved him. I was trying my hardest to speak to him of God because Jesus told his believers that he would speak through them to the world about who God was, who Jesus was, and what Jesus was about (John 15:26-27; 16:12-15). He was hearing God and seeing evidence of God, but was blind to it.

God speaks loudly! As a poet, the psalmist uses imagery of a lightening storm to describe the voice of God. We hear the voice of God in Scripture, but that is not the only place. God speaks in the love that grows in the lives of his children. Jesus said, "By this all people will know that you are my disciples, if you have love for one another" (John 13:35). The love of God produces good fruit in the lives of believers. Paul described the fruit of the Spirit as "love, joy, peace, patience, kindness, goodness, faithfulness, gentleness, self-control" (Gal. 5:22-23). As these grow in the lives of God's children God is speaking to the world about the validity of a transforming faith. Jesus was clear, "each tree is known by its own fruit" (Luke 6:44). He added in John, "By this my Father is glorified, that you bear much fruit and so prove to be my disciples" (John 15:8).

I think we live in such a communication world where texting is routine and immediate, where most people are able to read, where cell phones make calls or video talking mundane. This results in our thinking real communication must be in this same twenty-first-century form. Yet God has been speaking loudly long before cell phones, faxes, or even landlines. God speaks in what he has made, in his Word, in Jesus, and in the followers of Jesus who have his Spirit. Are we listening? Do we recognize the voice of God?

Lord, please help me to hear your voice and honor what you say. Teach me to distinguish your voice from the background noise or from the counterfeits to you. In Jesus, Amen!

❧ ❧ ❧

APRIL 23

The heavens declare his righteousness, for God himself is judge! (Ps. 50:6)

There are four very important concepts worth our consideration in this short verse. First, "The heavens declare. . . ." Paul saw this, and wrote about it to the church at Rome. He told them, "what can be known about God is plain to them, because God has shown it to them. For his invisible attributes—namely, his eternal power and divine nature—have been clearly perceived, ever since the creation of the world, in the things that have been made" (Rom. 1:19-20). We understand the heavens more than any other age. We know of countless galaxies that populate our universe. We see deeper into the heavens than ever before, able to count trillions upon trillions of more stars that Paul or the psalmist would have ever seen. We also know that the heavens work by very specific rules. We know precisely where Mars will be tomorrow or 57.34 years from now. We can compute this because the heavens run by laws of nature. These are irrevocable laws that do not change.

The heavens declare "his righteousness." This righteousness is the second concept in the verse. It is one of those "invisible attributes" of God that Paul described in Romans 1. We can think of righteousness as "consistency." It is seen in the universe, which operates around unchanging laws of nature. It is an unchanging trait of God that brings up the third concept: God.

God is consistent. God does not change. Sin is evil and leads to death. It always has, and it always will. God is good. Sin is the absence of good or the marring of good. Sin is a cancer on the purity of good.

This thought leads to the last concept: God is "judge." God rules above the heavens. He is not only the standard of good, but as the creator and sustainer of the universe, it is God who will bring sin to account. God must be the one to vanquish sin, for just as the heavens are resolute in their consistency, so is God in his righteousness. God can't morph into some other being that tolerates or venerates sin, any more than the moon can leave its earth orbit and start flying around Mars instead. That just isn't reality.

When we look at the stars at night, when we see the moon in its phases, we need to pause and think of the God of righteousness, of consistency. We need to thank him that we are judged by his righteousness, when we are forgiven of our sins by the sacrifice of Jesus. Jesus atoned for our sins, making our forgiveness justice before a righteous judge!

Lord, thank you for the death of Jesus that atones for sin. I accept the death of Jesus and trust you to deliver me from my sin and the powers of darkness, through Jesus my Lord, Amen!

❧ ❧ ❧

APRIL 24

Hear, O my people, and I will speak; O Israel, I will testify against you. I am God, your God. . . . I will not accept a bull from your house or goats from your folds. For every beast of the forest is mine, the cattle on a thousand hills. I know all the birds of the hills, and all that moves in the field is mine. "If I were hungry, I would not tell you, for the world and its fullness are mine." (Ps. 50:7, 9-12)

A lot of people wonder why God made people and what he wants from us. We tend to project human thoughts onto a non-human God. For some it makes sense that God made people because he wants our worship or attention. This is wrong, but it is not a new idea. The psalmist was addressing the same concern. Some people in his day thought God actually wanted or needed the sacrifices of animals. An ancient Mediterranean piece, *The Epic of Gilgamesh*, told the story of a Noah-esque flood. After the floodwaters abated, the gods were famished because no one had been able to sacrifice to them. This idea the gods "ate" the fragrances or residue of sacrifices was a primitive thought among Israel's neighbors, and doubtlessly some of Israel too.

The psalmist makes the obvious point: God doesn't need anything from people. He doesn't need our sacrifices. After all, he owns every animal. He doesn't need us to feed him, as if he could be "hungry." He owns everything.

God doesn't need our worship. He is not an egotistical being looking for sycophants to feed his ego or make him feel good about himself. He is not needy in the least. God isn't bored, looking for humans to entertain him or keep him company.

The beauty of the Godhead (God being the Father, Son, and Holy Spirit) includes the relationship and communication among the three eternal beings. God has "company" within the Godhead. No humans are needed.

So why did God make people? Scripture is clear: God made us to love us and give to us. He made us, giving Adam and Eve everything, including the Garden where they lived. In love, he ransomed humanity after our fall when we were in the grip of sin. We worship because it is right to do. God is worthy of our worship. We obey because it is best to do. He teaches us the ways that are right. We give to God because we know things are his and we are stewards. It reminds us that he owns everything. We trust in his provision when we give back to him from the first fruits of our labor.

Lord, we worship and adore you. We long to be in relationship with you. We long to give you our hearts, as we recognize and give back to you from the bounty you give us in Jesus, Amen!

❧ ❧ ❧

APRIL 25

But to the wicked God says: "What right have you to recite my statutes or take my covenant on your lips? For you hate discipline, and you cast my words behind you. If you see a thief, you are pleased with him, and you keep company with adulterers." (Ps. 50:16-18)

Amazingly, sometimes you can hear wicked people who are steeped in sin criticizing dismissively both God and faith. Some of God's most vocal critics are people who don't follow him. I have heard these people say, "Well, the church is full of hypocrites. After all, they violate this or that Bible command." Some people, while living in full violation of God's word, have the audacity to go to believers and indict the struggling believer for failing to measure up to God's standards. It is as if, by pointing out others' failures, one can justify one's own behavior.

But it doesn't work that way. The psalmist points out God's indignation over this. What right have the wicked and unfaithful to sit in moral judgment over the believer? People who do not have faith in God, and people who are living by their own standards rather than the lessons and instructions God has given, have no business sitting in judgment over anyone, much less one of God's followers.

These people are committing evil acts simply by holding up God's rules while not believing in them. It amounts to slander against those seeking God and doing the best they can to follow him. In the psalm the writer points out that those doing this may think God was either not present or was on their side. Not so. The psalmist issues a stern warning. "Mark this, then, you who forget God, lest I tear you apart, and there be none to deliver!" (Ps. 50:22). God wants people offering thanks to God, seeking to live right before him, not people living on their own and sitting in judgment on others (Ps. 50:23).

This psalm focuses me on living right before God, not simply in what I do, but in how I judge and treat others. I never want to be one who points to finger in accusation against others who might be transgressing the words of God, without recognizing that I have my hands full trying to live right myself. Jesus put it this way, "Why do you see the speck that is in your brother's eye, but do not notice the log that is in your own eye? Or how can you say to your brother, 'Let me take the speck out of your eye,' when there is the log in your own eye? You hypocrite, first take the log out of your own eye, and then you will see clearly to take the speck out of your brother's eye" (Matt. 7:3-5).

Lord, thank you for giving us insights into living. Thank you for the instructions you have provided. May we take them seriously as part of our faith and trust in you. In Jesus, Amen!

APRIL 26

Have mercy on me, O God, according to your steadfast love; according to your abundant mercy blot out my transgressions. Wash me thoroughly from my iniquity, and cleanse me from my sin! For I know my transgressions, and my sin is ever before me. Against you, you only, have I sinned and done what is evil in your sight. (Ps. 51:1-4)

Tradition teaches that this psalm was written by David as he was repenting from his sin of adultery with Bathsheba and the murder of her husband Uriah. This tradition is so old, that we find it inscribed on our oldest manuscripts of the psalm. The psalm certainly rings out as one written from such a crisis time of sin.

The phrase in this psalm that I always find stunning to contemplate is, *"Against you, you only, have I sinned."* How could he say that? After David has committed adultery, impregnated a woman not his wife, killed the woman's husband, who was a loyal friend, so that no one would know about David's sin, how could he say that against God alone has he sinned and done evil?

I am not ready to write this off as an error in David's judgment. I think David was right, at least in one way. While David sinned against others, his real sin was against God. Our "duty" to live righteous lives is one owed to God. God is the one we seek to serve. He is the one to whom we commit our lives. He is our king to whom we owe the utmost duty of service and loyalty. God is the righteous judge who must condemn sin to death. Sin's eternal consequences are God's responsibility. No one else can effectively put sin to death or rescue the sinner from the impending end to sin. God is the only one who is righteous and thus justified in addressing sin. When the adulteress was brought before Jesus for stoning, Jesus said, "Let him who is without sin among you be the first to throw a stone at her" (John 8:7). Hearing that, the people all left, except for Jesus. Jesus actually *could have* righteously stoned the woman for he was the only one there who was "without sin." Yet Jesus didn't. He showed compassion and forgiveness, something else only Jesus has the authority to dispense.

When we sin, we hurt others, and we hurt ourselves. There is a reason God has taught us what sin is, instructing us to avoid it. Sin is a dangerous and destructive disease. No good comes from it. It fosters pain and anguish to ourselves and to others. It is futile, not fruitful. When we sin, we come to God for forgiveness for our sins are against him. He is the one who told us how to live. He is the one we owe our lives.

Lord, we confess ourselves sinners before you. We have sinned in what we do. We have sinned in what we don't do. We are sorry, and pray you forgive us for Jesus' sake, Amen.

❧ ❧ ❧

APRIL 27

Behold, I was brought forth in iniquity, and in sin did my mother conceive me. (Ps. 51:5)

Anyone who does not believe in original sin just needs to spend more time around children. Even the best and most obedient and compliant child will teach us the same lesson. You don't need to teach a child to sin or misbehave. They come by it naturally. Our parenting efforts are always toward teaching a child to behave and live up to proper standards. One would think by the time the child becomes an adult, the whole "sin" thing would be conquered. As an adult, surely I would have enough self-control to stop sinning. After all, isn't it just a decision? After gorging over food, I am always good at thinking about how I will in the future eat in moderation, only to find myself once again gorging on the wrong day. Sin has an insidious power.

Paul wrote about the sins we commit and the forgiveness in Jesus, but he also wrote about the power of sin. We might call this Sin with a capital S as if the sin is a person or entity that holds power and control over people. This is the sin into whose power and grip we were born. Paul explained "Therefore, just as sin came into the world through one man, and death through sin, and so death spread to all men because all sinned" (Rom. 5:12).

Jesus broke the power of this sin over the believer, but until we are glorified in God's eternity, we are still living as people in the old body that was enslaved to sin. Sin still has a grip on us, even as it did Paul. Paul confessed, "I do not understand my own actions. For I do not do what I want, but I do the very thing I hate" (Rom. 7:15). Some scholars debate whether Paul was referencing his life before his conversion or after. I think that debate is academic, if not silly. Anyone who is sensitive to sin *knows* that is a true statement after accepting Christ. Before accepting Christ, most don't care too much about sin!

So as people "brought forth in iniquity" and conceived "in sin," what shall we do? How do I handle it when "I see in my members another law waging war against the law of my mind and making me captive to the law of sin that dwells in my members" (Rom. 7:23)?

Like Paul, we recognize that we are free from sin's power, even as it exercises its effects on us. "Thanks be to God through Jesus Christ our Lord! So then, I myself serve the law of God with my mind" even though our flesh at times succumbs to the power of sin (Rom. 7:25). We find the assurance of forgiveness and victory, even as we wage the battles for righteousness, although not always successfully.

Lord, our hearts desire to be true and faithful to you, yet we often seem unable to live consistent with that. Please continue to teach us to live in the victory of Christ over sin. We pray in his name, Amen!

❧ ❧ ❧

APRIL 28

Hide your face from my sins, and blot out all my iniquities. Create in me a clean heart, O God, and renew a right spirit within me. Cast me not away from your presence, and take not your Holy Spirit from me. Restore to me the joy of your salvation, and uphold me with a willing spirit. Then I will teach transgressors your ways, and sinners will return to you. (Ps. 51:9-13)

At its core, sin separates us from God. It also turns us from what we could be into something much less. God didn't place his commandments into this world as some arbitrary list of things to do or not to do. God explained to us, in these commandments, how we can live lives consistent with his nature and character. This is a part of us living with him. The unchanging God has a nature that is hard wired into us as creatures made in his image. The commandments are expressions of what how we need to live to be in fellowship with him

So as we sin, we make choices and do deeds that are at odds with God's will and purposes. These sins have a destructive force. They bring about evil consequences in the world at large as well as in the lives of the sinners. These deeds also separate us from God, alienating us from him just as certainly as sticking our hand in fire produces a burn. Fortunately, while our God is a just God who brings the destructive power of sin to a just end, he is also a loving and merciful God, seeking to bring our lives back into purity and fellowship with him.

As a sinner recognizing that, the psalmist prays to God to forgive sins. The psalmist wants God to create a clean heart, renewing a right spirit within. This is a plea for God to make us right, because we are powerless to do so on our own. It is a prayer God answered through the atoning death of Jesus. There we find the just answer to the problem of our sin. The sinless Jesus embraced our sin for punishment's sake, and we have redemption through his blood.

God can take the moral guilt away through Jesus, but many still wrestle with the personal shame associated with sin. That shame has no place in the redeemed believer. God can and will restore the joy of salvation. It is right for that, once the repentant believer stands in the grace of God. This also allows the next logical step of the forgiven: tell the lost about God's grace! Let the redeemed of the Lord share that redemption with the lost!

Lord, we confess our sin. We stand in the blood of Jesus, clothed in his righteousness alone, and we seek your sustaining touch to live with joy, in spite of our sin. Father, may we tell others of the good news of life in the Jesus through whom we pray, Amen!

❧ ❧ ❧

APRIL 29

For you will not delight in sacrifice, or I would give it; you will not be pleased with a burnt offering. The sacrifices of God are a broken spirit; a broken and contrite heart, O God, you will not despise. (Ps. 51:16-17)

Israel's God was not a primitive God who needed the blood of a bull or goat to be happy with people. The sacrifices God set out in his instructions to Moses were a foretaste of something much greater. The same foretaste was given to Abraham when he was instructed to offer Isaac, his son, to God, only to be stopped at the last minute because the real sacrifice would come later. As Abraham had prophesied to his son, "God will provide for himself the lamb for a burnt offering, my son" (Gen. 22:8).

If we think about it, how does killing an innocent lamb satisfy any real sense of justice for my sin or yours? The purpose of sacrifice is not to make an angry god happy. There is something deeper and more serious at play. We see that in the symbolism of the exodus itself. God's people were in slavery to a powerful ruler, the pharaoh of Egypt. God wanted to deliver the people from that slavery, and to do so required God's direct intervention. God did so, using a sacrificed lamb to distinguish his own people for the angel of death that would kill the firstborn in unmarked homes, shaking loose the power of pharaoh over the people.

God deeply rooted this symbolism into Hebrew history and it makes sense of one aspect of Jesus' purpose in dying. Jesus was the human/divine fulfillment of the lamb that ransomed God's people from slavery. Jesus rescued us from the slavery of sin, not of pharaoh. Unlike some lamb or goat Jesus was both fully human and fully divine. Jesus was an innocent who had no reason to die as a result of sin. Yet he did, on multiple levels. It was sin that sent Jesus to die; he didn't die of natural causes. He also bore the sins of the faithful in that death, through a voluntary assumption of our sins. He could die for others' sins because he had no sins of his own to account for.

God doesn't need humanity to offer sacrifices. God needs humanity to humbly accept the work of Jesus. That takes a broken spirit, one of confession and need. It takes a person who realizes how inadequate one's own actions are to seek the salvation from another (Jesus).

God calls us to wake up from a world numb to him, to sin, and to Jesus. He calls us to be acutely aware of sin, of righteousness, and of judgment. We are to know who Jesus is and what he has done on our behalf. Then we humbly walk before God with contrition and appreciation for the work in Jesus.

Lord, we need you. We need your forgiveness. We need your help. We are inadequate for the tasks of this life, much less the life to come. Without you, we are lost. Thank you for hearing our prayers and providing for us in Jesus, Amen!

❧ ❧ ❧

APRIL 30

Your tongue plots destruction, like a sharp razor, you worker of deceit. You love evil more than good, and lying more than speaking what is right. . . . But God will break you down forever. . . . The righteous shall see and fear, and shall laugh at him, saying, "See the man who would not make God his refuge, but trusted in the abundance of his riches and sought refuge in his own destruction!" (Ps. 52:2-3, 5-7)

I have tried many cases in which the theory of liability is that the defendant failed to warn the injured about what might happen. I had a case where the company didn't warn the rider on the mower that the mower blade kept rotating when the rider got off the mower. This caused a young boy to lose a hand. Another case involved a drug that was a "super aspirin" but caused a sixfold increase in heart attacks. The company never told anyone because it would affect their sales. You have an obligation to warn about harm associated with your products.

God has warned. No one can fault him for failing to warn. God has made it clear that sin has a price. If you fail to follow God, you will fall. If you trust in your riches instead of the Lord, you will be let down. If you think that deceiving people will enrich your life, you will find yourself broken. If you think lying works, your deceit will ensnare you. If you think slandering others will make you popular, you will find yourself the subject of slander.

God teaches the harms of sin; it's just that many don't listen. I remember growing up, my parents would teach me different things. I was taught not to hitchhike, even though it was popular in upstate New York when I lived there. While I could have done it, and many people did with no negative repercussions, I knew that my mom and dad had my best interests at heart. If they said not to do it, I thought I would be a fool not to follow their advice. I knew it was for the best.

So it is with God. God has warned everyone what will work in this life and what won't. He has told us about the negative consequences associated with unholy living. Those negatives may not arise immediately, but they will surely come. When we find ourselves stuck in the negative consequences of our sins, we need to plead to God to help us. It is time to repent and seek to do right. But we must never think that consequences are immediately erased. There are real consequences to sin and we deceive ourselves if we think otherwise.

Lord, give us wisdom to see your warnings, to understand your instructions, and to follow them, walking in your will, following the example of Jesus, in whom we pray, Amen!

❧ ❧ ❧

MAY 1

The fool says in his heart, "There is no God." They are corrupt, doing abominable iniquity; there is none who does good. God looks down from heaven on the children of man to see if there are any who understand, who seek after God. (Ps. 53:1-2)

We can classify the atheist into two categories. There are those who have made an intellectual (or often emotional) decision that there is no God. There are also those who are at best ambivalent, but God has no impact on their lifestyle. (This second group is akin to those who might accept there is a God, but give him no other regard. Jesus spoke of such saying "Lord, Lord!" but not doing what Jesus instructed [Matt. 7:21].)

We often think of atheists simply as those of the first group. Whether by virtue of education, environment, or emotion, there are those who think that this universe is all there is; that it came from itself (or had no cause); that we are fish plus time; that fish are stardust plus time; that "conscious thought" is simply a chemical and electrical reaction going on in the assorted chemicals that have aggregated into a form we call a "body"; that our values are similarly just chemical and electrical rules we give credence to, even though they determined by the physical laws of chemistry and electricity operating in our chemical soup we call a "brain"; and that "human dignity" is some label we use to stand for the concept that our sacks of chemicals ("bodies") that have accumulated over billions of years by the force of the rules of nature applied to the stuff of the cosmos are inherently more special than other collections of chemicals.

Many in this first group of atheists may try to live a moral or good life; many may choose not to. Either way, this group will not be seeking the will of God, for they don't acknowledge God exists.

The second group of atheists may actually outnumber the first group. These atheists live a life that effectively removes God from any consideration of reality. You might even ask them if they believe in God and they might say, "Yes," or "Maybe." But the reality of their life shows they don't. They live as the ultimate masters of their own lives, finding themselves as the center of things, letting their own desires dictate their choices and realities. This group also does not live seeking to do God's will and see his kingdom honored on earth as in heaven.

Both groups show a profound ignorance of the God who *is* there, along with the implications of that reality on who we are and why we are here.

Lord, may we see you, believe in you, and live for you. In Jesus' name, Amen!

❄️ ❄️ ❄️

MAY 2

They have all fallen away; together they have become corrupt; there is none who does good, not even one. (Ps. 53:3)

Words are funny things. Ultimately they are sounds that represent ideas. As such, words can have different meanings to different people or in different contexts. My idea of "Daddy" is certainly colored by who my dad was or wasn't. Other people may have a slightly different idea of the term.

So it is with the word "good." Good can mean different things at different times to different people. For many good is what we find useful, meaningful, helpful, beneficial, or something similar. Accordingly, we might say, "Helping an older lady cross the street is a good deed for the day." In that sense, lots of people do lots of good every day.

There is a concept of "good"; however, that goes beyond simply something beneficial or nice. There is a higher concept of good that is a description of God's purity or morality. Since God is a moral God, we need a word that represents the idea of his morality. The word we use is the word "good." In fact, it is the morality of God that infuses our more common usage of "good" with meaning.

It is in this sense that the word "good" occasionally finds expression in the Bible. For example, in this passage, the psalmist explains that no one does good. Not one person does even a good deed, as Paul explained it, referencing this psalm in Romans 3:11-12. We are not able to operate on God's moral plane. Our motives never have his level of purity, even if we are doing a magnificent deed. I might bring my wife flowers, which can be a good deed in a human sense, but my doing so might have a tinge of self-interest! I see that in my personal satisfaction at her smile, affirming me and my "good deed."

God has a level of purity far beyond mine or yours. God is "good" in ways that we can only marvel and dream about. We do not achieve such goodness, even though it inspires us to try. Jesus frequently directed people to this truth of God, teaching "there is only one who is good" (Matt. 19:17). Similarly, when a fellow ran up to Jesus calling him "good," Jesus replied, "Why do you call me good? No one is good except God alone" (Mark 10:18).

We are hardwired to understand good. The God who is a moral being, whose morality we call "good," made us in the God who is truly "good" and infuses the word "good" with meaning!

Lord, you are good! May we learn to model your goodness. In Jesus' name, Amen!

❧ ❧ ❧

MAY 3

O God, save me by your name, and vindicate me by your might. O God, hear my prayer; give ear to the words of my mouth. (Ps. 54:1-2)

For decades in my practice of law, people have come to me for help. They have been wronged, and hurt—physically, economically, emotionally and more. When they come, I try to help, but many times I have to turn them away. Often I find that the law or my skill set does not allow me to help them. I have sent away compelling hurts because I don't have the means to do anything else. Doctors undoubtedly have the same issue with medical situations. While some people go to doctors and get treated or cured, others go only to be informed there is nothing the doctor can do.

There is a great judge and physician who is not like our earthly lawyers and doctors. The Lord sits enthroned over the world, and he is able to help. He can heal the broken hearted. He can rescue the fallen. He can ransom the captive. He can deliver the trapped. He can strengthen the weak. He can forgive the sinner. He can save the perishing. He can vindicate the oppressed. He can comfort the grieving. He can embolden the reticent. He can lift up the downtrodden. He can love the unloved. He is Father to the fatherless. He is husband to the widow. He is guidance to the wanderer. He is wisdom to the foolish. He supplies the needy. He gives peace to the worried. He is all sufficient to the insufficient. He disciplines the unruly. He guides the lost. He gives joy to the sad. He gives patience to the impatient. He teaches kindness to the rough. He is faithful to the faithless. He is rest to the weary. He is resurrection to the dead. He is a harbor in the tempest. He is direction to the lost. He is sight to the blind. He is the answer for the questioner. He is light to those in darkness. He is freedom to the enslaved. He is clarity to the bewildered. He meets the needs of the needy. He feeds the hungry. He is the one who *always can meet any cry of our heart.*

This does not leave you and me out of the picture, however. In a sense, when Paul explained that we are the body of Christ (we are his hands, his feet, his mouth, his arms—1 Cor. 12:14ff.), we need to take seriously our ability to be God's vessel in meeting the needs of others. When we are able to help others, we need to see that we act for God. He will meet our needs, and use us to meet the needs of others. What an honor for us when he uses us to meet needs! Let's seek to do so in his name today!

Lord, please use us to meet the needs of others. May we have compassionate hearts for the world around us, even as you met our needs in Jesus, through whom we pray, Amen!

❧ ❧ ❧

MAY 4

With a freewill offering I will sacrifice to you; I will give thanks to your name, O LORD, for it is good. For he has delivered me from every trouble, and my eye has looked in triumph on my enemies. (Ps. 54:6-7)

This psalm speaks of making a "freewill offering" to the Lord. It is a thought carried over into the next phrase of giving thanks to the Lord. The psalmist knows God has brought deliverance and victory to the writer, so it is the writer's desire to sacrifice and thank the Lord.

I know this importance, at least part of it. God has brought me through many troubles in life, and he has sustained me through the attacks of many enemies. It makes me want to be thankful also. But I get a bit perplexed over sacrificing a freewill offering. First of all, we do not live in the temple era where I could take a dove or a gathering of my harvest and voluntarily sacrifice it on the altar. Furthermore, I know that God doesn't really need anything from me, so what good does it do to give him something?

Thinking through the passage, it readily occurs that one example of sacrificing is giving up a meal taking the money for the food and giving it in compassion to a work of God. This should never take the place of an obligation already made, or a tithe, for then it would not be a freewill offering. Of course, as hunger sets in, I tend to challenge my "sacrificial thinking," muttering to myself that God really doesn't need this from me.

And the psalm continues to stare me in the face. Finally, I begin to see an attitude at work here. It is calling me to show appreciation not simply through words, but through deeds. Of course, this is not because God needs or wants it for his own sake. This is for my sake. This is a part of God teaching me to have his heart and priorities. This is a chance for me to grow and become more Christ-like.

So I will look for opportunities to say, "thank you!" to God, not simply in my words but in my deeds. I can do it by showing compassion to others, by taking something that is mine and giving it to another in need, by forgoing a personal pleasure, or by some other means of personal sacrifice in the name of God. This is not to earn God's favor. It is not to become a "Super Christian." It is a simple response of gratitude.

Lord, thank you for the many blessings in my life. My family, friends, job, and more. You have rescued me, redeemed me, and loved me. I am grateful. In Jesus' name, Amen!

MAY 5

My heart is in anguish within me; the terrors of death have fallen upon me. Fear and trembling come upon me, and horror overwhelms me. And I say, "Oh, that I had wings like a dove! I would fly away and be at rest; yes, I would wander far away; I would lodge in the wilderness; I would hurry to find a shelter from the raging wind and tempest." (Ps. 55:4-8)

Growing up can be hard. It is hard when you are the child, and it is hard when you are the parent. As a child, I can remember times of hurt and heartache, at least as measured by a child. It may have been as simple as confronting a bad grade with mom and dad or failure at some project or event. As a parent, it can be hard when we see our children go through times of emotional difficulty. When their world seems to crumble around them, and we *want* to step in and rescue them. As the children pass into adulthood, it doesn't necessarily get easier. Our children experience setbacks and problems, and we want to intervene and protect them.

Sometimes the rescue is the right thing to do. But sometimes, it isn't. Sometimes our children (or us as children) need to learn the lessons that come only through experiencing the problems and living through them. I wish it weren't so, but it is. I know some children who never became responsible adults because their parents always bailed them out from difficulties.

This psalmist wanted a bailout, but God wasn't giving it! The heartache was real. The terror and fears were genuine. The desire of the psalmist was plain: escape! The psalmist wanted God to come rescue by removing the writer from the situation. Calling on the familiar image of a bird simply flying away from the face of danger, the psalmist wanted to flee. Rather than endure the storms of life, the psalmist longed for a quiet place.

Sometimes God grants such a rescue, but oftentimes he doesn't. Like a parent, sometimes God chooses to walk through the fires with us, rather than rescue us from the fires. (Remember Shadrach, Meshach, and Abednego? Read Dan. 3:20ff.) This is part of growing up.

Lord, we confess we often want you to run this world like Disneyland. We want everything to be great, fun, and joyful. Pain, difficulty, and hardship are not what we want. Yet we know that this world is not Heaven. We know it has problems. We pray for rescue from anguish, but yearn to be satisfied by your presence in the midst of sorrow and difficulty. Be with us, as you were with Jesus, in whom we pray, Amen!

MAY 6

For it is not an enemy who taunts me—then I could bear it; it is not an adversary who deals insolently with me—then I could hide from him. But it is you, a man, my equal, my companion, my familiar friend. We used to take sweet counsel together; within God's house we walked in the throng. (Ps. 55:12-14)

It's never nice when people who don't like you gossip about you, try to turn others against you, or set you up for failure. If you know someone has that propensity, and you know they don't like you, you are generally on the lookout for the maliciousness and guard against it. But it is a different story when someone who is your friend hurts you. With adversaries, you watch them. But friends you are supposed to be able to trust, and so you can turn your back to them, believing they "have your back." When a friend hurts you, we have the expression of being "stabbed in the back." It can be devastating.

So it is with the psalmist here. The writer acknowledges that if an adversary had been mean and abusive, that would not be surprising; it would be understandable. That is how enemies often behave. That is how they get the title, "enemy." But here the psalmist was attacked by a friend. It was a close intimate who wrecked damage on the writer's life. The friendship was a deep one, a religious one, one based in fellowship before the Lord. Yet the friend betrayed the trust of the psalmist. Unfaithfulness of a dear friend brings a unique pain.

What do we do when betrayed by a friend? The same thing we do when betrayed by an enemy! We take the situation before the Lord, praying for God's protection, God's deliverance, and God's mercies. That is the easy part. It is easy to seek God's help in difficulty. The hard part is the forgiveness. Jesus taught his church to pray for God's forgiveness as part of the believer's willingness to forgive others. "Forgive us our trespasses, as we forgive those who trespass against us" (Matt. 6:12). Forgiveness is hard for an enemy, and sometimes even harder with a friend's betrayal.

I can't read this without thinking of Judas betraying the Lord with a kiss. Only a friend gets close enough to use a kiss. The betrayal must have a special sting. Yet we know from the character of Jesus, that he stands ready to forgive anyone, including Judas. I have betrayed the Lord; we all have. That is my haunting thought on this psalm. Where Jesus is concerned, I know I am sometimes the betraying friend! Hence the Lord's Prayer—God forgive us, as we forgive those who sin against us.

Lord, have mercy on us. Forgive us for betraying you and being unfaithful. Help us to forgive our friends who have betrayed us. In Jesus' name, Amen!

�֎ �֎ ✖

MAY 7

But I call to God, and the Lord *will save me. Evening and morning and at noon I utter my complaint and moan, and he hears my voice. . . . Cast your burden on the* Lord, *and he will sustain you; he will never permit the righteous to be moved.* (Ps. 55:16-17, 22)

As we grow and age, everyone develops ways to handle life's problems. Some do well, others not so much. I know lawyers who yell their way through problems, hurling invectives against anyone within shouting range. I know some who drink their way through problems. Many experience sleepless nights. Some attend extensive counseling sessions with life coaches or psychologists. Anti-depressants are among the largest sellers in the pharmaceutical market. Now certainly some have a brain chemistry issue and need these drugs. Similarly, some are greatly helped by counseling, and the Scriptures speak to the value of godly counsel (Prov. 11:14). But even those resources, by themselves, are not the best way to address problems.

Problems need to be set before the Lord. It is something we need to do constantly. I am reminded of a fellow who was accused of using God as a crutch. His reply was, "Yes, but when you're crippled, you need one." The psalmist knew this, and was praying through problems at least three times a day. The Jewish day started in the evening at sundown, so for the psalmist to say *"Evening and morning and at noon I utter my complaint and moan"* is to say "all day long!"

God is not a magician who causes problems to disappear with a heavenly "Abracadabra." God "sustains" us. The idea behind this Hebrew verb includes supporting us and maintaining us. God doesn't make the problem disappear, nor does he let the problem win. God teaches us how to walk in victory. This doesn't mean avoid the medicines or counselors that might help. It means use them under the oversight of the Lord. Let the Lord be the ultimate resource. We need to pour out our hearts to him all day long. Then as we age, we find ourselves more and more reliant on the Lord for life. That is not a bad thing. To the contrary, we are all crippled in some way. We need a crutch. It's just a question of which crutch we will choose.

Lord, here are the problems I have right now. [List them!] Please sustain me. Give me wisdom. Give me strength. Provide light in the darkness. I trust in you as my rock and refuge. Embolden me to live this day confident in Jesus, Amen!

MAY 8

In God, whose word I praise, in God I trust; I shall not be afraid. What can flesh do to me? (Ps. 56:4)

In the 1950s, the United States addressed a fear of communism through a number of measures, including adopting "In God We Trust" as the national motto. This was to set America apart from the Soviet Union whose national faith was atheism. Since then, numerous groups have challenged this motto as violating the separation of church and state. The courts have upheld the motto with the Supreme Court writing in 1984 that the words, "have lost through rote repetition any significant religious content." In other words, people say "in God we trust" so much, it doesn't mean anything. That is sad.

The psalmist said thousands of years before the United States existed, "In God I trust." For the psalmist, it had meaning, and with meaning, it is a life changer. The psalmist knew that when one truly trusted in God, there was no fear of anyone or anything. God is far greater than anyone else, and, importantly, God is *trustworthy*! If God were greater, but not trustworthy, we would have a reason to fear. If God were greater but wasn't interested, we would have a reason to fear. If God were greater but was distracted, we would have a reason to fear. But that is not our God.

Our God is trustworthy. That means our God is interested and not distractible. We know this because of the life and death of Christ. God cares enough and is responsible to our needs such that at great personal cost, he would leave behind his existence in the form of God and take on human form. He would voluntarily suffer and die as a human to ensure our just forgiveness and redemption. This consummate act of love shows the ultimate care of a trustworthy God.

This enabled Paul to encourage believers with the fact, "we are more than conquerors through him who loved us. For I am sure that neither death nor life, nor angels nor rulers, nor things present nor things to come, nor powers, nor height nor depth, nor anything else in all creation, will be able to separate us from the love of God in Christ Jesus our Lord" (Rom. 8:37-39).

So we should affirm the psalmist, "In God I trust." Whatever we have before us in the immediate future, we rightly place it before the Lord with an affirmation that we want his will in those things, and are trusting in him accordingly. We will not be let down.

Lord, we trust in you. We want to walk in your will. Guide us and protect us, please. In Jesus' name, Amen!

MAY 9

Be merciful to me, O God, be merciful to me, for in you my soul takes refuge; in the shadow of your wings I will take refuge, till the storms of destruction pass by. (Ps. 57:1)

Umbrellas are amazing things. If the weather is simply spitting rain, I rarely use one, but when we have a torrential downpour, with pelting rain, an umbrella is critical. Becky keeps them in one place at our house, so one is always available.

We know the expression the "storms of life." There are storms of life where we need an umbrella. We might be able to get by without one when the problems are equivalent to spitting rain. We get a little wet, but we get where we are going and the rain passes. Sometimes, however, there are storms that rock our world. They flood our lives with hurt, worry, and misery. These are the storms where we desperately need protection. Just as you can find an umbrella in a certain place in our home, so an umbrella in life's storms can be found in one place—in God.

The umbrella metaphor works a bit better for our modern twenty-first-century America than the "shadow of your wings" analogy of the psalmist's era. While they didn't have umbrellas in ancient times, they saw the way a hen would protect her brood. There are times where we need God's merciful graciousness in protecting us from the onslaughts of this world. There are too many things beyond our control. We can't control most circumstances and we certainly can't control other people. Yet there is provision and protection in the care of God. The key for us is to avail ourselves of it.

Jesus used this same analogy concerning the people of Jerusalem. "O Jerusalem, Jerusalem. . . . How often would I have gathered your children together as a hen gathers her brood under her wings, and you were not willing!" (Matt. 23:37). Reading it, we see the importance of people's willingness to have God's protection. Like an umbrella in a closet, no matter how rough the storm is, if we don't take out the umbrella and use it, we will not benefit from its protection. So with our Lord. We need to seek him out with prayer in the storms of life. We also need to walk in his will. We will enjoy his protection as we do so.

As we grow, we learn the real challenge in life is to seek God's protection even when the storms of life are gone and the skies are blue.

Lord, please show us mercy. Be gracious to us. Protect us. May we run for the shelter of your wings, even when the skies are far from gray. In Jesus' name, Amen!

MAY 10

I cry out to God Most High, to God who fulfills his purpose for me. He will send from heaven and save me; he will put to shame him who tramples on me. God will send out this steadfast love and his faithfulness! (Ps. 57:2-3)

There are great reassurances in this psalm. It affirms a purpose in my life that is greater than anything I could devise. God has plans for me! Paul called them, "good works, which God prepared beforehand, that we should walk in them" (Eph. 2:10). When we consider God's plans for us, we should not get caught up in thinking these are only long range plans. God has plans for each day. He knows whom we will encounter today and tomorrow, and God has a purpose behind those encounters. He knows our opportunities each day, and he has a purpose for us in those opportunities.

If we realize this, and if we truly believe it, we wisely will choose to spend our days seeking to discern what are God's purposes for us. What are the good works that God has for us to do? We will search for them, pray for them, and try to walk in them.

But we might wonder, what if we can't do them? What if we are not up to the task of achieving those purposes God has for us? What if others get in the way of our accomplishing God's works? The psalmist assures us, that won't happen!

God not only prepares the works for us, but he prepares us for the works! "God is at work in us, to will and to work for his good pleasure" (Phil. 2:13). That is the significance of Paul saying that we are God's "workmanship" (Eph. 2:10). He assures us that we are who we need to be (and where we need to be) to fulfill his plans. If anyone or anything gets in the way, we need only to "cry out to God Most High," and *God* will rescue *God's* plans!

This is a part of God's steadfast love and faithfulness. God's purposes for us are not malevolent; they are good! God is kind and loving. He desires the best for us and his kingdom. We know this by looking at the gracious love demonstrated in Christ. God sought our good at great personal expense. We can be confident that having done so, his plans for us are nothing but the best.

So let's embrace the Lord. Let's embrace his plans—today, tomorrow, and over our lifetime. Let's call out for his victory in our lives, and pray against any impediment to his will. Then let's watch, with deep appreciation, his mighty hand in our lives.

Lord, we cry out to you for your purposes in our lives. Tune our hearts to hear your voice, to discern your will, and to honor your desires. Grow our faith to better walk in your service. In Jesus' name, Amen!

❧ ❧ ❧

MAY 11

My soul is in the midst of lions; I lie down amid fiery beasts—the children of man, whose teeth are spears and arrows, whose tongues are sharp swords. Be exalted, O God, above the heavens! Let your glory be over all the earth! (Ps. 57:4-5)

There is an interesting and instructive contrast in these two verses. Both make sense, but not nuzzled right next to each other. Many psalms recognize the precarious nature of God's children in a fallen world. Over and over we find in the Psalms a plea for God to protect the endangered writer. Sometimes the dangers are truly physical with one in the midst of enemies who seek to kill. Other times the dangers are more societal, with the enemies gossiping, plotting, or embarrassing the writer.

Regardless of the degree of danger, the Psalms frequently read from the perspective of one who needs God's rescue from people inflicting danger. The Psalms also often pray for God to destroy or bring to naught the persecutors.

But in this psalm, immediately following the concern of danger for the writer, we read the verse, *"Be exalted, O God, above the heavens! Let your glory be over all the earth!"* The psalmist recognizes that the real key to godly living is not Easy Street. Our goal as believers is not to have a cushy life that moves from one mountaintop experience to another, having success at all we do, friends among all we meet, health that never falters, with family and friends who never get sick and die. Our goal needs to be the glory of God spreading across the world!

It is not an accident that the first three phrases in The Lord's Prayer are not about the praying person, they are about the God to whom we pray: "Hallowed be *your* name. *Your* kingdom come. *Your* will be done." All of this is to happen "on earth, as it is in heaven." This is what we live for and should be willing to die for. Knowing this brings us to these two verses next to each other.

We might be in the middle of people who want to devour us. We might be in a place where we are threatened with being burned to a crisp, figuratively speaking. Our companions might be so vicious with their words, that we equate their teeth to sharpened swords. That would not be our choice for our lot in life today, but that is not our issue. Our issue is simple: God be glorified! If you are glorified by me being devoured, I am ready. If you are glorified by me being attacked, I am ready. If you are glorified by me being subject to malicious gossip and slander, I am ready. May God be glorified!

Lord, we seek your glory. No more, and no less. We give ourselves to that. In Jesus' name, Amen!

MAY 12

I will sing and make melody! Awake, my glory! Awake, O harp and lyre! I will awake the dawn! I will give thanks to you, O Lord, among the peoples; I will sing praises to you among the nations. For your steadfast love is great to the heavens, your faithfulness to the clouds. (Ps. 57:7-10)

There was a point in my life when I was singing in church on a Wednesday night. Normally the service had a singing time and then a teaching time, with a few prayers punctuating the service. This night was different. In the middle of a song, the preacher got up and interrupted the singing. He stopped the song and told everyone that he knew the melody and harmony were pretty. He knew everyone enjoyed singing the song. But did everyone realize that the song was being sung *to* the Lord? The words were not just about God, they were addressing God. The song was a prayer.

Praise often takes that form. There is a praising of God that is directed to the Almighty God. When we sing worship songs, we are ascribing worth *to* God. I am always a bit stunned when singing a song to God in church, only to have someone nearby whisper to me something like, "I'm excited about . . .". I want to ask that person, "Do you realize this song is a prayer? I am glad you are excited, but I am in the middle of a prayer to my God! I am singing *to* God. I have been taken into his throne room and am in the middle of proclaiming his greatness to all creation!" Of course, that is not my place, and I am likely guilty of much worse, so I smile, and get back to my prayer songs.

The psalmist understood that the faithful have a privileged calling to give thanks *to* God in music and song. We get to sing *to* God. We sing of his steadfast love and his faithfulness, and we can sing it *to* him. In many of our fine church songs, we sing about God, but we must have in our times of worship songs that are directed to God. It shouldn't be simply, "Jesus is good." We should also have, "Jesus, you are good!" There is a big difference in the two.

Think through our songs and hymns. Identify those that are directed to the Lord. Then let's bring those songs out, and sing them with gusto! Let's awaken the dawn with them. Let's sing to God before all the nations, leading others to his throne room. We cannot be in the presence of God worshipping him, and leave unchanged. His glory will transform us. Guaranteed.

Lord, we worship you as God and King. You are great in your steadfast love and faithfulness. We honor you as God Almighty who works wonders in Jesus' name, Amen!

❧ ❧ ❧

MAY 13

Do you indeed decree what is right, you gods? Do you judge the children of man uprightly? No, in your hearts you devise wrongs; your hands deal out violence on earth. (Ps. 58:1-2)

Israel spent most of its Old Testament history worshipping idols and other gods aside from YHWH God, the God of Abraham, Isaac, and Jacob. Many kept up worship of the true God, but combined it with worship of other local deities.

We don't generally have the problem of worshipping Mesopotamian gods as part of our religious life today, but that doesn't mean we don't have idols. Ours just wear other masks. An idol is anyone or anything take takes the worship and value that belong exclusively to the Lord God. We must guard against anything taking the throne of God. We should never make money, people, position, power, or anything our confidence. They must all be seen as tools and resources under the control of an Almighty God.

This psalm points out the destructiveness of having any other gods. Whether the psalm is using sarcasm in referring to powerful people as "gods," or is referring to the idols worshipped by many, is irrelevant to the point made. Only the true God will be proven true in all the things that matter. The true God judges rightly and justly. The true God devises right, not wrong. The true God seeks to bring peace, in the sense of destroying or restraining evil so that peace can be real and lasting.

We find this in our lives today. If we focus on God, on his will, and on his plans, we find a constructive building of his kingdom on earth, as it is in heaven. We find his plans unfolding in our lives in ways that bring blessings. We find true good coming into a dark world. If we focus instead on idols, the results are destructive. The idols will feed themselves, not the good of the kingdom. The love of money breeds greed and reaches for even more money. The over valuation of power creates a monster that will garner even more power on its way to corrupting the good.

This leaves me wanting to be very careful and thoughtful about my life. What am I valuing? What is worth my energy? What am I fearful of losing? Am I placing undue importance on anything when that importance that belongs to God? If so, it will not lead to good! I need to get this right.

Lord, we live in a vast world with more options for our time and energy than we can count. Please give us faithful hearts. Help us focus on you, placing you alone on the throne of our hearts. Be our one God. In Jesus' name, Amen!

MAY 14

Deliver me from my enemies, O my God; protect me from those who rise up against me; deliver me from those who work evil, and save me from bloodthirsty men. (Ps. 59:1-2)

Tradition holds that David wrote this psalm when he was running for his life. King Saul had sent his men with instructions to kill David (see, e.g., 1 Sam 19:11ff.). David fled, and cried out to God for protection and deliverance.

In my fifty-five years, I am fairly certain no one has tried to kill me physically. That said, many have sought to bring me to an end professionally, personally, and more. As life unfolds, we often find that there are those who have evil intent for us. I have found solace in David's psalms in times of intense struggles against others.

When I was out of law school, I went to work as one of fifty-five hires at a big international law firm. There were some amazing people there that are still my friends today. But there were also some who thought that of the fifty-five, maybe five would find themselves successful as partners. Among these, at least one set himself to ensure he would be one of the five, not only by working hard and doing well, but also by secretly torpedoing others. With malice, he tried to make certain that others did poorly. During this time, I was reading through the psalms monthly. In my reading program, this psalm came up on the twenty-ninth of each month. I remember well praying it, seeking God's protection.

I was not concerned for my life or death in a bodily sense. I was concerned about my life and death in a professional sense. I was concerned about my life and death in a financial sense. The prayer of David fit well with my concerns. I needed protection from God. I couldn't see where all my enemies were, and I couldn't discover the traps laid for me. But as smart as some of those folks were, none of them could outsmart the God of the universe! God is a protector like no other! This psalm later notes that God "laughs" at these who think they can scheme successfully against those God protects (Ps. 59:8).

As we consider the enemies that might be about our lives today, I rest with the assurance that the same God who protected me then, cares for me and will protect me today.

Lord, with gratitude in my heart, I thank you for being with me, every day, every week, every month, every year. You never cease to protect me from my enemies, many of whom I don't even know. Lord, I pray for you to continue to walk with me. With confidence in your care, I entrust you with my friends, my family, my job, and certainly with my enemies. In Jesus' name, Amen!

MAY 15

But I will sing of your strength; I will sing aloud of your steadfast love in the morning. For you have been to me a fortress and a refuge in the day of my distress. O my Strength, I will sing praises to you, for you, O God, are my fortress, the God who shows me steadfast love. (Ps. 59:16-17)

At different times in my life, I have had my main devotional time at night or in the morning. Obviously I have no clue when anyone might be reading this, but if it is in the morning, Great! If it is in the evening or some other time of day, still great!

The psalm speaks of singing the Lord's strength and his steadfast love in the morning. This is a marvelous time to do it. We can sing of his steadfast love in the morning, as he stood watch over us in the night. We also know that a full day arises before us with all the opportunities it will contain. If the day has splendid moments in store, we sing of God's strength and steadfast love. If the day has difficulties in store, we sing of the Lord's strength and steadfast love. It really doesn't matter what kind of day we are going to have. That is the beauty of the Lord's steadfast love. It is constant. It is reliable. That is what steadfast means. He will not let us down. His love and commitment to us is not seasonal. We can approach today in victory, knowing the victorious one supplies our strength and meets our needs.

The psalmist knows this from experience. The psalmist remembers how God has been a fortress and refuge. The memory of God taking care of deep and hard needs serves as confirmation for the love and care of the Lord. Of course, we live on this side of Calvary. We can see in the life of Christ, and certainly in his death and resurrection, the steadfast love of the Lord as well as his resurrection power and strength.

If we are reading this devotional in the evening, we read it backwards. We read it with trust in how we can sing of God's strength and steadfast love tomorrow. But we also sing it affirming the way the Lord was with us during this day. God has not forsaken us. He doesn't forget us, even as we might get so caught up in our day, that we fail to fully take into account his presence with us.

We remember that God has taken care of us with a steadfastness that moves us in responsive love. Oh, the greatness of our God, who supplies our needs, and tends to our souls!

We bless you Lord, our rock, our fortress, our provider! In Jesus' name, Amen!

❈ ❈ ❈

MAY 16

O God, you have rejected us, broken our defenses; you have been angry; oh, restore us. You have made the land to quake; you have torn it open; repair its breaches, for it totters. You have made your people see hard things; you have given us wine to drink that made us stagger. (Ps. 60:1-3)

There are times where we mess up. Seriously mess up. I can look back on my messes and see how I was foolish or rebellious, choosing my own way, rather than following the ways of God. In my practice of law, I have seen the untold things. I have taken tragic cases from people whose lives were ruined by someone who drove while intoxicated. Of course, the driver's life was ruined too. Among my family and friends, I have seen it as well. Choices made that are contrary to God's instruction inevitably lead to harsh and difficult consequences.

How one reacts to this state of affairs is interesting. Some react by blaming God! I have heard some say, "If God was a good God, he would ensure this wouldn't happen!" Those reactions seem immature and silly to me. God was and is good. He did his good and loving part by telling us what to avoid! He told us plainly how to live and how not to live. He warned us that bad things happen when bad things are done. We shouldn't blame God; he did his part. We made choices with eyes wide open.

Other react with the related idea, "If God were really forgiving, then he would forgive this and I wouldn't have these harsh consequences." Again, that is not God or the world in which we live. God *is* forgiving and will give up his glory, become human, and die as a human to justly give us forgiveness. But that never eliminates earthly consequences. Again, this should not be a surprise. God has warned us of this too. Paul was clear, "Do not be deceived: God is not mocked, for whatever one sows, that will he also reap" (Gal. 6:7).

So what do we do when we mess up? How do we face the messy consequences? First, with repentance. We confess our sins and trust in his forgiveness (1 John 1:9). Second, we lay the mess before him. Even though the mess is there, he will teach us how to live in the midst of it. While we have to face the consequences, we don't have to face them alone. He teaches, supports, and encourages. We are never forced to endure something without him. We flee to the God who saves us, even as we live through the messes we made!

Lord, I don't like messes. I hate the results of sin, and the problems that come. Help me remember this as I walk today. Let me make choices as you have instructed and taught me. Help me to walk in your will. In Jesus' name, Amen!

❄ ❄ ❄

MAY 17

Hear my cry, O God, listen to my prayer; from the end of the earth I call to you when my heart is faint. Lead me to the rock that is higher than I, for you have been my refuge, a strong tower against the enemy. (Ps. 61:1-3)

The psalms use wonderful language and imagery to speak to our souls and lead us in our walk with the Lord. What a marvelous start to this prayer. Calling on God to hear the prayer as a cry.

For me, sometimes prayer is, if not an obligation, at least something that is a discipline. Now that is a pity, and it certainly shouldn't be that way, but it is. I never think of having conversations with my sweet wife as something I just "need to do." It is a joy, a privilege, and an opportunity. If I don't have that time, I miss it. Often with God it is the same, but not always. This is an area in which I am growing as I get older. The more I walk with him, the more I talk to him in prayer, the more prayer becomes integral to all I do. I like the psalmist saying, "Hear my cry." I want my prayers to be cries from my heart, not simply obligations of my head!

The psalmist cries to God when "my heart is faint." I know those times. The heart is a finicky thing. It can soar in heights of joy, and come crashing down by circumstances that are really not that big a deal. My father was fond of saying, when someone spilled milk, for example, "If that's the worst thing that happens to you, you're going to have a great day!" He could put things into perspective. Perspective is easily lost on the heart. Emotions fluctuate for most everyone. Here the psalmist was with a "faint heart." We can read that as depressed or down! The solution was to cry out to God!

God does not simply leave us in our emotional puddle. He is one who can lead us "to the rock that is higher than I!" This is a marvelous picture! When my heart is down, I need to remember that God is the lifter of my soul! He picks me up. He takes me to a solid place, a rock, and sets me places I couldn't reach on my own. God is the healer of my heart, the moderator of my emotions, the protector of all things ME! He has been before, and he will be today. THANK YOU, LORD!

Lord, I do cry out to you. I cry out for your presence in my here and now. Please be present in my thoughts and emotions. Lead me to a rock higher than I. Lead me to places I can't reach on my own. Lead me to see and experience your love and forgiveness. In Jesus' name, Amen!

MAY 18

Let me dwell in your tent forever! Let me take refuge under the shelter of your wings. . . .
So will I ever sing praises to your name, as I perform my vows day after day. (Ps. 61:4, 8)

Growing up we moved around a lot. I was born in Dallas, but we quickly moved to Ft. Worth. Then New Orleans, Shreveport, Abilene, Memphis, Pittsburgh, Rochester, and Lubbock, Texas, all before age thirteen. The location changed a lot, but in my mind, I lived one place: home. Home was where my mom, dad, and sisters were. It didn't matter where it was geographically; it was still home.

I think of that as I join the psalmist in prayer, "Lord, let me dwell in your tent forever." Life takes me many places. Not only do I find myself living in different places, but I travel a lot as part of my job. I frequently find myself living one night in one hotel, then another night in a different one. But regardless of where I find my life, in Jesus, I find I can dwell in the tent of the Lord forever. My home is not based on the geography of the day; it is based on the presence of my Lord.

I want to be dwelling in God's presence regardless of where I am. I want to experience the rich fellowship of prayer, the exalted experience of worship. I want to sing songs to the Lord aloud with my voice or quietly in my heart. I want to find his plans and purposes and walk in them by his strength and with his guidance.

Then as storms come, I find shelter under his wings. As storms go, I still exist in his presence. This is my home. This is where I truly belong and live. It is a home I find through the resurrected Jesus. Jesus has opened the door and prepared for me a dwelling place in the midst of God. I have no right to be in his tent based on my own life. But with the forgiveness in Christ, I belong! He bought me, paying a great price, and so I can live in his presence forever.

This is some of the import of Jesus telling his disciples that going to the cross was him "preparing a place for them" in his "Father's house" where there are "many rooms" (John 14:1-3). He has prepared that place, and we are welcome. That is good, for that is where I want to be. That is my true home!

Lord, thank you for the invitation to make my home in your presence. It is where I want to live each day. I know I am there only by your mercy and grace, and I sing of that to the world that needs a home. May I share with them the way in Jesus, Amen!

MAY 19

For God alone my soul waits in silence; from him comes my salvation. He alone is my rock and my salvation, my fortress; I shall not be greatly shaken. (Ps. 62:1-2)

In the Hebrew original, the word "*af*" jumps out at you. It begins the first two verses. Verse one begins, "*Af* toward God silently waits my soul." Then in verse two we read, "*Af* he is my rock and my salvation. . . ." Verses five and six of the same psalm repeat the refrain from verses one and two, beginning also with "*af*."

What is the meaning of "*af*"? When placed at the start of a sentence like this, *af* calls attention to what follows, usually with the idea of "only" or "exclusively."

The psalmist puts the *af* at the start of these phrases to point out the importance that *only* with an eye toward God does the writer wait silently. God alone—exclusively God—provides the salvation, protection, stability, and more that the psalmist desperately needs. The psalmist is in turmoil. That point cannot be missed. There is no thought that God will remove the turmoil and make the moment one of sunshine, but the confidence is there that God will not let the psalmist be *greatly* shaken.

This psalm feeds my quiet time. I know that God rescues me from the things that shake up my life (whether greatly or minimally), and his rescue often comes through things I do, or actions I take. So how does that comport with silently waiting for the Lord? How do I mesh that with God *alone* as my rock and salvation? This is one important role of my devotional time. Often in times of meditation, quiet worship, and prayer, I better reflect on what God is doing, and what God is teaching me to do. In silent and thoughtful time with God, my vision becomes clearer. The anxiety that clouds my thinking dissolves away, even if for just a short time, and I am better able to understand what God says about my problems.

So I can be shaken, but not greatly. For God is there to bring salvation. He provides the stability that exceeds my quaking. He protects me in love. He refreshes me. He heals me. He quiets my soul. He shines light upon my path. He removes my fear. He shepherds me through life. I am not facing anything alone.

Lord, I need you to help me keep perspective on life. I let things shake me up, when those things fade away in your presence. As my shepherd, you are leading me beside quiet and restful waters. I need those daily. So in Jesus I pray, Lord, silently waiting for you. Speak into my life today please. Amen!

MAY 20

Trust in him at all times, O people; pour out your heart before him; God is a refuge for us. Those of low estate are but a breath; those of high estate are a delusion. (Ps. 62:8-9)

Trust is a funny thing. I link it to "rely." What I trust in is what I rely upon.

I find in my life I rely upon a lot of things. I rely on the money I have to provide a roof over my family, to enable me to see that our children are fed, clothed, and educated. I rely on my job to continue to replenish the money I rely on. I rely on the stability of our country to keep my job as one that is available. I rely on the politicians to ensure that our country remains stable. I rely on the military to fulfill the orders of our politicians. I rely on doctors to keep my family well, and heal us from sickness. I rely on medical schools to properly educate our doctors. This chain can go on and on.

It is good for me to meditate on this psalm. I need to take the time to reflect on the God on whom I *really* need to rely. God is *really* who sees that I have a job. The money we spend? It is God's. The job I enjoy? It came from the Lord. As we carefully consider our trusting and reliance, we are well served to remember that God is the source of all that we have. We are caretakers of what God has *entrusted* to us! God trusts us to use resources for God's purposes. Surely we are to then trust him who supplies such to us.

To live or think otherwise is to abuse God's things, and to rob him of the credit as the refuge and source of our security. We can exalt God as our rescuer and provider, or we can claim such titles for ourselves. People who live as if they are the source of their own sustenance are exalting themselves onto a throne that is not theirs.

God calls us to humble ourselves before God, letting him lift us up. We are not to live as proud people, thinking we are something on our own. Those so deceived are brought to nothing by God. Peter and James both quoted Proverbs 3:34, "God opposes the proud, but gives grace to the humble" (Jas. 4:6; 1 Pet. 5:5).

As the psalmist notes, rich and poor alike are a delusion or brief breath. We should never be sold on ourselves. Our trust needs to be in God. What we have, is his. We rely on him, and trust that he will work through this world to bring us where we need to be. This brings a humility that is honest and real. It makes us who we really need to be. I must learn to rely upon and trust our God who is reliable and trustworthy.

Lord, in humility we set ourselves before you. We rely on you to sustain and direct us. We live for you. What we have is yours. May we use it carefully in Jesus' name, Amen!

MAY 21

O God, you are my God; earnestly I seek you; my soul thirsts for you; my flesh faints for you, as in a dry and weary land where there is no water. So I have looked upon you in the sanctuary, beholding your power and glory. (Ps. 63:1-2)

I have been thirsty, really thirsty. Most people are at some time or another. We are a blessed people who generally have access to clean water, but we still experience thirst. Whether outside on a hot day, exercising to a point of exhaustion, or perhaps a combination of the two, we know what it is like to be thirsty. Who hasn't searched for a glass or bottle of water when thirsty? Few things taste or satisfy like a cool drink of water when parched. That makes thirst a marvelous metaphor for the psalmist.

Knowing the driving thirst that pushes one to seek out drink is like the psalmist's burning desire for the presence of God. The psalmist so needs the Lord, that the best illustration is that of a person hot and dry in a location with no water. The body suffers, the mind suffers, and the consuming need is to find some drink to bring life back to a wilting soul. Like the old adage, "seven days without prayer makes one weak," the psalmist knows there can be no life without experiencing fellowship with God.

This needs to be us! We should experience the deep need for the presence of God. We should know that we are not able to function without the power and glory we find in the presence of God. Of course, it would be horrible if we were to have this thirst, but have God nowhere to be found. Fortunately, we need not fear that, however.

Jesus explained, "Blessed are those who hunger and thirst for righteousness, for they shall be satisfied" (Matt. 5:6). He added that we can find the satisfaction to hunger and thirst in Jesus himself! Jesus said to them, "I am the bread of life; whoever comes to me shall not hunger, and whoever believes in me shall never thirst" (John 6:35). In beholding Jesus, we behold the "power and glory" of God that the psalmist recognized.

I want this to be me. I want to be thirsty for God. I want Jesus in my life. I want to love him, live for him, and become more like him. In John 7:37 Jesus said, "If anyone thirsts, let him come to me and drink." I am coming to Jesus!

Lord Jesus, I come to you thirsty and hungry. I need your righteousness. I need your love and compassion for the world. I need your love and compassion for me. I come to you with gratitude for the fullness you supply. Amen!

MAY 22

Because your steadfast love is better than life, my lips will praise you. So I will bless you as long as I live; in your name I will lift up my hands. (Ps. 63:3-4)

Our worship of God has a powerful profoundness when it is deeply rooted in our experiences with him. In this passage, the psalmist has praise on his lips that came from experiencing the steadfast love of the Lord.

Love is a common human experience. It is something everyone wants. We see it in various ways and depths. There, in the puppy love of young romance. There is the growing love of a committed relationship. There is the love of a friend for a friend. There is parental love that flows from parent to child, as well as love that a child has for a parent.

Love can vary in depth and commitment. The love that is most secure is one that is steadfast. This is a love that stands the test of time. It is an enduring love that works for another's good. It is not based on performance of the loved, but on a decision of the lover. The depth of this love runs deeper than life's circumstances. Steadfast love is firm and reliable. It is constant and unchanging. This is the love of God for his people. It is also the love that infuses life with significance. The psalmist says God's steadfast love is "better than life" because without such love, life is hardly worth living. But with it, life soars.

Because the psalmist had experienced the steadfast love of the Lord, the song of praise comes to the writer's lips. This is a reason to proclaim God's greatness (to "bless the Lord"). In God's name, that is, because of who he is and what he's done, the psalmist lifts hands in worship. Experiencing God's steadfast love permeates the psalmist so greatly, that singing is not enough. The psalmist is fully into praising God to the point of a physical response of worship.

We live millennia later than the writing of this psalm. More than the psalmist, we can and should sing of the steadfast love of the Lord. We live on this side of Golgotha. We know the depths of God's love like no time before, aware and experiencing the love that would cause Jesus to leave glory, become a human, subjugate himself in humility to other humans, dying a sinner's death to redeem us. We live acutely aware of our sins that are responsible for driving the nails into the Lord. We also live experiencing the great loving kindness of the Father, Son, and Holy Spirit who never give up, but constantly woo us with steadfast love. We have reason to praise God!

Lord, we praise you with all we are! There is no one like you! In Jesus' name, Amen!

❧ ❧ ❧

MAY 23

When I remember you upon my bed, and meditate on you in the watches of the night; for you have been my help, and in the shadow of your wings I will sing for joy. My soul clings to you; your right hand upholds me. (Ps. 63:6-8)

Sometimes I have trouble sleeping. It might be because of problems of the day. It might be because I am not tired. I have learned a solution for those times: meditation and prayer.

Over the years, I have learned passages of Scripture that I am able to recall without much trouble. Some of them are particularly good for insomnia-fused meditation. I will take a passage and, while lying in bed, eyes closed, prayerfully, contemplate the passage. It will move me to prayer both for understanding and for changes in my life. This passage gives us a good example.

The psalmist writes, "you have been my help, and in the shadow of your wings I will sing for joy. My soul clings to you; your right hand upholds me." I take this passage on a sleepless night and start with "you have been my help." I then prayerfully think through the many times God has come to my aid, thanking him for them. I search long and hard in my memory, breaking my life into phases. When did I see God's help while this age? Or while at this stage of life?

If still awake, I then meditate on finding myself in the shadow of his wings. Walking back through times of help, I consider how God has held me and protected me from people and events of life. With each, I sing quietly in my mind, a song of joy to the Father.

If still awake, I consider the phrase, *"My soul clings to you."* I work carefully and deliberately through the circumstances of life, purposely delivering all concerns into the Father's hands. In this way, I cling to him for his merciful protection, wisdom, and direction for the circumstances and people on my heart. I join these thoughts with thanksgiving for his strong hand that will handle all I have entrusted to him. Meditating on this passage brings to mind other Scriptures that reinforce what I am doing. I remember Paul's instructions to the Philippians not to worry in anything, but in all things, pray to God, seek him for his aid and deliverance, and be sure to thank him for the assuredness of his careful answers at the same time (Phil. 4:6).

If still awake . . . Actually, I have never made it past this and still been awake!

Lord, teach us to meditate and pray in the night, entrusting life to you. In Jesus, Amen!

❧ ❧ ❧

MAY 24

Hide me from the secret plots of the wicked, from the throng of evildoers, who whet their tongues like swords, who aim bitter words like arrows, shooting from ambush at the blameless, shooting at him suddenly and without fear. . . . But God shoots his arrow at them; they are wounded suddenly. They are brought to ruin, with their own tongues turned against them. (Ps. 64:2-4, 7-8)

Gossip is not a good thing. Not even when cloaked with, "Don't tell anybody, but . . ." or "I know you would want to pray about this . . ." Of course, there is a time to share information that will bring people to pray, and there is a certain sharing that is useful in dealing with a crisis. But we must be careful, because there is also a time where talking is not really about such solid motives, but instead is the fruit of a desire to spread something of interest. This can be destructive.

The psalmist was subject to intense words that might have been simple gossip or something even more extreme. It might be that people were spreading false rumors. Either way, words have an ability to light a forest fire that quickly rages out of control (Jas. 3:5). They can be destructive and hurtful. The psalmist equated these bitter words to arrows being shot in ambush. The talkers who were shooting the arrows were doing so without regard to consequence, *"shooting suddenly and without fear."*

The psalmist was hurt. He took his pain to the Lord in prayer, and was reassured. The actions of the wicked talkers would backfire! They shot their words as arrows, but the psalmist knew that God would shoot his own arrows at the wicked. They would be brought to ruin. Their own tongues would be turned against them. As the saying goes, "What goes around, comes around." Or, "It is a short road that doesn't have a turn in it." Or, "You reap what you sow."

I want to guard my words carefully. I want them to be "seasoned with grace" (Col. 4:6). I want control over the strong tongue. "No human being can tame the tongue. It is a restless evil, full of deadly poison. With it we bless our Lord and Father, and with it we curse people who are made in the likeness of God. From the same mouth come blessing and cursing. My brothers, these things ought not to be so" (Jas. 3:8-10).

Lord, help me know when to speak and what to say. Let my words build up, and not tear down. Let me encourage, not gossip. May I seek the good, and not spread the evil. Teach me to control the tongue and use my words for good, not evil. In Jesus' holy name, Amen!

❧ ❧ ❧

MAY 25

Praise is due to you, O God, in Zion. . . . O you who hear prayer, to you shall all flesh come. When iniquities prevail against me, you atone for our transgressions. (Ps. 65:1-3)

The Bible makes clear that sin disrupts the divine-human relationship. God is a pure moral God. He is also unchanging. It makes good sense that, as God is pure and unchanging in morality, moral impurity on behalf of humanity would disrupt the fellowship. Part of God's unchanging purity includes his justice. God is fully consistent. Sin brings on death as assuredly as rain brings on water. I know sin. I know it intimately. It has trapped and ensnared me. Sometimes I have walked straight into it, eyes wide open. I also know the separation of that sin as it poisons my relationship with the Almighty Pure One.

That same Almighty Pure One has a deep desire rooted in love to restore the relationship disturbed by sin. How shall that be done? It won't be done by me. My best efforts might produce a fairly genuine, although also fairly self-interested, apology. But how does an apology pay the just price of sin? It doesn't. Sin is a marring of the divine moral code. Sin merits death. It can't be allowed to prosper and breed.

So what is going to happen to my sin? Will I die with it or can something else rescue me? Three times in the Psalms we read of God himself atoning for our sins. God the Divine, who cannot leave sin unpunished, comes to the rescue of the sinner by atoning or satisfying justice for sin. On my own, I lose to iniquity. My sins *"prevail against me."* But in steps God. If one were to ask the psalmist, "How does God atone for your sins?" the answer would likely be, "I don't know!" Paul spoke of the "good news" (aka "gospel") about God's atonement in the death and resurrection of Christ as something that had been a mystery before (Rom. 16:25). God's atoning work was done through Jesus, and it wasn't until then, that people could understand how a just God atoned for the sins of his people.

The mystery is more than God saving the Jews through the work of Jesus. As the psalmist foretold, *"to you all flesh shall come."* The mystery of atonement included a mystery of God redeeming other nations of the world as well. Paul wrote of this in Ephesians 3:4-6: "When you read this, you can perceive my insight into the mystery of Christ, which was not made known to the sons of men in other generations as it has now been revealed to his holy apostles and prophets by the Spirit. This mystery is that the Gentiles are fellow heirs, members of the same body, and partakers of the promise in Christ Jesus through the gospel."

Lord, I stand in your atonement through Jesus with deep gratitude. In his name, Amen!

%* %* %*

MAY 26

Blessed is the one you choose and bring near, to dwell in your courts! We shall be satisfied with the goodness of your house, the holiness of your temple! (Ps. 65:4)

The Rolling Stones had a hit song with Mick Jagger singing over and over, "I can't get no satisfaction." As the song relates it, he tried, tried, and tried, but without success. He looked for satisfaction from knowledge, social status, or relationships, but reached a dead-end.

Satisfaction is an internal drive for most people. We want the peace that comes from it. We want the joy that comes from it. We want satisfaction! Many will mimic Mick's efforts of finding satisfaction from learning, from social acceptance, or from relationships. I know many who try to find it in careers or the money and influence that often accompany "successful" careers. Many try to find satisfaction in food, drink, or drugs. I even know a few folks who try to find satisfaction by education and occupying their minds with lofty matters. That is roughly akin to filling the Grand Canyon with spoonfuls of dirt. It isn't going to give full and final satisfaction.

The psalmist found satisfaction. It was found in the goodness of the Lord's house. How can this be? This was not because God has really great furniture. The satisfaction doesn't come from the food or refreshments God serves his guests. The key to the house of the Lord being satisfying is that God is found there. The presence of God is what makes the house good and the temple holy. The presence of God is what brings satisfaction.

Satisfaction comes from a relationship and fellowship with the Lord. If we do not have that fellowship, we know the emptiness that drives us to find more in life. If we have that fellowship, we know the peace that comes from God. That does not make the Christian life without drive. To the contrary, the drive is now drive with purpose. The drive is not fueled by a need to be satisfied. It is driven by a desire to find the things in life that God has directed for us. It is understood that God has worked in us and prepared us to be just the right people to do the very particular things that God has for us.

All Christians are in God's house. In fact, Paul says the church, which is the congregation of those in Jesus, has become the temple of God (1 Cor. 3:16-17). Or to put it as Jesus does, the believer dwells with God (John 17:20-21). We have access to the power of God, the wisdom of God, and the direction of God. We also have the peace of God that comes from satisfaction (Phil. 4:7). We just need to make the choice to walk in those things.

Thank you for our relationship in Jesus. We love you and seek to walk in your will. Amen!

❧ ❧ ❧

MAY 27

You visit the earth and water it; you greatly enrich it; the river of God is full of water; you provide their grain, for so you have prepared it. You water its furrows abundantly, settling its ridges, softening it with showers, and blessing its growth. You crown the year with your bounty; your wagon tracks overflow with abundance. The pastures of the wilderness overflow, the hills gird themselves with joy, the meadows clothe themselves with flocks, the valleys deck themselves with grain, they shout and sing together for joy. (Ps. 65:9-13)

We lose some of the punch of this passage in twenty-first-century America. It speaks to the visitation on earth of God the Ruler. If we were living in the time of the psalm, a visit of the king or ruler was not always the best thing! Kings typically traveled with their army, or at least a large retinue. They rarely came with their own supplies. They ate the fruit of the land, and required provisions from those along the way. This was not a time of recycling where the kings and their armies cleaned up after themselves either. There are references to the ancient kings and their courtiers lingering and doing as much devastation as swarms of locust. Their greed left a permanent mark on the resources of the landowner.

Not so with God, the King of kings! God visits and the land prospers. God doesn't rob the land and strip it of its resources. He enriches it. He brings water and causes the grain to grow. The psalmist draws a picture: while you could find the trail of an earthly king by seeing the destruction of the tracks where kings could make their own roads, cutting across fields and crops, God's passage was discerned by the opposite. Just look for the blessings of abundance that flow from God's tracks. You know God has been there because you see his residue that enriches the people and the land. His tracks don't destroy fields; they cause them to overflow with blessings.

No wonder, where God goes forth in peace among his people, there is joy. The hills are happy. The crops are abundant. The livestock are well supplied. There are songs of joy.

Reading this, who wouldn't want a visit of such a king? My mind immediately flashes to Revelation 3:20 where the King of kings declares, "Behold, I stand at the door and knock. If anyone hears my voice and opens the door, I will come in to him and eat with him, and he with me."

Lord, I open the door of my heart to you today. Please come in! I want to be a good host, and am glad to give you all that I have. Thank you for teaching me how to give. It is a joy to fellowship with the God who gives! In Jesus' giving and holy name, Amen!

❧ ❧ ❧

MAY 28

Shout for joy to God, all the earth; sing the glory of his name; give to him glorious praise! Say to God, "How awesome are your deeds! So great is your power that your enemies come cringing to you. All the earth worships you and sings praises to you; they sing praises to your name." (Ps. 66:1-4)

Sometimes it's time to shout for joy to the Lord! There are days where his people need to proclaim his greatness loudly, thanking him for his deeds. Here it is commanded!

Our worship for God is not a command without merit, it is the logical response of people who see and know God. Think of the glory due him. Think of who he is and what he has done. I get real personal on a psalm like this. I am thankful to the Lord for the great things he has done with my family. While many in the world thank God for rescuing them from difficulties in their families, I am thankful for God giving me a magnificent family of blessing: my parents, my siblings, my wife and children—all great blessings from God over a lifetime. Similarly, I live in a marvelous land, where I enjoy the freedom to worship, to parent, to work, and more, on a level not realized by most people today or in history. I live in a secure land where many have sacrificed to ensure that such freedom and safety will remain. Our family has an abundance of food. We have opportunities for a great education. My job is a job where I get to use my talents to help others. I have time to read and study in the word, and opportunities to share that with others. I know God, and have a meaningful relationship with him. He has blessed my life and given me purpose. I have seen his victory over those enemies that would thwart his will.

As I write this, I am mindful of impressive believers whose blessings have taken a different form. For those whose family of origin has been damaging, I have seen them blessed by the rescuing and healing God. For those who haven't had sufficient money for the opportunities of education, food and life's provisions, etc., I have seen them praise God for his abundance in their want.

God doesn't work the same in all our lives, but all of us have reason to be thankful. There is much to praise God for, and there is a time where we should stop and shout our praises to him.

Lord, I do loudly proclaim to the world that you are an AMAZING God. You love and nurture us. You provide for us, call us, empower us, and put us to work for your kingdom. You are a GREAT God and we LOVE YOU! In Jesus, your greatest provision, Amen!

MAY 29

Come and see what God has done: he is awesome in his deeds toward the children of man. He turned the sea into dry land; they passed through the river on foot. There did we rejoice in him, who rules by his might forever, whose eyes keep watch on the nations—let not the rebellious exalt themselves. (Ps. 66:5-7)

This is written with an imperative. That means that this is a command or instruction! We are not simply invited to come and see what God has done, we are instructed to do so. This gets an explanation mark—Come and see what God has done!

This includes a call to read and study the word. In the pages of the Bible, we glimpse the hand of God working through thousands of years of history. Inspired by the Holy Spirit, we read of God acting through the nations (Exod. 34:24). He brings world powers onto the stage, and he readily dismisses them when their time is finished (Job 12:23; Rom. 13:1). He also works in the life of the individual, tending to the loss of a widow (Luke 7:11-17), bringing offspring to the barren (Gen. 25:21), ministering to the hurting (Matt. 11:5), healing the sick (Matt. 12:22), hearing prayers (Gen. 20:17), supplying needs (Matt. 6:8), teaching wisdom (Matt. 5:2ff.), and more.

God has wrought his greatest act in the incarnation, death, and resurrection of Jesus. This is a magnificent direct intervention into the time of humanity on earth, and also a direct intervention into our eternal destiny. Through Christ, we are justly brought into a direct relationship with the Almighty.

When we come and see what God has done, we get a glimpse of what he can do through us. We also get a confidence for what he will do in the future. *Today* the God who wrought wonders in the past, can do wonders through me. He can use me to minister to others, to bring his blessings to a world in need, and to express his love to people unloved. I can be confident that as I do so, God will also be working for me through the lives of others. This is the God we love and worship.

So COME AND SEE what God has done! Not an option, but a command! Doing so will change us.

Lord, you are good, and you have done magnificently. I fear often we fail to glorify you for your great deeds, writing them off to something lesser. Forgive us when we do. May we rightly glorify you for all good things. In Jesus' name, Amen!

❧ ❧ ❧

MAY 30

I will come into your house with burnt offerings; I will perform my vows to you, that which my lips uttered and my mouth promised when I was in trouble. (Ps. 66:13-14)

I know lots of people who have said to God, "Get me out of this trouble and I promise I will . . . ." Trying to cut a deal with God is not a new thing! Is that something the psalmist referenced in this passage: "*I will perform my vows , , , my mouth promised when I was in trouble*"?

Confession: I have never been a big fan of this type of deal-making. Deal-making seems to imply that there is a good I will do, but only if God does me a favor first. If God doesn't, then I won't do the good. It strikes me as spiritually immature, and I want to be more mature than this. I want to do right because it's right. Spiritual infancy is nothing to be proud of. Spiritual maturity should be our goal.

I think this passage is not the kind of deal we typically hear about. This passage grows out of the broader context of this psalm. This psalm speaks of God refining the writer like one refines silver. Silver is refined by fire, which is a metaphor in the psalm for times of difficulty that God uses to bring growth and maturity to his children. Of course, we might think this unduly harsh. It might not comport with our sense of kindness. Maybe we think God should gently mold us into what we should be with gentle words of encouragement and positive reinforcement. I actually believe God does that. But it is not always that simple, and we are not always that moldable!

As parents, Becky's and my philosophy on discipline was to use the least harsh discipline available that would do the job. If a stern look got the point across, a stern look was given. If it took a firm voice, then a firm voice. If it took time-out, then a child was placed in time-out. As our children got older, we grounded where necessary or removed privileges (television, cell phones, the car, etc.).

I hope we got those parenting ideas not only from our families, but also from a studious contemplation of the Lord's working with his children. God has disciplined me. I have needed it. It has been the way he has captured my otherwise preoccupied attention. It is the way he has forced my focus back where it belonged. This is not because God is a tyrant. It stems from the opposite. God loves us enough to bring us to spiritual maturity, even when our bent might be spiritual laziness.

It is from that refining that the psalmist speaks. God captures attention through discipline. The writer realized that, promising God to be more serious about living right, about growing up spiritually. That is a good thing. Those are promises to keep!

Lord, I want to grow before you, and keep my promises in Jesus' name, Amen!

❧ ❧ ❧

May God be gracious to us and bless us and make his face shine upon us, that your way may be known in all the earth, your saving power among all nations. Let the peoples praise you, O God; let all the peoples praise you! (Ps. 67:1-3)

This passage contains a very ancient Hebrew blessing. In Numbers 6, Moses instructed Aaron to recite this blessing over the people of Israel: "The LORD bless you and keep you; the LORD make his face to shine upon you and be gracious to you; the LORD lift up his countenance upon you and give you peace." This blessing is no human creation. God taught the blessing to Moses for Aaron and his sons to use. God promised that as the blessing was given, God would fulfill the blessing on the people.

We might ask, "Why this indirect process? If God wants to bless his people, why doesn't he just do it? Why should there have to be a request first? Isn't this inefficient?" It seems to me that several things are in play. First, when we ask God for the blessings, then as they come, we are aware he gave them, and we more readily recognize him and thank him. That is not important because God needs the ego stroking of our gratitude. It is important because it keeps us living humbly before our God. It helps us keep him on the throne where only he belongs.

There is a second reason I believe we are to call down God's blessings. God has set up this world as a place for us to work to his glory. Adam and Eve were instructed to tend to the Garden of Eden (Gen. 2:15). Once they were expelled from the Garden, that charge was not changed. They were still to work the ground, but this time, instead of abundant food, they were going to have to work among the thorns and the thistles for their bread (Gen. 3:17-19). We struggle in this world to make it a better place, yet this is our responsibility. It is hard, and we don't succeed well if we do it alone. So we ask God for his help, as part of our work in this world. We need his blessings and strength. He stands ready to provide it, but it is our responsibility to ask. That is how we get done what we are to get done, and make this world a better place.

Let's call on God to bless us. Let's ask him to be gracious and merciful. Let's ask him to shine his face, to bless us, as we work to reflect his love to our fallen world. In this way, not only will we grow in our praise, but the world will as well.

Lord, please be gracious and shine on us. Grant us your peace in Jesus' name, Amen!

❧ ❧ ❧

JUNE 1

Let the nations be glad and sing for joy, for you judge the peoples with equity and guide the nations upon earth. Let the peoples praise you, O God; let all the peoples praise you! (Ps. 67:4-5)

At first blush, this seems to be a psalm everyone would cheer and applaud. But if one carefully considers it, the cheering might lessen! The part that might give people heartburn is that God judges the people with "equity."

Many people don't really think God should judge in equity. It is as if they don't want God to judge at all. If someone has sinned, they want God to overlook it, or at least not judge too harshly. Many people who are not believers, and perhaps some who are believers, give short shrift to the idea of God judging the nations in the Old Testament. On a certain level, it seems God instructed the Israelites to destroy entire nations, including women and children. How could that be equitable or fair?

It all depends upon the standard for "fair." If it's fair that sin brings death, then if in eternity that death occurs less than a hair's breadth before it would otherwise, it seems fair to me. The question then becomes why does God execute just punishment on some but not others. Again, we have to understand that God might have reasons in his eternal plan for others to have a stay of execution for what again is less than a millisecond when viewed from eternity.

Equity does have God destroying all people, BUT FOR the Cross of Christ! In Jesus, God's equity is fully met, and there is redemption for those for whom equity demands death. This is what we might call and "equitable mercy." God's justice—his equity—finds expression in the atoning death of Christ, and we find mercy for all who live and die under that atonement.

Now in Christ, we have a reason for the nations to be glad and sing for joy! Now we have a reason for the people on earth to praise God! We have equity and mercy in Jesus. We have redemption. We have no need to fear an awesome God who justly condemns, yet mercifully lets live. We see the love of God hand in hand with his justice. There is no favoritism here; all are called to Jesus. All are equally able to live the life of the redeemed. Let the redeemed of the Lord say so, and let the people praise the saving, equitable God!

Lord, you are amazing! You walk in consistency. You walk in mercy. You walk in justice. You walk in love. Lord, we praise you. We are a people who get to walk redeemed by the sacrifice of Jesus. May we shout to the world what you have done. Use us to reach the nations in Jesus' name, Amen!

JUNE 2

God shall arise, his enemies shall be scattered; and those who hate him shall flee before him! As smoke is driven away, so you shall drive them away; has wax melts before fire, so the wicked shall perish before God! (Ps. 68:1-2)

I don't understand people who set themselves against the Lord. I am a fairly competitive person, and I don't generally like to get into battles I can't figure out how to win. No one is going to beat the Lord. It's just not going to happen.

No doubt some people don't yet believe there's a God. (Eventually everyone will see there is a God. Unfortunately, for many, it will be after their death.) These people war against God, in part, because they don't think he is there. It is as if their mission is to disprove him by declaring war, and showing God's failure to defend himself. On one occasion I had a professor who challenged the "absurdity" of my faith by this approach. He asked me to agree he could hit me on the head with a hammer and if there was a God, I could ask him to stop it. I have found most of these types of people are warring against God to help themselves overcome a devastation in their life where they perceive God failed to rescue them. Hence, they want to show he isn't there, perhaps even as a statement to him about his refusal to show up when needed.

Some people, however, are believers and still set themselves against God. These people are harder for me to understand. These are folks who know God, know his instructions, know what he expects, and live with a callous disregard, if not outright rebellion to such. Why would anyone in their right mind be an enemy of God? Do they think God is unaware of their choice? Do they think he doesn't care? Do they think he is too pre-occupied with weightier matters? Are they trying to call him out? Is this their way of taunting him? Is it a childish temper tantrum, the spiritual equivalent of a toddler stomping his or her feet at a parent?

I can't play psychologist for others, but I can look at my own life. I know there is no future in wickedness and sin. I know that the Lord will see that sin meets its end. I know the Lord pays attention. He cares what I do. He is ready to bless holiness, even as he is ready to drive away sin. The only real question for me is a personal one. Why would **I** set **myself** against God? It is **not** a winning proposition!

Lord, please forgive my rebellion. Give me the smarts to walk holy and faithfully before you. Teach me the walk of the righteous. Then use me to work for your kingdom in this world. Teaching others about the treasures in store for those aligned with you, even as your enemies are scattered. In Jesus' name, Amen!

❄ ❄ ❄

JUNE 3

Sing to God, sing praises to his name; lift up a song to him who rides through the deserts; his name is the LORD; exult before him! (Ps. 68:4)

This passage calls on us to praise God with songs. We are to lift up songs based on who God is and what God has done. We are to exult before him in song. How many songs do you know that lift up God for who he is and what he's done? Here are some of my favorites:

- "Oh Lord, you're beautiful! Your face is all I seek. For when your eyes are on this child, your grace abounds in me. . . . When I'm doing well, help me to never seek a crown, for my reward is giving glory to you." (Keith Green)
- "At the cross, at the cross, I surrender my life. I'm in awe of you. I'm in awe of you. Where your love ran red and my sin washed white, I owe all to you; I owe all to you, Jesus." (Matt Redman and others)
- "Thank you for the cross, Lord. Thank you for the price you paid, bearing all my sin and shame, in love you came, and gave amazing grace. I thank you for this life Lord. Thank you for the nail pierced hands. Wash me in your crimson flood. . . . Worthy is the Lamb seated on the throne. I crown him with many crowns. You reign victorious, high and lifted up." (Hillsong Live)
- "My heart has storm clouds raging deep within. The prince of Peace came bursting through the wind. The violent sky held its breath. And in your light I found rest. Tearing through the night, riding on the storm, staring down the fire, my eyes found yours. Shining like the sun striding through my fear. The Prince of Peace met me there. You heard my prayer." (Hillsong United)
- "Healer of my soul, keep me at even'; keep me at morning; keep me at noon. Healer of my soul." (John Michael Talbot)
- "O sacred head now wounded, with grief and shame weighed down. Now scornfully surrounded with thorns thy only crown. How art thou pale with anguish? With sore abuse and scorn? How does that visage languish which once was bright as morn? What language shall I borrow to thank you dearest friend? For this thy dying sorrow, thy pity without end? Oh make me thine forever. And should I fainting be, Lord let me never, never outlive my love for thee." (Traditional hymn)

Do you have these songs? If not, download them! If yes, sing to God! Do you have others? SING TO GOD! It meshes our hearts and emotions with our thoughts bringing all to God's glory. As we sing to him, he changes us to his glory!

Lord, thank you for song. The way it expresses our hearts and minds. We sing praise to you in Jesus' name, Amen!

❊ ❊ ❊

JUNE 4

Father of the fatherless and protector of widows is God in his holy habitation. God settles the solitary in a home; he leads out the prisoners to prosperity, but the rebellious dwell in a parched land. (Ps. 68:5-6)

A core concept we understand in the Trinity is that God is a God of relationships. Inherent in God is a relationship among Father, Son, and Holy Spirit. Beyond that we see God making people in his image and walking in relationship with them (Gen. 2-3). God cares enough about his relationship with people that he became a human, lived from infancy into adulthood, worked among us, walked among us, befriended us, and died for us. These are the actions of relationships.

Another core concept of God revealed to us in Scripture is his desire and readiness to help those in need. Jesus was constantly helping those in need whether they were hungry (Matt. 15:32-39), sick (Matt. 15:29-31), needing advice (Luke 10:38-42), confused (John 14:8-11), or even sad (John 11:17-27).

What happens when you combine God being a God of relationships and a God who desires to help those in need? You get understandings like those of the psalmist in this passage. To the fatherless, God becomes a Father. To the widow God becomes protector. God is a God of relationships, and he takes those relationships seriously. God is a God who meets needs, and he takes those needs seriously. That brings me to me.

I remember when I moved to a brand new location as a twelve-year-old boy. I knew no one. I had no friends. It was brought to my attention at church that Jesus wanted to be my friend. That sounded too good to be true. I sought out that friendship, and it was there for the asking. God really did want to come into the life of a young man and be present in a very real sense. He came and has never left. He has faithfully been my friend through good times and bad. He was there at the death of my father. He was there at the birth of my children. He has never forsaken me, but has met my needs and helped me outgrow my spiritual childishness. (He continues to help me do that!)

This is our God. A God of relationships who longs to be intimate with us in a daily fashion. He wants to interact with our world and bring us to the fullness we can have in this life. "Greater love has no one than this, that someone lay down his life for his friends" (John 15:13). Those are the words of my best friend, Jesus. After saying those words, he gave his life for me. That is my God.

Lord, thank you for being my friend. Thank you for your love and constancy. Help me show my love to you too! In Jesus' name, Amen!

❧ ❧ ❧

JUNE 5

You ascended on high, leading a host of captives in your train and receiving gifts among men, even among the rebellious, that the LORD God may dwell there. (Ps. 68:18)

This verse gives a picture of God as the victorious king! God has come down on earth and conquered. He returns on high, leading a host of people who are now subject to his kingship. Those people, even ones who were rebellious, give gifts to the Lord their king. They come into his kingdom and serve the Lord God in his dwelling.

That is our God. He is a conquering God who has won over our hearts and souls. We gladly follow him in victory and dwell in service to him as our Lord and king. But like so many things in Scripture and life, there are two sides to this passage and to God's victory. The other side is given in a delicious turn of this passage by Paul in the letter to the Ephesian churches. In a section where Paul is urging the believers to walk in a manner worthy of their calling, he says, "Therefore it says, 'When he ascended on high, he led a host of captives,' and he gave gifts to people" (Eph. 4:8, my trans.). As I translate the passage, Paul's quotation from the psalm stops at "captives." The ending phrase "and he gave gifts to people" is Paul's add and turn on Psalm 68:18. Instead of our giving gifts to God, as the psalm states, Paul shows the other side of the equation. God gave gifts to us, his "captives!"

This is our God. After winning our souls, after receiving our captive lives, God gave us gifts that *we then use* for him as we give him gifts! Look at the gifts Paul describes: "He gave the apostles, the prophets, the evangelists, the shepherds and teachers, to equip the saints for the work of ministry, for building up the body of Christ, until we all attain to the unity of the faith and of the knowledge of the Son of God, to mature manhood, to the measure of the stature of the fullness of Christ, so that we may no longer be children" (Eph. 4:11-14).

What a God. What a king! He gives gifts to his people. He builds his people. He moves to make his people grow. He is no mortal king who uses people toward his own end. He brings things together for the good of his people.

I know now what to do for my King! I am going to live my life for the good of his kingdom, for the good of others. I will live to bring others into his kingdom. I will live to serve those by helping them become more like Christ. My God has given me gifts, and he wants to use me to give gifts to others. He wants the same for you!

My Lord and my King. With joy in my heart I live to serve you by serving others. Bring people into my life with whom I can share your gospel! In Jesus' name, Amen!

JUNE 6

Blessed be the Lord, who daily bears us up; God is our salvation. (Ps. 68:19)

We all know crisis. Those times when we are stunned, when we are unsure about what might happen, when we don't know what to do. Those are times when God becomes a rock and provides much needed stability, wisdom, direction, and salvation.

Then there are other times. I readily confess some of what disturbs me most are the small things. These are things that really make no difference in the grand scheme of life, but they happen often, and seem to disturb me tremendously. It might be as small as an inability to handle a work matter successfully, or the turmoil associated with a problem that needs resolution but can't be readily resolved. It can often be associated with the fear of the unknown. If I am uncertain about what may or may not happen, I fret needlessly with an unsettled feeling in my gut. These are the problems that still need God as my rock. I need the confidence from knowing God is there, and is watching out for me. I need to know that when I set these even minor concerns before him, he is there, and he caring. He will bear me up in such circumstances and see that I come out the other side a better, more Christ-like person, and that his kingdom will be advanced.

Of course, the times where everything is going well can be the most challenging from a perspective of living under God's protection. When I was a college student, Amy Grant sang a song about the tough times, "Lord, I'm really glad you're here. I hope you feel the same when you see all my fears and how I fail. I fall sometimes. It's hard to walk in shifting sand." She cries out, "Lord, help me lift my hand so you can lift me up." That prayer struck me then, and still does today. There are days when I can't even lift my hand so God can lift me up. Days when he needs to help me lift my hand so he can lift me up. But that isn't the main line delivered to me in that song. The song has tucked away a subtle line that is set apart from the trying time that inspired the song. This line prays for God to teach me to stay in his loving arms, seeking his help, "even when my skies are far from gray."

That is my challenge, but it is the reality of life and his love. I need God as my salvation, God to bear me up, every day—awful days, challenging days, and great days! I need God daily!

Lord, thank you for being there. Please help me to seek you every day. Be there in my greatest struggles, but let me lean on you also when life seems grand. I want to share the joys of life in your arms as well as life's difficulties. Thank you for such constant love and caring. In Jesus' name, Amen!

❊ ❊ ❊

JUNE 7

Our God is a God of salvation, and to GOD, *the Lord, belong deliverances from death.* (Ps. 68:20)

On February 1, 2004, I was teaching my class at church, but my earthly father's health was a constant thought in my mind. He had suffered a stroke about a month earlier and had been hospitalized since. He was unable to speak or communicate significantly, and we were uncertain about the stroke's outcome. While I was teaching, someone came into the back of class and indicated that I needed to go the hospital. I cut class short and raced there. My dad died about fifteen minutes after I arrived.

I had been praying for God to restore my father's health. I was not ready for him to die, nor was the rest of the family. In spite of our many prayers, dad died. I realized then, as I do today, that my prayers were not unanswered. The Lord delivered my father from death. He restored my father's health in ways it could not be restored in this life. This is the salvation of the Lord.

Our God is a God of salvation. He is a God who guides us through the door of death into the eternity of the redeemed. It is a place described in a vision revealed to John and recorded in Scripture for our benefit. "Behold, the dwelling place of God is with man. He will dwell with them, and they will be his people, and God himself will be with them as their God. He will wipe away every tear from their eyes, and death shall be no more, neither shall there be mourning, nor crying, nor pain anymore, for the former things have passed away" (Rev. 21:3-4).

God is not a stingy God, straining out as many as possible to keep heaven as small as possible. As a God of salvation, he works toward and desires for all to come into his presence through Christ and dwell with him. God is in the saving business. And he wants his business booming! (2 Pet. 3:9).

I am in God's family, just as my earthly father is. I will one day join my father on the other side of glory. In the Old Testament, one of the expressions of death was, "and he was gathered to [or 'slept with'] his fathers" (1 Kgs. 11:21, 43; 14:20, etc.). I like that expression. I am confident that upon my death, I will be gathered to my father. I hope my children take the same solace upon my death—that they will know that I am not removed from their lives forever, but as our God is a God of salvation, a God who brings deliverance from death, so they can one day be joined to me on the other side of glory as well.

Lord, thank you for salvation in Jesus and eternity together. We long for the rejoining of us with loved ones who have gone before. In Jesus, with confidence, we say, Amen!

JUNE 8

Your procession is seen, O God, the procession of my God, my King, into the sanctuary—the singers in front, the musicians last, between them virgins playing tambourines: "Bless God in the great congregation, the LORD." (Ps. 68:24-26)

Where are you in God's procession? As a victorious king, God is pictured in the psalm as the subject of a majestic parade! There are singers, musicians, young women, and a host gathered together in a great congregation. They are blessing the Lord God, singing and proclaiming his greatness.

I want in the parade. I know about the greatness of God. I have experienced it firsthand. He took a naïve, young boy who had little idea of what greatness could lie ahead and heard the boy's voice cry out for God. God not only heard my cry, but he acted on it. In big ways. God inspired me to holiness, inspired me to grow. He reached out and protected me, even as he gave me challenges that taught me to rely first on him, before any other, including myself. He steered me through sin and sin's snares, to understand his grace, even as he impressed upon me his holiness and the importance of how I live. He revealed himself in greater measures, inspiring me to worship him. He taught me that worship was not a show. It was not just some emotional outpouring. He led me to worship as a deliberate effort merging my mind and heart, thoughts and feelings, intellect and emotion, into a proclamation of his worth, at least as much as my feeble efforts could muster. God brought me into adulthood, knowing that I needed him in my work. He guided me into a career that allows me to use talents he gave me. He blessed me as a parent, entrusting me with five children to love and protect, modeling as best as I was able, the love I knew from my heavenly Father. He gave me the lessons of loving my wife as Christ loved the church, leading in sacrificing to ensure that she could be all that she chose to be before God. He gave me the hope of eternity, comforting me in the loss of loved ones, as I await the glory after this life.

In the midst of all of this was the incarnation, life, death, resurrection, and promised return of Jesus Christ. These historical realities and future assurances formed the basis for all the actions of God in my life, described in the above paragraph.

So I want in on the parade! I want to sing of the goodness of the Lord. I want people to hear my voice and join the parade. I want to play the instruments of life, plucking the strings that reverberate the deeds of the Lord. Come join me in this parade!

Lord, we celebrate your victories in Jesus! We sing and bless you in his name, Amen!

❧ ❧ ❧

JUNE 9

Summon your power, O God, the power, O God, by which you have worked for us. . . .
Rebuke the beasts that dwell among the reeds, the herd of bulls with the calves of the
peoples. Trample underfoot those who lust after tribute; scatter the peoples who delight in
war. (Ps. 68:28, 30)

Some days more than others, I need to cry out, "Summon your power,
O God!" Often I seem to get by on, if not remote control, at least the general
power of God. But occasionally, something rears its head seeming to require
some extraordinary power of God.

Each morning, I like to pray the Lord's Prayer. It is a marvelous start
to the day to praise God in three stanzas (declaring his name holy, praying
for his kingdom and will) followed by three stanzas of prayer for God's work
in my life (for daily bread, for forgiveness, and deliverance from temptation).
That prayer is a marvelous gift from the ministry and teaching of Christ.
Beyond that prayer, though are the moments and events in life that shake
the foundations.

The foundation-shaking events happen when there is a medical issue
of life and death. These events happen when job security is lost. When a
loved one seems to have jumped of the deep end. When violence or drugs
or some other demon seems to intervene and take control of a person or
situation. These types of events are never simple, and they never seem to
get fixed in a moment. Instead, they are long-term problems that need long-
term assistance. For me, these are "Summon your power, O God" times.

How great is God's power? Is it sufficient for my big problems? Consider what Paul had to say about the power of God. It is the power through
the cross of Christ to forgive sins and bring harmony between people and
God (1 Cor. 1:18, 24); the power that resurrected Jesus from the dead and
will do the same for us (1 Cor. 6:14); the power that keeps us from being
crushed amidst affliction. When we are perplexed, it keeps us from despair.
When we are persecuted, it builds us up (2 Cor. 4:7-9) and enables us to
minister to others (2 Cor. 6:7). The power of God shows itself perfect when
we are weak (2 Cor. 12:9).

The power of God is "immeasurably great toward us who believe"
(Eph. 1:19). There are days when I know I need that. Of course, every day
is a day I need that, whether I realize it or not.

Lord God Almighty, thank you for the mighty work of your power in the life, death,
and resurrection of Jesus. Thank you for making that work in me. Thank you for constantly
bringing that same power into my challenges in life. I need you. In Jesus' name, Amen!

❧❧ ❧❧ ❧❧

JUNE 10

Save me, O God! For the waters have come up to my neck. I sink in deep mire, where there is no foothold; I have come into deep waters, and the flood sweeps over me. I am weary with my crying out; my throat is parched. My eyes grow dim with waiting for my God. (Ps. 69:1-3)

This passage speaks to me about timing. God's timing is not mine, and that can be very frustrating.

I know God hears my prayers. I know God knows when I am hurting or in trouble. I know God is a God who cares. I know he is my rescue, my rock, my fortress, my deliverer. I know he won't let anything separate me from his love. I know he has numbered the hairs on my head. I know he knows each of my days before they have come to be. All of that is revealed to me in his word and has been confirmed to me in my life. But this psalm is also very real and has also been confirmed to me.

God has different timing than I do. On some things it doesn't matter. I just need to learn to be patient. But what about when things are crashing around me? What about when things are terrible and are making a shipwreck of life? Why does his timing need to be so different then? Consider the psalmist.

The psalmist writes at a time where the waters have come up to the neck. God's timing didn't rescue when the waters were ankle deep or up around the knees. He wasn't saving once the waters reached the waist or even chest. God is still holding back his deliverance when the waters have reached neck high! The psalmist is sinking! There is no foothold. There is no way the psalmist can get out of the water alone. The water just gets deeper, and the flood is coming. For a long time, the psalmist has cried out to God. The psalmist's voice is gone from crying. The writer's eyes are dim, whether from tears or loss of sleep. Where is God? Why must his timing be so different?

The psalmist knows the answer, even in the midst of the cry. It is explained in verse 13, "At an acceptable time, O God, in the abundance of your steadfast love answer me in your saving faithfulness." God's timing isn't ours. But his is right. Ours isn't. He is God. We aren't. He does things his way for his eternal plans. We need to be okay with that and wait on the Lord.

Lord, you don't do things as I would. You don't always do things as I would like. It is hard sometimes for me to say it, but I am glad. I rest in you and trust in your timing. In Jesus' name, Amen!

❧ ❧ ❧

JUNE 11

Answer me, O LORD, for your steadfast love is good; according to your abundant mercy, turn to me. Hide not your face from your servant; for I am in distress; make haste to answer me. Draw near to my soul, redeem me; ransom me because of my enemies! (Ps. 69:16-18)

This is one of my favorite pleas to the Lord in the Psalms. I like it for what is says and how it says it. It asks God for an answer and asks him to take action. Sometimes action is sufficient for me, but sometimes I really need some understanding, too.

I liken this world to a massive Sudoku puzzle. Sudoku is a three-dimensional puzzle that has one solution. When properly solved, it has the numbers one through nine in each line going across, each line going down and in each box that is formed upon the grid. Now if you've never done a Sudoku puzzle, you may not understand, but if you have, you know how tough they are. In my mind, I see the world as a massive Sudoku puzzle that, when history is complete, will have God's answers perfectly formed in each row and box. The Sudoku puzzle works perfectly by the power and knowledge of God. Here is the rub, though. God let's us pick our number in the puzzle. God may desire me to be an eight, but I can chose to be a seven. You can choose too.

Somehow, with all of us getting to choose our own numbers, God still gets the Sudoku puzzle to work. To put it in more practical terms, everyone makes their own choices, but Peter still decided to deny the Lord three times before a rooster crowed, just as God proclaimed ahead of time.

How does God do it? Those are the ways of the Lord. I know he put this universe into play a long time ago. He set the knobs of physics such that by nature's own laws, certain things would be set into motion (the cataclysms of weather, etc.). I also know that God will let things happen in my life not only because of what I need, but others need as well. Keith Green sang, "I pledge my head to heaven for the gospel." He is right. I want God to use my life to sculpt the lives of others. If my life or death can better bring the Sudoku puzzle numbers where they need to be, I am at peace. I will die one day, and I hope my death will be one that brings others into alignment with God's will.

So with each day and each crisis, I know there is a God, and I want his deliverance, but sometimes I want his answers. But what I already know is that his answers are wrapped up in his actions. His actions are his answers. I need to be satisfied with that.

Lord, please use me. Make my life what it needs to be for the good of your kingdom. Use every day of my life and even my death to bring people to you. In Jesus' name, Amen!

❦ ❦ ❦

JUNE 12

You know my reproach, and my shame and my dishonor; my foes are all known to you. Reproaches have broken my heart, so that I am in despair. I looked for pity, but there was none, and for comforters, but I found none. (Ps. 69:19-20)

In my legal work, I have had the chance to try and help people who have had their reputation wrongly destroyed. I think of one case in particular, where my client was a godly man. Of course he wasn't perfect, but a godly man of extraordinary talent and devotion. He was also my friend. This man was set to a godly calling and, by God's grace, exceeded all expectations. But all was not well in the political circles that revolved around the work of this man. There were those who were offended by his accomplishments, and they sought to bring him down. It was as if they wanted to disgrace him and so bolster themselves. And so they went to work.

My friend was maliciously defamed. His name was besmirched and his reputation set upon in ways that reminded me of ravenous wolves ripping flesh from a carcass on the Discovery Channel. It brought pain to my friend, his family, and his friends. It brought damage to the greater work he was doing.

In the midst of that work, I came upon this passage of psalms. I thought immediately of my friend. I found this psalm a salve. For thousands of years, there have been those who are godly who have wrongly experienced reproach, who have had to bear up under undeserved shame, and whose honor has been displayed dishonorably.

While these psalms are often personal, this is a psalm that should speak to us beyond our own concerns of self. As God's body on earth, as God's people, we need to find those who are wrongly reproached and take up their cause. We need to see where the enemies of goodness and right are impugning the honor of God's children and defend them. We need to bring pity and care to those wrongly hurt. This is our opportunity to do so in the name of Christ.

We saw in Jesus one who not only stood by those wrongly dishonored (Luke 10:40ff.), but one who also stood by those who were "rightly" abused (John 8:3-11)! We should all carefully and prayerfully examine our lives. How do we stand? Do we reach out to the popular, or will God find us reaching out to everyone: popular or isolated, at ease or in distress? May God use us as we attentively look to be his hands on earth.

Lord, many of your people are hurting. They seek comfort from you. May we be your hands and voice for them. May we give them comfort, not simply by praying, but by taking action in Jesus' name, through whom we confidently can announce Amen!

❧ ❧ ❧

JUNE 13

My frame was not hidden from you, when I was being made in secret, intricately woven in the depths of the earth. Your eyes saw my unformed substance; in your book were written, every one of them, the days that were formed for me, when as yet there was none of them. (Ps. 139:15-16)

One strong directive in my life has stemmed from my mom telling me from an early age that she had prayed God would give her a son (she already had my sister) and that she had told God if he would, that she would dedicate the son back to the Lord. Because of this, she explained to me, she was confident that God had important things planned for me to do, and I better pay attention with my life and see that I get them done. She would tell me stories of people in the Bible who wasted what God gave them, stories of those who honored what God gave them, and stories of those who were a mixed bag. She told me it was up to me to live up to what God wanted, so I could fill the role in this world he had for me. Needless to say, with each of my children I have prayed the same prayer of gratitude and dedication within minutes of their births.

Today's passage instructs me that while I will always be grateful for a mother who reinforced God's calling so strongly, God's calling is not unique to me. It applies to all of his children. There is not a person alive who follows the Lord for whom it's not true. None of us was hidden from God as our DNA was put together. God never needed a sonogram to know our gender. He wasn't waiting until we came into the world to see if we had hair. God wasn't guessing about our weight, size, or even birth date. God wasn't lost or bewildered about us after our birth either. He has advance knowledge of our lives. He knows the good things that will happen. He knows the bad. He knows the good choices we will make. He knows the bad.

This doesn't mean that we have no choices in life. We do. We select how we live and what we do. So do others. (This is one of the reasons bad things happen to good people!) We have the assurance, however, that God knows these things and has configured time and space where we are given opportunities to live for him in ways that are unique to each of us. God has "good works," as Paul calls them in Ephesians 2:10, and God has already prepared for us to walk in them. This means that everything that we have, everything we don't have, all of our talents, all the scars we bear from bad history, all of these make us who we are today! And today the God who has known us from the womb is wanting to work in each of us! He has a job for you and me to do!

Lord, it is a great honor to be known by you, loved by you, empowered by you, and directed by you. I pray that today I can follow your direction and fulfill your purposes. In Jesus' name and for his sake, Amen.

JUNE 14

Let heaven and earth praise him, the seas and everything that moves in them. (Ps. 69:34)

Have you ever wondered how the seas praise the Lord? How the fish praise him? How the heavens and earth praise him? If we figure that out, is there anything we can learn from the praise of these non-human, and even non-living things? Without question!

The heavens, earth, seas, fish, and more praise God by being who and what God made them to be! They praise God even without a conscious awareness of who or what he is. Consider fish. Fish praise God by being the fish he made them to be, swimming the seas performing the "job" God gave them. For scavenger fish, that is cleaning up the sea. God gave some fish the role of population control. They praise God when they eat mosquitoes, bugs, and of course, other fish. (Thank God for their praise in eating mosquitoes and keeping their populations under control!) Some fish fulfill God's plan by supplying themselves as food, both to other fish and other creatures (birds, people, bears, etc.). Fish perform their roles assigned by God when they breed and populate the waters. Fish being true fish are praising God, even though they don't know it in a humanly conscious sense, because they are fulfilling his plans for them. They show what an incredible planner our God is. They show the remarkable way the world can work when people do as God made and instructed them.

The heavens are not conscious, but they praise God. For example, when the sun radiates heat as the Lord intended, it fills its function to the glory of God. As the sun's rays give energy for photosynthesis, they praise God the designer. When the moon affects the tides, it fulfills its important role affecting currents, weather, biological life, and more. As the heavens operate with mathematical precision, they and all of nature operate in a cause/effect relationship. They praise God doing what God set in motion and reflecting the nature and invisible qualities of the Lord God (Rom. 1:20).

Everything brings praise to God by being what they were made to be. Plants and animals praise God when they become food for people and animals. They are being what they were made to be. (Of course this doesn't mean that any conscious being should be needlessly tormented! Even as we raise animals and kill them for food, it should be done responsibly.)

Do we learn from non-human praise? Absolutely! We learn the importance of being humans! We know we can praise God when we do God's work to God's glory. So we praise God not just in church but in life! When we serve others, love and invest in our families, work responsibly in our jobs, enjoy recreation in proper measure, we praise God!

Lord, let everything praise your name! May I join the world in doing so in Jesus, Amen!

❦ ❦ ❦

JUNE 15

Make haste, O God, to deliver me! O LORD, make haste to help me! (Ps. 70:1)

God's timing is not always my timing. I know from many psalms, as well as from life, that suffering and bad things do not always pass quickly—even though I know all things do pass. Scripture teaches the importance of patience, but I tend to be one who wants to learn that lesson as quickly as possible! So I like passages like this one: Hurry God!

This psalm reinforces to me how God loves to hear the honest prayers of our hearts. God is not looking for theological correctness in our prayers. He is looking for honesty from a submissive spirit. If we have doubts, we can have those honestly before the Lord in prayer. If we are worried, we can express those worries before the Lord in prayer. If we are angry, with a submissive spirit we can express that anger to the Lord in prayer. God is not blind to our emotions. He made us emotional beings. He wants to teach us to live with our emotions in ways where the emotions are not controlling us; rather, we function with them taking their rightful place. Emotions can motivate us, teach us, give us endurance, move us in sympathy, and more. The key is to make sure the emotions are not trumping reason!

So with God, there are times when I am in a hurry. I tell him so! I tell him, "Lord, I am in a hurry! PLEASE help me NOW! HURRY GOD!!!" These are the conversations that get written in lots of capital letters with lots of exclamation marks.

As I work through these things with God, I don't do so in rebellion to him or his will. I think of Jesus telling his followers that God is like a Father who has his children ask for bread. He won't give them a rock! God is not a vengeful and trickster Father to his children. I have seen my children grow up, and I have seen them mature in their requests. I hope I do the same with the Lord, but he *always* wants to hear my heart. I pray my heart, always trying to add that my overall concern is growing in him and being used for the good of his kingdom and will.

This is one reason I love the Lord's Prayer. It has my personal needs, but always puts God first! It begins with praise, praying that God's name be honored, his kingdom expanded, and his will done. THEN it moves to my needs. In prayer we need to be mindful of priorities, but we pray our heart before God and trust him with the answers. I do pray, "HURRY PLEASE, GOD" when that is my heart. And if he hurries, I say, "Amen!" And if he doesn't, but he says, "Be patient," I say, "Amen (and help me please)!"

Lord, thank you for wanting to hear my heart. Help me to be honest in prayer. In Jesus' name, Amen!

❧ ❧ ❧

JUNE 16

Let them be put to shame and confusion who seek my life! Let them be turned back and brought to dishonor who delight in my hurt! Let them turn back because of their shame who say, "Aha, Aha!" (Ps. 70:2-3)

One of America's most famed lawyers and jurists was Supreme Court Justice Louis Brandeis (1856–1941). Among his legion of quotable sayings is one from 1914: "Publicity is justly commended as a remedy for social and industrial diseases. Sunlight is said to be the best of disinfectants; electric light the most efficient policeman." The principle makes sense. Disclosure is healthy; secrecy breeds problems.

Over and over in the life of the psalmist we read about the suffering that came from the hands of disingenuous people. We all have had times (or will if we live through the middle school years) when people have maliciously said or done things to hurt us. We will find in life some who will gossip, spread rumors, deliver innuendos, plot evil, and cause distress in our lives.

The psalmist prayed for sunlight, that great disinfectant. The request was that God would reveal bad motives, bring to naught the plans of the devious, and illuminate the deceptions of others. This might seem vindictive, but it needn't be. In the New Testament, in the life and teaching of Jesus, we have a more mature explanation for what we should be seeking.

Jesus told us to pray for our enemies and persecutors (Matt. 5:44). This is not a prayer of vengeance. We aren't asking God to bring pain and misery to those causing us pain and misery. We pray for God to reveal truth, and ultimately drive the wrongdoer to repent, turn away, and seek forgiveness. After all, if we carefully examine ourselves, we will find that we have been guilty in the past, if not for similar sins then for at least the seeds of such sins. We certainly have been guilty of many sins of equal magnitude!

We prayerfully ask God to forgive our sins. We need to be in a posture of forgiving those who sin against us. In the Lord's Prayer, we pray, "Forgive us our sins as we forgive those who sin against us," and we do well to remember Jesus' teaching that came on the heals of that prayer, "For if you forgive others their trespasses, your heavenly Father will also forgive you, but if you do not forgive others their trespasses, neither will your Father forgive your trespasses" (Matt. 6:14-15). So as we see abuse, let's remember, sunlight is the key. Let's pray for God to reveal truth and bring sinners to repentance. Let's be ready with our own forgiveness as well!

Lord, reveal truth in life, move sinners to repent and forgive us all in Jesus, Amen!

❧ ❧ ❧

JUNE 17

May all who seek you rejoice and be glad in you! May those who love your salvation say evermore, "God is great!" But I am poor and needy; hasten to me, O God! You are my help and my deliverer; O LORD, do not delay! (Ps. 70:4-5)

Say and do! That's a good motto to live by. Or we might word it as the old adage, "Practice what you preach!" The psalmist in this passage follows that sage advice.

The verses begin with the prayerful recognition that all who seek God can rejoice and be glad in him. As Jesus pointed out, "Ask and it will be given to you; seek, and you will find; knock, and it will be opened to you. For everyone who asks receives, and the one who seeks finds, and to the one who knocks it will be opened" (Matt. 7:7-8). We can be confident that as we seek the Lord, we will find him. We can rightly rejoice if we are seeking God. He is not hiding. We will not miss him!

But the psalmist doesn't simply teach us that those who seek God find God. The psalmist then practices this principle. The psalmist begins actually seeking God. The psalmist seeks God from the middle of a mess. The psalmist self-describes as "poor and needy." I have seen many reactions from those in need. I have seen them wallow in self-pity, strike out in anger, get lost in bewilderment, blindly grasp for straws, shut down in depression, check out in some drug- or alcohol-induced stupor, but none of that for this psalmist. This writer knows how to not only "talk the talk," but how to "walk the walk."

The psalmist knows that the neediness needs to go before the great Lord God! God is the deliverer. God is the needed help. Compare the difference between God as help and the options I described above. With God, it is not a pity party, it is a truthful setting of needs before God. Self-pity draws attention to us. Here the attention is given to God. It is like fasting (something we can do when in need to drive our focus to God). Even there, Jesus taught that when we fast we shouldn't contort our faces to make it about us (Matt. 6:16-18). We keep the fasting between us and the Father. It is about him meeting our needs, not about us displaying those needs to others. Similarly, we don't strike out in anger when in need. We confess sin; we meaningfully seek God's will and deliverance. Neediness shouldn't fuel bewilderment, but an urgent seeking for God's direction. We needn't grasp for straws but should purposefully find godly counsel and direction. Rather than shutting down in depression, we should lay our emotions before the Lord and let him mold us through them. Alcohol and drugs make problems worse. Get lost in praise and worship instead, and watch God give strength and power. Seek God. You will find him.

Lord, we set our needs before you. We seek your help. Please. In Jesus' name, Amen!

❀ ❀ ❀

JUNE 18

*In you, O L*ORD*, do I take refuge; let me never be put to shame! In your righteousness deliver me and rescue me; incline your ear to me, and save me! Be to me a rock of refuge, to which I may continually come.* (Ps. 71:1-3)

There is an adverb in this passage that speaks to me: "continually." The idea behind the adverb is something that occurs repeatedly. It happens over and over. This is my God as my rock of refuge. I can come to him over and over for stability in crisis and help in life's raging storms. He is always there. He never goes on vacation. He never tires of my needs. He never finds me to be a pest. He doesn't denigrate my problems as inconsequential. He doesn't minimize my needs.

No human could be a good substitute for God on this. Many might be glad to be there most of the time, but eventually each person would say, "Come on. You got this! Just come to me on the real serious matters!" This is why one of my good friends (Bob) was never too comfortable praying. Bob would tease me, "I figure God is good for three or four of my prayers each year. I don't want to waste one on something that's not crucial."

I would tell Bob, "God is not that way!" Think of God as a Father. What father doesn't want his children to come to him with their problems, be they few or many? Bob told me "My father didn't!" I had to back-track. "Okay," I replied, "Maybe not your father, but YOU as a father certainly care that way for your children!" On this he agreed. (Bob is a GREAT father!)

God is not a shabby dad apathetic about his family. He is a provider Father, an interested Father, a doting Father, even. God wants to be there for his children. If he cares when a sparrow falls, if he's numbered the hairs on our heads (Matt. 10:29-30), then he wants to be there for us when we are nervous, scared, sad, or worried; just as he does when we are confident, at peace, happy, and secure.

God is a rock. What a pity if we should ever fail to go to him at any moment we need a stable place to stand and endure. God will infuse us with wisdom, strengthen us with power, steady us with firmness, and send us back into the fray to handle things with his aid. Continually!

Lord, we do need you as our rock. We need you daily, hourly, minute-by-minute. Thank you for being there as a constant loving Father. In Jesus' name, Amen!

JUNE 19

*Blessed be the L*ORD*, the God of Israel, who alone does wondrous things. Blessed be his glorious name forever; may the whole earth be filled with his glory! Amen and Amen!* (Ps. 72:18-19)

This passage reminds me of two songs that seem on the surface to have nothing in common. The first one makes sense. From *Fiddler on the Roof*, the song is "Miracle of Miracles," also called by its repeated line, "Wonder of Wonders." Motel the tailor sings the song after receiving permission to marry Tevye's oldest daughter, Tzeitel. He dances around the stage (or screen, if watching the movie), equating the wondrous events to God saving Daniel from the lions, tearing down the walls at Jericho, softening pharaoh's heart, parting the Red Sea, and other wonders in Scripture. God was doing something in the life of Motel that was spectacular. He gave him the bride of his dreams. He sings, "But of all God's miracles, large and small, the most miraculous one of all is the one I thought would never be. God has given you to me."

The unlikely second song I relate to this is "Double Vision" by Foreigner. Evidently the song wasn't inspired by alcohol, as some might think, but by a collision in a hockey game that left a player with double vision. Regardless, the song comes to mind for me because of its constant usage of the phrase, "double vision."

The same events can be seen from two different mindsets. We can look at a set of events, say that of Motel the tailor, and see it as a wondrous miracle of God. Or we can see it without considering God and simply see Motel as a persuasive fellow who was able to convince Tevye, a soft-hearted fellow, to reverse directions and give Motel the hand of Tzeitel in marriage. Double vision: is it the hand of God or human hands?

I write this as our daughter-in-law is in labor about to give birth to our first granddaughter. Is this marvelous new life a gift from God? Or is she simply the laws of nature coming to a successful conclusion after an egg was fertilized and carried to term?

The psalmist tells us that God alone does wondrous things. We may be able to see them as natural occurrences, but we know that God set nature into motion. The laws of nature were written by the Creator of nature. James in the New Testament wrote much the same thing, "Every good gift and every perfect gift is from above, coming down from the Father of lights with whom there is no variation or shadow due to change" (Jas. 1:17). Wonder of wonders!

Oh wondrous Lord, we honor you as a wonder-working God, giving us your love daily. We thank you in Jesus' name, Amen!

JUNE 20

I have been as a portent to many, but you are my strong refuge. My mouth is filled with your praise, and with your glory all the day. (Ps. 71:7-8)

If asked, I suspect a lot of people might not know what a "portent" is. The idea behind the Hebrew word so translated is something that is extraordinary, a wonder, or even a mystery. Believers should be portents to an unbelieving world. You and I should be portents.

This always reminds me of a Keith Green song from my youth, "Because of You." Keith makes the point that when people see him as a portent, he, as the psalmist does above, knows it is because God is his strong refuge. He sings, "People smile at me and ask me what it is that makes them want to be just like I am. So I just point to you and tell them, 'Yes it's true, I'm no special one, I'm just one man.' . . . Yeah, it's because of you I can raise my hands and reply and say, 'I'm happy because of you.' "

My job is trying lawsuits. I have tried some on a national stage, with news media present, with lots of money on the line, with lawyers from around the world watching; these are generally considered stress generators by the legal community. Stress can turn many trial lawyers into impatient shouters. Others get lost in alcohol and drugs as coping mechanisms to alleviate the stress. A lawyer friend of mine who is also a psychologist has watched me try a number of cases. She has repeatedly asked me, "Aren't you dying inside? How can you do this over and over again? Why doesn't this drive you crazy like everyone else?" I am a portent to her (and others who just aren't so vocal). I tell my friend, as I tell anyone who might ask, it's like Keith Green says—it's like the psalmist says—I am this way because God is my strong refuge. If I am doing what God wants me to do, I am at peace. I don't have to care about the outcome. That is God's job. My job is to do what he says, pray for his will, and trust him. If I am supposed to win the big case, may God make it so. If I am to lose it, I am at peace.

People of faith should be a portent to the world. The world doesn't have what we have and should be stunned at our strength and confidence in life. Our confidence is not based on ourselves; it is based on our God. Our God lights our path, ensures our success, and gives us grace in the midst of our failures. This gives the believer something the world doesn't have. It makes us a mystery to those watching. Then as they ask us why, may we always point to the Lord! May our mouths be filled with praise giving him glory!

Lord, you have called us to be portents. You have our backs! You have our fronts and sides too! May we show the world in the face of life's problems that you make the difference. May we be the portents you have called us to be. To Jesus' glory, Amen!

❀ ❀ ❀

JUNE 21

My enemies speak concerning me; those who watch for my life consult together and say, "God has forsaken him; pursue and seize him, for there is none to deliver him." . . . But I will hope continually and will praise you yet more and more. My mouth will tell of your righteous acts, of your deeds of salvation all the day, for their number is past my knowledge. . . . So even to old age and gray hairs, O God, do not forsake me, until I proclaim your might to another generation, your power to all those to come. (Ps. 71:10-11, 14-15, 18)

The psalmist impresses me. Reaching a point in later life, the psalmist finds life not so clearly blessed by the Lord. Maybe it is poor health. Maybe it is isolation. Maybe it is an inability to make ends meet. We don't know with certainty what happened in the psalmist's life, but his enemies claimed God abandoned him.

The psalmist doesn't rebel against God. We don't read verses taking God to task for God's failures. There is not an indication that God is at fault. Instead, the psalmist reacts to the difficult situation by reaffirming praise to God and continuing to live, trusting in the salvation of God. This means that the psalmist praises God, remembering all the ways God has worked in the writer's life. There are more than the writer can count, remember, or even realize, but there is no doubt who has been at work—God! This God is not failing in the psalmist's later years. Life just comes in cycles. The psalmist knows that and waits for God's hand to be evident again.

I am also impressed at the *reason* the psalmist gives for wanting God's blessings. The psalmist wants to use the blessings to proclaim to a younger generation more praise to the Lord. This is an important part of aging, and it is important all along the way. High school students have much to say to middle schoolers. College students will have a listening audience among high school students. Young professionals have experiences with God they can share with college students, high school students, and more.

As we age, we have a responsibility to those behind us. They may not see the hand of God as we do. We who know God need to give godly advice to the coming generation. I am continually amazed at how those younger than I have the questions and issues I had at their age. I need to share what God has taught me. I also need to experience God today to be able to share tomorrow!

Lord, thank you for your hand in my life. Thank you for walking with me, enlightening and teaching me, and enabling me to share your blessings with others. In Jesus' name, Amen!

❧ ❧ ❧

JUNE 22

I will also praise you with the harp for your faithfulness, O my God; I will sing praises to you with the lyre, O Holy One of Israel. My lips will shout for joy, when I sing praises to you; my soul also, which you have redeemed. And my tongue will talk of your righteous help all the day long. (Ps. 71:22-24)

What do you do well? What talents did God give you? Can you sing? Play piano or guitar? Do you write poetry or stories? Can you do calligraphy? Are you a ball player of some kind? Are you a thinker? A planner? Whatever gifts and skills you have, use them to praise God!

The psalmist was a harp and lyre player. So the psalmist used the harp and lyre to praise God. The psalmist also "shouts" for joy "singing" praise for God. The psalmist used the tongue to talk of God's greatness and righteousness.

We should not get so caught up in the specifics that we fail to grasp the message. The psalmist is declaring that everything we have is called to give praise to God. I don't know many harp players, but I know lots of people who have generous hearts. I don't know many good at the lyre, but I know many good at law. In any station of life, with any gift, we can always find an opportunity to act with glory going to ourselves or to the Lord. That is the psalmist's challenge. Find everything at your disposal as a chance to give glory, honor, and credit to God.

Are you a big tipper? Write a note on the bill blessing the server in the name of God. Are you skilled in serving others? Serve them well, and let them know we worship a serving God. Are you friendly to strangers? Bless them in the name of God. Are you gifted as an encourager? Encourage people in the name of Jesus! Are you a natural teacher? Find ways to teach people about our Father. Are you a leader? Lead people in ways that reflect God's leadership. Also show you are led by someone greater than yourself.

God gave you your talents. God gave you your opportunities in life. Don't be bashful about giving him credit. Don't be timid about doing well and giving him the glory. Don't hesitate to receive compliments, but turn them into praise of him who is really responsible. Then when you are doing well, let your reward be one of giving glory to the Father.

Lord, there is no one like you, no one even remotely close. You are the hope of our heart. You give us joy in the present. You have taught us to live and given us reason to sing. May we lift you up in praise in our words and deeds. In every way may we give you glory before a world that desperately needs you. In Jesus' name, Amen!

❧ ❧ ❧

JUNE 23

Give the king your justice, O God, and your righteousness to the royal son! May he judge your people with righteousness, and your poor with justice! (Ps. 72:1-2)

Politics is a nasty business. People equate it to sausage. We live with the end product, but nobody really wants to see how it's made. Not many people hold political office, and I suspect many in political life are not in a daily walk with the Creator God. But whether politicians are or aren't, every believer has a responsibility to pray for those in power.

It was the authority of the Roman government that put the innocent Jesus to death. The Roman Caesars and their administrative chiefs would oversee the martyrdom of many in the early church, including the apostle Paul. Yet that same Paul wrote to the church at Rome, the seat of governmental power in the New Testament world, "Let every person be subject to the governing authorities. For there is no authority except from God, and those in authority that exist have been instituted by God. Therefore whoever resists the authorities resists what God has appointed, and those who resist will incur judgment" (Rom. 13:1-2).

Christians are called to pray for those in governing positions. Christians pay their taxes and don't lie or cheat on them. Christians abide by those laws that do not interfere with faith. Christians in democratic countries like America have a stewardship chance to vote, and that is important. It is an action that goes with prayer.

In America, we pray for three branches of government. We have the executive branch. These are the president and vice president on a federal level. On a more local level, these are governors, mayors, and the like. In the legislative branch we have senators and members of congress/representatives on both a federal and state level. Communities will frequently have city councils. In the judicial branch, we have trial judges and appellate judges.

In all of these areas, Christians have a responsibility to pray. We should pray for justice, especially for the poor, weak, and those unable to speak up for themselves. Justice more frequently leaves them behind. We should pray for laws that recognize God's priorities. These laws need to function so that life is valued, regardless of age, gender, and nationality. Law should enable unhindered worship with freedom. Law should foster and promote peace and opportunities for people to grow and prosper. These opportunities should be available to everyone. Law should protect people from evil. We have a lot to pray for!

Lord, establish goodness and justice in our land. Bless those in power. In Jesus, Amen!

❧ ❧ ❧

JUNE 24

For he delivers the needy when he calls, the poor and him who has no helper. He has pity on the weak and the needy, and saves the lives of the needy. From oppression and violence he redeems their life, and precious is their blood in his sight. (Ps. 72:12-14)

Reading this passage out of its immediate context, it appears to be speaking of the actions of God. God delivers the needy when they call. God helps the poor and those without a helper. God pities the weak and needy. God redeems the life of his children from oppression and violence. But read within the context, something else becomes apparent.

This passage is about a righteous king! It is the righteous king who cares for the needy and poor. A righteous king helps the helpless. A righteous king saves lives from oppression and violence. A righteous king rules and uses his power to do the things God does. The righteous king's agenda should mirror the agenda of *the* righteous King of kings.

Of course, in most political systems today, we don't have kings. In America, we have politicians, but they are representatives of the people. The United States is a government of the people, for the people. Regardless of the job title, however, the righteous politicians and rulers of our day should still seek to mirror the agenda of the King of kings. People in power should do this. It is a good political platform!

This mirroring should not lie only at the door of politicians, but as we are a government of the people, this is what righteous people should do period. I want to deliberately live this way. I want to find opportunities to deliver the needy when he calls. One of our daughters gives food coupons and gift cards to beggars seeking food. I need to figure out ways to help the poor and those who are helpless. If I see violence, I need to step in and defend. I need to find ways to salvage those oppressed.

This means my life is about more than my family and me. It extends beyond my friends. I am quick to try and help my friends and neighbors, but this mindset expands that group tremendously. I am suddenly in the world of Jesus' parable of the good Samaritan. That story was birthed from a lawyer's question, "Who is my neighbor?" asked after Jesus gave priority to the commandment, "Love your neighbor as yourself" (Luke 10:25-37). Our calling is to help those in our path in need of help. As we mirror God's agenda, we are mirroring God's heart. This is a good thing.

Lord, there are a lot of hurting people. A lot of people in need. You have blessed us with resources and gifts we can use for the least of our brothers and sisters. May we see the needs and with unselfish hearts reflect your generosity as we mirror your agenda. As our Lord Jesus modeled to us, may we model to the world with honor to our Lord, Amen!

JUNE 25

For you, O Lord, are my hope, my trust, O LORD, from my youth. (Ps. 71:5)

Some people think of faith as an old person's thing. Young people are to sow oats. Young people are more into fitting into the crowd, and less about "spiritual matters." Religion can wait, many think. It's more suited for my parents. Some young people even believe themselves smarter than others and have figured out there is no need for (or no such thing as) God. Sometimes children reach adolescent years, and turn from God. Many students from homes of faith head off to college and quit going to church, perhaps thinking church can come later. After all, they reason, college is a time for study and fun, and that doesn't happen in church.

These people are missing out—tremendously. There is something incredible about growing up with trust in the Lord. As we grow, our minds develop patterns and ways of thinking. We are more tuned into things that we can learn. (Ever heard of the difficulty of teaching an old dog new tricks?) As our brains develop, infusing them with faith and a walk with the Lord transforms all of life. It develops our thinking differently.

Setting aside neurological development, walking with the Lord since youth delivers an entirely different kind of blessing. Walking in the ways of the Lord sets us on paths that are quite different from paths of rebellion to God. The proverbs speak of God making "straight paths" for those who are trusting in the Lord (Prov. 3:5). It is a simple fact that roads lead somewhere. Generally, good roads lead to good places and bad roads lead to bad ones. Trusting in the Lord keeps you on good roads. This ensures success in life.

Finally, trusting in the Lord at a young age builds up faith credits in your faith bank that you will need to draw on later in life. I remember events when God came through for me as a twelve-year-old boy. I remember praying to God at all ages of life, teenage years to now. Over and over God heard my prayers. I look back, and seeing this instilled in me faith that I have needed later in life. I know that my redeemer cares. I know he is involved in my life. I know he hears my prayers. He has done so all my life. My trust in him is not in vain. I have had it since youth!

Everyone, every day has an opportunity to trust the Lord. We can regret not doing so earlier in life, but we must never fail to use today to trust him. It changes who we are, puts us where we should be, and gives us strength and confidence for the job at hand!

Lord, in you I put my trust today. I trust you to take care of my family, my friends, myself. I trust you to provide for me, to give me direction, and to teach me your ways. I trust you with all I am and all I have. In Jesus' name, Amen!

JUNE 26

When I thought how to understand this, it seemed to me a wearisome task, until I went into the sanctuary of God; then I discerned their end. (Ps. 73:16-17)

Some things aren't easily understandable. This is a psalm in which the writer is perturbed over how wicked people seemed to be on easy street compared to the hard roads of the psalmist. It doesn't seem fair or right. The psalmist can't get over the fact that God seems to let the wicked and arrogant prosper. It stirred up envy in the psalmist. In verse after verse, the psalmist details the sins of these people living selfishly at the expense of others. The wicked were even taunting God, claiming God is ignorant of what goes on in the world (Ps. 73:11). Instead of receiving God's judgment, these folks seemed to increase in riches and in what the world would term "blessings."

Meanwhile the psalmist began questioning the virtuous life: "All in vain have I kept my heart clean and washed my hands in innocence" (Ps. 73:13). The psalmist was at wits' end until coming into the presence of God. In God's presence came insight and wisdom. The writer confesses such in the passage for today.

Life for the wicked may look marvelous on the surface, but it isn't. It may seem successful, but it isn't. It may seem perpetually happy; it isn't. The wicked will be swept away, just not on the day of the psalmist's choosing! It is from God and in God's timing.

In the presence of God, the psalmist had insight into both the wicked and the psalmist's own heart. He saw he was guilty of envying the wicked and doubting the role of God. "When my soul was embittered, when I was pricked in heart, I was brutish and ignorant; I was like a beast toward you" (Ps. 73:21-22). Nevertheless, God was patient. God brought the psalmist peace and strength, and gave him wisdom: "I am continually with you; you hold my right hand. You guide me with your counsel, and afterward you will receive me to glory. Whom have I in heaven but you? And there is nothing on earth that I desire besides you. My flesh and my heart may fail, but God is the strength of my heart and my portion forever" (Ps. 73:23-26).

What an awesome God. The writer came to realize the issue was never about how God was treating the wicked. The issue was only about how the sinful psalmist trusted and relied upon God. Being in God's presence taught that valuable lesson. I need to spend more time in the presence of God.

Lord, teach me where my focus should be. Help me be concerned with my sin, not that of others. Help me to honor you with my thoughts and deeds. In Jesus' name, Amen!

❧ ❧ ❧

JUNE 27

For behold, those who are far from you shall perish; you put an end to everyone who is unfaithful to you. But for me it is good to be near God; I have made the Lord GOD my refuge, that I may tell of all your works. (Ps. 73:27-28)

For more reasons than I can count, it is important to me to grow closer to the Lord. This passage contrasts those who are far from God, calling them "unfaithful" with those who are near God, who make God their refuge. Those close to God tell of his works.

When I am close to God, I learn his wisdom and ways. His will grows clearer to me. People often ask me, "How do I know what God wants me to do?" in reference to some situation or another. Many would like God to be a divine GPS direction system, an app they can download to their phone to pull up when in doubt about which direction to go. God doesn't work that way. He is not our Siri or Google Map app. God has given us instructions that reveal his character, ethics, and priorities. He has also modeled that in the life, death, and resurrection of Jesus. As we practice, study, and learn the ways of the Lord, we draw nearer to him. We understand his will better. He works to renew our minds, so we can make godly decisions, not simply follow a phone app.

Another reason to draw near to God is wrapped up in worship. As we spend time before the Lord in his sanctuary, not a physical place, but one we experience through devotional worship, we better see him in his glory, better see ourselves in our humanity, and appreciate God's redemptive work in Jesus. This draws us near to him, infusing us with an appreciation of his power and love. Knowing the power of God emboldens us in our faith. Knowing the love of God teaches us how to love. Our lives are changed in the presence of God.

I wonder if this is behind a line in the story of Enoch in Genesis 5:24: "Enoch walked with God, and he was not, for God took him." God always provides us a chance to grow closer to him. Enoch experienced that firsthand. I want to be nearer to God today than I was yesterday. I want to know him better and love him more deeply.

This is our choice. Those far from God choose to be unfaithful. You cannot be unfaithful and draw near to the Lord. Unfaithfulness denies God in his essence. How do we draw near to someone we don't trust? If someone is not close to God, it is not God's fault! The psalmist also says, "I have *made* God my refuge." Again, this is the psalmist's choice to draw near to God. I know what choices I need to make today. I want to draw near to God.

As the old hymn prays, *"Draw me nearer, nearer precious Lord to the cross where thou hast died. Draw me nearer, nearer, nearer precious Lord, to thy precious bleeding side."*

❧ ❧ ❧

JUNE 28

Remember your congregation, which you have purchased of old, which you have redeemed to be the tribe of your heritage! (Ps. 74:2)

You are not an afterthought. You aren't someone who stumbled into the kingdom and care of God. You are the end of his deliberate planning. He chose you before he ever made the world, to be complete and whole in Jesus Christ. Paul said it this way, "Blessed be the God and Father of our Lord Jesus Christ, who has blessed us in Christ with every spiritual blessing in the heavenly places, even as he chose us in him before the foundation of the world, that we should be holy and blameless before him" (Eph. 1:3-4).

It was never enough that God should choose his people. His people could make choices too. We read that in the story of Adam and Eve, and we experience it in our own lives. Unfortunately, the history of humanity is one of choosing rebellion over God. That choice is not without effect, and we should not be surprised. Cause and effect is the order of things. The core effect of our sin is a bondage to the consequences of sin. These consequences include alienation from a perfect God and a bondage to the sin we have committed. Sin is sticky. It doesn't let us go. Its road is one that should not shock anyone. God sends evil to die. Cause and effect is at work in the law of sin and death.

So God's people had to be redeemed. Someone needed to rescue sinners from death and separation from the God of life. God did that in Jesus. Paul continued his explanation of God's redeeming work in Ephesians 1:7-8: "In him [Jesus] we have redemption through his blood, the forgiveness of our trespasses, according to the riches of his grace, which he lavished upon us, in all wisdom and insight."

The psalmist knew God had redeemed his people. God "purchased" his people from "of old," as Paul said, "before the foundation of the world." Of course, for centuries *how* God redeemed his people was a mystery. There were clues. Passover was a powerful message of God's sacrificing a lamb to bring his people out of bondage into the Promised Land. The Day of Atonement placed sins of the people onto a sacrificial animal who bore those sins away from the congregation. People were taught to sacrifice innocent animals for their sins. All of these foreshadowed the mystery of redemption. In Christ, the mystery was revealed. Paul finished his thought in Ephesians 1:9-10 noting that, in Christ, God was "making known to us the mystery of his will, according to his purpose, which he set forth in Christ as a plan for the fullness of time, to unite all things in him, things in heaven and things on earth." We are not an afterthought. We are the climax to God's great salvation drama.

Lord, thank you for the redemption from sin in Jesus Christ. Amen!

❀ ❀ ❀

JUNE 29

Your foes have roared in the midst of your meeting place; they set up their own signs for signs. (Ps. 74:4)

The people of God are peace-loving people. At least we should be! We are charged to be peacemakers (Matt. 5:9). We are taught to love our enemies and pray for our persecutors (Matt. 5:44). The fruit of the Spirit includes kindness (Gal. 5:22). So it might come as a surprise that there are foes and adversaries of God and his kingdom. Because we love peace, we tend to think all others must as well. A history lesson on the twentieth century should teach us otherwise (Hitler, Lenin, and Mao Zedong alone killed many more millions than we will every know). For that matter, reading the news in the twenty-first century informs us of the evil and hatred in the world. Mass shootings and bombings, hate crimes of different measures, rape and sexual exploitation are all too common.

Some of these wicked people are simply uninformed about God and his mercies. They have deliberately chosen to purse an agenda antagonistic to the Lord. While some we label "demented" and others "mentally ill," I believe there are some who are outright evil.

Scripture teaches that there are powers and principalities of darkness seeking to disrupt and destroy God's plans for the world. Readers of 1 Peter 5:8 are warned: "Be sober-minded; be watchful. Your adversary the devil prowls around like a roaring lion, seeking someone to devour." Paul explained to the Ephesians, "we do not wrestle against flesh and blood, but against the rulers, against the authorities, against the cosmic powers over this present darkness, against the spiritual forces of evil in the heavenly places" (Eph. 6:12).

Are we to fear these evil forces? We should certainly have a healthy respect for them. This is no game we are in. It is a cosmic battle. We are not alone in it; we are forces for the victorious God. God has given us the weapons we use to fight evil.

Paul urges us to stand against these spiritual foes with the weapons of spiritual warfare: "Take up the whole armor of God, that you may be able to withstand in the evil day, and having done all, to stand firm. Stand therefore, having fastened on the belt of truth, and having put on the breastplate of righteousness, and, as shoes for your feet, having put on the readiness given by the gospel of peace. In all circumstances take up the shield of faith, with which you can extinguish all the flaming darts of the evil one; and take the helmet of salvation, and the sword of the Spirit, which is the word of God, praying at all times in the Spirit, with all prayer and supplication" (Eph. 6:13-18).

Lord, make us wise. Help us wield your weapons rightly. Use us in your battle, and please protect us as we battle in your name. Through the victorious Jesus, Amen!

❧ ❧ ❧

JUNE 30

Yet God my King is from of old, working salvation in the midst of the earth. (Ps. 74:12)

God is working salvation in the midst of the earth. That is a formidable thought. Somehow with people having freedom to make their own decisions, God is at work bringing salvation to his people. God knew Judas would betray the Lord Jesus, even though it was Judas' choice. God didn't make Judas sell Jesus out for 30 pieces of silver. But God was at work when Judas did it.

God is working salvation in the midst of the earth. This alters my perspective on a lot of things that happen in this world that make no sense to me. We live with such a limited view that we are unaware of the reasons that make sense to God. We live in a massive piece of complicated machinery we call "earth and history." This machine is one that God knows intricately. I am one small item within that machine, and God has given me tasks I am to do. These tasks help the larger machine work with God's precision. Now I might choose not to do the tasks God has given me. Of my own volition, I might rebel against him or sin in some way. God has foreknowledge of this, however, and has built redundancy into the machine. Where I fail, another will succeed. God's plans will not be thwarted by my actions!

God is working salvation in the midst of the earth. This helps me walk in faith when things are not what I would choose. God's plan is not to make my life a Disney World experience. God's plan is to use the life I've committed to him for the higher calling of working salvation. In the early church, that meant a martyr's death for many. They knew that was a small price to pay for God's work. Death on earth to a believer is a graduation ceremony to a better eternity. It is not feared.

God is working salvation in the midst of the earth. Earth is my planet; this is very personal to me. God is working salvation in me and through me. He is the author of my salvation in Jesus; he is the perfecter of my salvation as well (Heb. 12:2).

God is working salvation in the midst of the earth. This is my calling. I want to be his helper. I choose to be in his service. I want to seize opportunities to share his salvation to a lost world. I want to see those in need, and bring them the good news that Jesus Christ died for their sins, bringing them salvation.

God is working salvation in the midst of the world, and I am amazed.

Lord, you are a saving God, of that there can be no doubt. We worship you for your salvation. We thank you for it. Help us to share it in Jesus, Amen!

❧ ❧ ❧

JULY 1

Yet God my King is from of old, working salvation in the midst of the earth. You divided the sea by your might; you broke the heads of the sea monsters on the waters. You crushed the heads of Leviathan; you gave him as food for the creatures of the wilderness. You split open springs and brooks; you dried up ever-flowing streams. Yours is the day, yours also the night; you have established the heavenly lights and the sun. You have fixed all the boundaries of the earth; you have made summer and winter. (Ps. 74:12-17)

There is something different from the God of Abraham, Isaac, and Jacob, who has revealed himself in Scripture to the gods of Israel's neighbors and other contemporary cultures. Others saw gods wrapped up in nature. They saw Baal as the god of storms and thunder, not too unlike the Vikings who had Thor as the thunder god. The Egyptians had Ra as the sun god, riding across the sky, much like the Greeks and Romans had their sun god driving across the sky in his chariot. Not so the God of the Bible.

The God of the Bible isn't a part of nature; he rules nature; he is responsible for nature. One point of the creation poem in Genesis 1, much like the creation poetry in this passage, is this very thing. God is not bound up in the ocean, the sun and stars, the seasons of harvest or any other natural thing. God is from old. He existed before nature and is responsible for nature. Paul would explain that nature reflects God's invisible attributes (Rom. 1:19-20). God divided the sea; he isn't the sea. God has authority and dominion over all the fishes in the sea, even the greatest (the Hebrew word "Leviathan" could be anything from a whale to a mythical sea creature, to a crocodile in the Egyptian Nile). God is the reason night and day exist. The sun and stars are not God; they are all part of a cosmos that God set up.

Still, the most provocative part of this passage isn't that God is beyond nature. It isn't that God set nature into motion or that he is greater than nature and its parts. The most provocative part is that God is at work in our world to rescue his children. The God beyond nature enters into nature because of his love and compassion for his children. He does so for children who are in need, and he brings them salvation or rescue from the small things of life as well as the great struggle for full redemption.

We worship an amazing God. As we contemplate the world and nature, the amazing intricacies of biology, the expansive universe, we need to pause and marvel at the God who is responsible for all that, and steps into it day-by-day, minute-by-minute, knowing our name, what we need, and coming to our rescue.

Amazing, Almighty Lord, we are in awe. Thank you for your love. In Jesus' name, Amen!

❧ ❧ ❧

JULY 2

Remember this, O LORD, how the enemy scoffs, and a foolish people reviles your name. (Ps. 74:18)

It amazes me how many people think they are smarter than God. Oh, they don't say it that way with words. They say it with actions. Some think they are so smart they have figured out that there is no God. It's mildly ironic, that these folks think they are smarter than God, because they think there is no God. All of these scoff over the idea of God, in one way or another. Lest I be that way myself, I like to dwell on this passage.

This passage is best understood if we understand a core feature of much Hebrew poetry: parallelism. Hebrew poetry is not known for rhyming. That is a feature of much of English poetry. A defining mark of Hebrew poetry is parallel phrases. For example, the poet will say a phrase, then say another phrase that closely mirrors or contrasts with the first phrase. In today's verse we have a parallel repetition in the two phrases, *"the enemy scoffs"* and *"a foolish people reviles your name."* Realizing that, we can explore the meaning of the poem's phrasing recognizing that "the enemy" is a parallel to one who is "foolish." The "scoffing" parallels to "reviling" God's name. These pieces are part and parcel of each other.

An "enemy" of God is an easy concept to understand. It is someone who sets him or herself against God, someone who stands before God in denial or confrontation, or even someone who chooses to work against God rather than for God. But the psalmist is giving us greater insight into an "enemy" of God. The psalmist equates the enemy of God here to a "fool." A Hebrew "fool" is one who is senseless, who has no real religious perception. The fool isn't generally a conscious "enemy" of God as we might understand the word, but the psalmist says the fool is an enemy nonetheless. One who is not consciously aware of God, who doesn't acknowledge him, is set against God just like an enemy.

Continuing to look at the parallels, we see that the enemy "scoffs," while the fool "reviles." The Hebrew idea of "scoffing" includes our concept of "taunting" (see Judg. 8:15) or "defying" (1 Sam. 17:10). We can see how an enemy of God would be one who might taunt him, or openly defy God. The deeper understanding is found when we add the shaded meaning of a fool who "reviles" God. To "revile" God is to "spurn" or "despise" him, often accompanied with an unbelief in him (see Num. 14:11). It is to treat the Lord with "contempt" or "scorn" (1 Sam. 2:17; 12:14).

This passage teaches that the enemy of God is not just the one who is conscious of God and openly rebels against him. One who foolishly acts as if there is no God is also rebelling and is not different than one who openly taunts God. I don't want to be either!

Lord, help me be conscious of you. Help me honor you every day. In Jesus, Amen!

✵ ✵ ✵

JULY 3

At the set time that I appoint I will judge with equity. When the earth totters, and all its inhabitants, it is I who keep steady its pillars. I say to the boastful, "'Do not boast,' and to the wicked, 'Do not lift up your horn; do not lift up your horn on high, or speak with haughty neck.'" (Ps. 75:2-5)

How often have you heard or thought, "God is not fair! If he were fair than so-and-so would get what's coming to him or her. Evil people prosper while the good people don't. There's something wrong with such a God!"

I was teaching on this concept when an elderly gentleman in class came up to me afterwards and said, "God balances the books; he just doesn't do so at the end of every day." This man had wisdom and a pithy way of illustrating the truth of today's passage. God does judge. He does set things right. But he has his own accounting schedule. *"At the set time that I appoint I will judge with equity."*

That doesn't mean that God is out of control in the meantime. To the contrary, should the earth totter, God keeps it steady. We need to remember that God's timing takes into account things that are far beyond our own. God promises this world will work out in accordance with his will. In the process, however, humanity gets to make their own choices. This can be a bit difficult to understand, but we might see it better with a biblical example of Judas Iscariot, the apostle that betrayed Christ for thirty pieces of silver.

Jesus prophesied that Judas would betray him. Before Judas approached the Jewish rulers with an offer to betray Jesus, Jesus already prophesied to that effect (John 6:70-71). Judas later went to the chief priests and officers and cut a deal to betray Jesus for money (Luke 22:3-6). Judas began looking for the opportunity to betray Jesus, even after Jesus called Judas out, declaring the coming betrayal (Luke 22:21). Satan was at work; Judas was at work; and God was at work. Had God balanced the books immediately, Judas would have been struck dead for even thinking about betraying the Lord. Once he reached an agreement with the rulers, immediate justice would have altered histories course. But God let the injustice go for the time being. It was necessary to bring God's plan to fruition. That did not make God the author of the injustice. That was the choice of Judas and the influence of Satan. Jesus warned Judas and Judas chose to ignore the Lord.

In this passage, God warns me how I should live. I see God's assurance he will balance the books, and I trust that God's timing is the right timing for his purposes.

God, you know what to do and when to do it. Help me grow in trusting patience. Help me remember you are the omniscient God. In Jesus, Amen.

❧ ❧ ❧

JULY 4

It is God who executes judgment, putting down one and lifting up another. For in the hand of the LORD there is a cup with foaming wine, well mixed, and he pours out from it, and all the wicked of the earth shall drain it down to the dregs. (Ps. 75:7-8)

This passage gives a marvelous illustration of the Old Testament metaphor of God's judgment as a cup being poured out. Isaiah also spoke of the "cup of God's wrath" and the "cup of his staggering" (Isa. 51:17, 22). Similarly Jeremiah 25:15 spoke of the "cup of the wine of wrath." Ezekiel called it a "cup of horror and desolation" (Ezek. 23:33).

The cup will be dispensed as one of judgment upon all the wicked of the earth. In absolute terms, that really means everyone in history, with one exception. History gives us one person who was not wicked at all—Jesus Christ. Yet Jesus willingly came with the express mission of taking up our cup of judgment. Jesus took that cup, and would drink it to the dregs. This was a cup of sins' consequences. Sin separates from God. Sin is a terminal condition that brings death. Sin brings the full judgment of God.

As Jesus took the cup, Jesus bore our sins and our judgment. It produced separation from the Father and death (Mark 15:34, 37). Jesus went to the cross drinking the cup to its dregs, fully suffering God's judgment. Before going, Jesus prayed, asking God to take away the cup from him (Mark 14:36). Some see in this a sudden reticence of Jesus to die. I have always thought of it a bit differently. We know that even though Jesus was fully God and fully man, Jesus set aside a measure of his God-ness in becoming human (Phil. 2:5-7). That only makes sense. No human brain could contain the mind of God! Even Jesus spoke of things God the Father knew that Jesus didn't (Matt. 24:36). So with that in mind, I wonder how much of the post-cross story Jesus knew. He certainly knew of the resurrection (Matt. 12:40). But in the midst of the experience, how and when God would remove the judgment, the separation and death, might not have been clear within his mind. Jesus would have to trust God to do what he must do to bring the mission to fruition.

So Jesus prayed for the cup of judgment to be taken away, but with a willing heart for everything necessary to affect our redemption. Jesus willingly and in faith, took isolation from the Father, took on death and the powers of darkness that rule the kingdom of sin, and did so to prepare a door for us to the Father's house (John 14:2-3). There is much cloaked in mystery, but of one thing we can be certain. There could be no greater gift of love prompted by a confidence in the Father than Jesus willing going to the cross. Our cup of judgment has been emptied. There is no more.

Thank you so much, Lord Jesus, for drinking the cup of judgment on my behalf. Amen.

❀ ❀ ❀

JULY 5

Make your vows to the LORD your God and perform them; let all around him bring gifts to him who is to be feared. (Ps. 76:11)

Have you ever made vows to God? Some people make vows to God when they are in trouble, "God, if you will fix *ABC*, then I will start going to church regularly." Sometimes the particular problem is linked to a certain sin, bringing forth a variation on the vow, "God, if you will rescue me from the consequences of this sin, then I promise I won't sin again!"

There may or may not be a place for such vows. I am not a particular fan of deal making with the Almighty, but this is a different type of vow referenced in this passage. This is the vow as a gift to God. It's not a tradeoff, giving God something in return for his divine rescue; it is something done out of love and respect for the Lord. These are good vows to make, and it is important to keep them.

A biblical example of these vows is the Nazirite vow found in Numbers 6. This vow was to abstain from alcohol (or eat grapes), and from getting a haircut. This vow was taken for a specified time, and at the conclusion of the vow, there is a commitment to offering certain sacrifices to the Lord (one for sin, one for peace, one as a burnt offering). While under the Nazirite vow, one was to refrain from intentional contact with the dead. These sacrifices could be increased if one so vows, in excess of what the normal Nazirite vow required.

Samson was designated a Nazirite from birth to death (Judg. 13:7). Samson was not to have his hair cut and was to abstain from all alcohol. Samson was specially set aside by God to save the Israelites from the hostile Philistines. Rather than walk in his vow, Samson visited vineyards, touched dead carcasses, and eventually had his hair cut (Judg. 14:5-9; 16:17-19). Things did not turn out well for Samson. His failure to takes his vows seriously coincided with a failure to walk with God seriously.

Paul and others in the New Testament church took Nazirite vows for a period. For a period of time, Paul took a Nazirite vow, and he also paid the sacrifices for other churchmen who had taken the vow (Acts 21:23-24). Many think that since Jesus said not to take an "oath" that we should not take vows to God (Matt. 5:33-37). A vow, however, is not the same as an oath (in English or in the New Testament in Greek). We don't swear by heaven or earth, but live by a "yes" or "no." We can, however, make a vow to God to fast for a meal, a day, etc., to not drink alcohol, to have study time, or a number of things. But if we do take such vows, the motive should be right, and the vow should be kept!

Lord, you give us so many incredible gifts, and it seems feeble to even think we might give you anything. Help us see where we might bless you with gifts, In Jesus, Amen!

JULY 6

I cry aloud to God, aloud to God, and he will hear me. (Ps. 77:1)

This is one of those passages that should make everyone want to read their psalms in Hebrew. It is not overly complicated, but it is beautifully crafted with a touching emphasis. We can get some of it by breaking down just a few Hebrew elements. First, we note two of the Hebrew words for speaking, one that denotes the voice, and gives the idea translated by the English Standard Version as "aloud" and a second that denotes "crying out" or "appealing." Also of note, the Hebrew uses a prefix that conveys motion to or toward something. Now with those elements, let's consider today's devotional passage. Because it often takes several English words to convey the Hebrew idea, I am grouping the English phrases to show each Hebrew word.

The psalmist says,

\my voice aloud/ \toward God/ \I cry out/

\my voice aloud/ \toward God/ \and he hears/ \toward me/.

These seven words read delicately together to contrast and explain a psalmist who is crying out vocally *to* God, and God is hearing *to* the one crying out loud.

Prayer is a two-way street. We cry aloud toward God. God listens toward us. The crying in this psalm can be so intense, as it is here, that it is actually out loud or vocal. This is no an aimless moaning. It isn't an empty wailing. It is an out loud, vocal appeal made directly to God, with the sound sent his way.

God responds with a serious personal listening that is directed. God's listening is not a general listening for anything that may be happening on planet earth. God doesn't simply overhear us because our wailing is so loud. God directs his hearing toward us, hearing our pleas and registering them in a personal way. He gives us personal attention.

We tend to be just self-centered enough to often lose track of this significance. Most of us would have trouble getting an audience with the president of the United States or another world leader. Often we have trouble on the phone getting an audience with the right person to hear our complaints! But the God of the universe gives us a personal audience and listens to our most personal concerns. We serve an amazing God!

Lord, thank you for listening to me. Thank you for hearing my voice. Thank you for caring for my concerns. I praise you as an amazing God, and am honored to know you as Father and friend. In the name of Jesus, Amen!

❧ ❧ ❧

JULY 7

In the day of my trouble I seek the Lord; in the night my hand is stretched out without wearying; my soul refuses to be comforted. When I remember God, I moan; when I meditate, my spirit faints. You hold my eyelids open; I am so troubled that I cannot speak. I consider the days of old, the years long ago. I said, "Let me remember my song in the night; let me meditate in my heart." (Ps. 77:2-6)

Troubles come in different forms and intensities. Some troubles are a nuisance, metaphorical flies that need a good swatting. Occasionally, however, we come across troubles that are severe. These can include significant health problems, events that threaten to rend the fabric of families, economic problems with no apparent solution, issues at work or school that eat away at our emotions, the tragedy of death that leaves a hole that will never be filled, and more. These are problems like the psalmist faced, ones so significant that the writer couldn't sleep or speak. The psalmist was so distraught that even trying to pray was difficult, as the mind wondered and the "spirit" was faint.

Rest assured, even if we are not experiencing such trouble today, it will come. It does for everyone. What can one do in such a time? Unable to do much more, the psalmist decided to put the brain to work, thinking about what God had done before. The psalmist sought to remember God's deeds, meditating on them, turning them over and over.

When I think of what God has done, my thoughts fall into two groups: ways he worked faithfully in my life, and ways he worked in history. In my life, I have found events some might write off to "luck," but I know better, God has answered my prayers and brought me deliverance. He hasn't always rescued me immediately from my crises, but he has never failed to walk through it with me, teaching me and giving me strength. I have always been a better person on the other side of the troubles. I feel sorry for people who live without regard to God, for when their problems come, they are robbed of experiences that give them great confidence and strength.

Beyond me personally, the hand of God in history is one of rescue in the face of disaster. The life of Christ, the incarnate God, is the supreme example. In the midst of scorn and abuse, abandonment from people and divinity, Jesus took on the burden of humanity's sin, and died. Of course, we know the end of that story, it was good news for us, and resulted in Jesus meeting his personal goal, that of redeeming his people. This too was the hand of God in the midst of difficulty. Jesus was not spared intense troubles, nor was he abandoned by God. This speaks to me.

Lord, be with me in life's troubles, please. May I seek you in the small ones as well as the cataclysmic ones. Build my memories and trust for that day, please. In Jesus, Amen!

❧ ❧ ❧

JULY 8

Your way, O God, is holy. What god is great like our God? You are the God who works wonders; you have made known your might among the peoples. You with your arm redeemed your people. (Ps. 77:13-15)

"Holy" is a word we use a lot in religion. It is found in Scripture, in songs, and in prayer. The Hebrew word translated "holy" is *qadosh*. It conveys the idea of something that is not ordinary, something that is singled out, commanding respect and generally awe-inspiring. Old Testament priests were to be "holy" (Lev. 21:8). They were not ordinary Israelites, but were separated out and consecrated to God. They were to live in a way that commanded respect, ministering for the Lord who made them priests. The place in the tabernacle and temple where only the high priest could enter, and he only once a year, was called the "holy of holies" or the "most holy" place. It was segregated out from ordinary places of ordinary people, and even the ordinary places of holy priests! On another scale, the Israelites themselves were called to be "holy," because they were set out from among all peoples by a holy God to be special among the nations, uniquely entrusted with Scripture and the lineage of the Messiah (Rom. 3:2; Gal. 3:7-8).

So armed with a background of the word holy, we come to today's devotional passage. God's *way* is "holy." What does it mean that our Lord's *way* is holy? This references not only the paths God walks (metaphorically speaking), but also the manners or ways of God.

We can safely say that God does not do ordinary things in ordinary ways. God is no mundane God. We worship the God of uniqueness. Our God is one who does the stunning. Now we may not see it. The deeds of God may be hidden. Or they may be wide open, visible to the world. Either way, no one is as great as our God; no one works his wonders.

None of the gods invented by people care for all of humanity as does the Lord God. None of those gods would sacrifice themselves to save the weak and needy as well as the strong and mighty. The Roman and Greek gods might have become enamored with one or two humans and gone to great lengths for a relationship, but all people equally? No one! Who could imagine a God that would care for us as the Father does?

If we believe this, we will have no trouble choosing to follow the ways of God as he has revealed them to us. The world may tell us some things are okay, or even good, but if God has instructed us otherwise, we can readily choose the Lord's ways. We would know they are best for us, even if they aren't the ways of the world. God's ways, after all, are holy!

Lord teach me your holy ways that I might walk in them through Jesus, my Lord. Amen!

JULY 9

Give ear, O my people, to my teaching; incline your ears to the words of my mouth! I will open my mouth in a parable; I will utter dark sayings from of old, things that we have heard and known, that our fathers have told us. We will not hide them from their children, but tell to the coming generation the glorious deeds of the LORD, and his might, and the wonders that he has done. (Ps. 78:1-4)

Every school-age person knows about learning. We start learning early and continue through high school, many through college, and some through graduate school. Does the learning end there? Hope fully not! We should be learning all the time, and not just reading, writing, and arithmetic. The psalmist writes on the importance of our listening and learning about the Lord and his works, and then passing that knowledge on to the coming generations. We can learn of the works of the Lord through Scripture as well as through the lives of the faithful. Both have merit, and both are important. But both can be ignored, and such ignorance is damaging.

This passage makes me want to be both a good student and a good teacher. I want to be a good student because I want to learn of God. I want to know him better and have a greater depth of understanding. That will enable me to more readily see his hand at work, more quickly and precisely determine his will, more readily express to him my gratitude and praise, and more successfully teach of him to those wanting to learn.

The role of teacher is not one that some of us might have, in a real sense it is a responsibility of everyone. Parents are to teach their children about the Lord. We should readily teach those in our circles of influence about who God is and what God has done. If we fail to teach, then it is the equivalent of hiding the works of God, and we would certainly never want to be guilty of that.

Some types of knowledge are more important than others. The Gospel of John quotes Jesus in prayer to the Father about Jesus' followers, saying, "This is eternal life, that they know you the only true God, and Jesus Christ whom you have sent" (John 17:3). I want to teach knowledge of God and Jesus to my family and friends, not hide it. Who would want to hide the truth of eternal life? Of course, to teach it, I must know it. I must first learn it. The passage tells me that if I am going to know it, I will need to listen. I need to find the sources that teach of such things and "give ear." Listening, learning, and teaching are important goals for me.

Lord, may I seek out sources of insight into you, your work, and your ways. May they illuminate my mind, and may I teach my children, grandchildren, and any others who would listen. In the name of Jesus my Savior, Amen!

JULY 10

Blessed is he whose help is the God of Jacob . . . who keeps faith forever; who executes justice for the oppressed, who gives food to the hungry. The LORD sets the prisoners free; the LORD opens the eyes of the blind. The LORD lifts up those who are bowed down; the LORD loves the righteous. The LORD watches over the sojourners; he upholds the widow and the fatherless, but the way of the wicked he brings to ruin. (Ps. 146:5-9)

In 1965 the Beatles hit the radio waves with the song "Help!" The song begins, "Help! I need somebody. Help! Not just anybody. Help! You know I need someone. Help!!!" I loved the song as a boy, but it wasn't until much later in life that I realized the truth of the lyrics. Perhaps the truth to me exceeded the mindset of Lennon and McCartney when they wrote it. I need help beyond that which a human can give me. Fortunately, there is one who wants to help.

Passages like today's psalm confirm for me that God chooses to help his people. God's role in our lives is not to take from us, but to give to us. For those who are in need of good things, he gives good things. To those who are pursuing evil things, he brings their pursuits to a dead end. I want to find myself, literally or poetically, among those in need of God's help, looking to him to satisfy those needs.

"*To the oppressed, he gives freedom. The LORD sets the prisoners free.*" I do find myself oppressed, not often by the world, but certainly by the circumstances of the world. I find that life easily becomes a treadmill that I run. God can deliver me from the treadmill. I may still do many of the same things, but not because I am enslaved or bound to do those things. I do them now with purpose. I do them for my Lord and his kingdom. I am not running a treadmill going nowhere, I am running to the endpoint designated by my God!

"*The LORD opens the eyes of the blind.*" Physically, my eyes work fine, at least as long as I wear my glasses. But I walk in a world of deception. The world can appear one way, with its charms and deceits, when reality lies under the surface. God shows reality. He opens my eyes to see his hand at work and the truth of this life.

"*The LORD lifts up those who are bowed down.*" Life can bend us down. We can also walk with humility, bent down on our own. God lifts those bent from life. God graces the humble. I need not be proud and boastful. I need to humbly seek to serve my Lord. Like the rest of the passage encourages, we are called to be righteous and to lean on God regardless of life's circumstances. He will be our provider. He helps the helpless.

Lord, I am helpless without you. I cannot ever be who or what I need to be, without you. Help me Lord Jesus. I pray in your name, Amen!

❧ ❧ ❧

JULY 11

In the sight of their fathers he performed wonders in the land of Egypt, in the fields of Zoan. He divided the sea and let them pass through it, and made the waters stand like a heap. In the daytime he led them with a cloud, and all the night with a fiery light. . . . Yet they sinned still more against him, rebelling against the Most High in the desert. . . . In spite of all this, they still sinned; despite his wonders, they did not believe. So he made their days vanish like a breath, and their years in terror. When he killed them, they sought him; they repented and sought God earnestly. They remembered that God was their rock, the Most High God their redeemer. (Ps. 78:12-14, 17, 32-35)

The lesson from the story of God with the Israelites in the wilderness after leading them from Egypt is instructive. God performed incredible miracles, things most people would beg for a chance to see. The reaction of the people was positive at first, but soon turned to grumbling, which in turn became disbelief.

They people grumbled because as they got from God, they wanted more. They were not satisfied to see miracles that would still be spoken of over 3,000 years later; they expected God to be their "On-the-Spot Magic Show." They knew that God could provide; he did so with the manna, with birds, and with water from the rock. That's what they came to expect. And when God wasn't treating them as one might expect from a waiter at a five-star restaurant, they grumbled. This led to rebellion and disbelief. After all, if there was a God worth worshipping, wouldn't he be doing more spectacular miracles? God's reaction, and the natural effect of sin in this world, was death, despair, and trouble on the unthankful grumblers. The interesting thing is that *only then* did the people turn to God. Times of trouble brought forth faith, when God's blessings and miracles didn't.

This gives me great pause. I would love a miracle working God at my beck and call. I would love to see immediate healing of sickness, turning two fish into thousands, and bringing back life to those who have died. Wouldn't that inspire faith? Or would it? God didn't make this a Harry Potter world, subject to spells that defy the laws of nature. Can God eclipse those laws? Certainly! But more often he works through them. That is the way of things. I should be able to see God's hand in nature, see how he weaves together the fabric of this order and produces the tapestry of blessings in my life. I should be able to give him glory for such providential care. I do *not* want to seek God only when times are difficult. I want to honor him 24/7, 365 days a year, until my life is over.

Lord, help me to seek you when the sun is out and life is bright. Instill in me appreciation for you in the common things of life, even as you have blessed me with the greatest miracle of life in Jesus. Amen!

❧ ❧ ❧

JULY 12

Their heart was not steadfast toward him; they were not faithful to his covenant. Yet he, being compassionate, atoned for their iniquity and did not destroy them; he restrained his anger often and did not stir up all his wrath. He remembered that they were but flesh, a wind that passes and comes not again. (Ps. 78:37-39)

As a twelve-year-old boy, I asked the Lord Jesus to be my God, to forgive me of my sins, and to live within me, teaching me, guiding me, and using me for his glory. It was a life-changing experience that I remember forty-five years later.

During that forty-five years, I have lived in fellowship with God, but have also been unfaithful to him. I have learned that sin can be tricky and sticky. The trickiness of sin is the way it can snare you. It has an allure that can draw you closer and closer until you find yourself in it up to your neck. It is sticky because as you get caught in its web, it doesn't let you go easily. God would be fully in his rights to bring damnation upon me, if not eternally, certainly in this life, because of my unfaithfulness, but thankfully, that is not our God.

Our God is a merciful and forgiving God. He seeks redemption, restoration, and a healthy relationship with us. Even when we are unfaithful, if there is any road for our redemption, God will find it and use it. The psalmist says God "*he restrained his anger often and did not stir up all his wrath.*" That doesn't mean that sin doesn't have earthly consequences. It does. God's "wrath" is a concept that aligns with the pain, misery, and sometimes horrific consequences of sin. But God doesn't stir up *all* his wrath. Thankfully his mercy shines through. God acts, knowing we are human. He knows we are feeble. He knows we are prone to sin. Does this make our sin okay? Can we let down our guard and dabble with sin? Heavens no. Sin is serious business. Its consequences still remain serious.

I can confidently say that after fifty-seven years on earth, there is not one sin I have committed where I am glad I did it. I see the effects of sin clearly, and I am certain that no sin is a good thing. No sin is "worth" is. It would be a marvelous thing if life had a "sin eraser" where one could go back and erase past sins so they never happened. God has erased those sins from eternal consequences, but they still bear fruit in this life. I am thankful God works in spite of my iniquity. He works in my life with the tricky and sticky sin. I am thankful for his steadfast love and mercy.

Lord, forgive me my sins. Please. Give me strength to live holy before you, in Jesus, Amen.

❀ ❀ ❀

JULY 13

O God, the nations have come into your inheritance; they have defiled your holy temple; they have laid Jerusalem in ruins. (Ps. 79:1)

Have you ever seen someone with magnificent promise, dash it to pieces by poor choices and a disregard for God? It happens every day, as it has for ages gone by.

On a larger than human scale, this passage invites us to consider the city of Jerusalem, a city of promise. God accepted the temple Solomon built as the place for sacrifice and honoring his name. Jerusalem was called the City of God, and much it was called to be. It could and should have been a light set on a hillside. It could and should have been a beacon to the nations. It could and should have shown forth the truth of the Lord God if Israel for the world to see. But such was not the case.

That city, with that potential, soaked up God's blessings and ultimately turned its back on God, instead chasing after other gods. Rather than upholding God's law, the city persecuted the downtrodden and took advantage of the weak. The city didn't demonstrate God's justice, but put justice up for sale, going to the rich at the cost of the poor. God sent warnings to the city. Prophets came and said that the city would not garner God's blessings and protection if it didn't live right. But the people laughed at the prophets and martyred them. The city, after all, knew better than the old superstitions of those religious "prophets." So God brought judgment. God brought the city not just to its knees but into ruins. The city was destroyed and the survivors taken to a foreign land, or dispersed into the surrounding countries.

This story of the city is not too different from what I've seen with some obstinate or misinformed people. I have seen some with magnificent promise, blessed by God with skills, opportunities, sharp minds, education, resources, fame, and more—people with a voice that could be heard, and instead of speaking for God, they turned their backs. Some "learned" God was just an old superstition. Others found other things more captivating than God. Still others simply ignored him, getting so caught up in his blessings and gifts, they ignored the giver.

Those people, with all their potential and all their chances to change the world for the better, over and over are brought to ruin, albeit in different ways. Their potential is spent on things of little to no merit. Their opportunities are squandered for personal gain. Their focus turned to debauchery rather than building.

I don't want to be that way.

Lord, make me an instrument of yours, doing your will with the opportunities you've given me. Help me keep my focus and purpose, finishing this life faithfully in Jesus. Amen!

❧ ❧ ❧

JULY 14

Do not remember against us our former iniquities; let your compassion come speedily to meet us, for we are brought very low. Help us, O God of our salvation, for the glory of your name; deliver us, and atone for our sins, for your name's sake! (Ps. 79:8-9)

The Old Testament realized the predicament of humanity. We are sinners by nature and practice. Try as we might, we can't stop sinning. That sinning is not simply a crime with which society has to deal, sin is a transgression against a holy God. It is more than serious.

The New Testament clearly teaches that God forgives sin through the death of Christ. As Jesus himself said, "No one comes to the Father except through me" (John 14:6). This is the way God has forgiven all sin, that of the child and the adult, that of people who lived before Jesus and those who lived afterwards. Everyone who is forgiven has their forgiveness rooted in the atoning death of Jesus.

Paul emphasizes this point in Romans explaining that the death of Christ shows God's faithfulness because of promises like that found in this psalm. As Paul put it, "All have sinned and fall short of the glory of God, and are justified by his grace as a gift, through the redemption that is in Christ Jesus, whom God put forward as a propitiation by his blood, to be received by faith. This was to show God's righteousness, because in his divine forbearance he had passed over former sins" (Rom. 3:23-25).

The psalmist in this passage prays for God to forgive sins, seeking God's compassion. God's atonement is needed, and asked for "for your name's sake." The psalmist knows that it will take God's righteousness based on God's character ("name") to bring forgiveness. God would never be able to forgive based on our name or character. How can the character of a sinner be used to justify forgiving a sinner? That is a dog chasing its own tail for sure.

But in Jesus, forgiveness is a different story. Now based on God's character, a river of righteousness flows forward, washing away sins of all who come into contact with it. This is the forgiving God of mercy. He never loses his justice, but that justice and mercy meet at the cross. There we find a righteous forgiveness. There we find deliverance from the death of sin. There we find peace. Let's meet at the cross and stand amazed, enveloped by the grace of our God of salvation.

Help us, O God of our salvation. For the glory of your reputation, deliver us. We repent of our sins, and seek your mercy. We plead the death of Christ, and claim it as our atonement, and as we stand by grace forgiven, we give you praise and thanks in Jesus, Amen.

※ ※ ※

JULY 15

Give ear, O Shepherd of Israel, you who lead Joseph like a flock. You who are enthroned upon the cherubim, shine forth. Before Ephraim and Benjamin and Manasseh, stir up your might and come to save us! (Ps. 80:1-2)

No longer living in a culture with shepherds and sheep runs the risk of us losing some terrific metaphors in the Bible. Over and over we read of God as shepherd and his people as sheep. This should be a great solace to believers, especially as we see what kind of shepherd God is.

Shepherds were to ensure the safety of their flocks. Shepherds found adequate food and water. Unlike goats, which generally can find the best feeding grounds, sheep need to be led to their food. Sheep need water once a day, and again, must be led to the water. Early on, sheep learn the voice of their shepherd and can respond to their call. Societies that still keep sheep in this way can intermingle two flocks, and the sheep of one will separate out, discerning their master's voice. It is not surprising that the master of sheep became a metaphor for a spiritual overseer or pastor.

This passage speaks of God as Shepherd leading his flock, lighting the way, and saving the sheep as necessary. Micah 5:2 prophesied that from Bethlehem would come God's shepherd for the sheep. Jesus fulfilled this prophecy (Matt. 2:6), and took this metaphor and expounded upon it, as he related it to his role before God for the followers that he labeled his flock. Jesus felt the compassion and concern of a shepherd (Mark 6:34). Jesus explained he was a good shepherd willing to lay down his life for the safety and well-being of his sheep (John 10:11). This was because the sheep, we followers of Christ, actually belonged to the shepherd. He was no mere hired hand (John 10:12). Similarly, Jesus as a good shepherd is known by his sheep, just as he knows us. We hear his voice and follow his lead (John 10:14). Not surprisingly, in the early Christian sermon in our New Testaments as the book of Hebrews, we read of Jesus as "the great shepherd of the sheep" (Heb. 13:20). In the vision of Revelation, we have a final prophecy of Jesus as shepherd who will guide us "to springs of living water" as God wipes away every tear (Rev. 7:17).

This is our God and shepherd. God the shepherd cares, nurtures, feeds, protects, and secures us in Jesus, the Great Shepherd. This should surprise no one, since God and Jesus are one. Who wouldn't want to be a sheep under God's protection and care?

Lord, Shepherd of believers in Christ, thank you for your love, care, feeding, and protection. Thank you for knowing us by name, watching us every moment of every day, and securing us eternally in your presence. Through our Great Shepherd we pray, Amen!

JULY 16

O LORD God of hosts, how long will you be angry with your people's prayers? You have fed them with the bread of tears and given them tears to drink in full measure. You make us an object of contention for our neighbors, and our enemies laugh among themselves. Restore us, O God of hosts; let your face shine, that we may be saved! (Ps. 80:4-7)

Sometimes songs are born out of great difficulty. This is no less true for many of the songs to the Lord that are in our Scriptures, that educate us, help us express our human concerns and fears, and guide us in our prayers and praise. Here is one of those songs.

We don't know the details that brought this song forth, but the circumstance must have been dire. The psalmist is experiencing tribulations that have driven the writer to tears. This must have been a matter of public disgrace, as if the people had relied upon God, only to have that reliance dashed. The cynics close to the situation saw and laughed, sensing the disgrace and rubbing it in.

I suspect most everyone can relate to circumstances and times that are troublesome where we turn to God and express our faith in him. We trust him, and we live, relying on his to rescue us, only to find ourselves defeated and in even greater trouble. We wonder, "Where is God? Is he there? Is he angry? Is this something I did wrong? Is this righteous punishment? If not, why do bad things happen to good people? What kind of God would let this go on?"

Some of those questions are readily answered; some are not. We can answer, "Where is God? Is he there?" Yes! He is here! He is not an absent God, regardless of how we might feel. Hopefully, we can also answer, "Is this something I did wrong? Is it righteous punishment?" We must always look honestly at whether or not we have sinned. Sometimes we deceive ourselves and don't readily see our sin, but when we have sinned, we need to confess the sin and try to make it right. The answer to, "If this isn't a result of sin, then why do bad things happen to good people?" is a bit more difficult. We can say, "They do." But *why* they do is often beyond our reach. We know that God is going to make time turn into eternity in a way consistent with prophecy. He will bring his sheep home, and will execute justice. How he gets there, sometimes means that good people have to endure bad things. Sometimes those bad things come from the evil deeds of others. Sometimes not. Finally, we can answer, "What kind of God would let this go on?" with "A kind and loving God who will walk with us in suffering, hold us up, and in the best timing redeem us and the situation." This is our God to whom we pray:

Restore us, O God of hosts; let your face shine, that we may be saved in Jesus. Amen.

❧ ❧ ❧

JULY 17

Sing aloud to God our strength; shout for joy to the God of Jacob! Raise a song; sound the
tambourine, the sweet lyre with the harp. Blow the trumpet at the new moon, at the full
moon, on our feast day. (Ps. 81:1-3)

If one were to ask about the commands in the Bible, many would
think, "Ugh, those are a bunch of difficult things people have to do." Or if
one was thinking about the Old Testament law, one might think, "Those
were a bunch of obscure rules that really make no sense." Some might even
think, "Commands are God's limits on what we can do, that keep us in line,
but also keep us from the fun of the world." Billy Joel had this concept in
his song "Only the Good Die Young" singing, "I'd rather laugh with the
sinners than cry with the saints. The sinners are much more fun." But if
we think this way, we are wrong!

Today's passage is a fun command! God is telling his people to have
a party! This is not an aimless party to occupy the mind while the world
is forgotten. It is a party with a purpose that enriches the participant. It is
a party of music, celebration, and feasting. We celebrate God, shouting for
joy, singing loudly with full band accompaniment. God has commanded a
celebration among his people!

What is there to celebrate? The mighty works of God! Sit and make a
list. What has God done worthy of celebrating? Can you rattle some off? If
you are having trouble, think of biblical things, the creation of nature, the
creation of people in relationship with God, the incarnation of Jesus, the
miracles related in Scripture, the resurrection of our Lord and Savior, the
known second coming and final redemption. Lots of things in the Bible are
worthy of celebrating God!

In our lives, it is no less so. As I write, I cannot see where a reader's
life is at this instant. But for many, they can find cause to celebrate in their
family. I have five children and, at the time of writing, one granddaughter.
That is great cause for celebration. We can celebrate the godly marriages of
our family and friends. Jesus celebrated marriage, performing his first public miracle at one (John 2:1-11). We celebrate good jobs, good schools, good
friends, and more. The key to celebrating any good thing is recognizing that
all good things come from God (Jas. 1:17). Our celebrations should not be
the *things*, but should be the God behind the things!

Scripture teaches there is a time to laugh and dance (Eccl. 3:4). God
commands it, so let's do it! Let's celebrate our God!

Lord, you are worthy of our best parties. You deserve songs of joy and all the celebra-
tion we can muster. We love you and shout in your honor! Celebrating in our Jesus, Amen!

❧ ❧ ❧

JULY 18

My people did not listen to my voice; Israel would not submit to me. So I gave them over to their stubborn hearts, to follow their own counsels. Oh, that my people would listen to me, that Israel would walk in my ways! I would soon subdue their enemies and turn my hand against their foes. (Ps. 81:11-14)

Isn't this an amazing passage? God declares in this psalm that there are people who deny him, who deny his existence, who deny his care; people who deny God's instructions, deliberately choosing their own path instead. Then when things go bad, some of these people will shake their fist to the skies saying, "How could a good God let this happen?" Some even use this as their justification for saying there is no God, because, according to their reasoning, if there were a God, he wouldn't allow such problems.

God says that if people choose not to be in submission to him, but instead choose to go their own way, then he lets them go their own way! It reminds me of the old saying, "Be careful what you ask for, you might get it!" When we disregard God, he is fully right in disregarding us. This is not some passive-aggressive behavior of God where he is pouting over being snubbed so he responds in kind. It is something altogether different.

This is like an umbrella that God extends in protection over those who walk with him in his way. If people choose not to walk with God, they step out of his umbrella of protection and are left to handle the elements on their own. They make that choice in spite of God's warnings to the contrary. God does not chain people to him such that they can't make choices of how and where to walk. People can choose to be in step with God or to go it alone. Of course it isn't always easy walking with God. But we always have his strength and direction to teach us and protect us along the way.

Daily, we have that precise choice. We choose to follow God or not. Paul warned the Galatians about this, saying, "Do not be deceived: God is not mocked, for whatever one sows, that will he also reap. For the one who sows to his own flesh will from the flesh reap corruption, but the one who sows to the Spirit will from the Spirit reap eternal life. And let us not grow weary of doing good, for in due season we will reap, if we do not give up" (Gal. 6:7-9).

Happily, if we walk away from God, and he delivers us over to our stubborn hearts, we can also rest assured that God is doing so to draw us back to him, or to bring us under the umbrella in our analogy. This is an interesting life!

Lord, thank you for your compelling love. Thank you for the many ways you reinforce our learning and growing. I pray I will have a soft heart to you, learning things the easy way! In Jesus, Amen!

❧ ❧ ❧

JULY 19

God has taken his place in the divine council; in the midst of the gods he holds judgment: "How long will you judge unjustly and show partiality to the wicked? Give justice to the weak and the fatherless; maintain the right of the afflicted and the destitute. Rescue the weak and the needy; deliver them from the hand of the wicked." (Ps. 82:1-4)

This passage has an important message that is often lost because of the clumsy way our translators have to put it into English. At first glance, it seems as if this is a polytheistic (i.e., belief in more than one god) passage, as if there is some council of gods in the heavens and capital "G" God hands down wrath.

Instead, we should see this as the "divine council" being the ruling congregation of Israel. These are the people who we would consider the powerful community leaders like we read of in Numbers 27:16-17 and 31:26. They are the "gods" referenced above. They were to bear God's image to the people. They were to be God's voice, in effect, little "g" gods.

Now see the punch of this passage. The divine God comes into the council of these Israelite leaders who were to be his appointed judges and leaders for the people, and the divine God wants to know why the leaders were judging unjustly in God's name. He quizzes them on why they would show partiality to the wicked. He upbraids them and calls them to account. He instructs them to give justice to the weak and fatherless. To treat fairly the afflicted and destitute. He instructs them to come to the aid of those who are weak and needy. He wants them to intervene and deliver those in the grasp of the powerful.

I take this passage to heart. It is not lost on the believer in Christ that we are the image of Christ in this world. We are his hands and feet. We are his body bringing his love and message to a lost world. We are the city on a hill shining his light into a dark world. We are the salt of the earth carrying his power and flavor into a culture in desperate need. We are the council of "gods" not in the sense that we are divine, but in the sense that we reflect him. We are to care as he cares, love as he loves, give as he gives.

So this passage is important. I need to examine my life in light of this warning and instruction. I better not show favoritism to the popular, powerful, rich, and elite. I better show value, love, and respect, readily bringing aid, and helping those who need it. May God see me treating everyone equally, as I go out of my way to rescue the needy.

Lord, thank you for showing your heart to me in Jesus. Thank you for the chance to reflect your heart in this fallen world. May I do so diligently and with care. In Jesus, Amen.

❧ ❧ ❧

JULY 20

O God, do not keep silence; do not hold your peace or be still, O God! For behold, your enemies make an uproar. . . . They lay crafty plans against your people. . . . They say, "Come, let us wipe them out as a nation; let the name of Israel be remembered no more!" For they conspire with one accord . . . the tents of Edom and the Ishmaelites, Moab and the Hagrites, Gebal and Ammon and Amalek, Philistia with the inhabitants of Tyre; Asshur also has joined them. . . . (Ps. 83:1-8)

Over and over we read in Scripture that God made an everlasting covenant with Abraham and his descendants (e.g., Gen. 17:7). Other peoples come and go, but there will always be identifiable descendants of Abraham. This is amazing to think about. So amazing that for many, it is evidence supporting the truth of the God of the Bible.

Many people have tried to destroy the Israelites, yet we have millions of Jews still alive today. As this psalm recounts, the Edomites, Ishmaelites, Moabites, Hagrites, Gebalites, Ammonites, Amalekites, Philistines, and more tried to wipe out all of the descendants of Abraham. We know they were not successful, any more than Hitler or more modern efforts have been. Also unsuccessful were the efforts of those between the time of the psalm and more modern history like the Babylonians, Persians, Seleucids, and others who sought to assimilate the Jews.

Even if there weren't such deliberate attempts to destroy the nation of Israel, consider simply the ravages of time. Those nations of today's passage are gone, even though they sought to destroy Israel. Have you met a Gebalite or Hagrite lately? Of course not.

God is good and faithful to his promises. We see that in the presence of the Jews today, and we see it personally in our lives. Preservation of Abraham's offspring was not the only promise our faithful God has made. He has made many to you and me. Consider his promise about your sin—it won't last! "He has granted to us his precious and very great promises, so that through them you may become partakers of the divine nature, having escaped from the corruption that is in the world because of sinful desire" (2 Pet. 1:4). Are you worried? God promises peace. "Peace I leave with you; my peace I give to you. Not as the world gives do I give to you. Let not your hearts be troubled, neither let them be afraid" (John 14:27). Are you in need? "My God will supply every need of yours according to his riches in glory in Christ Jesus" (Phil. 4:19). Consider the Jews, and know God will not fail to keep his word.

Lord, I find your faithful love amazing. It is hard to fathom that a people you blessed with a promise four thousand years ago still live in that promise. I smile living in the promise of Jesus, through whom I pray, Amen!

❧ ❧ ❧

JULY 21

How lovely is your dwelling place, O LORD of hosts! My soul longs, yes, faints for the courts of the LORD; my heart and flesh sing for joy to the living God. Even the sparrow finds a home, and the swallow a nest for herself, where she may lay her young, at your altars, O LORD of hosts, my King and my God. Blessed are those who dwell in your house, ever singing your praise! (Ps. 84:1-4)

This is one of my favorite psalms out of all one hundred and fifty. It gives me joy and peace. It expresses my deepest desires and calls me to a place of worship. It gives me insight into God's love for us as it inspires my own love and respect for him. This psalm is engraved in my heart and worthy of every one of us memorizing.

The psalmist knew of the dwelling place of God as the temple, and writes that way. But Israel knew, as we know today, that the temple was a symbol of God's dwelling. The God of Israel never lived in a man-made building. Even as Solomon called the temple the dwelling place of God, he proclaimed it was a metaphor, "But will God indeed dwell on the earth? Behold, heaven and the highest heaven cannot contain you; how much less this house that I have built" (1 Kgs. 8:27). The dwelling of God is his presence. That is what my soul longs for, no faints for—the presence of God.

God's presence is frightening in a way, as Isaiah experienced (Isa. 6), but it is also a place of love, healing, comfort, and peace. We know that the presence of God has the Lord Jesus seated at his right hand (Eph. 1:20). Jesus is no less the fearsome God, but he also went to great lengths to express his friendship to me. He wept when his friends were hurting (John 11:33-35). He fed the hungry, ministered to the sinner, spent time with little children, confronted and controlled the demons, blessed the needy, healed the sick, honored family, taught and modeled love, and so much more. This demonstration of God Almighty's love for me is my comfort. I want to be in the presence of my God, more than any place on earth.

Looking at the temple, the writer saw a nest of small birds, and noted how even those were at home in the presence of God. The sparrows would have their children and rear their children at God's feet. I want to do the same. What a great blessing to be with my family in God's presence, to worship and proclaim the great and mighty God, my Father and Friend!

Lord, draw me into your presence. Let me seize every opportunity to come into your presence in worship and praise. Just to have the joy of being before you transforms me and puts me at peace. You offer me insight, encouragement, strength, and direction as I gaze at your beauty. Thank you, Lord Jesus for making it all possible. Amen!

❧ ❧ ❧

Blessed are those whose strength is in you, in whose heart are the highways to Zion. As they go through the Valley of Baca they make it a place of springs; the early rain also covers it with pools. They go from strength to strength; each one appears before God in Zion. (Ps. 84:5-7)

Psalm 84 expresses the overwhelming joy of the writer at being in the midst of God's dwelling. Speaking of the temple, the psalmist writes that he "longs, yes faints" for the temple courtyards. It was an opportunity to sing and worship God. That singing and worship become "highways to Zion" in the heart.

Those highways, those times of worship, bring forth not only praise to God, but blessings to the worshipper. Worshippers find strength in God. "*As they go through the Valley of Baca they make it a place of springs.*"

We miss some of the significance of that in the English. In Hebrew, *baca* (בכא) references "balsam trees," and referred to some Holy Land location now unknown. But as you say it, it sounds like the Hebrew word for weeping or wailing (*bacah* -בכה). This is the point of the psalmist. Being in the dwelling of God takes the weeping moments of life and makes them nourishing springs for growth. This is the transformational power of communing with God.

As we spend time in God's presence, in worship and praise, we see changes. The change isn't to the circumstances of life, but to how we live in those circumstances. I have seen this firsthand. Struggling with school, relationships, parenting, work, friendships, economics, and so much more, I have come into God's presence in praise and been changed. I have been blessed in ways that give me joy in the journey. God gives me strength to endure. He gives insight to live, and faith to do so with rejoicing.

As the psalmist explained, walking the roads to Zion, moving into praise before God, strips away the weak moments in my life, converting them into nourishing moments, and making me stronger. The answers to life are found in God and his presence. Why would I want to go anywhere else?

So in this passage, I find the reasons to get up and go to church on sleepy mornings. I find the reason to enter into worship when my mind wanders. I find the time for prayer when time seems scarce. I find the songs of worship on my playlist and I make them songs of my heart. Praise the God who turns tears into nourishing springs.

Lord, I love being with you. I need you. Every day. In Jesus I pray, Amen.

❧ ❧ ❧

JULY 23

O LORD God of hosts, hear my prayer; give ear, O God of Jacob! Behold our shield, O God; look on the face of your anointed! For a day in your courts is better than a thousand elsewhere I would rather be a doorkeeper in the house of my God than dwell in the tents of wickedness. For the LORD God is a sun and shield; the LORD bestows favor and honor. No good thing does he withhold from those who walk uprightly. O LORD of hosts, blessed is the one who trusts in you! (Ps. 84:8-12)

The psalmist would rather be a doorkeeper at the temple than live in the most luxurious dwellings of the wicked, and for good reason: God bestows favor and honor; he withholds no good thing from his followers who walk uprightly. Who wouldn't want to be constantly in the presence of such a God? This psalm has ministered to me during the rougher times of life. It is a psalm that has compelled me to worship and seek God.

I wonder how Paul might have considered the psalm in light of his arrest in the courts of God (Acts 21:26ff.). Paul awoke one morning and went to the temple, to God's "courts." This was the "blessed place" where even a sparrow found a home. The psalmist said, "better is one day" in the temple courts "than a thousand elsewhere." Yet, this turned into one of the more difficult days of Paul's life in Jerusalem. Jewish enemies in the temple accosted Paul. They dragged him from the temple and began to kill him when a Roman tribune intervened. The tribune had Paul bound in chains, but gave Paul the chance to make a speech to the Jewish crowd. That turned into a riot with the crowd chucking dirt and stones at Paul. The tribune then ordered Paul to be tortured by flogging, a most horrific and often lethal torture, which Paul avoided only by invoking his rights as a Roman citizen.

This could not have been the day Paul had hoped for when he went into the lovely courts of God, yet the real beauty of Psalm 84 is not the beauty of the courts. It was not court architecture or the GPS location that made the courts so wonderful. It was the presence of God. The worship of the God of Hosts is what turns tears to springs. Being in the presence of Almighty God is the blessing. So, while Paul ended his wretched day in captivity, he ended it strong because the Lord stood by Paul that night in the Roman barracks. "The following night the Lord stood by him and said, 'Take courage, for as you have testified to the facts about me in Jerusalem, so you must testify also in Rome' " (Acts 23:11).

With the presence of God, Paul was ready for the next day.

Lord, it is better to be in your presence, especially when my days are upended and times are desperate. Thank you for giving courage, hope, and strength. In Jesus' name, Amen.

❧ ❧ ❧

JULY 24

I wait for the LORD, my soul waits, and in his word I hope; my soul waits for the Lord more than watchmen for the morning, more than watchmen for the morning. O Israel, hope in the LORD! For with the LORD there is steadfast love, and with him is plentiful redemption. (Ps. 130:5-7)

I am not good at waiting. It is hard for me to be a patient driver, especially if the car in front of me isn't at least going the speed limit. I like fast food because it's immediate. Even in a normal restaurant, I am generally ready to order the moment I sit down. Waiting is hard.

But, waiting is a virtue! Paul gives "patience" on his list of the fruit of the spirit (Gal. 5:22). Patience is a trait of God (Rom. 9:22), was an apostolic practice (2 Cor. 12:12), and should be a pursuit of the believer (Col. 1:11).

I am eight years older than my younger sister. That made me old enough to adore her from her earliest days. There was not much I wouldn't do for her as she grew up. I took the big brother role seriously. However, when I was in high school and she in elementary school, she took to pestering me. It got to be rather frustrating. In my quiet time, I realized that this might be God teaching me patience, a virtue that doesn't come readily to me. Every time my sister pestered me, I tried to thank God for the chance to grow in patience. Perhaps because my sister quickly grew out of that stage, and as I referenced at the start of this devotional, I failed to get my full dose of patience!

Waiting is not a choice when walking with God. God will not be rushed. He operates on his time and his schedule. I can recall more than once when God was teaching me a lesson through life's circumstances, and my prayer to him was, "Okay, I got this already, let's move on!" God knew better. Part of waiting for God includes hope and faith. When we are forced to wait, we can make some choices. We can say, "God isn't interested." Or, "God doesn't care." Or even, "God isn't there!" These are positions that are inconsistent with our faith and hope in the Lord. The right position is that of the psalmist. "I will wait for the Lord, trusting in his goodness and timing, knowing his patient love, and plentiful redemption."

Have you found areas of your life that demonstrate impatience? Maybe God is placing something nearby to teach you patience. I want patience. In fact, I want it yesterday! I can't wait to get patience! But wait, I will. It seems to be part of the learning. But I take heart. The watchman waits for morning, and eventually morning comes. I will wait for patience, and trust the Lord to grow that fruit in me. He is faithful to the work of his hands.

Lord, help me be patient, trusting in your timing, your care, and your redemption. In Jesus' holy name, Amen.

❧ ❧ ❧

JULY 25

Steadfast love and faithfulness meet; righteousness and peace kiss each other. Faithfulness springs up from the ground, and righteousness looks down from the sky. (Ps. 85:10-11)

All of the words in today's meditation are powerful biblical words. They describe God and are traits encouraged in people.

Steadfast love, *chesed* in the Hebrew, is hard to put fairly into one English word. It conveys a covenant loyalty, with mercy and loving-kindness. After Joseph interpreted the dream of pharaoh's chief cup bearer, explaining that the man would be released to prison and restored to his position, Joseph asked the cup bearer to remember that Joseph had successfully interpreted the dream, and work toward getting Joseph out of jail. Following through on such a promise Joseph called an act of *chesed* or kindness and loyalty to an agreement (Gen. 40:14).

Faithfulness, *emet* in the Hebrew, is fidelity or truth. It is frequently used in tandem with steadfast love (*chesed*). The two belong together as strong reliable pillars. If we act with kindness and faithfulness, we live a demonstration of God's character. God is the one who is loyal and faithful, full of mercy and truth. These traits coincide in God, and we should strive for them to meet in us as well.

Righteousness (*tzedek* in the Hebrew) fits with peace (*shalom* in the Hebrew) in much the same way. God is righteous through and through. There is no sin in him; there is no wrong in him. He is not 99.99 percent righteous, he is fully righteous. Yet at the same time, this God of righteousness is able to give peace to his children, through the sacrifice of Jesus. That sacrifice is a righteous way to put anyone at peace with God and ourselves. Faithfulness is then described as springing up from the ground meeting the righteousness from the sky. These important concepts are pictured in metaphors. Faithfulness is pictured as something growing from the ground, while righteousness streams down as the sun's rays.

I read these images, and weigh these important words and ask myself, are these readily apparent in my life? What can I do to grow in these virtues? How can I show myself loyal to God and others? How can I better live in truth? Is the pursuit of righteousness important to me? Have these traits found me at peace? God is the source of all these things, and I need to stay close to him and make these priority pursuits!

Lord, thank you for your steadfast love and faithfulness I have found in life and especially in Jesus. Thank you also for the righteousness of Christ and peace in Christ. Please help me to grow in these traits, for Jesus sake, Amen.

❧ ❧ ❧

JULY 26

Incline your ear, O LORD, *and answer me, for I am poor and needy. Preserve my life, for I am godly; save your servant, who trusts in you—you are my God. Be gracious to me, O Lord, for to you do I cry all the day. Gladden the soul of your servant, for to you, O Lord, do I lift up my soul.* (Ps. 86:1-4)

Nobody wants to be poor! One look at the television or Internet demonstrates the desires for riches. There are even some "evangelists" that tell you God is bent on giving his followers riches if they have enough faith and will give to a certain ministry. God does not see "poor" quite the way we do. There is a lesson here.

The biblical ideas behind being "poor" are important ones, and we do well to consider the word carefully. In our age, we generally use "poor" to refer to "poverty," a lack of money or resources. The Hebrews did as well (e.g., Exod. 22:24). In Hebrew thought, however, the same word we translate "poor" also referred to someone who was humble or, in a sense, the opposite of "haughty" or arrogant. So in 2 Samuel 22:28 we read, "You save a humble people, but your eyes are on the haughty to bring them down." The word normally translated "poor" is here translated "humble." It is someone who is not proud or arrogant. This person doesn't view himself or herself as rich in status, character, or otherwise. This is not a lack of self-esteem, but it is a recognition that our value is not self-earned. It is something bestowed by God. We should not be arrogant, but should see ourselves as "poor and needy" as the psalmist does. This is the person who, whether possessing lots of money or little, knows that their true needs in life are met by God and God alone. In Isaiah 14:32 we again see the word normally translated "poor": "The LORD has founded Zion, and in her the afflicted of his people find refuge." Here the word is translated "afflicted." The poor person is one who is not equipped to handle what life has thrown at her or him.

Where should such a person turn? The psalmist says, "Turn to the Lord!" Seek God's deliverance. Seek his resources for handling life's problems. He is RICH! He has what we need, and he longs to help us.

In this sense Jesus said, "Blessed are the *poor* in spirit, for theirs is the kingdom of heaven" (Matt. 5:3). Jesus knows that when we come to God, God will hear and answer. It is so much better to be "poor in spirit" than haughty and self-sufficient!

Lord, I am weak and needy in so many ways. I do not have what it takes to face all the challenges of this life. Impoverished in spirit, I seek you for life's needs. Please teach me, guide me, empower me, and bless me to walk in your ways bring glory to Jesus. Amen!

※ ※ ※

JULY 27

You, O Lord, are good and forgiving, abounding in steadfast love to all who call upon you. Give ear, O LORD, to my prayer; listen to my plea for grace. In the day of my trouble I call upon you, for you answer me. (Ps. 86:5-7)

At times, I have found myself in a place where I am acutely aware of both my need for God and my sinfulness. It is a horrible predicament. You need God's loving compassion, his help, and his intervention in the crises of life, and yet you feel way too guilty to ask for it! In these times we want to pray to God, but how dare we ask for God's help when we have so clearly disregarded his will and instructions in life!

From today's passage, I have learned an important lesson for times like these. God is first and foremost a forgiving God. He wants us to come to him in our sin, confess that sin, and repent of it. Even that can be hard, however, because our repentance can sometimes ring hollow. This is especially so when it is a sticky sin that clings to us and is hard to shake. Consider, for example, overeating. (I pick the sin of gluttony because it is fairly non-judgmental, but my same reasoning holds true for all sorts of addictive sins.) After a gluttonous bout, in the satiety of the moment, we might be able to repent, but knowing we are just a hunger fit and good opportunity away from repeating the sin makes it a bit tougher! How do we repent of something if we reasonably anticipate doing the sin again?

We struggle with this, but the answer is not really hard to find. The answer is: be honest before God and use best efforts to walk right, empowered by his Spirit. We come to God and try to confess our sin with repentant hearts, and to the extent we fear we aren't fully repentant, we confess that and repent of it as well! God is faithful and abundant in steadfast love. He wants an honest people who come to him in need, including in need of forgiveness. He is not a checklist God who simply checks off where we succeed while drawing a red circle where we fail. God is integrated in our lives, working within us to bring forth his creation in fullness. He wants to make us in the image of his Son. He is at work, and longs for us to come to him for that work.

So in those times where we are needing God, but also cognizant of being steeped in sin, we have this passage telling us that we come to God for forgiveness of the sin, and also setting our needs in front of him. Do not let sin prevent you from seeking God and his help. He needs to help us with our sin, as much as he needs to help us with our crises. We should come to him with both, as the psalmist does.

Lord, we confess to you our sin. We repent, and seek your forgiveness in Jesus. We need your rescue from sin as well as the crises of life. May we never fail to turn to you! Amen!

❧ ❧ ❧

JULY 28

There is none like you among the gods, O Lord, nor are there any works like yours. . . .
For you are great and do wondrous things; you alone are God. Teach me your way, O
LORD, that I may walk in your truth; unite my heart to fear your name. (Ps. 86:8, 10-11)

In boxing, there is a basic combination called the "one-two punch,"
"the old one-two," or the "one-two combo." It is what boxers learn first, a
jab (a type of punch referred to as a "one" in boxing parlance) followed by a
cross (another type of punch commonly called a "two" by boxers). They are
both sensible punches, but fit well in a combination because the jab can set
up the cross. This passage is like the old one-two.

The "one" in this passage is the recognition that there is no one like
God. God is unique, truly one of a kind. No one has his knowledge and
insight, his heart of compassion and concern, or his power and might. God
has a plan for humanity and for his followers that will bring us through
the pitfalls of life victoriously, placing us in his eternal presence with all
that entails. God has the means to see that his plan is successful. He will
see it to completion.

Just as there is no one like our God, by extension, there are no works
like his. His ways and works are those that bring his plan to fruition. These
works are, accordingly, "great and wondrous." God's works shine light in
the darkness. They find peace in turmoil. They find grace in frustration.
They bring love into selfish hate. They bring forgiveness into bitterness.
The works of God are unique, just as God himself.

Recognizing the "one" of God's great and marvelous works brings us
to the "two" in this passage: God teach me your ways! As we realize that
the great and awesome God has great and awesome ways, then we naturally
seek God to teach us those ways so we may walk in them. Why would we
want to walk in anything less than the great and wondrous ways of our all-
powerful, unique God?

God can teach us to be the light. We can learn his peace and share it
to others in turmoil. We can experience his grace, readily dispensing it to
those who are frustrated. When we confront selfish hatred, we can model
selfless love. When the root of bitterness has sprung up and is bearing the
nasty fruits it brings, we can interrupt with a forgiving spirit, destroying
the bitterness at its source.

The old one-two! God is great; there are no works like his. So let's
learn and do them!

Lord, teach me your ways. Remove from me any arrogance that thinks I might have
a better way. I want to walk in yours! In Jesus, Amen!

❧ ❧ ❧

JULY 29

He established a testimony in Jacob and appointed a law in Israel, which he commanded our fathers to teach to their children, that the next generation might know them, the children yet unborn, and arise and tell them to their children, so that they should set their hope in God and not forget the works of God, but keep his commandments; and that they should not be like their fathers, a stubborn and rebellious generation, a generation whose heart was not steadfast, whose spirit was not faithful to God. (Ps. 78:5-8)

With the birth of each of my children, there was a special moment when they were placed in my arms. Holding each in wonder and amazement, I prayed silently, dedicating each one to the Lord, pledging myself to try and teach them of God, both in my words and by modeling God and his love. I asked that God would keep them in his care.

This was not something done out of the emotion of the moment. I had planned it. It was important to me. I knew that my children were a gift from God and that I was their earthly father with a chance to give meaning and significance to the Father in heaven. I have not always succeeded in being the father I would like to be, but good fathering has taken my energy, been my priority, and continues even as my children are in adulthood.

The Bible was never simply a "To Do" list of dos and don'ts. God didn't lay out instructions and leave it there. It is a book of many things—poetry, songs, narratives, theology, laws, letters, and more. It gives the history of God's interactions with earlier generations. The Bible tells parents to teach their children about what God has done. We have a responsibility and our failure to do so has real consequences. If each successive generation fails to know and understand the Lord and his ways, God will be forgotten in their lives. Maybe they won't lose the big idea of God, but they will not know God makes a day-by-day difference in life.

Some of the differences between a generation knowing God and not knowing God are set out in this passage. God gives us hope, and fulfills that hope in his timing. Failure to embrace God dulls that hope, if it still exists at all. Failure to teach God in his glory results in disobedience as people fail to respect, know, and honor God's instructions. Such disobedience brings ruin, for the ways of God are for our good. Failing to know and remember God produces stubbornness and rebellion. We no longer are sensitive to him, and we begin to think we know better than such superstitions.

So if we have children, we dedicate our children. We dedicate ourselves to teaching our children. It is important in more ways than we know.

Lord, help us teach the generations about you, your love, and your truth. In Jesus, Amen.

❋ ❋ ❋

JULY 30

But you, O Lord, are a God merciful and gracious, slow to anger and abounding in steadfast love and faithfulness. Turn to me and be gracious to me; give your strength to your servant, and save the son of your maidservant. Show me a sign of your favor, that those who hate me may see and be put to shame because you, LORD, have helped me and comforted me. (Ps. 86:15-17)

Sometimes things in life are really stressful and tough. There are times where we desperately need the favor of God, but God's final rescue and solution are likely a long way off. These problems don't resolve in a night.

The psalmist was in this situation. Knowing the problems wouldn't go away immediately, the psalmist asked God for a "sign" of his "favor," something that would show the enemies that salvation was coming.

I have always been a bit hesitant to ask God for a sign of his favor, but that doesn't mean I shouldn't! Let me explain. Jesus teaches us to be patient and to trust in God (Matt. 6:25-34). Sometimes I fear that asking God for a "sign of his favor" demonstrates impatience. While it might be impatience, it doesn't have to be. Sometimes it is merely seeking God to give you encouragement along the way while you wait in patience. I don't think the teachings on patience should preclude asking God for a sign of his favor.

In reflection, I think my hesitancy also stems from Jesus, after his arrest, going before King Herod. Luke tells us that "When Herod saw Jesus, he was very glad, for he had long desired to see him, because he had heard about him, and he was hoping to see some sign done by him" (Luke 23:8). But in the next verse we read that Herod "questioned him at some length, but he [Jesus] made no answer." Similarly, in Mark 8:11-12 we read of Pharisees arguing with Jesus and seeking a sign to test him. Jesus remarks negatively about such a seeking of signs. I don't want to ask God for signs as a test. That is not what we should be about either. But that is not the only reason to ask.

I think it's okay when we are in the midst of a long and difficult challenge, to ask the Lord to bestow a showing of his favor as a means of encouragement. I think he is already bestowing favor, so it's almost just asking him to open our eyes! It might not seem proper, but our Father is an encouraging God. He is not a genie in a bottle granting wishes, but he will give you signs of his favor to help you in the face of life's enemies!

Lord, give us pure hearts as we seek your encouragement in daily life. May we see your signs of favor, even as we live and pray in Jesus, the greatest sign of your favor! Amen!

❧ ❧ ❧

JULY 31

Of Zion it shall be said, "This one and that one were born in her"; for the Most High himself will establish her. The LORD records as he registers the peoples, "This one was born there." (Ps. 86:5-6)

This psalm speaks of those born in Jerusalem as blessed by God. I like to think of this in its prophetic sense as it speaks of what God does in the heavenly Jerusalem.

In Jesus' letter to the church in ancient Philadelphia, given in the Revelation to John, Jesus affirms the ones who conquer in the name of God in their recorded by God in his holy city. "I will make him a pillar in the temple of my God. Never shall he go out of it, and I will write on him the name of my God, and the name of the city of my God, the new Jerusalem, which comes down from my God out of heaven, and my own new name" (Rev. 3:12).

These passages, and others like them, speak of a special relationship between God and his people that gives solace and encouragement. The people of God are not an afterthought. Jesus distinguished the believers from those, "whose name has *not* been written before the foundation of the world in the book of life of the Lamb who was slain" (Rev. 13:8). Revelation 20:15 reiterates, "And if anyone's name was not found written in the book of life, he was thrown into the lake of fire." Paul recognized these were believers in Christ as he wrote the church in Philippi about those who, "labored side by side with me in the gospel together with Clement and the rest of my fellow workers, whose names are in the book of life" (Phil. 4:3).

What is this about God having our names written down in his book or register? Our relationship with God is not transitory. It is not an afterthought. We are not just whispers of flesh that pass quickly in the corridors of time on earth. We are a people with names. We matter to God. He knows our names and he calls us by name. Jesus said, the shepherd "calls his own sheep by name and leads them out" (John 10:3). Isaiah 43:1 explains that God "created you," "formed you," and "called you by name" because you belong to him.

This is amazing to think about. God knows my name. God has a direct interest in me as me. Though I am not even a speck in the universe, nor in the vastness of time, God has written my name down with care and nurture intended for me. I am awash with gratitude.

Lord, it really is hard to fathom the depth of your love and attention. I am grateful beyond measure, and I stand amazed that you care so deeply. Keep me focused on bringing glory to your name, even as you have written down my own. I pray in the name of my Savior Jesus, Amen.

AUGUST 1

There is none like you among the gods, O Lord, nor are there any works like yours. All the nations you have made shall come and worship before you, O Lord, and shall glorify your name. For you are great and do wondrous things; you alone are God. Teach me your way, O LORD, that I may walk in your truth; unite my heart to fear your name. (Ps. 86:8-11)

Israel lived amidst pagan nations with pagan gods. The pagans believed that gods were regional in power and existence, tied to particular areas or rulers. Each pagan ruler and area claimed gods they believed favorable to that ruler or area. When people left the territorial reign of the god, they left the power of the god. We might think of it in the more common Greek thought of Poseidon as the god of the sea. If you are on the sea, you hope and pray for the protection of Poseidon. If you are fully inland, he's not too much help! So it was with the contemporaries of Israel.

But Israel was taught differently. Even though they often held the beliefs of their pagan neighbors, the revealed God of Israel was no local or tribal God. The Lord God was the God of heaven and earth—all of heaven, and all of earth! There was no little "g" god like the Lord God. He wasn't only the God of Israel, "all nations" would come and worship him. After all, he "made" all the nations.

Today we see this incredible truth borne out. You don't find followers of the tribal gods of Israel's neighbors around the world. There is no large cult of Ba'al, no Asherah poles found worldwide. There are not the tribal gods of the Ammonites or Perizzites. But today, all around the world, in the faiths of Christianity, Judaism, and even Islam, the God of Abraham is honored (albeit there is a major difference in how that God is understood among the faiths).

So with a great and wonderful God, a God that far exceeds those of the other nations and tribes around Israel, what was the psalmist to do? What are we to do? The psalmist made the smart choice. We read the request, *"Teach me your way, O LORD, that I may walk in your truth; unite my heart to fear your name."*

Shouldn't we want to know the ways of the one true God, the one whose reign exceeds anyone's conception of God? This is the God of truth. He is a real God who has real ways. He will be the victorious God when this world is over. I want to learn the ways of this God and walk in his truth!

Lord, you are worthy of the title God, and there are no others. I don't wait until the end of days to proclaim you Lord; I do so with great joy today. Teach me your ways and help me walk in your truth. There are many distractions, and I need your help in Jesus, Amen.

❧ ❧ ❧

AUGUST 2

I give thanks to you, O Lord my God, with my whole heart, and I will glorify your name forever. For great is your steadfast love toward me; you have delivered my soul from the depths of Sheol. (Ps. 86:12-13)

Gratitude is an important trait, one we teach our children and one we hope to have ourselves. When people do nice things for us or when they help us, it is important to show gratitude, to say a meaningful, "thank you!" Many times that even involves writing a thank you note or email. Gratitude is not as much about the giver, as it is about the one who receives the gift.

I want to have an attitude of gratitude toward the Lord. He has done so much for me. At times, that flows easily. I can remember exceptional times in life where I gazed up into the sky with an exuberant, "THANK YOU!" to the Lord. There are other times, however, when the gratitude is a bit harder to come by. It's not that I am spiteful to the Lord, but when difficulties come, I am often more bent on making it through the difficulties than I am expressing thanks to the Almighty.

One part of my law practice has been dealing with a dreadful terminal cancer caused by asbestos. It is called mesothelioma. People who contract this disease have little hope of surviving for long. Among the many victims I have represented, a number are believers. Here they are, with a cancer that often provides only six to eight months survival after diagnosis, and in the midst of struggling to make sense of it, trying to find what treatment may give the best chance for a longer survival, trying to be a rock for their loved ones, trying to get their house in order and often plan a funeral, these believers more times than not have shocked me. I will ask them sincerely, "How are you doing?" It is staggering how many say, "I am so blessed. I am so thankful to God . . ." and they proceed to tell me how and why.

Having a thankful heart in the midst of crisis, when others would despair, I find inspirational. It proceeds from a recognition of God's steadfast love. His love is not limited by disease, whether terminal or not. His love flows until the day we die, and beyond. He has delivered our souls from darkness after death. He is the reason so many early Christian martyrs, including most of the apostles, held firm their faith, staring their earthly demise in the face while awaiting the blessed confidence of resurrection.

Lord, I owe you a debt of gratitude beyond my ability to express. It leaves me wondering how to show my gratefulness for your love. Help me show appreciation by the ways I treat others and share of your love. In Jesus I pray, Amen.

❧ ❧ ❧

AUGUST 3

On the holy mount stands the city he founded; the LORD *loves the gates of Zion more than all the dwelling places of Jacob. Glorious things of you are spoken, O city of God.* (Ps. 87:1-3)

The Old Testament indicates a great devotion from God for "Zion," here a reference for the city of Jerusalem (sometimes "Zion" references a specific hill in Jerusalem). The psalmist holds up Jerusalem as a location God loves more than all others. It might seem odd that God would favor one city over against another. We don't normally think of God as particular about geography. I suggest two areas for deeper thought.

First, it was a geographical location where Jesus was betrayed, crucified, buried, and resurrected. These events didn't happen in the ether, but in a location with history. Two thousand years before Jesus, God called Abraham to sacrifice his son, sending him to a specific geographical location, Mt. Moriah (Gen. 22:2). There, right before the sacrifice, an angel stopped Abraham, saying God would provide the sacrifice. It would be God's son, not Abraham's. Mt. Moriah became the threshing floor of Araunah, where the angel stopped the plague on Israel that resulted from David's sin (1 Chr. 21:15). This same physical location then became the place of Solomon's temple (2 Chr. 3:1). This same spot was the area from which Jesus was sent to Pilate and Calvary. God, filled with his foresight, saw Zion through eternity's eyes. From Zion God redeemed humanity.

A second area for deeper thought is that the "city of God" takes on a new meaning after the work of Christ. In Revelation, Jesus spoke a letter to the angel of the church at Philadelphia, an ancient city that was located in modern Turkey. Jesus called "the city of God" the "New Jerusalem, which comes down from God out of heaven" (Rev. 3:12). Then in the final vision of Revelation that set forth the end of days, John saw "the holy city Jerusalem coming down out of heaven from God" (Rev. 21:10). John called the city "the holy city, new Jerusalem, coming down out of heaven from God" that was "prepared as a bride adorned for her husband" (Rev. 21:2).

Can there be any doubt about God's love and devotion to the plan of salvation, a real time and space event that happened in a geographic space? Can there be any doubt of God's love and devotion to the church, purchased by the blood of Jesus? God's love for Zion is a story of God's love for me!

Lord, thank you for your love from long ago that will last to the end in Jesus, Amen.

❧ ❧ ❧

AUGUST 4

O Lord, God of my salvation; I cry out day and night before you. Let my prayer come before you; incline your ear to my cry! For my soul is full of troubles, and my life draws near to Sheol. (Ps. 88:1-3)

Many psalms are born out of pain and anguish. There is something about difficult times that drives us to God. When times are great, we seem to have everything under control, but when life gets crazy, when we are hurting, when we are unable to see to the end of a matter, when the things we thought were reliable prove unreliable, when we aren't healthy, when we can't understand the difficulties we face, when our "soul is full of trouble," then we seek the Lord, fearing we can't get where we need to be on our own.

God is the solution. Events in life may be crazy, but God gives wisdom that pierces through the craziness, giving light to darkness, and truth to illusion. When we are hurting, we find consolation in God, realizing that he understands hurt, and stands by us faithfully in our pain. Our inability to see the end of a crisis or other concern becomes an exercise in trust and hope when God enters the picture. God is not surprised by the future. God isn't living in doubt about what may come. The future is the past to God. He knows how things will turn out, and has assured us that all will be okay in the final accounting. This is our assurance from a resurrected Jesus. God defeats even death. When things we relied upon prove unreliable, we find in God the answer. God is the ultimate in reliability. He doesn't change. He was the same yesterday as he is today and as he will be tomorrow. He maintains a steadfast love that is unchanging.

God's timing isn't always ours, but we trust it is the best timing for his will to unfold. We also know that he loves and protects us in spite of anything that may come. When we face difficulties, with God they are opportunities to grow in faith, holiness, focus, and the fruits of his spirit (love, joy, peace, patience, kindness, goodness, gentleness, and self-control).

God is our "Go-to" when times are difficult. My chore is to see him as my "Go-to" when times are great! I need him no less when I am healthy, happy, and prosperous, I just don't seek him as readily!

Lord, do help me cry out to you, not only when times are difficult, but also when they are the best of times. I want to be in your hands 24/7 in Jesus, Amen!

AUGUST 5

But I, O LORD, cry to you; in the morning my prayer comes before you. O LORD, why do you cast my soul away? Why do you hide your face from me? Afflicted and close to death from my youth up, I suffer your terrors; I am helpless. (Ps. 88:13-15)

For most of my life, I have had my quiet time in the evening, generally right before I go to bed. Many friends told me their quiet time worked much better in the morning, but for me, evening was best. My friends would tell me, "I need my quiet time before I face the day." I would answer, "I need mine to clear my head and heart so I can sleep!" It wasn't until the last five years that I figured out I could have both!

Morning is generally a time where I think about what the day has planned, and deliver it to the Lord in prayer, entrusting him to see that the day brings his kingdom to greater fruition, brings more glory to his name, and sees his will done in my life. This is the time to entrust my day to his mercies, giving to him the matters that weigh heavily on my heart. Some days will be better and some days will be worse, but all go to him.

In today's passage, we have the psalmist starting his day with the Lord, and not just a difficult day for the writer, a horrible day is anticipated in the midst of a horrible season. The psalmist feels alone. It seems one of those days where you wonder if prayer does anything at all, other than bounce off the ceiling and come right back. The psalmist feels God has cast the writer off. It is as if God is purposely avoiding, and maybe even punishing, the writer. "*I am helpless.*" It seems nothing can be done.

These are true feelings of the writer, and this psalm teaches me that God is big enough to handle my true feelings. If I feel alone and rejected, even though it isn't true, it is okay to tell God how I feel. If I feel scared, I can tell God. If I feel lost, I can tell God. If I feel God has abandoned me, I can tell God. If I feel my prayers are ineffective, I can tell God. If I feel desperate, I can tell God. If I feel bewildered, I can tell God. If I feel doubt, I can tell God. If I wonder about my faith, I can tell God. God knows you and he knows me. He knows we are human and subject to human feelings. He knows our frailties. God loves us as we are, even as he transforms us into what we can be.

God had not abandoned the psalmist. God had not chosen an ill moment to play hide and seek. The psalmist's prayers were not going unanswered. It only felt that way. There are dark and difficult days. We have a God who wants to hear how we are feeling, and he will be with us and never forsake us regardless of how things feel or seem.

Lord, please help me be honest with you about all my feelings. Thank you for your steadfast love in Jesus, Amen.

❧ ❧ ❧

AUGUST 6

I will sing of the steadfast love of the Lord, *forever; with my mouth I will make known your faithfulness to all generations. For I said, "Steadfast love will be built up forever; in the heavens you will establish your faithfulness." (Ps. 89:1-2)*

"Trust me!" Those words are sometimes scary. If you have a real important problem that you are not able to take care of personally, and you go to someone for help, when that person says, "Trust me, I got this!" it is reassuring, but also not always convincing. As a lawyer who has handled people's problems on a daily basis for over three decades, I can tell you that most folks are quite antsy, even after I tell them, "Trust me, I will handle this for you." They *want* to trust me, but some problems are so serious that they are still nervous.

Since Adam and Eve in the Garden of Eden, humanity has had a huge problem. People are ensnared by sin, and that sin brings death and separation from God. There could be no greater human problem, especially when you consider that people were made to be in a relationship with God. Almost everyone has had this deep awareness that there has to be more to life than simply living. We look for meaning; we think there must be meaning. I'm rather confident no other living organism has this pre-wired awareness that there is meaning in life, and that we can and should search for the meaning that is missing. Humans are uniquely made in God's image, and made to live with God in relationship. So when we are not, we sense something missing or not as good as it should be. Long before this psalmist wrote, God told his followers, "I know about the problem of sin and separation, trust me. I got this!" God told Adam and Eve he would work out the problem through Eve's offspring (Gen. 3:14-15). God told Abraham the same (Gen. 12:2). Over and over in the voice of the prophets God reminded people of his promise.

God didn't fail any of those people who entrusted this problem to God. Slightly over 2,000 years ago, in a move few could have foreseen, God emptied himself and was incarnated into a human life. He came as a baby named "Jesus," meaning "God is salvation." Jesus was God, coming to save. Jesus lived a flawless life unmarred by sin, keeping himself in full fellowship with the Father. Jesus died a humiliating and unrighteous death, was buried, but defeating death itself, was physically resurrected, walking the earth for weeks, witnessed by hundreds, before ascending into heave with a promise to return. Paul says that in the death of Jesus, we who trust in him have the problem fixed! But not just us, God was fulfilling his promise to the psalmist and others. God's steadfast love was faithful and honorable, and God solved the problem for everyone. God was faithful to all generations. Amazing if you think about it.

Lord, thank you for your steadfast love shown in Jesus, in whom we pray, Amen.

❧ ❧ ❧

AUGUST 7

You have said, "I have made a covenant with my chosen one; I have sworn to David my servant: 'I will establish your offspring forever, and build your throne for all generations.'" (Ps. 89:3-4)

When I was young, there was a song we occasionally sang, "My Jesus Is Coming Soon." The chorus proclaimed, "My Jesus is coming soon; Morning or night or noon; Many will meet their doom; Trumpets will sound. All of the dead shall rise, Righteous meet in the skies; Going where no one dies; Heavenward bound." At one youth event, there was a barbershop quartet set to sing that song. They said they were none too fond of the lyric, "Many will meet their doom," so preferring to stay on the positive, they were changing it to "Many will meet their groom." This happened about the same time the group 2nd Chapter of Acts came out with "The Prince Song" (worth downloading!). These songs focused on the return of Jesus.

It is a reassuring thing to know that God will be bringing this earth to a full conclusion at some point, and that the believers will be transformed to a new heaven and new earth (2 Pet. 3:8-13). This finish to things is not a nothingness or void. It is God reigning, enthroned on high, a new heavens and earth, with Jesus at God's side reigning as King of kings and Lord of lords. Jesus as an offspring of David, in his earthly existence, means that this promise of God is fulfilled in Jesus who reigns eternally. None of this is God's afterthought. All of this was part of his majestic plan contemplated before he even made this world. It is God's way of uniting all things in heaven and on earth in Jesus Christ (Eph. 1:3-10).

You and I plug into this promise very directly. In this entire plan, God planned our adoption through Jesus' blood. This was and is the will of God (Eph. 1:4-6). We are no Plan B. We are intended for this blessing. In a metaphor, we are the bride of Christ, getting ourselves ready for this eternity (Rev. 19:7-8). We need to clothe ourselves in the purity of Christ, knowing that upon his return, the king who reigns eternally will be worshipped by us, the believers who are his bride.

I know Jesus said we will not know when this all happens. He will come as a thief in the night. But we are to live as if it is any moment now. This means our focus is always on eternity and our preparation for it. I suspect I will live today quite differently if I think Jesus may be coming back any minute! There are lots of things I might do differently! I want to take this seriously, and worship the Lord who will be King forever!

Lord, help me to live right before you focused on your promises in Jesus, Amen.

❀ ❀ ❀

AUGUST 8

Let the heavens praise your wonders, O LORD, your faithfulness in the assembly of the holy ones! For who in the skies can be compared to the LORD? Who among the heavenly beings is like the LORD, a God greatly to be feared in the council of the holy ones, and awesome above all who are around him? O LORD God of hosts, who is mighty as you are, O LORD? (Ps. 89:5-8)

Oh to get a glimpse of God in his eternal heavens! No one could be the same afterwards. Scripture tells of two who got glimpses, the prophet Isaiah, and John, who recorded the Revelation. The visions amaze me.

In Isaiah chapter 6, we read about Isaiah's encounter. He dated it to the year King Uzziah died. Isaiah saw God lifted up high on a throne. His robe had a hem or train that filled the temple. Flying around the Lord were angels singing antiphonally to each other, "Holy, holy, holy is the LORD of hosts; the whole earth is full of his glory!" The Hebrew word for "holy" is *qadosh*. It denotes something that commands respect, is awesome and removed from common usage. The word emphasizes the "otherness" of that which is holy. There is a twenty-first-century tendency to think of "holy" as a description of very ethical behavior. While actions can certainly be "holy" (or "profane"—common), the word goes beyond simple behavior. It is rooted in something extraordinary.

The building shook in awe as the angels sang praise to the enthroned Lord. Immediately, Isaiah realized how utterly lost and sinful he was. Of course, Isaiah knew that Judah's King Uzziah (aka "Azariah") had arrogantly gone into God's earthly temple to burn incense, and God gave him leprosy as punishment. No doubt Isaiah was concerned about the results to him as he was beholding the Lord sitting upon his real heavenly throne. Isaiah, however, did not suffer from Uzziah's proud heart, nor did he suffer Uzziah's consequences. Isaiah's reaction was to fall to his face and cry, "Woe is me! For I am lost; for I am a man of unclean lips, and I dwell in the midst of a people of unclean lips." God then provided the sacrifice to clean Isaiah up, before sending Isaiah on his mission to speak for God.

In Revelation 4, we read John's experience. John saw the angels worshipping the Lord, along with deceased followers of God from the Old and New Testament era. The angels sang, "Holy, holy, holy, is the Lord God Almighty, who was and is and is to come!" while the people cast their crowns before God (who would wear a crown before God?), declaring God holy.

The psalmist had it right. No one is worthy of the praise of our God.

Lord, in our own feeble way, sinful as we are, we offer you our praise. Cleanse us and save us. In Jesus, Amen!

❧ ❧ ❧

AUGUST 9

You have a mighty arm; strong is your hand, high your right hand. Righteousness and justice are the foundation of your throne; steadfast love and faithfulness go before you. Blessed are the people who know the festal shout, who walk, O LORD, in the light of your face, who exult in your name all the day and in your righteousness are exalted. For you are the glory of their strength. (Ps. 89:13-17)

I love the ways the Bible reveals God to us. How on earth, are we humans supposed to understand someone as God? God is all things superlative. He is the strongest, the most knowledgeable, the kindest, the most mysterious, the most ancient, the most _____—fill in the blank. God is not of this natural order, but created the universe and all that is in it. God is not physical in our sense of the word. God is not a captive of time and space. How are we to ever get an accurate idea of God?

Through scripture, God has revealed himself in ways that we can understand. We get passages like this, where we read of God with a "mighty arm" and "strong hand." Of course, God has no arms or hands as we know them, but this helps us understand that he is a working God, strong and able to do things that could not otherwise be done.

To describe God's throne as having a foundation of righteousness and justice is again a metaphor. We have an understanding from this that God's reign, his power, his majesty, what sets him uniquely in a place of worship is rooted in righteousness and justice. God is an ethical God and his ethical standards are those from which we derive words like "righteous" and "moral." God's character determines what is good. We can look to God to get the definition of good and right. Justice is a comment on the integrity of God. God is not one way one day, and something different on another. God is just, or consistent in his character and reign.

God has revealed himself in this way, but not all people acknowledge him. Some would rather have their own sense of righteousness and justice. Others have this sense not knowing from where it comes. Often they see it woven into the universe, but don't know why. Still others disregard righteousness and effectively flee from it.

But those people who see God as he has revealed himself, carry a particular blessing. There is a festal shout, a reason to celebrate, when we know God as the righteous and just God. When we live our lives oriented to the enlightenment that comes from knowing God as he revealed himself, we are strengthened by his strength. We live in joy and confidence that comes from him!

Lord, teach us your ways. Show us your strength. Lead us in righteousness in Jesus, Amen.

❧ ❧ ❧

AUGUST 10

I have found David, my servant; with my holy oil I have anointed him, so that my hand shall be established with him; my arm also shall strengthen him. The enemy shall not outwit him; the wicked shall not humble him. I will crush his foes before him and strike down those who hate him. My faithfulness and my steadfast love shall be with him, and in my name shall his horn be exalted. (Ps. 89:20-24)

David's story is fascinating. He was selected by God to lead Israel, even though he wasn't an obvious choice. David's success came from trusting God.

His training was as a shepherd, tending to the family sheep. While one might not think this an ordinary path to making history as a king, it served David well. David knew the importance of hands-on care. He faced fears in the night, and fought off wild animals, trusting in God for the courage and ability to do so. He spent time outside gazing into the heavens, contemplating with awe the God who made the stars and yet had time for David and humanity. David took these gifts to work for the country. When bringing food to his brothers who served in the king's army, David saw Goliath come out and taunt the Israelite army. David understood this as a taunt against God, and dispatched Goliath easily. Later, David was anointed king, long before he ascended the throne. The prior king, Saul, sought to kill David, and had David on the run hiding in caves and barely eking by. These hard times produced in David even greater faith, seeing God protect him and bring him through the most trying times.

Knowing these marvelous things, it is not surprising to see David blessed by God, but that is not the whole story! David also had his problems. David could be proud, and that pride cost the nation of Israel a lot (2 Sam 24:10ff.). David committed adultery with Bathsheba, the wife of one of his trusted soldiers and friends. David committed murder rather than confess and accept responsibility for his sin. David was no minor sinner!

So how do these two sides of David match up to the promise of God? Scripture tells us he was a "man after God's own heart" (1 Sam. 13:14). David was devoted to God in prayer and praise. David carried compassion and humility into his daily walk with God, and was deeply concerned for fairness and justice. All of us have our sins and shortcomings. We should never take them lightly. Thinking of David underscores my need to purify my heart before the Lord. I want to be one after God's own heart, knowing that even in my sin, the Lord will be able to bring blessings.

Lord, create in me a clean heart. Renew a right spirit within me. Teach me your ways and your will and bring me to your service, fit for your purposes in Jesus. Amen.

❊ ❊ ❊

AUGUST 11

How long, O LORD? Will you hide yourself forever? How long will your wrath burn like fire? Remember how short my time is! For what vanity you have created all the children of man! What man can live and never see death? Who can deliver his soul from the power of Sheol? (Ps. 89:46-48)

Can you imagine how frustrating it would be to live as a believer in the centuries before Christ? We who live in the twenty-first century have a huge knowledge advantage over those who lived then. This is related, in part, to a concept theologians call, "progressive revelation." Just as we learn differently as we age, so God has revealed (taught) people about him, his work, and life in general, as society and culture has aged. Even though there is little difference in people in the ways we feel, in what we want, etc., people today have a greater knowledge and awareness base than people of even a hundred years ago. Can you imagine the differences between people of the 1200 BC Bronze Age in Canaan and the Roman era of AD 200?

So thinking about this passage, I am appreciative of the greater revelation God has given us since the psalmist wrote. Since the resurrection of Jesus, we live in what the Bible calls, "the last days." Paul explained that Jesus was the "mystery" that God "kept secret for long ages" (Rom. 16:25). In Jesus we have a righteousness unknown since the Garden of Eden. Righteousness was not just in the life of Jesus, but also comes into the lives of all who put their trust in him (Rom. 5:12-14)

Unlike today's passage, I can never ask if God will hide his face forever. I might feel like he is hidden, but I know from the experiences of Jesus that no such thing could happen. When Jesus was on the cross bearing humanity's sin, the sky darkened as God hid his face, but that was temporary. The cup of God's wrath passed, and Jesus arose from the tomb victorious over death. Paul explained that as Jesus defeated death, so he brings all who put their trust in Jesus into the same victory over death (1 Cor. 15). I no longer need worry, as the psalmist did, over who can deliver me from death. God delivers me from death as he did Jesus.

Still, even living in the last days, with thousands of years of culture, knowledge, and understanding, we are not fit to know everything. More will be revealed upon death. Paul says we see and understand like looking in a dim mirror, but then we will see fully (1 Cor. 13:12). We don't know what our bodies will be like after death, but that will be revealed when it occurs (1 Cor. 15:35ff.). We can trust the Lord for that!

Lord, thank you for your love and revelation. I trust you for today, tomorrow, and eternity in Jesus, Amen!

❧ ❧ ❧

AUGUST 12

Lord, you have been our dwelling place in all generations. (Ps. 90:1)

The first home I bought was in a subdivision in Houston, Texas. The home was built to last—for maybe fifty years or so. It was built in a way where I could have likely lived in it until death. I might call it a one-generation home. Oh, it would likely survive longer, but not without a lot of major rebuilding. When one goes to Europe, one can find homes that were built to last for hundreds of years. That impresses me. Yet this psalm points to a more stunning truth. God is the dwelling place for *all generations.*

Isaiah 41:4 puts it this way, "Who has performed and done this, calling the generations from the beginning? I, the LORD, the first, and with the last; I am he." This is bizarre! What home is built to last for all generations? What home never needs repair or rebuilding? If we think of a generation as forty years, then we have about fifty generations since the birth of Christ. If we want to go back to Abraham, we have another fifty generations, giving us around a hundred generations of people in the Abrahamic/Christian covenant who have found in the Lord God a dwelling place. The generations come and go. A hundred before, a hundred after, the numbers don't matter. He is the same God then, now, and tomorrow. We have a dwelling place that never changes. God's "throne endures to all generations" (Lam. 5:19).

Go to any major city of the world, and you can find homeless people. Not so in the kingdom of God! Everyone has a home, a dwelling place. In the Lord, everyone has all that "home" implies. We have protection. We have family. We have the things needed for life. Isaiah also prophesied that the dwelling place in God would forever be one of God's righteousness and salvation (Isa. 51:8). This is ours as it was the generation before ours. This will be there for the generation to come, should the Lord tarry. What an amazing heritage!

Pre-Jesus generations knew the blessings of God, but they didn't understand how we would get into God's dwelling place. A way had to be prepared for us, the way of the Lord. That was done by Jesus going to the cross. He prepared a way for us into his Father's house, our dwelling place for all generations (John 14:1-4)! This also solved the mystery of how God would unite the Jews and Gentiles in one kingdom.

Glory to God in the highest! God, who has been our dwelling place in all generations is due "glory in the church and in Christ Jesus throughout all generations, forever and ever" (Eph. 3:21).

Lord, what an honor to dwell in your house, in you. We are honored to be in Jesus joining the generations of history in your holy care. Amen.

❧ ❧ ❧

AUGUST 13

Before the mountains were brought forth, or ever you had formed the earth and the world, from everlasting to everlasting you are God. You return man to dust and say, "Return, O children of man!" For a thousand years in your sight are but as yesterday when it is past, or as a watch in the night. (Ps. 90:2-4)

We live by clocks. Alarms awaken us. We have times to be at work or in school. We set appointments that start and end with certain hours or minutes. Our calendars reserve dates months and years in advance. We keep track of the earth rotating the sun, marking birthdays and anniversaries. We can tell one another what we were doing when the earth was last in virtually this same position last (i.e., where was I one year ago?). We know seasons, counting off the summers, autumns, winters, and springs. Time is part of who we are.

Not God! God works in our universe, but God exists outside space and time. There is no sun which God orbits to measure years. There is no digital watch God wears to make sure he isn't late for this, that, or the other. God is an unchanging being that exists in eternity. In between the smallest division of time we can conceive or measure, we find God in eternity. Before an electron can move in the slightest around a nucleus, God is in eternity.

This is one reason it is silly to ask questions like, "How can God hear the prayers of all the people on earth at once?" God is not captive to our time. God's eternity is not suspended because the earth is orbiting the sun. God has eternity not just between each breath, but constantly. He can and does know us through and through. He can and does keep track of every subatomic particle that courses through a universe of billions and billions of galaxies and countless stars. We have trouble thinking of this because to say "we are brief in this life" is an understatement of immense proportion.

Having a God who exists in eternity beyond time is important to me. It gives me awe and wonder over the greatness of God. It makes a bit more sense of how he can care for me in the midst of caring for so many others, all while keeping track of what seems an infinite number of things. God's eternity is infinite. It is part of what makes him God.

So today, I will go to my Father humbly with amazement and wonder, trusting him with my minutes and days. He is fully trustworthy in this!

Lord, as a creature of time, I have trouble understanding your existence in eternity. But even the little I know, brings me great amazement and comfort. Thank you for your love and care. Please help me use each second of my time to your glory. In Jesus' name, Amen!

❧ ❧ ❧

AUGUST 14

You have set our iniquities before you, our secret sins in the light of your presence. (Ps. 90:8)

Today's passage I think of as "good news/bad news." First, the bad news: God knows all my sins, even the ones I don't like to think about! There are dark things that we all do and have done. I have yet to meet anyone who hasn't had moments of sin in life that are beyond humiliating. If you are old enough, you know the depths of sin. If you aren't so old, you will. Sin is a sad thing that brings hurt, guilt, shame, and often devastating consequences. It is something we don't like to show or share. The darkest sins are ones we shove deep into our past, hoping to not think of them and careful they are not discovered. Yet they are there, and God know each one.

Furthermore, God not only knows my sins, he has set them before his eyes. He has considered each one and given due thought to it. My sins in all their horrific reality are on display before the purity of God's divine presence. Think about all of that in front of a perfect God who stands ready to judge the sin. Knowing the consequences of sin are death, this should be a frightful reality. That is the bad news. Now for the good news.

God knows all my sins, even the ones I don't like to think about! No, this isn't a typo. I know I gave the same fact for both good news and bad news. The news that is bad is also the same news that is good. It is good because the God who sets those sins in his pure presence, ready to judge them, judges them in light of the death of Christ. Jesus has already paid the penalty for my sins, so God can be just when he examines those sins, and then decrees my forgiveness in Jesus. Furthermore, because God knows all my sins, when God gives me forgiveness, the forgiveness is not limited to certain sins of which God is aware. I need not worry that he gave us limited forgiveness for the select sins he knew about. God knows all of my sins and they are very real to him.

There is more good news! Scripture teaches us that God not only knows our sins, and forgives those sins in Jesus, but God also works to grow us out of the patterns of sin in our lives. Many of our sins are inadequacies in life, and many of them are ingrained patterns of sin. In all of those sins, God is at work transforming us into the image of his perfect Son. This is something God does little by little, day by day. Because God knows each of our sins, he knows where to go to work and what work needs be done. What an amazing God we serve!

Lord, I confess myself a sinner. I know that you know the full depths of my sin, but I still confess it openly in repentance. Thank you for forgiveness in Jesus, Amen.

❧ ❧ ❧

AUGUST 15

Teach us to number our days that we may get a heart of wisdom. (Ps. 90:12)

I started praying this passage once a month when I was a young man in my twenties. Something scary happened. God answered the prayer, at least the part about teaching me to number my days.

We live in a crazy demanding world. The busyness of life starts early. We begin school at a very young age, with all that it entails (homework, papers, extracurricular activities, etc.). Then we leave school and go into the job market, and finding work also consumes much of our time and energy. When family comes into life, there is a whole new set of demands on our time. Marriage takes time, if it is going to be healthy and strong. Parenting takes time if we want to do it right. Upkeep of a home—from doing the dishes to mowing the lawn—takes up a lot of energy and time. All of this happens for many while they are also trying to work outside the home. Of course, hopefully there is also some time for personal sanity, including time to exercise, get a haircut, and eat! Did I mention answering emails? This busyness often leaves people at the end of their day exhausted, ready to sit on the sofa and watch the television until they are ready to close their eyes. Then they sleep less than they should and wake up the next morning to get back on the treadmill and do it all over again.

The psalmist interrupts this treadmill, injecting the truth that we will gain wisdom from numbering our days. We must somehow get into our conscious minds, in a way that it stays there, that each of us are on a countdown. There are a certain number of days each of us will live. Maybe we live a full seventy-five years, and if so, those days may seem numerous early on. At birth they are just under 27,400. But by the time we're twenty, they're already down to just over 20,000. I first typed this at age fifty-five. If I last to age seventy-five, I was down to 7,305. I am editing it a year later. Now I am under 7,000! Of course, a lot of people never live to age seventy-five. The numbers can be quite small for all of us.

There is a lot I want to get done in this life. There are a lot of people and things needing my prayers. I still have a lot I want to read; a lot I want to write. There are people very dear to me, and I want to spend time with them. I have goals that are important, more important than a lot on which I spend my time.

If I number my days, and I think through the implications, it changes the way I live those days. I want to do the important things. I want to do the things of God. These are the things that have lasting value. God help me number my days and grow in wisdom!

Lord, teach me to number my days, and live each moment wisely. In Jesus' holy name I pray, Amen.

❧ ❧ ❧

AUGUST 16

Satisfy us in the morning with your steadfast love, that we may rejoice and be glad all our days. (Ps. 90:14)

A good night's sleep is important. Modern neuroscience teaches that the brain restores good chemistry during sleep. We know the results of that. After we have a good night's sleep, we feel rested, rejuvenated, and ready for the challenges of a new day. While not everyone is a breakfast eater, for most, it is an extremely important meal. It gives energy for the body to go with the well-rested body and mind getting the person ready for a strong day!

Today's Scripture adds to that. When we awaken, we are well set for the day if, in addition to physical and mental rest and nourishment, we come before God thinking about his steadfast love. It is a breakfast for the soul, and a necessary breakfast at that. Thinking through God's patient, enduring love gives us what we need to make it through day by day.

Consider starting each day with a reflection on how much God has loved us. He pays attention to our needs, from the day we are born (actually even before that!) until the day we die, God supplies us out of his abundant love. He tends to our physical needs, but also our emotional needs. God has given us instructions on how to live, with the assurance that when we walk in his path, while the road will not always be easy, it will ultimately be the best road for us. Walking God's path means we find ourselves in his will. We can experience his blessings, and share those blessings with others.

God's love for us extends beyond the physical. It extends to the spiritual as well. In God's love we have the assurance that the mistakes of yesterday are forgiven, and grace abounds for today. As we wade into deep waters, God's sovereign hand guides us. He doesn't fail us. He never has, and he never will. This enables us to call on his name when times are difficult and we can rest in God's steadfast love. It affirms that we belong to him and he indwells us, caring for us as a parent does a child.

Thinking through these things each morning will set us on a course of victory in Jesus for the day. We know that God will meet our needs, so we needn't worry or panic. We know in faith that he will calm the storms, or at least secure our feet where we can walk on water through the storm. When we think of his steadfast love in the morning, we think of HIM in the morning. We think of how he wants to work through us for the day. That is a recharging of our batteries that will lead us into his will, with all that entails.

Lord, lead us into your love. Teach us to trust you. Help us live out our faith deeply entwined in you. Thank you for that love in Jesus, Amen.

❊ ❊ ❊

AUGUST 17

Let your work be shown to your servants, and your glorious power to their children. Let the favor of the Lord our God be upon us, and establish the work of our hands upon us; yes, establish the work of our hands! (Ps. 90:16-17)

You are a builder! I am a builder! We are all builders, whether we know it or not. We are building our lives. We build our lives by the choices we make and the things we do each day. The real question is how are we doing at building our lives? Are we making a solid home, fit for dwelling, or are we building a shack that is in shambles?

Any good building has a few core requirements. First, the building needs a good foundation. I learned this more fully early in my legal career when I handled a case over whether the foundation of a million-dollar house was poorly designed. The homeowner was convinced that the failing foundation was the reason he was unable to sell his home. He didn't want it, and neither did anyone else. The walls had cracks, and all the putty in the world wouldn't cover them up or prevent them from returning. If the foundation wasn't fixed, even though the house had luxurious fixings inside, it was destined for the wrecking ball.

Jesus taught us that when we build our lives, we need a firm foundation just like a home. The best foundation, Jesus explained, was one that is built on him. When we see the work of the Lord in Jesus, we see his glorious power provided for us, his children. It is the power of building our lives on the truth of Jesus. We can build our lives on the lessons and teachings of Jesus. Most importantly, we can live our lives through faith in the cross of Jesus, where we find life worth living through sacrifice, first his, and by example, our own. We take up our cross and follow him, giving of ourselves for the betterment of others.

A second requirement for a good building is using good materials. We don't want to build a fair-weather home that comes down around us when the winds of trouble arise. A solid and lasting house comes from living (building) by the will of God. This is how we build our lives where they last with God's blessings. Paul spoke about the need to build up the body of Christ carefully, saying, "Now if anyone builds on the foundation with gold, silver, precious stones, wood, hay, straw—each one's work will become manifest, for the Day will disclose it, because it will be revealed by fire, and the fire will test what sort of work each one has done" (1 Cor. 3:12-13). This is also true in each of our lives. If we want God to establish the work of our hands, then we need to be wise builders. We need to build on the foundation of Jesus with the materials of God's will.

Lord, let us see what you have done in Jesus and in our lives. Let us then build our lives to your glory in Jesus, Amen.

❧ ❧ ❧

AUGUST 18

He who dwells in the shelter of the Most High will abide in the shadow of the Almighty. I will say to the L*ORD*, *"My refuge and my fortress, my God, in whom I trust." For he will deliver you from the snare of the fowler and from the deadly pestilence. He will cover you with his pinions, and under his wings you will find refuge; his faithfulness is a shield and buckler. You will not fear the terror of the night, nor the arrow that flies by day, nor the pestilence that stalks in darkness, nor the destruction that wastes at noonday. A thousand may fall at your side, ten thousand at your right hand, but it will not come near you.* (Ps. 91:1-7)

This is one of my favorite psalms. It speaks to me in ways that make me read it over and over again. I like the ideas and pictures that are painted in these verses.

I want to "dwell" and "abide" in the shelter and shadow of the Almighty. By "abiding," I do not plan on moving! I want to live there. I may foray out into the world, of course taking the Almighty with me, on mission for him, but I always return to my home, dwelling in the Almighty's shelter.

This dwelling is not simply one of "God," but it is the shelter of the "Almighty." I live in the care and custody of the greatest one there is. He is greater than any problem; he is their solution. He is greater than any fear; they melt away in his presence. He is greater than any hurt; he is balm for the pain. I dwell in the Almighty!

I say to the Lord, "My God in whom I trust" because my life in him is built on trust and faith. I trust him to take care of me today, tomorrow, and eternally. Without him, I am left trusting myself or others. At that point, I am in trouble! But trusting in him brings peace. He is not only the "Almighty," on a personal level he is my Lord and God.

The images the writer uses to show God's protection and care are beautiful. Though there are traps in life, into some of which I will undoubtedly fall, God will be there to deliver me. God will cover me with his wings like a bird does her chicks, protecting me and feeding me. God is my armament. He is a shield to block the assaults of the enemies. I need not fear the attacks of any, day or night. Even disease is not to be feared with our God. I may die of cancer one day, but living in my God that death is simply a graduation into his eternity. No fear here, just faith and gratitude. That is the life of one who dwells and abides in the Almighty!

Lord, thank you for your ever-present love. Thank you for all it entails. Thank you for extending your Almighty-ness into my life, directly involving yourself for my benefit and that of your kingdom. May I never fail to dwell in you, through Jesus, Amen!

AUGUST 19

Because you have made the Lord *your dwelling place—the Most High, who is my ref-*
uge—no evil shall be allowed to befall you, no plague come near your tent. (Ps. 91:9-10)

Wow! Look at today's passage again. "*Because* you have made the Lord
your dwelling place, no evil shall befall you." I have three reactions to this.

First, I am struck by the need to dwell in the Lord. The picture painted
is like God is an umbrella. When I am walking in his will and ways, when
I am attentive to his direction, sticking with him as I walk, then I have protection from evil in the world. Of course the obverse of this is what happens
when I choose to live outside the protection of the Lord. Those times where
I choose to dwell in the world rather than the Lord, I am opening myself to
the pain and destruction of the evil in the world. I have lived long enough
to see people, some of whom are dear to me, who have chucked overboard
their lives with the Lord for one reason or another, and without fail, their
lives have become shipwrecks. We see a select few seeming exceptions to
this passage, where someone dwells outside God's will and seems to have a
marvelous life well put together, or where someone dwells in God but seems
to have no end of problems. But those are rare exceptions in this life. They
do, however, lead me to my next reaction.

Second, I have seen exceptions! I have seen those who dwell in the
Lord and suffer tremendously. I have seen evil come against them. Is the
passage wrong? No, it is not wrong. In the larger context of Scripture, there
is nothing to indicate that the precious ones walking in God's will never
suffer tragedy or difficulty. In fact, the opposite is told. Jesus, the most precious and perfect of any human, suffered grievously. Furthermore, he told
his followers they would suffer too. He asked them to take up their own
cross and follow him. The point of Scripture is not that God's children don't
suffer. The point is that when they suffer and endure, they come out from
the other side with more faith, more holiness, more of what they need to
be God's tool in their day. Paul deemed it an honor to suffer for the cause
of Christ. Evil doesn't get its way with believers. Evil can do its worst, but
God is still bringing out the best.

Third, I am thankful to the Lord for his care and attention. He hasn't
made this world heaven. Heaven is in our future. We are in a world of pain
and difficulty, but as believers in the Lord we face that with joy in our
hearts and hope in the Lord. That makes all the difference in the world.

Lord, help us wait on you until the day you come. Let us put to death our sinful ways
to dwell securely in your love. In Jesus, Amen.

❧ ❧ ❧

AUGUST 20

He will command his angels concerning you to guard you in all your ways. On their hands they will bear you up, lest you strike your foot against a stone. You will tread on the lion and the adder; the young lion and the serpent you will trample underfoot. (Ps. 91:11-13)

After being baptized, as Jesus was beginning his ministry, he went into the wilderness where he was tempted by Satan. As Matthew sets out the temptations, it began with Satan asking Jesus to turn stones into bread as proof of his divinity. Jesus responded, "It is written . . ." and then quoted Deuteronomy 8:3 that "man shall not live by bread alone." Satan then tempted by quoting Scripture himself. This psalm passage is the one Satan turned to, although he didn't quote the whole passage.

Satan took Jesus to the pinnacle of the temple and urged Jesus to jump off. He said to Jesus, "It is written . . ." and he then quoted, "He will command his angels concerning you, and On their hands they will bear you up." Jesus shut down this temptation quoting Deuteronomy 6:16, which instructs us not to test the Lord.

There is something wrong when we read these scriptural promises in a way that turns them into tests of God. If we think we can find a promise in Scripture, set it out in our lives, and order God to respond, we need to be careful. It becomes too easy for us to act like we are God in that circumstance, making the Lord do what we say and bind him to, rather than us letting him tell us what we need to do to follow his will. God is not our genie or bellhop, carrying our luggage where we want when we want. God is God. That fact should fill us with a measure of shock and awe.

Side note: Isn't it interesting that Satan knows his Scripture well enough to quote it to Jesus? It is the story going back to the Garden, Satan takes what God has said and tries to twist it into sin. This sets me on my guard. I want to be a good student of God's word, careful to rightly understand it and teach it.

While Satan tried to misuse Scripture with Jesus, the reply of Jesus is notable. Jesus not only set the Scripture aright within the greater doctrine of a godly life, but also fulfilled the rest of the Scripture that Satan didn't quote. By not letting this Scripture be taken out of its biblical context of how we should live, Jesus didn't stumble, but instead trampled the serpent. Jesus defeated the enemy. There was not a temptation that captured Jesus' heart or mind. Jesus walked in victory, and so do we when we knit our lives to Scripture and to him through our faith and trust.

Lord, we want to walk in your victory in our lives. We want to do your works, shine your light, and proclaim your glory. Help us to do so, Lord, in Jesus' name, Amen!

❧ ❧ ❧

AUGUST 21

Because he holds fast to me in love, I will deliver him; I will protect him, because he knows my name. When he calls to me, I will answer him; I will be with him in trouble; I will rescue him and honor him. (Ps. 91:14-16)

This passage is both instructive and reassuring. It teaches that deliverance from the problems of this life comes from holding fast to the Lord. Protection from the dangers in this life comes from knowing who God is, what he has done, and what he can do. Answers to life's predicaments come from asking God. Rescue from life's troubles comes from being with the Lord. While this teaches me, it also brings me comfort.

Countless times in Scripture we see God's children holding fast to him in love and being delivered. Joseph was grabbed by his brothers who sought to kill him, then sold into slavery instead, almost as an afterthought. Yet God was with Joseph and delivered him, placing him into a place of great responsibility in Potiphar's house. Again, Joseph was in need of deliverance when Potiphar wrongly had him thrown into jail. God again came to his rescue and delivered him to an even higher position, second to Egypt's pharaoh. In spite of great distress, God caused all that Joseph touched to find success.

God's protection is easy to trace in Scripture. Over and over those who knew God went through difficult circumstances but found his protection. David, long before he became king, was the subject of King Saul's manhunts. Saul wanted David caught and wanted him killed. David fled through the wilderness, hid in caves, and found food where he could. God protected David, however, and at the right time, Saul was dead and it was David ascending the throne of Israel.

The Israelite Elkanah had two wives, Peninnah and Hannah. Peninnah had children, but Hannah was barren. Year after year, Hannah prayed for a child, and ultimately God answered, and the great prophet Samuel was born at just the right time.

Elijah was hunted by King Ahaz and Queen Jezebel, in deep trouble for the chaos he caused when confronting them. But God was with Elijah, feeding him, and keeping him safe. Ahab and Jezebel died horrible deaths, but God sent a fiery chariot to take Elijah from this world.

These aren't just stories from the past. God has delivered me, protected me, answered me, and rescued me. God doesn't save his people from every trouble, but he does rescue us in our problems! We learn faith in this. This is a tough life. We learn to hold close to the Lord, and we find deliverance. That is more than enough.

Lord, may we hold close to you and walk in your marvelous love and care in Jesus. Amen!

❧ ❧ ❧

AUGUST 22

It is good to give thanks to the Lord, to sing praises to your name, O Most High; to declare your steadfast love in the morning, and your faithfulness by night, to the music of the lute and the harp, to the melody of the lyre. (Ps. 92:1-3)

Every so often in history there have been major shifts in Christian music. While we don't have written history beyond the New Testament for the first hundred years or so of church music, we start getting some information fairly soon thereafter. Some of the earliest shifts included melodic singing, antiphonal singing, and more. By the time of the Reformation Martin Luther decided that the music of the church was too limited and he began putting Christian lyrics to melodies one would hear in bar taverns. The church recoiled, but today those hymns like "A Mighty Fortress Is Our God" have become church staples.

When I was young, there was a new movement of contemporary Christian music. It came out of the hippie movement of the late 1960s and early 1970s. These songs crept into our youth group, and found their way into our record collections. These were songs that transformed my life. They became the soundtrack of my walk with the Lord in those young years. Songs from Keith Green, John Michael Talbot, 2nd Chapter of Acts, Phil Keaggy, Michael Card, Amy Grant, and the list goes on.

Since that time, the modern music of the church has changed a good bit, evolving just as secular music does. There are songs that come out now that minister to my soul. They praise the greatness of God, proclaim his steadfast love and faithfulness. They bring the singer and listener into a tighter bond, calling forth a reliance on God for all of life's burdens. For example, Hillsong has a tremendous set of songs that pour into my life. "Prince of Peace" is a cry for God's touch in the midst of a crazy world. I can get lost in worship, regardless of what is happening in the world or my life singing, "Worthy Is the Lamb."

In the midst of these songs, many of which now form the backbone of our worship services, I have renewed my appreciation for the old hymns from my youth. I find reverence and awe singing "Holy, Holy, Holy." I can find tears in my eyes singing the proclamation, "It Is Well with My Soul" (especially knowing the backstory to that song). I am moved singing "Abide with Me."

If you don't have a soundtrack and assortment of songs to sing to the Lord in the morning and evening, you are missing out. As the psalmist said, this is "good!"

Lord, you have gifted your church with many to write and perform songs that draw us deeper in our walks. Thank you. Bless them. Help us take advantage of this in Jesus, Amen.

❧ ❧ ❧

AUGUST 23

How great are your works, O LORD! Your thoughts are very deep! The stupid man cannot know; the fool cannot understand this. (Ps. 92:5-6)

Three and one-half pounds! Yes, that's right 3½ pounds. That is the average weight of a human's brain. Out of that brain, we have the gray matter that keeps our heart beating, moves our muscles, senses feelings sent from our nerves, and stores memories. On top of that, we have gray matter that works to process thought. That's really not that much.

It is rather remarkable, when we think about it, that we are even able to think about it! But we can and do think. In some cases, we can think fairly clearly. We are able to know that if we have two apples, and we are going to get two more, that we will have enough apples to give one to each of our four friends.

Sometimes our thoughts are not so clear or quick. There are some people in this word who think their brains are potent enough to contemplate the eternity of truth, and determine that there is no God. There are others who know there is a God, but have the audacity to speak on his behalf, believing they have him and his plans figured out. Then there are some who are bewildered by all of this, and think there is no chance a 3½-pound brain can come to any real conclusions. How do we make sense of this? What is the biblical view of this?

The mind is not an afterthought. It is an amazing creation of God. It makes humans different from other living beings. We are able to contemplate things that other creatures can't. This doesn't mean our minds are perfect. To the contrary, Scripture teaches that our minds have fallen under the control of sin. Yet in that, God is at work in the believer renewing the mind (Rom. 12:2). This allows the mind to better discern the will of God, testing matters to see how they fit into God's plans.

One time I overheard my son explaining a unique feature of Christian faith related to the mind. He was speaking with my mom, his grandmother, and he explained, "Scripture teaches that we understand God mainly through his revelation. While we can find truths about God by analyzing the world, God has provided the fuller truth to us in revelation because we are unable to discern rightly without that." I was impressed! That is the biblical position stated better than I could.

We have a God whose ways are beyond ours. His thoughts are far from thoughts we could have. If we think we understand God, we are foolish. There are limits to understanding inherent in our 3½-pound brains! What we can understand is what we are taught by him.

Lord, thank you for revealing yourself to us in Scripture and in Jesus. Amen!

❦ ❦ ❦

AUGUST 24

The righteous flourish like the palm tree and grow like a cedar in Lebanon. They are planted in the house of the LORD; they flourish in the courts of our God. They still bear fruit in old age; they are ever full of sap and green, to declare that the LORD is upright; he is my rock, and there is no unrighteousness in him. (Ps. 92:12-15)

There is a lot to be said about good, old-fashioned, righteous living. Righteous living involves the whole person, heart, mind, and body. Our heart is the start of righteousness. Jesus taught as much when he explained that it was not enough not to kill your enemies. We shouldn't even hate them. We should love them and pray for them. From our hearts issue forth our actions. Part of righteous living is getting our hearts aligned with the heart of God. It means purifying our hearts of selfishness, ingratitude, envy, anger, etc.

Our hearts are not the only place where we need to work on righteousness. As integrated wholes, our hearts, minds, and bodies are all interrelated. We help our hearts when we help our minds. (What we do with the body affects us heart and mind as well.) Our minds are battlefields for righteousness. We need to understand who God is and what he has done. As we grow in that understanding we will increase our trust in him. As we recount the ways he has worked in our lives in the past, we will increase our faith for his actions in the future. Our bodies often become the acting out of the heart and mind. We need to be careful with them. If there are areas of temptation, avoid them. Alcoholics know better than to hang around bars. Believers need to be careful where they take their bodies.

We should be ridding ourselves of any love or attachment to things unholy, like gossip, sexual immorality in the mind, or other impurities. This is often more easily said than done. How to move the heart from unrighteousness to righteousness is a lifelong endeavor. Still that doesn't mean there are not definite steps we can take. For starters, we need to be careful what we feed our hearts. What we see, who we hang around, what we listen to, where we invest our time and energy, all of these things feed our hearts. We want to be feeding our hearts good things, not bad. The more we flood our hearts with good things, the less room there is for unrighteousness. Paul gave good insights in this to the Philippians, speaking to heart, mind, and body when he wrote, "whatever is true, whatever is honorable, whatever is just, whatever is pure, whatever is lovely, whatever is commendable, if there is any excellence, if there is anything worthy of praise, think about these things. What you have learned and received and heard and seen in me—practice these things, and the God of peace will be with you" (Phil. 4:8-9).

Lord, may we be righteous. Purify our thoughts, renew our minds, strengthen our bodies. In Jesus, Amen.

❦ ❦ ❦

AUGUST 25

*The L*ORD *reigns; he is robed in majesty; the L*ORD *is robed; he has put on strength as his belt. Indeed, the world is established; it won't totter. Your throne is established from of old; you are from everlasting.* (Ps. 93:1-2)

This is a marvelous ancient Hebrew poem whose beauty is best appreciated if we read it as such. The defining mark of Hebrew poetry was writing in stanzas that run parallel to each other. Sometimes the parallel stanza means a similar thing, but using different words, draws an interesting emphasis. Sometimes the parallel stanza means the opposite, allowing the opposition to add shades of meaning. The parallel stanza may even be just a further step from the first stanza, adding nuance in the process.

Here we have eight stanzas, all of which are related and parallel. The first two stanzas make up the first picture (I will put the stanzas in parenthesis to best make this easy to follow): (1) The LORD God reigns, (2) his clothing is MAJESTY. God doesn't wear anything so mundane as a human does. After all, God is not flesh and blood. God's clothing is majesty, an awe-inspiring greatness unequalled anywhere in all of space and time. The second two stanzas run parallel to the first two. (3) The LORD is robed, (4) he has put on strength as his belt. Stanzas 1 and 3 both fit. God reigns and God is robed, a sign of reigning. Similarly, stanzas 2 and 4 fit each other. God is clothed in majesty and strength.

The last four stanzas also fit each other. They are set as a complement to the first four stanzas. These last four stanzas begin with "Indeed," and add, (5) the world is established and (6) it shall never be moved. Then we have the last two stanzas working together. (7) God's throne is established from of old; (8) God is from everlasting. Putting these four groups (1 and 2, 3 and 4, 5 and 6, and 7 and 8) together gives us the key to the passage.

The LORD reigns and is robed. The earth doesn't reign, but it is "established" and won't totter or quake. We see the earth. We live on it and know it. It hasn't gone anywhere and isn't going anywhere tomorrow. In a similar way, though we don't see him, God's reign is established. God's reign is going nowhere. He has always been in control and always will be. He is strong and majestic. None of that is leaving. None of that is changing. The God we worship is Lord of all. He is exalted high and always shall be.

Lord, we praise you as awesome God. We are humbled to be allowed to praise you and honored to be your children. We lift you up as majestic and strong, and lean on you for our lives daily. In Jesus' mighty name, Amen.

❧ ❧ ❧

AUGUST 26

Your decrees are very trustworthy; holiness befits your house, O LORD, *forevermore.* (Ps. 93:5)

Have you ever been to a church service where people in the audience let out an "Amen!" to something said in the sermon? Maybe just in the ordinary course of living you've heard someone affirm something another is saying with an "Amen!" Of course, most everyone ends prayers with an "Amen!"

We might consider "Amen" part of the English language, but it goes back thousands of years into ancient Hebrew. It is the word that confirms or supports something. In various forms, the word is often translated as "trustworthy," "faithful," "truly," or "amen." It is a supporting word lending affirmation to something as being true and reliable.

We have "amen" in this passage (in a noun form; we usually translate the adverb form as "amen"). It is found in the word "trustworthy." The writer gives an "amen" to the decrees of God. Those decrees are trustworthy and reliable. To use a modern saying, we can "go to the bank" on them. We should study those decrees and apply them in our lives. As Paul said, they are "profitable for teaching, for reproof, for correction, and for training in righteousness," that each one belonging to God "may be complete, equipped for every good work" (2 Tim. 3:16).

The amen to God's decrees is not always echoed by the world. In fact, the world is often at odds with God's decrees. Certainly some of the decrees God delivered were clearly for a time and place, and we know that today is different. A clear example of that is the dietary laws of the Old Testament. God explained to Peter that those laws were not binding upon all people as Peter was about to be used in Cornelius' conversion (Acts 10). But those instructions and decrees that are important to holiness, are important to us today. We need to make our prayerful decisions about such things, knowing, as the psalmist pointed out, holiness befits the house of the Lord.

Before leaving the psalm, note the last word—"forevermore." Holiness is an attribute of God, who exists forever. It is the right behavior for God's people who are made in his image, and called into relationship with God forever. So we join the psalmist with a hearty, Amen!

Lord, may our lives reflect the AMEN we affirm in your decrees. May we live in your holiness forever. In Jesus the holy and righteous one we pray, AMEN.

❧ ❧ ❧

AUGUST 27

O Lord, God of vengeance, O God of vengeance, shine forth! Rise up, O judge of the earth; repay to the proud what they deserve! O Lord, how long shall the wicked, how long shall the wicked exult? (Ps. 94:1-3)

Hmmmm. . . . Lots of people have trouble with passages like today's. Who wants to read, much less think, about God as a God of vengeance. We want to think about a God of love. We want to tell the world that God is kind and loving, seeking to forgive and save the lost. We cringe over calling God a God of vengeance. It makes him sound bloodthirsty and mean. Anyway, doesn't Jesus put to rest notions of God as a harsh retributive God?

I think many of our thoughts come from the comparatively cushy and comfortable lives we live. We are not living through the atrocities of tyrants who torture and murder to advance personal power and agenda. Hopefully we never see firsthand the evil of rapists and killers. Most of us never experience pure evil and the pain and misery it brings. If we read in the news reports of killings in Kosovo, for example, where Serbian soldiers rounded up defenseless young ladies and, as reported by the BBC, killed those daughters in front of their mothers, then maybe we cry for justice in these atrocities. Letting these atrocities go without an answer would reinforce such behavior.

But God's justice goes beyond those types of atrocities. God's vengeance reaches to all sin. God is a God of justice. That is a character trait of his that isn't going away. That means that sin is punished; sin brings death. That means that wrongs are wrong, and not whitewashed into right. God doesn't play justice, he defines justice. We may not see it immediately, but it happens in God's timing. He doesn't balance the books of justice second by second, but he balances them nonetheless.

The blessing and the good news, no the GREAT news, is that the God of vengeance and justice *is also* a God of love and mercy. God wants to bring mercy to everyone. God wants to bring forgiveness to everyone. God wants everyone to walk in his grace and mercy. Here is where we find the cross of Jesus. It is that nexus point where God's vengeance and justice collide head-on into God's love and mercy. By Jesus taking the vengeance of God, taking the cup of God's wrath, taking the punishment of sin, all on our behalf, God is able to extend his mercy and love to us, while never sacrificing his character as a just God. We need to acknowledge God's justice and vengeance, for without it, we have trouble ever understanding the cross of Jesus. God's justice is right. His mercy is grace.

Lord, we acknowledge you as a God of vengeance, and we thank you that vengeance has passed from us in Jesus. We pray others will turn to you as well. In Jesus, Amen.

❧ ❧ ❧

AUGUST 28

They say, "The LORD *does not see; the God of Jacob does not perceive." Understand, O dullest of the people! Fools, when will you be wise? He who planted the ear, does he not hear? He who formed the eye, does he not see? He who disciplines the nations, does he not rebuke? He who teaches man knowledge—the* LORD*—knows the thoughts of man, that they are but a breath.* (Ps. 94:7-11)

Look at the polls. Most people in the United States believe in God. I am not sure, however, that most people think that God is paying attention! My litmus test for this idea is how people live and what people do.

This passage pointed out the foolishness of anyone who thinks God isn't paying attention. God is the reason we have ears; do we think him deaf? God is the reason we have eyes; do we think him blind? God is the one who oversees the nations rising and falling; do we think him apathetic to our lives?

I read today's passage and write of those that believe one thing, but seem to live another, but then warning bells sound in my head. I am haunted by my memory of the Pharisee who looked over at a sinner and prayed, "God, thank you that I am not like that sinner." Jesus did not have good things to say about that haughty Pharisee (Luke 18:10-14).

So I try hard to take these passages and consider them from a personal angle. Where is my life inconsistent with a true belief in God? Do I think I'm smarter than God? Do I fail to see him as my teacher, thinking I find wisdom on my own instead? Do I think I see the world better than God? Do I think my thoughts about me, the world, reality and truth, and God are correct, even when set against the truth of God in revelation?

If I am going to accept that God is who God claims to be. If I am going to accept that the Bible gives me genuine revelation of God. If I am going to believe and trust in that revelation, then it is going to sculpt what I do and believe, not the other way around. I won't be defining who I think God is, I will be seeking to understand God as he has revealed himself. I won't be letting my brain dictate reality, I will use my brain to better understand the reality of the revealed God in my world.

God needs to be at the center of my thoughts. Here is wisdom: Removing confidence in my ability to find truth apart from God, and putting confidence in God to teach me truth.

Lord, I am guilty of putting myself in the center too often, when you are the rightful center of all things. Help me to look to you, learn from you, and live for you in Jesus, Amen.

❧ ❧ ❧

AUGUST 29

Blessed is the man whom you discipline, O Lord, and whom you teach out of your law, to give him rest from days of trouble, until a pit is dug for the wicked. For the Lord will not forsake his people; he will not abandon his heritage. (Ps. 94:12-14)

There are great illustrations in life of the power of discipline. I have seen animals do amazing things because they have been taught through discipline, both affirmative and negative. Some amazing achievements of athletes illustrate the power of disciplined workouts and practices. The disciplined lifestyles of certain people have propelled them to accomplishments not achieved by the ordinary person. Many adults today readily acknowledge much of their success in life came from living under parents who carefully disciplined, teaching right, wrong, work ethic, and motivation.

I have also seen the negatives from a failure of discipline. I have seen dogs run out into the street into oncoming cars. I have seen people whose lives have fallen apart because they never learned to say "No!" where "no" was important, people whose lives became limited because of lacking discipline in exercise and diet. Many people have difficult lives because they lack the discipline necessary to make hard choices and follow through.

Spiritual life is not too different when it comes to discipline. We need to learn and incorporate into our lives the discipline to do right, to live in love, to flee immorality, to stand up to injustice with determination, to answer hate with love, to trust in the face of doubt, to pray in crisis, to answer fury with patience, and to be at peace in the midst of turmoil.

How do we get there? When we commit our lives to the Lord, he takes us at our word. He doesn't let us come into a committed relationship without his working in our lives. He disciplines us as a parent does a child. He teaches us right from wrong. When we choose right, he affirms us with positive reinforcement. When we choose wrong, he teaches us the wrongness, often with painful consequences! Paul explained that this discipline is an important way that God keeps us distinct from the world (1 Cor. 11:32). The writer of Hebrews explained that God's discipline proceeds from his love. "And have you forgotten the exhortation that addresses you as sons? 'My son, do not regard lightly the discipline of the Lord, nor be weary when reproved by him. For the Lord disciplines the one he loves, and chastises every son whom he receives'" (Heb. 12:5-6). Let us thank God for discipline and walk in its blessings as we grow before our Lord!

Lord, we do thank you for disciplining us. We pray we learn your lessons and become the people you want us to be. In Jesus we pray, Amen.

AUGUST 30

When I thought, "My foot slips," your steadfast love, O LORD, held me up. When the cares of my heart are many, your consolations cheer my soul. (Ps. 94:18-19)

Where do you turn in times of need? Do you have a safety net that will keep you from falling? If you are a child of the King, the answer is "Yes!" Randy Stonehill penned a song with the chorus: "I turn to you, like the night turns into morning. I turn to you when I feel like trouble's knocking at my door. I turn to you, and through all the years, you've never turned away. And I am always turning back to you." I like that song.

I also like the way the psalmist has expressed God's care and protection. The writer doesn't say, "My foot slips, so I cried out to God and he saved me." Nor does he say, "The cares of my heart are many, so I seek your help, and you send consolation to cheer my soul." There is nothing in the way the psalm is written to indicate that God's protection and consolation are linked to the cry for help.

The relationship between psalmist and the Lord is such that the "pleas for help" are inherent in the relationship. The writer already leans on God. So when the writer's foot slips God is already there, protecting and holding the psalmist up. The writer is already close to the Lord so when "the cares of my heart are many," the consolation of God is already flowing.

I want to be in such a relationship with the Lord. I want to be in constant communication with him. We live in a day where smart phones and social media make instant communication with friends possible, but I want even more closeness with the Lord than that. This closeness is possible, through Jesus Christ.

Right before his arrest and crucifixion, Jesus spent a good bit of time in prayer. A long section of that prayer was written in John 17. In his prayer, Jesus prayed that his followers would know that while Jesus would leave the world in a physical sense, that Jesus would take up residence in his children and be "in us" (John 17:22-26). Jesus used similar language in speaking to the church at Laodicea saying, "Behold, I stand at the door and knock. If anyone hears my voice and opens the door, I will come in to him and eat with him, and he with me" (Rev. 3:20).

With Jesus dwelling inside us, communication with the Lord can be an ongoing dialogue, not needing the cell reception our social media might need. It is why Paul can tell the Christian to "pray without ceasing" (1 Thess. 5:17). That is a relationship we can trust.

Lord, help me to stay in ongoing dialogue with you. Thank you for being there for me. In Jesus, Amen.

❧ ❧ ❧

AUGUST 31

Oh come, let us sing to the LORD; let us make a joyful noise to the rock of our salvation! Let us come into his presence with thanksgiving; let us make a joyful noise to him with songs of praise! For the LORD is a great God, and a great King above all gods. (Ps. 95:1-3)

I love the songs of devoted worship. I am not sure there was ever a better song penned than "Holy, Holy, Holy." But those aren't the only songs we need in our worship vocabulary. We also need songs of "joyful noise!"

We all know how the melody and lyric of songs can affect the way the song moves in our hearts. It can even affect our own moods. There are times for songs of mourning, but there are also times for songs of joyful dancing. We should never think of one category as belonging to our times of worship and the other belonging to times outside of God. God gets both!

We have reasons to make a joyful noise to the Lord. We have a lot to be thankful for. We are the recipients of so many good things. The greatest, of course, is the forgiveness and love we find in Jesus. This alone should move us to great rejoicing and happiness. Moreover, we have the promise of eternity. This life isn't the end of our existence. When we die, death has no sting. We, and so many of our loved ones in Jesus, are assured a glorious resurrection. It will be so great, that as our Rabbi Paul taught, the sufferings we have to endure in this life, are nothing compared to the glories that will be revealed to us after this life is over (Rom. 8:18). Many of us have marvelous families to be thankful for. The food we eat, each breath we take, the days of good health, the opportunities of citizenship and life in this world are so abundant. All of these good things are gifts from our God and Father, and each is a cause for rejoicing with a joyful song.

God is no policeman, waiting to catch us in a speed trap. God is no harsh taskmaster, looking to get us to do his work for him. God is no weak God, needing our provision to keep him going. God is no poor God, needing our money to get his message out. God is no limited God, keeping some semblance of power as long as we are in the right place at the right time. God is a great God. He is a King above any other thing or person we might ever worship or highly regard. We can bring joyful noises to him and to the world, proclaiming the truth of who our God is. It is a reason to sing happily and with gusto!

Lord, we lift your name on high. You are great and treat us with undeserved love. Our gratitude isn't adequate, but we bring it to you in Jesus, knowing you are worthy of it and much more. Amen!

❧ ❧ ❧

SEPTEMBER 1

Oh come, let us worship and bow down; let us kneel before the Lord, *our Maker! For he is our God, and we are the people of his pasture, and the sheep of his hand. Today, if you hear his voice, do not harden your hearts, as at Meribah, as on the day at Massah in the wilderness.* (Ps. 95:6-8)

Meribah and Massah weren't high spots in Israel's life. Israel had been enslaved in Egypt for centuries, and at a particularly bitter time when pharaoh was forcing infanticide on them, God brought forth Moses. By God's grace, Moses had a peculiar childhood, raised as one of pharaoh's own in pharaoh's court. A boil turn of events led the adult Moses out of Egypt into the wilderness of the Sinai Peninsula. There Moses encountered the Lord in a burning bush. God sent Moses to rescue the Israelites. Through the working of miracle after miracle, the people were finally released. As the Israelites fled Egypt, pharaoh had second thoughts. He took the world's largest and mightiest military force of the day in pursuit. God parted the Red Sea, rescued the Israelites, and routed pharaoh's forces.

God's provision was amazing. Having rescued the people, God guided them, promising to bring them into the Promised Land, a land of abundance. By a pillar of fire in the night and a pillar of smoke by day, God led the Israelites through the harsh wilderness. When they hungered, he gave them free bread (manna). One of their encampment sites had no water, and the Israelites got thirsty. The people started defaming God and Moses. Evidently God's accommodations were not up to their standards at this part of the journey. The people grumbled, "quarreling" with Moses and "testing" the Lord. God stepped in and instructed Moses on how to get water from the rock by hitting it with his staff. Moses then named the place "Massah and Meribah, because of the quarreling of the people of Israel, and because they tested the Lord by saying, 'Is the Lord among us or not?'" (Exod. 17:7).

The psalmist rightly warns us about Meribah and Massah. We believers have been delivered from a slavery to sin and its curse of death. God assures us that he has a Promised Land awaiting us, secured by the death and resurrection of Jesus the Messiah. God guides us through this life, feeding us and meeting our needs. As the psalmist says, we are the sheep of his pasture, and he tends to us as a shepherd, leading us and seeing to our sustenance. Heaven forbid we should be like the hardhearted Israelites who grumbled against the Lord, not satisfied with his provisions. We know that this is not the Promised Land, and we shouldn't pretend it is. We are his people and we follow him with joy to the end of our journey.

Lord, please soften our hearts. Thank you for your perfect provisions! In Jesus, Amen.

❧ ❧ ❧

SEPTEMBER 2

Oh sing to the Lord a new song; sing to the Lord, all the earth! Sing to the Lord, bless his name; tell of his salvation from day to day. Declare his glory among the nations, his marvelous works among all the peoples! For great is the Lord, and greatly to be praised. (Ps. 96:1-4)

The psalmist urges us to sing to the Lord, and to tell of his salvation from day to day. God is at work, day to day, in many ways in our lives. We should be aware of it, praise him for it, and tell others about it.

God's work in our lives each day is evident. God is behind our provision each day. Of course, we may want to take credit for that. We may think that because we have money and a job that we can buy our own food, so God wouldn't get credit, but believers know better. I would not have my job, but for the Lord. I would not have my parents and family, but for the Lord. I would not have the peace of mind to live, but for the Lord. God is the reason we have anything that is good. So, let's be daily in our gratitude. Jesus taught his followers to pray each day for their "daily bread," rather than once for all time. We rely on the Lord each day for our sustenance. Praise God!

God also works daily molding us into the kind of person we should be. He takes us like a potter takes a lump of clay, and fashions us into vessels for his service. God hasn't fixed me all at once; it is an ongoing process that takes time. Paul spoke of how we are transformed into a likeness of Jesus as we grow in the Lord in glory. "And we all . . . beholding the glory of the Lord, are being transformed into the same image from one degree of glory to another" (2 Cor. 3:18). I can see ungodly traits, thought patterns, practices, and habits in my life that need the transforming touch of God. I am thankful that he is doing that for me on a day-by-day basis. Praise God!

God works in my life each day to bring me into kingdom service for him. When I tendered my life to the Lord, I decided that I would not live for ME, but I would live for HIM. Jesus also taught his followers to pray that God's kingdom would come. We want to play a role in that. We want God to use us for his good works and for his purposes. Our ultimate long-term, medium-term, and short-term goals should be to be used by God!

So we have God at work in our lives each day. We should not be silent about that. Let us find someone and tell them how God is working in our life. Let us declare his glory and marvelous works to the world we encounter. Praise God with me!

Lord, thank you for working in me today. Use me in your service in Jesus, Amen.

❧❧ ❧❧ ❧❧

SEPTEMBER 3

Splendor and majesty are before the LORD*; strength and beauty are in his sanctuary.* (Ps. 96:6)

Look what we find when we are in the presence of the Lord! We find splendor, majesty, strength, and beauty! That alone should make us want to draw near to the Lord, find him in his sanctuary, and enter into praise in his presence. That will be our entrance into the blessings of his splendor, majesty, strength, and beauty!

When I was younger, I was listening to one of my favorite preachers, Don Finto, teach on worship. He used this passage and suggested that if splendor, majesty, strength, and beauty are found in the sanctuary and presence of God, shouldn't we all want to spend time in his presence?

I look at my life, and see my great need for God's strength. If I am going to be the father I need to be, the husband I need to be, the teacher I need to be, the lawyer I need to be, the believer I need to be, I must have God's strength. There is too much risk, too much pressure, and too much room for fear or failure, for me to live this life successfully on my own.

Since I am in need of God's strength, it is important that I spend time in worship, seeking him in his sanctuary. Worship needs to be more than simply being at church singing for melody's sake or because I like the songs. Worship means an intellectual and spiritual acknowledgment of God in his splendor, and majesty. Worship involves seeing, understanding, and acknowledging God's beauty.

This is a big part of what we are to be about in our corporate assemblies of worship, but it shouldn't be found only there. In my alone time, I need to draw near to God and gaze upon his beauty. God has done the necessary work to allow us to approach him. The writer of Hebrews explained, "we have confidence to enter the holy places by the blood of Jesus, by the new and living way that he opened for us through the curtain, that is, through his flesh, and since we have a great priest over the house of God, let us draw near with a true heart in full assurance of faith" (Heb. 10:19-21). We don't come into God's presence and leave empty-handed. We worship a God who gives gifts. We get his strength and more. As we "with confidence draw near to the throne of grace," we find "mercy and find grace to help in time of need" (Heb. 4:16). I need to spend more time in God's presence!

Lord, through Jesus Christ, our crucified Savior, we come before you in your holiness. We gaze upon your beauty and your splendor. Please give us the strength, mercy, and grace to walk in your ways each day. Amen!

❄ ❄ ❄

SEPTEMBER 4

Ascribe to the LORD, O families of the peoples, ascribe to the LORD glory and strength! Ascribe to the LORD the glory due his name; bring an offering, and come into his courts! (Ps. 96:7-8)

Are you a giving person? Some people are natural givers, while others have to work on it. We worship a giving God, and he calls us to become like him. All of us need to learn to be givers.

In this passage, the psalmist instructs us to bring offering into the Lord's courts. We are told to give to God. What can we give the God who has everything? In the Old Testament days, before the destruction of the second temple, the people could bring God sacrifices. Those sacrifices were never really gifts for God, though. He didn't need them. They were in place for people. They taught people to be attentive to their sins and short-comings. They taught people to be aware of the need for God. They taught people to be thankful to God. But we are remiss if we think the God who made all cattle needed a human to bring him a bull for slaughter.

There is something, however, that we are able to bring to God, that is ours to give. It isn't a "thing," but it is something greater. We can bring God our heart and all it entails, and give that to him. When we do, we bring God our obedience, and give that to him. We bring God our attitudes and give those to him. We bring God our fears and worries, and trust those to him. We bring God a fierce dedication to his kingdom and a determined dedication to being used by him for his kingdom's good. We bring him our praise, worship, and adulation. We sing to him songs of our hearts, expressing our trust in him, expressing his greatness, adoring his steadfast love and lifting up his unique holiness. We tell a world in desperate need of God about who he is and how he loves each person, and thereby bring to God the honor of our speaking of him to those in need. We bring God our prayers, daily acknowledging who he is and with gratitude, acknowledge what he does in and for us. We give God our tithes from the first fruits of our resources.

These are things that we can and should bring to the Lord. They are things he has left up to us. Of course, with our God, we are not surprised that even in these things we bring and give to him, he gives back to us. We aren't able to give God anything without there being a direct blessing to us. Whenever we give, we receive—pressed down and running over (Luke 6:38). We worship a giving God. I want to be more like him!

Lord, thank you for your innumerable gifts to me. I want to give back to you. You deserve all I have. Forgive me when I get greedy with you and fail to give to you. In Jesus, Amen.

❧ ❧ ❧

SEPTEMBER 5

Let the heavens be glad, and let the earth rejoice; let the sea roar, and all that fills it; let the field exult, and everything in it! Then shall all the trees of the forest sing for joy before the LORD, *for he comes, for he comes to judge the earth. He will judge the world in righteousness, and the peoples in his faithfulness.* (Ps. 96:11-13)

Does the idea of God coming to judge the earth cause you to rejoice and sing for joy? Does it help or hurt knowing that God will judge the world in righteousness? Does God's faithfulness in his judgments sound like a good thing? It should!

Judgment is a strange thing. Some don't like the sound of judgment and feel that God is a harsh God if his judgment finds someone guilty. Others don't mind the judgment of God because they feel that, at least compared to others, they seem pretty good. These folks figure that if God judging "in righteousness" means that our good deeds and our bad deeds get put into a balance, and as long as our good outweighs our bad, we get thumbs up.

Both of these camps are missing the biblical teaching of God judging in righteousness and faithfulness. For starters, we need to understand that God is not only the judge, but he is also the standard. God sets the standard for "good" and "evil." Judgment is not based on how are we compared to another. It is based on how are we compared to the Lord! God made us in his image, and we are charged with *his* ethics and morality. Our holiness should be an earthly representation of God's moral character. This was what Jesus exhibited. To fail to do this even once is to fail altogether.

Paul set out God's righteous judgment simply: to those who persistently do good, they have eternity with the Father; to those who don't obey and are self-seeking, they get wrath (Rom. 2:6-11). Now if that was all Paul said, we would be in trouble. After all, no one does good all the time. In fact, even our best deeds seem to be tainted with at least a little bit of selfishness. So God's principles of judgment, his righteousness, is not good news for anyone. There is, however, more to the story, and that is the good news. Paul explained that God's righteous judgment is met fully by Jesus Christ. If anyone is found "in Christ" or with the righteousness of Christ, then such a person is fully righteous before God. We are found in Christ when we put our trust in him (aka "faith"). If we are in Christ, our sins are justly forgiven because the full debt has been paid. Jesus explained it before Paul, saying, "whoever believes in the Son of God will not perish, but have everlasting life" (John 3:16). At the end of that famous chapter of John is the rest of the story: those who don't, on them "the wrath of God remains" (John 3:36). That is the justice and mercy of God.

Lord, thank you for Christ. I trust him to take care of my sin before you. In Jesus, Amen.

❧ ❧ ❧

SEPTEMBER 6

The LORD reigns, let the earth rejoice; let the many coastlands be glad! Clouds and thick darkness are all around him; righteousness and justice are the foundation of his throne. Fire goes before him and burns up his adversaries all around. His lightnings light up the world; the earth sees and trembles. The mountains melt like wax before the LORD, before the Lord of all the earth. (Ps. 97:1-5)

There is great news today. The Lord reigns!

The world might be in trouble. We know there is evil all around. There are wars, famines, terrorist attacks, and human rights are violated, but the Lord reigns. He sees and knows. He reaches out to those hurting and offers comfort. He will make all things right in time. Evil may stalk the world, holding a good bit under its control, but right will win in the end. In the war between Good and Evil, God will be victorious.

Our country might be in trouble. (This is true regardless of which country is your country.) The economics aren't always soaring. The political parties aren't always trustworthy. The politicians aren't always the kind of public servants we would want. The courts aren't always fair. The country's morality may be failing. But, the Lord reigns! He sets up politicians and pulls them down. He sustains his people through economic and political hardships. Some of the greatest growth of the early church came during the times of Roman persecution. God will not let any of the country's maladies stop his kingdom's advance.

Our families might be in trouble. We might have loved ones who are sick. We might have loved ones in rebellion against God. We might have loved ones who are captive to some addiction. We might have loved ones who have turned callous. Regardless, the Lord reigns! He knows what is at stake, and he promises to answer our prayers. He knows who is sick and whether healing is best at this time, later in this life, or best of it comes in the next life. He knows about addiction and is working toward helping those stuck find release. He knows rebellion and is on the case of the rebellious, seeking to bring them back into a vibrant fellowship.

We might be in trouble individually. Work, school, relationships, so many things can wreck our days and attitudes. But the Lord reigns! We can seek him out. He is a refuge, a teacher, a counselor, a friend. He will answer us in the time of need, and nothing can separate us from his love for us.

The Lord reigns! Let the earth rejoice. Let the people of God be glad!

Lord, you are the reigning God. Reign in our hearts, victorious in Jesus, Amen!

❧ ❧ ❧

SEPTEMBER 7

The heavens proclaim his righteousness, and all the peoples see his glory. (Ps. 97:6)

Sometimes things are so obvious, they don't register to us. We know the old saying, "He can't see the forest for the trees." This idea that some people can't find a forest because all the trees in front of their eyes seem to get in the way is not novel. It happens more often than we think. I think it especially common with the handiwork of the Lord.

The psalmist understood that the heavens proclaimed God's righteousness. I like to think of righteousness as linked closely to consistency. Both righteousness and consistency are reliable in outcome. God's righteousness doesn't change, and is fully reliable. In the same way, the heavens are quite reliable from the perspective of the psalmist and even today. We see the North Star in the northern sky. It doesn't change in some fickle way tricking us by becoming the South Star some nights. The three stars that align in Orion's Belt will be aligning there again tomorrow. There is a marvelous consistency and reliability in God's righteousness and in the heavens.

Paul noted this aspect of the world in Romans 1:20, linking creation to God's nature and also eternal power. "For his invisible attributes, namely, his eternal power and divine nature, have been clearly perceived, ever since the creation of the world, in the things that have been made." If these realities are the forest, the psalmist points out the problems some people have with the trees!

The psalmist points out that all people see God's glory. There is no one who doesn't gaze into the sky. Everyone has seen the night sky and stars. Everyone is familiar with the sun rising in the east and setting in the west. This is the glory of God reflected in his created world. The problem is a lot of people who see the glory of God do not understand it to be *his* glory they see. They think it a cosmic accident, or some natural event with no substance beyond its physical features. Often these are the same people who rail against the idea of God asserting, "Why doesn't he show himself?" Aside from the incarnation of Christ, we see the invisible God in his visible creation. We should see it and be in awe.

As I think through this passage, I wonder where I have my own blind spots about God. Where is God working in my life that I tend to see as something else? God has assured me that in the midst of this troubling life, he will be teaching, guiding, and protecting me. Where is he doing this at this moment that I am simply writing off to coincidence, good fortune or bad fortune, or something else? I want to see God's hand!

Lord, open our eyes and soften our hearts, that we might see you moving in our lives and give you the glory and honor due your name. In Jesus we pray, Amen!

❧ ❧ ❧

SEPTEMBER 8

O you who love the LORD, *hate evil! He preserves the lives of his saints; he delivers them from the hand of the wicked. Light is sown for the righteous, and joy for the upright in heart. Rejoice in the* LORD, *O you righteous, and give thanks to his holy name!* (Ps. 97:10-12)

Lots of people think of love and hate as opposites. They aren't. When we love the Lord, we hate evil. Paul says much the same thing in his instructions to the church at Rome. "Let your love be genuine; abhor ['hate'] what is evil" (Rom. 12:9). Genuine love hates evil because of what evil is and what evil does.

Love is a godly trait, but when that love turns inward in an insidious way, it becomes evil. Evil is a cancerous distortion of that which is good. For example, speaking the truth is a good thing. It is a godly thing. But when we speak falsely, rather than truthfully, we are doing evil, not good. Truth is good; lying is evil. Similarly, we can consider sexuality as an example. In God's instructions for marriage, sexual expression is a holy and good thing. But when that sexuality finds expression outside of marriage, that which is good becomes evil. If we want to eat some good food, that can be a good thing, a real blessing from the Lord. But overeating and gluttony becomes evil. Taking the resources and money God has placed at our disposal and using it to further God's kingdom is a good thing. But taking that money and wasting it or using it for destructive reasons is evil.

We can walk in holiness or evil. Generally, we mix the two up fairly well! If we stop and think about it carefully and prayerfully, however, we realize that loving God is loving good. That should in turn, stir up a hatred of evil. Why hatred?

As an aberration of God, evil is destructive. As good as good can be and as good as good can do, evil has the opposite effect. Evil leads to bad consequences as certainly as sticking your hand in the fire leads to burns. It is the reason evil is evil. If evil worked to God's good purposes, we would not call it evil. We need to stand against evil and fight against its role in our lives, in our families, and in our areas of influence.

Paul told the Galatians to avoid any deception about this. "Do not be deceived: God is not mocked, for whatever one sows, that will he also reap. For the one who sows to his own flesh will from the flesh reap corruption, but the one who sows to the Spirit will from the Spirit reap eternal life. And let us not grow weary of doing good, for in due season we will reap, if we do not give up" (Gal. 6:7-9). Let us be children of love. Let us hate evil!

Lord, don't let me fall into temptation. Please deliver me from evil. Develop in me a strong distaste for evil so I might walk and lead others in righteousness. In Jesus, Amen.

❧ ❧ ❧

SEPTEMBER 9

Oh sing to the LORD a new song, for he has done marvelous things! His right hand and his holy arm have worked salvation for him. The LORD has made known his salvation; he has revealed his righteousness in the sight of the nations. He has remembered his steadfast love and faithfulness to the house of Israel. All the ends of the earth have seen the salvation of our God. (Ps. 98:1-3)

Have you ever tried to get something known to the world? It is possible with the Internet. Some people become overnight sensations. For those who predate the wonders of the worldwide web, it was not always so. While it's still not easy today, it used to be a lot harder! If we go back to the days before television, it was harder still. Predate newspapers and moveable print, and worldwide fame was even harder to come by.

It has always stunned me that the word of Jesus Christ and Christianity became the world phenomenon it is today. Think about it this way. Some fellow, of whom we know next to nothing about for the first thirty years of his life, at least after his infancy, lived in the hills of a backwater province in the Roman Empire, walking around for three years telling people who would listen what he thought about God and the Jewish faith. His main followers were some uneducated fishermen and a few well-intentioned, but not too socially regarded women. The man offended the power structure of this minor religion in this hill country province and they used the Roman power structure to kill him.

That should have been the end of it. But it wasn't. Somehow this rumor started that the fellow came back from the dead after three days. Roman soldiers had stood guard over his enclosed tomb, but to no avail. His body was gone, with only his burial clothes remaining. Some of his followers, who at first disassociated from him at his arrest for fear they might too come to a violent end, became adamantly convinced that this fellow had come back from the dead and even charged them to give up their own goals, plans, and desires, living in jeopardy to tell the world that this fellow had died and was resurrected because he was the unique Son of God. He was deity himself.

Surely, such a preposterous idea wouldn't go far. It would be labeled some superstition of uneducated people in the hills of Judea. It would most assuredly die out when those who followed it were subject to forfeiture of all their property, wealth, family, and even their own lives. Yet it didn't die out. It didn't stay in the hills of the backwater country. Within a few decades, it was thriving all over the known world. It is still thriving today, and some think this coincidence.

Lord, you have made your salvation known. We are in awe. In Jesus, Amen.

❄ ❄ ❄

SEPTEMBER 10

Make a joyful noise to the Lord, *all the earth; break forth into joyous song and sing praises! Sing praises to the* Lord *with the lyre, with the lyre and the sound of melody! With trumpets and the sound of the horn make a joyful noise before the King, the* Lord! *(Ps. 98:4-6)*

This psalm seems a bit out of my reach! I don't have a lyre, and I couldn't play it if I did. I don't play the trumpet or any other horn. I couldn't coax a melody out of those instruments if my life depended on it. But that is not the full thrust of the psalm, so I digest it a bit more fully, and find it actually fits my abilities after all!

The constant beat in this psalm is not what instruments to play or when to play them. The drumbeat is one of praising God in every way with everything! The lyre, trumpet, and horns are marvelous examples, but they are not exclusive. We need to praise God with all that we have. We need to bring our resources, our talents, our creativity, our dedication, and our time to bear in praising the Lord. We join the earth in the chorus of exalting our God.

This is not a burden for the child of God; it is a joy. Our songs are joyful noise. These aren't just songs we sing, but also the song that proceeds from our lives. My voice is not the only instrument of praise of God. I can praise him with my life.

Here is where those "other instruments" come into play. The way I treat someone who is harsh to me, is a chorus of praise to the God who gives me joy. The way I help the orphan is a verse of praise to the God who has the heart of fathering the orphan. They time I give to someone who is panicked and uncertain how to move forward is a song of honor to my God who is seeking to help those who are in dire straits. The love that I share with my family is a refrain of God's love being reflected in both my role as a husband and a father. My faithful response to one in need of love is a melodic tune in harmony with God's faithful love to me. Walking peacefully through the storms of life shows me tuned into the Prince of Peace who stills the storms. My kindness to a stranger in need echoes the sound of Jesus' teaching about the Good Samaritan.

There are many ways in my life to sing new songs of praise to my God. I may not play the lyre, but I have instruments galore to bring to the symphony of praise to our God in this life and world. Praise God!

Lord, may I praise you with my life. All of me, all of life, all the time. May I live to your honor and glory, singing from my heart. In Jesus' most worthy name, Amen.

❧ ❧ ❧

SEPTEMBER 11

The LORD reigns; let the peoples tremble! He sits enthroned upon the cherubim; let the earth quake! The LORD is great in Zion; he is exalted over all the peoples. Let them praise your great and awesome name! Holy is he! (Ps. 99:1-3)

Elvis Presley had a hit song about the effect that falling in love was having on him. He asked, "What'sa wrong with me? I'm itchin' like a man in a fuzzy tree. My friends say I'm actin' wild as a bug. I'm in love. I'm all shook up." He was so shook up his hands were shaky, his knees were weak, and he had trouble standing up.

We know what it is to be shaking. It can happen when something scares us, awes us, or touches us. The psalmist calls it forth as a response to the Lord reigning. "*Let his people tremble,*" he writes, equating it to the image of an earthquake. The great and awesome Lord, high above all peoples, sits enthroned as ruler. We don't think about fearing God because we live two thousand years after the kind and loving Jesus from whom we seem to have nothing the fear. But we are remiss if we don't think carefully about God in his holiness reigning on high.

He is to be feared. Not because he might lash out. He doesn't have a short fuse. There is nothing arbitrary about him that we need to fear. But he is great and awesome. He has his will and purposes. He abhors the proud and abusers in this world. He cares for the wounded, the underprivileged, the humble, and those in need.

As I consider this, I am moved to alter my attitudes about some things. First, I need to be careful not to take the Lord for granted. He is not just my safety net for when I fall. He is my Lord, and I am pledged to his service. It is how I have chosen to live my life. Second, I need to realize that this world doesn't exist for me or revolve around me. It exists as an expression of God's love and will. God is taking a world that is a mess and is working to bring his kingdom to make things right. Third, I think it is appropriate for me to cringe when I hear people use "God" lightly, as if God damning people is not a real thing. Fourth, I need to regularly fall before the Lord in awed worship, remembering who he is and proclaiming his greatness.

Being shook up didn't start with Elvis. God is a holy and awesome God. That should make all of us tremble.

Lord, you are great and holy. I am unworthy to say your name, to sing your praises, or to even address you in prayer. Yet by your love and compassion and the great sacrifice of Jesus, I am able to do so with the confidence that you want to hear my prayers. That shakes me up even more. May you be blessed by my life today. Amen.

❧ ❧ ❧

SEPTEMBER 12

*The King in his might loves justice. You have established equity; you have executed justice and righteousness in Jacob. Exalt the L*ORD *our God; worship at his footstool! Holy is he!* (Ps. 95:4-5)

Many Hebrew words are translated "worship." One targets the idea of *service* to the one worshipped. Another focuses on the idea of *fear or awe* toward the one worshipped. A third emphasizes the idea of *seeking* the one worshipped. Still a fourth targets the idea of *ministering* to the one worshipped. Yet the main Hebrew word translated worship paints a different picture. The word gives the picture of lying prostrate with your face on the ground. It is a word that conveys many of the same ideas of the other worship words, but with a different picture.

When we come into the presence of God, we fall prostrate before him because of his greatness. Just as Isaiah fell before God claiming, "Woe is me! For I am lost; for I am a man of unclean lips, and I dwell in the midst of a people of unclean lips" (Isa. 6:5), so we rightly fall face first before the Lord. This awe is similar to what John experienced in the Revelation when he saw the Lord. He "fell at his feet as though dead" (Rev. 1:17). An element of our worship needs to be falling prostrate before the living God, the King of kings. If we don't see him with such awe, we should ask why!

The worship response of falling facedown before the Lord naturally includes the idea of service. We fall because God is Lord. Facedown is a form of obeisance, which means we are giving deference to the wishes or desires of the Lord to whom we bow. We recognize our role as servants, ready to engage however our Lord instructs us. Isaiah was ready to follow the Lord's commands. So was John. The same should be for me. When I worship at God's footstool, facedown, prostrate on the ground, I am putting myself at his service, waiting to hear his command.

We are privileged to get to worship the Lord. We don't stumble into his presence, we are invited. An invitation to the Oval Office to meet the president pales in comparison to the honor of being invited into the presence of the Lord. We have such an accommodating Lord, that we must guard against ever taking him or our worship opportunities for granted.

Lord, King of kings, faithful and steadfast, righteous and just, we worship and honor you. We are unworthy to sing your praises, but are honored you invite us into your presence, where we may. Put us to work. Let us serve to your glory in Jesus, Amen.

❧ ❧ ❧

SEPTEMBER 13

Moses and Aaron were among his priests, Samuel also was among those who called upon his name. They called to the LORD, *and he answered them. In the pillar of the cloud he spoke to them; they kept his testimonies and the statute that he gave them. O* LORD *our God, you answered them; you were a forgiving God to them, but an avenger of their wrongdoings. Exalt the* LORD *our God, and worship at his holy mountain; for the* LORD *our God is holy! (Ps. 99:6-9)*

How well do you know your Old Testament stories? They are marvelous and rich, edifying us in many ways as we read and learn from them. They are a part of the "Scriptures" that Paul told Timothy were useful for training us in righteousness, along with teaching us, correcting us and equipping us for God's works (2 Tim. 3:16-17).

In today's passage, the psalmist appeals to the stories of Moses, Aaron, and Samuel as ones that teach important truths. These three were "priests," meaning they were in the service of God. Their lives were built around the mission of God. These three are ones that "called upon the name of the Lord." This means that they sought out God for who he is. They sought God as God, the restorer of Israel, the righteous leader, the one who gives instruction and direction.

God answered their call. He spoke to Moses and Aaron through a cloud. He spoke to Samuel in a voice in the night. His speaking included giving the Israelites the laws and statues for their nation. This was not a small thing, but was something that the three were careful to keep.

None of the three were perfect. They each made mistakes. God, however, was not demanding their strict perfection. When they erred, he was quick to forgive. God did this even as he avenged the holiness of his love and purity against the rebellious Israelites.

Seeing these stories, and knowing what happened, the psalmist uses them to instruct readers. We should strive to be like the Old Testament heroes, Moses, Aaron, and Samuel. We should see that we are enrolled in God's service, seeking to further his mission. We should call upon God in this life. We should ask for his help, seek his face, and try to walk in his blessings for his good purposes. We should be listening for his reply. When we sin, our attitude must not be rebellious or haughty but one of repentance, seeking his forgiveness. In this we exalt in him and worship our holy Lord.

Father, thank you for the stories of the Bible showing how you worked in the lives of other humans. May we be inspired, and may we learn the lessons of the faithful. In the faithful Jesus, Amen.

❧ ❧ ❧

SEPTEMBER 14

Make a joyful noise to the LORD, *all the earth! Serve the* LORD *with gladness! Come into his presence with singing! Know that the* LORD, *he is God! It is he who made us, and we are his; we are his people, and the sheep of his pasture.* (Ps. 100:1-3)

When young David returned from war, victorious over the harsh Philistine neighbors of the Israelites, the women were dancing in the street singing "songs of *joy*" with tambourines and other instruments (1 Sam. 18:6). It was a parade! After Jacob had stolen away with his wives and children under cover of night from Laban, his harsh father-in-law, Laban caught up with him and scolded him for denying the family a going away party that would include "*mirth* and songs" (1 Sam. 31:27). When the writer of Ecclesiastes decided to try out what the world had to offer, he recounted, "I said in my heart, 'Come now, I will test you with *pleasure*; enjoy yourself'" (Eccl. 2:1). After King Jehoshaphat and his army returned from war with lots of treasure and booty, they "returned, every man of Judah and Jerusalem, and Jehoshaphat at their head, returning to Jerusalem with *joy*, for the LORD had made them rejoice over their enemies" (2 Chr. 20:27).

Each of these vignettes has a word that I italicized—*joy*, *mirth*, and *pleasure*. That is the word that is in today's psalm passage. In the psalm it is in the instruction, "Serve the LORD with *gladness*." No one likes the person who gives grudgingly. Any parent can tell tales of children who respond to chores or instructions with a good or a bad attitude. Those who gladly do what is asked leave a different impression than those who do the same thing, but grumble, and do it with a poor attitude.

As we consider the ways we seek and serve the Lord, we should also consider our attitude in what we do. When we give our tithes to God, do we do so with gladness? Is there joy in our hearts? Do we celebrate the moment? Maybe we don't tithe with dancing or a parade, but do we have a heart that rejoices over the chance to serve the Lord? How about with our holiness? When we are faced with opportunities to sin or to be in righteous service to the Lord with our time, talents, or bodies, do we grudgingly do right or do we find the joy in service?

I want to serve the Lord with gladness. I want my life to be one of song and appreciation, in the big things and the little. I am his, and I want to do as he wishes, with joy in my heart.

Lord, forgive me for the times where my attitude has not been right with you. Help me to appreciate each opportunity to serve you. May I serve you with joy. In Jesus, Amen.

SEPTEMBER 15

I will sing of steadfast love and justice; to you, O Lord, *I will make music.* (Ps. 101:1)

I was in college, attending a Wednesday night worship service. The music was phenomenal, after all my college was in Nashville, Tennessee, also known as "Music City." We had the blessings of some amazing worship leaders, including some of the early contemporary Christian recording stars. Michael W. Smith, Amy Grant, Brown Bannister, and many others were either leading the singing, or sitting in the pews with us keeping melody and harmony. There were new songs being written and tried out that would become modern Christian classics. Those were heady times!

I was a bit stunned then, when in the middle of a song, our preacher stood up and told everyone to stop singing for a moment. He interrupted a verse to speak to us about what we were doing. As best I remember his words, he explained, "Do you realize what you are doing? This is a marvelous song. It has a very catchy hook. The harmonies are great and it's fun to sing. We have a full church, and the sound is amazing and even entrancing. But do you realize what you are doing? You are singing *TO GOD!* This is not a time where you are simply singing a song. You are addressing the King of the Universe, God of the Ages, the only Lord and Savior. If you realize this, then you are praying right now in your worship. You aren't here for entertainment. We aren't clapping for the 'show.' We are entering into the very presence of God on a spiritual dimension to sing *TO HIM.*"

I was stunned. I had not realized that before. If I had, I wouldn't have been leaning into my friend in the middle and saying, "I love this song!" Who would be talking to God or singing to God and interrupt the conversation to tell a friend about the aesthetics of what was going on? It was the twentieth century equivalent of speaking to the Almighty, only to stop and text a friend.

This snapped me to attention, and my worship has never been the same since. Recently, I didn't cringe, but I did pause when during worship after we sang three prayers to the Lord, a minister got up and said, "Now it is time to move into prayer." I thought, "But we have been in prayer!"

We need to be thoughtful in our worship. Songs to the Lord are songs to the Lord. As the psalmist said, "I sing to you, O Lord!" Songs are never about the melody or the show. That is Broadway or the concert hall. Not worshipping the Lord.

Lord, move me to a better understanding and practice of worshipping you. In Jesus' holy name, Amen.

❧ ❧ ❧

SEPTEMBER 16

I will ponder the way that is blameless. Oh when will you come to me? I will walk with integrity of heart within my house; I will not set before my eyes anything that is worthless. I hate the work of those who fall away; it shall not cling to me. A perverse heart shall be far from me; I will know nothing of evil. (Ps. 101:2-4)

These words offer profound advice for holy living. These are simple affirmations that should become a mantra we live by.

The passage begins by a decision to think about right and wrong. Rather than blindly walk through life, or just doing what seems right, the psalmist sees the value in thinking it through. Reading the verses carefully show this is not a thinking through that rationalizes what one really wants to do. It is a careful and prayerful reflection on what is blameless and worthy of our efforts.

The passage continues with the need to live carefully at home. A lot of people put on their best behavior in public, but when the eyes of the world are not watching, out comes a lesser behavior. That is not the decision of the holy. We need to focus on being people of integrity. We need to live right when we are at home, just as much as when we are in public.

The passage then speaks about visuals. The psalmist says be careful with what we put before our eyes. We should take this to heart, especially in an age when there is so much garbage available. Jesus also explained how important it is that we guard what we see. "The eye is the lamp of the body. So, if your eye is healthy, your whole body will be full of light, but if your eye is bad, your whole body will be full of darkness. If then the light in you is darkness, how great is the darkness!" (Matt. 6:22-23).

The passage then speaks to the people that will influence the writer. The psalmist will not live influenced by others who "fall away," but will hate their lifestyle and works. Those are not the deeds that will influence the psalmist!

The goal of the psalmist is a pure heart, and flowing from that, a good life and ethic. These are great instructions. To put them in everyday language, "I am going to think carefully about how I live. I will be the same in private as I am in public. I will be careful about what I see, read, or watch. I will be careful about whom I hang around that can influence me. I will work for a pure heart."

Lord, please help me walk right before you. In Jesus, Amen!

❧ ❧ ❧

SEPTEMBER 17

Whoever has a haughty look and an arrogant heart I will not endure. (Ps. 101:5)

Scripture talks a lot about arrogance and pride. The volume of passages tells me both that the traits are really damaging and that people easily fall into that trap.

What is it about pride that is so destructive? For starters, it completely distorts reality. Pride is a haughtiness in who we are and what we can do. It is an arrogant, overweening view of ourselves and our talents. If we were comparing ourselves to other people, and if there were no God, some might have a basis for arrogance. But there is a God, and that changes everything.

Because there is a God, we should realize that our talents and achievements are by God's grace, not our merit. God gave me the parents I have; I didn't select them. God gave me my skill set. God set opportunities in front of me. God moved people in and out of my life to affect who I am. If I have achieved anything of merit, the credit and glory go to God, not me. When we walk in arrogance, we rob God of glory due him.

Arrogance on our part also represents a failure to focus on God's work. Scripture teaches us that God is at work through his people. That means that the role I play on this earth in however many years God gives me, should be centered on his desires and plans for me. If he wants me to accomplish great things in the eyes of the world, so be it. If he wants me to quietly sit in a corner and pray for others to accomplish great things, so be it. My goal is to do his plans. Therefore, there is no basis for comparing me to anyone. There is only a reason to compare me to what he wants me to be.

A further destructive power of haughtiness stems from its fake sense of fulfillment. This is the way it makes us feel. All of us were made to be in the image of God, walking in a relationship with God. There is a higher calling for each of us, higher than the mundane existence of simply living out life. When we walk with God, we find joy and fulfillment that exists independent of life's circumstances. Pride, on the other hand, gives this illusory sense of worth or merit that makes us feel as if we have accomplished or become something of note. This is a poor substitute for the real value of walking with Christ.

Of course, we walk with Christ in the humility of knowing that we are inadequate, not accomplished. We find him when we cry out for his love and security. He becomes our model. He sets us on a course of humble service to the Father and his kingdom.

Lord, may I never boast in anything except the cross of Jesus, and your constant love. Through Jesus I pray, Amen.

❧ ❧ ❧

SEPTEMBER 18

Unless the LORD *builds the house, those who build it labor in vain. Unless the* LORD *watches over the city, the watchman stays awake in vain. It is in vain that you rise up early and go late to rest, eating the bread of anxious toil; for he gives to his beloved asleep.* Ps. 127:1-2)

I need to read this psalm regularly. It needs to be in my mind because it needs to affect my choices in life.

My life is a house. If I design and build my life, it is frightful. If my decisions are based on what I want, more times than not, they will not be the best decisions. If I am the strength for my life, I will not withstand the storms of life. If I am my own moral compass, I will often be adrift in currents of immorality. My life needs to be built by my God. I need to base my decision on his will. I need his strength. I need his teachings on what is right and wrong.

My family is also a house. If I design and build my family, my family will suffer. If I love my wife in my own ways, my selfishness will not allow her to flourish as she should, and our family will suffer. If I fail to be an attentive father, if I let my desires and needs trump those of my children, they will not have the confidence of a father's love that will help them become the people they can become. My family needs to be built by God. I need to let the love of Christ teach me to love my wife. It means I readily sacrifice my comforts and what seems best for me, to care for my wife. Taking care of her becomes my first priority. I need to rear my children in the nurture and admonition of the Lord. They need to understand the "capital F" Father's love (as one of my daughters calls God) through the loving efforts of me, their "lowercase f" father.

My calling is a house. If I see life as my own Disney World, where I ride what I want, eat what I want, and rest when I want, I am living a charade that does little good. God has placed me in the world to do certain good works for him. Some of those are achieved through my job, just as they were through my schooling before I became employable. My efforts need to be in finding the jobs God has for me, and doing those to his glory using the tools he's given me for those very reasons.

I can build my houses, but if I do, I build in vain. I want God to build my house. I want him to build my life, my family, my job, and my calling. I can try my hardest on my own. Go to bed late, wake up early. Be a workaholic, but it won't bear the right fruit. That comes from God alone.

Lord, build my house. Take my life, family, and calling. Make them yours in Jesus, Amen.

❧ ❧ ❧

SEPTEMBER 19

Hear my prayer, O Lord; *let my cry come to you! . . . I am like a lonely sparrow on the housetop.* (Ps. 102:1, 7)

Sometimes in life we feel alone. Very alone. We look for friends and they seem non-existent. We try to find a support system, but to no avail. We look for companionship to share the journey, but find even those nearby are distant. In the words of the psalmist, we are like a lonely sparrow, sitting on the housetop.

In those times, we have a unique opportunity. We can cry out to the Lord. We may seek out the companionship from one who loves us and readily seeks to support us in life. We often think of Jesus as Lord, and that is important and correct. But Jesus taught us he was our friend as well. In his incarnation, Jesus didn't live as a Lord to be served by others. He lived making friends and being a friend.

Jesus ate with his friends, walked with his friends, talked with his friends. He taught his friends. He served his friends. Consider how Jesus described his own sacrifice for his followers. Jesus described his death as an act he was taking for his friends. "Greater love has no one than this, that someone lay down his life for his friends" (John 15:13). Jesus was making it clear, that even though he was Lord God, he was our friend. He put it bluntly, "I have called you friends" (John 15:15).

There is something uniquely intimate about our friendship with Jesus. He may not seem present with us physically, but he is present in an even greater way, albeit a bit more mystical. Jesus resides "in us." When Jesus was about to leave his friends for the cross, he had a last supper with them. At the dinner, he tried to explain that he would be gone physically, but a time would come where he would be with them in a different way. "I will not leave you as orphans; I will come to you. Yet a little while and the world will see me no more, but you will see me. Because I live, you also will live. In that day you will know that I am in my Father, and you in me, and I in you" (John 14:18-20).

What does this mean to me day-to-day? I am never alone. The presence of Jesus is real. He is my friend and constant companion. He is both with and in me. I can talk to him at any and every moment. I don't need an "and one" to have him join me at a function. He will be there. I can't go anywhere that I don't have my friend. As the old hymn says, "What a friend we have in Jesus . . ."

Lord, we are honored to have you as our friend. Your caring interest in our lives and our feelings is amazing. Help us to sense your presence and thrive in you. Through Jesus, Amen.

❧ ❧ ❧

SEPTEMBER 20

Save us, O LORD our God, and gather us from among the nations, that we may give thanks to your holy name and glory in your praise. (Ps. 106:47)

This passage comes at the end of a long set of verses that recount the story of the Exodus. The psalm reminded the people that God had shown his favor, in spite of the many Israelite sins. Early in the psalm we read, "both we and our fathers have sinned; we have committed iniquity; we have done wickedness" (Ps. 106:6). Importantly, each time the psalmist points out Israel's sins, he points out the continuing salvation of God.

The sins are recounted all the way back to the time when the Israelites were fleeing Egypt. "Our fathers, when they were in Egypt, did not consider your wondrous works; they did not remember the abundance of your steadfast love, but rebelled by the sea, at the Red Sea" (Ps. 106:7). Yet in spite of the sins of rebellion, God saved the people. "Yet he saved them for his name's sake" (Ps. 106:8). God's salvation was then praised by the same rebellious people. "Then they believed his words; they sang his praise" (Ps. 106:12).

The memory of the people was short, however, and sin became prominent again. "But they soon forgot his works . . . they had a wanton craving in the wilderness, and put God to the test in the desert" (Ps. 106:13-14). The people were jealous of Moses and Aaron. They forgot God, and made the golden calf. The sin got so bad that Moses had to intercede, and stop God from destroying the people. The people continued to sin, not trusting God to deliver them safely into the Promised Land, so God punished that generation, giving them what they wanted, and not letting them enter the land. Over and over the psalm continues to give specific examples of Israel's sins and the resulting punishments. Each time the people would cry out and then the Lord would deliver them.

The psalm was written at a time when the people were again suffering for their sins. They had been dispersed among the nations, losing possession of the land God had promised. The psalmist writes a confessor psalm, for the people to pray, trusting God to save his people again.

It is powerful to think through humanity's unfaithfulness to God. Over and over each generation brings forth their own times of short memory and sins. God never ignores the sins, but constantly works to woo his people back to forgiveness. This should become personal to us. We need to live with diligence in our faithfulness, remembering and honoring the work of God in our lives.

Lord, you have been faithful, even as I haven't. I confess my sin and pray for forgiveness in Jesus, my Lord, Amen.

❦ ❦ ❦

SEPTEMBER 21

Let this be recorded for a generation to come, so that a people yet to be created may praise the LORD: that he looked down from his holy height; from heaven the LORD looked at the earth, to hear the groans of the prisoners, to set free those who were doomed to die, that they may declare in Zion the name of the LORD, and in Jerusalem his praise. (Ps. 102:18-21)

WRITE IT DOWN!!! Take what God is doing in your life, and secure it in a form where the next generation has it! We have a responsibility to do so. The psalmist did it, and we are blessed because of it, over 2,500 years later!

This is the genesis of this personal book of devotionals. It is a way of writing down what the Lord has done in my life, through the devotional times I have shared with him. I want my children to know these things. I want my grandchildren to know these things.

There is a spectacular God who has taken me through valleys too deep for me to cross on my own. He has put me on mountaintops I could never scale. He has taken me out of sin's vicious grip, and put a clean heart in me. He works to renew my mind, and focus me on kingdom issues. He found me in solitude, and brought me into fellowship and friendship. He took my sins, paid for them, and cast them as far as the east is from the west. He found me in mourning, and gave me comfort. He found me weak, and gave me strength. He found me wandering, and gave me direction. He found me sad, and instilled in me a deep joy. He found me fidgety and worried, and gave me peace. He took my fears, and replaced them with faith.

This is the work of the Lord in my life. I praise him, and want all to know he is worthy of all praise. He can change your day, your week, your life, your eternity. He is the God of fixes. He is the God of purpose. He is the God of love. He is the God we desperately need.

I suggest you write down somewhere the ways God has set you free. Record for a coming generation the ways God has ministered to you. Make it known and not only others but you yourself will be blessed. It does us good when we reflect on such things as we write them down. Then when we come back years later and see them, we are amazed anew at the hand of the Lord. Write them in the margins of this page if it helps. Record the faithfulness of the Lord!

Lord, we give thanks to you. Help us to fulfill our responsibilities to the coming generations, letting them know you are the difference maker in life. In Jesus' name, Amen.

❧ ❧ ❧

SEPTEMBER 22

He has broken my strength in midcourse; he has shortened my days. "O my God," I say, "take me not away in the midst of my days—you whose years endure throughout all generations!" (Ps. 102:23-24)

Live long enough and you will have a health scare. The psalmist did, and we read the cries to the Lord for aid.

Because we have learned many of the miracles of science and medicine, we have a tendency to look to doctors in our health crises, and that is a good thing. God has made skilled doctors and given them a gift of healing. God is responsible for medicine and the science of our universe. They are tools he has given us to fight disease and the effects of our fallen world.

Does that mean we do not need to cry out to the Lord? Do we simply go to the ER or some medical expert? Heavens no! We do both! We use the tools God gave us (doctors, medicines, procedures, medical devices, etc.), and we thank him for them. But we don't use them in isolation from prayer.

We seek God's intervention in all ways. We want him to give us wisdom on where to go and which doctors to use. We want him to give the doctors alert minds, and good judgment in diagnosing and treating us. We want the medical technicians and other health care professionals on top of their game as they treat our loved ones. We want the Lord to step in as necessary, especially where science and medicine fall short.

Is this an effort to live forever? Absolutely not. After Adam and Eve sinned and fell from God, there was a guard put around the tree of life so they couldn't partake of it. This is part of the story where we are instructed that God does not let us live forever in this sinful condition and this sinful world. We will all meet our end, unless we are alive at the Lord's second coming. But there is no sting to death, and we confidently expect the resurrection that awaits all who are in Christ.

Still, that doesn't mean we are in a hurry to leave this life. There are burdens that God has put on our hearts that we want to meet before leaving. I don't want to leave this life until I have done all I need to do for my wife and children. This means that not only should we be praying to God for life and health but we should show him by our lifestyle that we doing what we can to honor that prayer—fewer donuts and more exercise! Then when our race is done, we head home for the victor's crown we can cast before our victorious Lord.

Father, give us health to meet this world as we should. Then bring us home in Jesus, Amen.

❧ ❧ ❧

SEPTEMBER 23

Of old you laid the foundation of the earth, and the heavens are the work of your hands. They will perish, but you will remain; they will all wear out like a garment. You will change them like a robe, and they will pass away, but you are the same, and your years have no end. (Ps. 102:25-27)

I was only four years old when we were headed home after church in Abilene, Texas. During the service we had sung the song, "How Great Thou Art." In the car, Mom said that she loved that song, and that she wanted that song sung at her funeral. I remember thinking, "I MUST remember this Kathryn (my sister) isn't paying attention, so this one is on me!" I suspect because of that powerful moment, this song has always captivated my attention.

The song begins recounting the wonders of creation and giving God praise for it in the chorus, "Then sings my soul, my Savior God to thee. How great thou art. How great thou art." The second verse recounts the reality of death of Christ on behalf of the believer, ending again with the chorus, "Then sings my soul . . . How great thou art. . . ."

The final verse shifts to the future and speaks of the end of days. "When Christ shall come with shout of acclamation, and lead me home, what joy shall fill my heart. Then I shall bow with humble adoration, and there proclaim, my God, how great thou art." The chorus is then sung one last time.

This passage from the Psalms inspires both the first and the last verses, but is missing the integral middle. It is the middle that infuses all the rest with its great meaning. It is the middle that is great news. The psalmist lived before the events of the middle; we live after. We get to see more fully what the end of the story looks like, and it makes this psalm even greater for us to consider.

If this world ended without Jesus having resolved the separation between people and the Lord, then the end would be unspeakably tragic. But Jesus did come, and he perfectly resolved the sin problem separating us from God. Now we know, as Paul explained, that this earth will be changed like a robe, but into another perfect world, one where we who also will change, will live in perfect fellowship with God. Paul was as confident in this as he was in the resurrected Jesus that he saw on the road to Damascus. Paul changed his whole life on his confidence that Jesus had come, bore his sins, died, was physically resurrected, ascended to heaven with a promised return to take his children home. Paul would sing with us, "Then sings my soul, my Savior God to thee, how great thou art!"

Lord, we sing your praise, the God of creation, sacrifice, and future hope in Jesus, Amen.

❧ ❧ ❧

SEPTEMBER 24

Bless the LORD, O my soul, and all that is within me, bless his holy name! (Ps. 103:1)

This is an easy refrain that rolls of the tongue, "*Bless the LORD, O my soul, and all that is within me, bless his holy name!*" But that short phrase in the middle packs quite a punch, if we think about it. Let, "all that is within me" bless his name. Now that's a serious goal!

It takes a solid commitment to go to church each Sunday. It may take a total of three to four hours, if you count getting ready, driving, etc. Out of 168 hours in a week, that is roughly 2 percent of our week going to church. For "all that is within me" to bless God's name, must mean more than being regular in church attendance.

Quiet time! We know quiet time. It is that time like now, when we stop what we are doing and spend time devoted to God. That is surely time blessing the Lord. Maybe we spend five minutes a day, maybe we spend thirty. We may be adding as much as another one to three hours a week, blessing the Lord. Still, we're only up to 4 percent of our time!

I suspect that the psalmist wasn't talking about time, at least not directly. I think the psalmist wanted there to be no part of one's life or being that isn't bent and focused on praising God. That means that I praise God with my mind. I spend my days learning and using my mind, but doing so out of the intent of bringing praise and glory to God. What I feed my mind should be done carefully with an eye toward praising God. Similarly, with my will, I need to learn the discipline to make praising God and bringing him glory how I choose to direct my actions.

Now bringing God glory doesn't mean always being in a Bible study or prayer session. When I was in college, my major professor Dr. Harvey Floyd read us a poem he'd come across. I don't remember it with precision, but it was fairly close to, "One day, one ordinary day, while I am washing the dishes, doing laundry, feeding a baby, or cooking dinner, my Lord will come back. How I'll have wished he found me knocking on a door, telling someone about Jesus. God have mercy on me." Dr. Floyd was sad as he read the poem. He rightly explained that praising God is not only found in evangelism, church, and Bible study. The Christian who is doing dishes, taking out the trash, and changing diapers is doing work that praises God. Those are not lesser chores. They are holy, important, and necessary when they are done to God's glory.

We are to seek to praise God with all we do. Let all that is within me bless his name!

Lord, we bless you as the incredible God. May we bless you by doing all we do in honor of and inspired by the Lord Jesus, through whom we pray, Amen.

❧ ❧ ❧

SEPTEMBER 25

The Lord *is merciful and gracious, slow to anger and abounding in steadfast love. He will not always chide, nor will he keep his anger forever. He does not deal with us according to our sins, nor repay us according to our iniquities.* (Ps. 130:8-10)

There is amazing balance in this verse. It marvelously expresses the character of God and his interactions with his followers. God's actions are rooted in his character, just as our actions are rooted in our character.

God's character shows one who is merciful and gracious, a beautiful phrase in Hebrew (*rachum veh chanun*). It is God's own attribution of who he is, as God delivered the phrase to Moses when the Lord passed before him on Sinai (Exod. 34:6). The Hebrew word for mercy is intertwined with the idea of compassion. As an adjective, "gracious" in the Old Testament is used only for God. It also contains the idea of compassion as well as "favor" or even "pity." God is one who cares deeply for us. This is no shallow momentary feeling of God; it is deeply ingrained in who he is. He is a caring, compassionate God of mercy and pity. He loathes the human condition, and desires to do something about it. Here is the balance and key.

God knows us, better than we know ourselves. God does not let us live this life in a false reality. He teaches us truth, even if it hurts in the process. We are a people addicted to the idea that we are the important ones. We may not say it in these words, but we live as if what is happening to us is most important. We think a loving God would make our lives easy. We think he would strip us of any disease. He would eliminate any pain. Many people who don't believe in God use this as their key argument. They say, "A loving God would not allow the pain in this world." This whole focus that comes quite natural to fallen humans is premised on a false assumption: that we are the center of concern. The world revolves around us. The truth is, it doesn't. God will teach his children that, even though breaking the "self-addiction" is a painful thing.

How does God teach us? How does he set us free from the deceitful addiction? He corrects us, he chides us, he shows us some of the consequences of our sins, and the anger the sin rightly stirs in him. Here again we see the balance. As a merciful and compassionate God moving in pity and care, he doesn't deal with us as severely as our sin deserves. He deals with us as needed to teach us and correct us. It is like the parent who disciplines a child with the least strident discipline needed to correct errant behavior. What a marvelous God!

Lord, merciful and gracious, thank you for your care and love. Continue to teach and reinforce in us that it is all about something much greater than ourselves. In Jesus, Amen!

SEPTEMBER 26

For as high as the heavens are above the earth, so great is his steadfast love toward those who fear him; as far as the east is from the west, so far does he remove our transgressions from us. As a father shows compassion to his children, so the LORD shows compassion to those who fear him. For he knows our frame; he remembers that we are dust. (Ps. 130:11-14)

Sometimes I take a few minutes and reflect on the sins in my life. I don't like to do it for long. They are really atrocious and shameful. I have done some things that I deeply regret, and would love to have another shot at getting some key things right. But there is no rewind button, and I am left a broken person, longing for the future and wanting to forget the past.

This is one reason why I love the apostle Paul. He had lived a very righteous life in some ways, certainly measured against many others around him. Yet he was acutely aware of horrible sins in his life. In some ways, they seemed to haunt him. Paul called himself the "foremost of sinners" (1 Tim. 1:15). He had played a significant role in persecuting the church, and had personal responsibility for the murder of Stephen, the first Christian martyr. He pointed out that his sinful past as persecutor made him unworthy to be an apostle (1 Cor. 15:9).

Yet Paul had an encounter with the resurrected Jesus that changed everything. The gospel exploded into Paul's life bringing with it, a forgiveness of sins and a righteousness that exceeded Paul's wildest imaginations. Paul understood for the first time, how a righteous and unchanging God could maintain his righteousness and offer forgiveness to we fallen people who have done and still do atrocious things. This was a righteousness that comes by relying upon the punishment meted out to Jesus as one that was rightly our own. We come before the Lord and accept his offer of forgiveness in Jesus and he is faithful to forgive us.

Paul's key explanation, one that has changed the world for many of us, is found in the famous words of Romans 3:21-25: "But now the righteousness of God has been manifested apart from the law . . . the righteousness of God through faith in Jesus Christ for all who believe. For there is no distinction: for fall have sinned and fall short of the glory of God, and are justified by his grace as a gift, through the redemption that is in Christ Jesus, whom God put forward as a propitiation by his blood, to be received by faith. This was to show God's righteousness." Oh our compassionate and amazing God, sending our sins as far away as words can express.

Thank you Lord for your amazing love and sacrifice for me. Through Jesus, Amen!

❧ ❧ ❧

SEPTEMBER 27

Bless the LORD, O you his angels, you mighty ones who do his word, obeying the voice of his word! Bless the LORD, all his hosts, his ministers, who do his will! Bless the LORD, all his works, in all places of his dominion. Bless the LORD, O my soul! (Ps. 103:20-22)

This is a magnificent call to bless the Lord. The shape of this passage is majestic and personal. The call to bless the Lord begins with a cry for angels to bless him. Angels are heavenly beings at God's command. They minister to God and he uses them, among other things, in some roles among us on earth. These are the awesome creatures set before the throne of God in Isaiah's vision of God's throne room (Isa. 6). John saw them in the revelation of the throne he recorded in Revelation 4. In Isaiah and Revelation, we see them singing praises to God, and the psalmist rightly calls them to bless him.

The psalmist refers to the angels as the "mighty ones" who are blessing the Lord by doing "his word." They hear the voice of God and obey. This is an important part of blessing God. Blessing God is not simply singing songs of praise, as we might do on Sunday, or as we read in Isaiah and Revelation. Praising God is also listening to God, and doing as God instructs. This blesses the Lord when we make him the Lord of our lives. After setting this blessing out from the mighty heavenly beings, the psalmist projects out from the angels to the "hosts" and to "ministers" who also bless him by doing his will. Like the angels, blessing God is not simply calling out his greatness in voice. It is showing his greatness by following him in deed. It is making his priorities our priorities. It is making his mission our mission. This is making God our Lord.

It is like the subtle play on words Jesus had with his disciples when he was teaching them the importance of serving each other. John 13:13-14 records Jesus telling them, "You call me Teacher and Lord, and you are right, for so I am. If I then, your Lord and Teacher, have washed your feet, you also ought to wash one another's feet." The disciples were calling Jesus "Teacher" first and then "Lord." Jesus shifted the emphasis saying he was first "Lord" and then "Teacher." It is because Jesus is Lord, because God is Lord, that we follow his teaching and do what he says.

The psalmist doesn't leave this passage calling on the angels, hosts, and ministers to bless the Lord. The psalmist calls on all of his works in all places to bless the Lord. The psalmist then brings the passage to the personal end. After calling on all from heaven to all reaches of all dominions, the psalmist calls out "Bless the Lord, O *my soul*." As all for all the others, may I make the Lord God my Lord God and do as he says. My Lord and Teacher.

Father, you are my Lord. May I live to show it! In Jesus, Amen.

❄ ❄ ❄

SEPTEMBER 28

I will sing to the LORD as long as I live; I will sing praise to my God while I have being. May my meditation be pleasing to him, for I rejoice in the LORD. (Ps. 103:33-34)

Twenty-four hours, that's 1,440 minutes or 86,400 seconds. That's what you have in a day. Depending on what time you are reading this, you don't really have that much time left. But think of it for tomorrow if you must. Or think of it as any other day. With 1,440 minutes in a day, how are you going to spend them?

I want to make sure in every twenty-four-hour time period that I commune with my Lord. It is good to thank him in the morning, praying for the day to come, seeking his will, asking his blessings, and calling on his strength. I like to thank God before every meal. He is the reason we have food. He causes crops to grow and animals to breed. He blesses world economies. We see how he has done much of this through the marvelous insights of science, and we should praise him for it. I want to come before the Lord each evening, before closing my eyes for sleep, I want to think through the day. Thank God for the victories and blessings. I want to lay out the problems and concerns I have that, if it weren't for my confidence in him, might keep me tossing and turning in the night. I want to thank him for protection and pray for my family, my friends, my loved ones, and for me.

These are times that are dear. They redeem the value of the 1,440 minutes each day. Even in this, though, I need God's help. I want my meditation and prayers to be pleasing and right before the Lord. I don't want them to be from my selfishness of assertion of my will. I want to sculpt them around him and his will. I want this meditation time to be fruitful for his kingdom, as he works in and through me, answering those prayers that are aligned with his purposes.

I pray that my meditations and thoughts would be pleasing to him. Paul told the church at Rome that the Spirit helps us in our times of prayer (Rom. 8:26). This is part of Jesus' promise that God would abide in us. "If anyone loves me, he will keep my word, and my Father will love him, and we will come to him and make our home with him" (John 14:23). We are not alone; we are inhabited by the Lord. His Spirit works within us teaching and leading us in our communications with the Divine. This is an amazing blessings and answer to the psalmist's prayer.

Lord, I want my time with you to be valuable. I want my prayers and devotions pleasing in your sight. I want to lift you up, and serve you. Even that I can't do without your help, however, so help me to praise you in my life. Trusting in Jesus, I pray Amen.

❧ ❧ ❧

SEPTEMBER 29

Oh give thanks to the Lord; call upon his name; make known his deeds among the peoples! (Ps. 105:1)

This passage is a scriptural waltz! The waltz is a centuries-old dance marked by a three-count featuring smooth sliding or gliding steps. Here we have a smooth transition between a three-count instruction. It is our spiritual waltz for the day.

Step one: give thanks to the Lord. This is a marvelous start to our dance. We begin by thanking God for who he is and what he's done. This isn't hard, but it does take some time. It means we are reflective on our station in life, what things we are thankful for, and the place where credit goes. It removes pride or arrogance, because we see our God responsible for our blessings. We also work hard to find ways to thank him, even for our struggles. We all face difficulties of various degrees. We all have faith struggles. Everyone has lows in life that are right on the heels of the highs. We need to be reflective and thankful to God for his presence in life's difficult moments. This is also the smooth transition to the next step in our waltz.

Step two: call on the Lord's name. As we consider the problems and difficulties we face, it is good and right for us to call upon the Lord. Our problems might be solved by people and events on earth, but we must never forget that the solution came from the Lord! He moves in others. He moves in events. He opens doors. He closes doors. He is our help at any moment, and we should call on him. Jesus taught his followers that God delights in hearing our needs and requests. He waits for us to lay them before him so we learn his will, and that he is the giver of all good things (Luke 11:11-13; Jas. 1:17). In our waltz, we begin thanking God, from this we slide effortlessly into calling upon his name, seeking him as the difference maker in our lives, and then we move into the final step.

Step three: make known God's deeds to the world. We know God's works; we have thanked him for them. We have seen them up close and personal. What's more, we know how God is able to answer our cries for help. We have called on him and experienced his presence. Now we have a call to take what we know and have experienced, and proclaim it to a lost world. There are people all around us who need to know that God is alive, that God is already blessing them, and that God seeks a relationship. Our three-step waltz is not done until we finish this third step. Then we are ready to start all over again! Tomorrow we dance again. We will have more to thank him for, more to ask him for, and more to proclaim! What a God!

Lord, we thank you. We seek your help. We want to take you to the world. In Jesus, Amen.

❧ ❧ ❧

SEPTEMBER 30

Seek the LORD and his strength; seek his presence continually! (Ps. 105:4)

There is a tremendous song with lyrics by two biblically great names, "Paul David" Hewson (aka "Bono"). The song is "I Still Haven't Found What I'm Looking For." I don't know what brought forth the song, but it echoes in my head along with today's passage. In the song, Bono sings about how he knows the salvation of Christ, he knows a relationship with God. He knows sin and forgiveness, but over and over we hear his refrain, "I still haven't found what I'm looking for." I think the same can be said by the psalmist.

We are instructed in today's passage not only to seek the Lord, but to seek his strength, and to seek his presence continually. The presence of God is not something we experience and then we sign off, like we might a website. It is one where we seek God, and do so continually. We are not satisfied. We are never fully done.

I need God every day. I need him in good times and bad. I need him in times of sin and times of faithfulness. I need him in times of sickness and health. I need him in times of worry and peace. I need him in struggles and on easy days. There is another old hymn that proclaims, "I need thee every hour." It is true.

So I seek God. This is not a treasure hunt with little chance of success. He is not playing hide and seek, trying to keep us in the dark. He wants to be found. Jesus assured us that when we seek him we will find him. "Ask, and it will be given to you; seek, and you will find; knock, and it will be opened to you. For everyone who asks receives, and the one who seeks finds, and to the one who knocks it will be opened" (Matt. 7:7-8).

The nice thing is when we find God and his presence we get his strength. There are some things that can't be done without the strength of God. How good are we at forgiving people who have really hurt us? It calls for God's strength! How about overcoming temptation? We need God's strength. How about walking in faith in the face of fear and danger? Again, with the strength of God we walk straighter and with confidence.

Have you found what you are looking for? In some sense, I have. I found the Lord. But in another sense, I still haven't. I need God's strength anew. I need God's presence again and again. He is integral to all I am doing today and every day.

Lord, I need your presence. I desire nothing but you. I offer you all I have to know you better. I know it's all because of your love and strength that I live and grow more Christ-like. That is my hope in whom I pray, Amen.

❧ ❧ ❧

OCTOBER 1

Remember the wondrous works that he has done, his miracles, and the judgments he uttered, O offspring of Abraham, his servant, children of Jacob, his chosen ones! (Ps. 105:5-6)

It is easy for us to live in the present and in the immediate future. We know what is happening in the present. It is our current reality. If things are going well, we enjoy it. If things aren't, we struggle through it. If the moment is thrilling, we are excited about it. If things smell of doom, we worry about it. In whatever frame of mind we have, we experience the present minute-by-minute as it passes by.

We also focus well on the immediate future. We anticipate what is coming and have learned that we can often change it or alter it. We can think about what we are going to eat. We think about what time we get out of school or off work. We contemplate our spare time and what we will do with it. We make weekend plans, and look forward to them. For some, contemplating the distant future is also part of life, although maybe not as great a part. We do think about school, work, and even retirement as we consider the future. We think about marriage, children, and grandchildren.

Today's passage tells us also to think about the past. Some people think about hurts in the past or wrongs that have happened to them. That is not what the passage is saying. The passage calls on people to think about the past in positive ways. Think about what God has done to pave the way for your present and future. Telling the Israelites to think about Abraham and the "children of Jacob" (their forefathers) with an emphasis on "his chosen ones" is a call for the readers to think about their history in God's hands. Abraham was early Israelite history, but the phrase "his chosen ones" brought the history current and included the listeners to the psalm. It even includes us. It is a call to think about God's hand from ancient history to modern and personal history.

The Christian equivalent is to think about the work and miracle that God did in Christ. Think about the early church and the Christian believers. Those of ancient days and those in our immediate history. Think about the people that God used to bring us to a relationship with him. Prayerfully reflect on the hand of God that holds us today.

Thinking about the role of God in the past affects our thinking about today and tomorrow. We more readily see the hand of God at work. We consider what he is doing and how he might use us. We think about fitting into his will in our future.

Lord, make our minds sharp about your hand in the past, as we watch your hand write our history today and tomorrow. In the mighty name of Jesus, Amen.

❧ ❧ ❧

OCTOBER 2

*My days are like an evening shadow; I wither away like grass. But you, O L*ORD*, are enthroned forever; you are remembered throughout all generations.* (Ps. 102:11-12)

This passage dances in my mind like an impressionist painting. The impressionists played with light, trying to accurately depict it, especially in the way it would shimmer and change as time passed. This passage is one that when I was young, was an intellectual affirmation of, "Yes, we don't live very long." As I have aged and find my sixth decade getting closer each year, I begin to see a different shade in the passage. I begin to see my days will dim like the shadows in the evening.

Aging does funny things to one. It plays with our health; we all know that. Backs stiffen, aches appear in joints we had never thought about before. Aging also plays with our priorities. Things that might have been important before, take on a greater intensity. I am reminded of when I asked our son to read a certain book, and he thoughtfully said to me, "Dad, if it means a lot to you, I will read it, but otherwise, I will pass." He explained, "I figure I will live fifty more years. If I read a book a week, then I have 2,600 books left to read. I need to prioritize those, and I'm not sure this one makes the list on its own."

I look at my life, and those books I can read are likely fewer than half that number. Considering it makes me think twice about spending time watching mindless television when I could spend that time in so many more fruitful ways. One time I was visiting with an elderly saint named Ken Kitchen. A delightful Brit, Ken was telling me his concerns about what he does with his time. A well-published Egyptologist and Old Testament scholar, Ken told me, "Mark, I'm in my late seventies. I have ideas in my head I need to put into books. It would take forty years to write all these. I will snuff out before that! I need to make choices on what I write and what dies with me."

These are amazing comments on the truth about time and aging. We will all wither away, and it comes a lot faster than we think. Days can be long, but the years zoom by. I am thankful that in the midst of this whirring life, there is my God, enthroned above space and time, reaching his finger into our world, helping me live each day, giving me direction and guidance, and ultimately gathering me up to take me to eternity with him. Some fear death. Some think dying the worst thing that can happen in this life. With the Lord, we realize life is a joy, but it is brief. Death is welcome, not because we hate our lives, but because however great this world is, it pales in comparison to the eternity awaiting us.

Lord, thank you for eternal life in Jesus. May I live to make the days of this short life count, serving you through Jesus, Amen.

❧ ❧ ❧

OCTOBER 3

Some wandered in desert wastes, finding no way to a city to dwell in; hungry and thirsty, their soul fainted within them. Then they cried to the LORD in their trouble, and he delivered them from their distress. He led them by a straight way till they reached a city to dwell in. Let them thank the LORD for his steadfast love, for his wondrous works to the children of man! For he satisfies the longing soul, and the hungry soul he fills with good things. (Ps. 107:4-9)

Psalm 107 speaks of different experiences by Israelites who went into exile. It uses great imagery to describe many experiences of life. Today's passage speaks to people who experienced desert experiences. These people were living in desert wastelands when God came to their rescue. Their experience is a metaphor for our "desert times" of life when nothing seems to grow.

When life is full, we are amazed at its opportunities and blessings. We grow; things change, and optimism abounds. But life is not always so grand. We also face times that are the exact opposite. We face times where things look bleak. Everything seems to be a grind. Nothing seems to prosper. We fight just to keep our heads above water. We miss any thrill in living. Emotionally we go dry. Things seem futile, and we struggle to find purpose. Each day seems to take forever, and the future looks like a dead end.

I have found those dry times appear in different phases of my life. I have walked through dry times socially. There are dry times we experience in our families. We have dry times at work. We have spiritual dry times, struggling to make sense of things. We have emotional dry times, when we can't muster the emotional energy to do much more than exist.

When we get stuck in those times, we need to cry to the Lord. God the Deliverer rescues us from the desert. He doesn't snap his fingers and set us in another place, but he leads us "by a straight way" to life! God will intervene and give you purpose. He will feed you, nourishing you back to health. God will redeem the desert experience and use it to drive your focus on him.

As God does, we have another reason to praise him. We get to observe firsthand the steadfast love of the Lord. God's faithfulness brings an oasis of life into our deserts of dryness. He gives meaning to what we are going through, and restores life.

Father, it is sometimes hard to put into words the dryness we experience. As we walk in our deserts, please keep our eyes on you. We need you to bring us life. We need you to feed us and nurture us. We thank you for your steadfast love. In Jesus, Amen!

❊ ❊ ❊

OCTOBER 4

*Some sat in darkness and in the shadow of death, prisoners in affliction and in irons, for they had rebelled against the words of God, and spurned the counsel of the Most High. So he bowed their hearts down with hard labor; they fell down, with none to help. Then they cried to the L*ORD *in their trouble, and he delivered them from their distress. He brought them out of darkness and the shadow of death, and burst their bonds apart. Let them thank the L*ORD *for his steadfast love, for his wondrous works to the children of man! For he shatters the doors of bronze and cuts in two the bars of iron.* (Ps. 107:10-16)

Psalm 107 speaks of different experiences by Israelites who went into exile. It uses great imagery to describe many experiences of life. Today's passage speaks to people enslaved in darkness. These people were living in bondage when God came to their rescue. Their experience is a metaphor for our "bondage times" of life when life seems hopeless and dismal.

There is joy in life lived in freedom. We romp around during days of productive happiness, and even chores are a pleasure, not a duty. We enjoy our friends, see opportunities galore, and put smile emoticons on our texts. We laugh, smell the flowers, and stand in amazement at the world God has made and the blessings he's given us. But there are other days that aren't so nice.

The dark days hit all of us at some time or another. Often these days are brought about by our own errors and sins, but not always. Sometimes it is simply life. These are the days where we see no light at the end of the tunnel, when we groan inwardly, or when we seem all alone facing our struggles. We don't understand what's happening. It can affect our appetites. (Either we can't eat, or we eat ourselves into oblivion.) We feel chained to bad circumstances, and life seems futile. Our enemies (inward and outward) have the upper hand, and we are helpless to defeat them.

When we are stuck in these times, and we can't find a way out, we need to cry out to the Lord! We need to call on his name. We must have his light in our darkness. We must have his hope to anchor our soul in the reality of his purposes for us. We must redouble our commitment to walking his path and seeking his face. Ultimately, that is where our deliverance will come from. There is no prison built that will hold back God. No chains can bind us if he sets us free. God is the answer to our days of darkness.

Lord, keep our eyes trained on you so when we enter dark times, we never lose sight of our hope in you. Come to our rescue. Deliver us from the chains that would hold us back from serving you in joy. Bring us into your glorious light. In Jesus' holy name we pray, Amen.

🌸 🌸 🌸

OCTOBER 5

My heart is steadfast, O God! I will sing and make melody with all my being! Awake, O harp and lyre! I will awake the dawn! I will give thanks to you, O LORD, among the peoples; I will sing praises to you among the nations. For your steadfast love is great above the heavens; your faithfulness reaches to the clouds. (Ps. 108:1-4)

So many of the psalms are similar to today's passage. They are calls to praise God. This one emphasizes the personal decision to praise God. It is not one that begins instructing others to come into a time of praise. It starts with the psalmist giving a self-instruction to praise! This is good personal coaching on holy living!

It is important that I tell myself to praise God. It draws my attention to purposeful actions and purposeful living. If I break down areas of praise, I can better explain it. Consider first, praise at church. I can easily go to church and go through the motions, even with a level of enjoyment. I can sing the songs, enjoy the melodies, even be moved by the lyrics. I can listen to the prayers with awareness that they are good prayers. I can listen to the sermon, even finding things that inspire me. I can do all of this, but not really spend my efforts directing my praise to the Lord.

It is a deliberate decision I need to make. I need to sing my songs to him and his glory, not sing them based upon me. I need to engage him in prayer, not simply listen affirming the prayers. I need to magnify the Lord over truth I hear in a sermon, not just listen for things that affect me.

This is the same in another area of praise, my daily living. I can eat my meals, be a good parent and husband, prepare my lessons for church, and work hard at my law firm. But that doesn't mean I am living in praise to the Lord! I need not only to eat my meals but be thankful to him for them. My parenting needs to be focused on glorifying God, not only for the chance to parent my children, but for the instructions, guidance, patience, kindness, and many other aspects of parenting that come from God and are to his glory. I can love my wife as Christ loved the church, giving myself up for her as part of my praise to the giving God. I can prepare lessons for church while praying that God will be praised by my efforts. I can give my best efforts at work because I am working to his glory.

This psalm gives us a marvelous self-help lesson for a God-focused life. I am going to praise God! I'm going to do it when I wake up, as I go through the day, and upon my pillow at night. I am going to credit him for the good things in life, and seek his help in life's difficulties. We worship an awesome God, and I plan on doing it purposefully!

Lord, I praise you for your love, care, support, and direction. I praise you in Jesus! Amen!

OCTOBER 6

Be not silent, O God of my praise! For wicked and deceitful mouths are opened against me, speaking against me with lying tongues. They encircle me with words of hate, and attack me without cause. In return for my love they accuse me, but I give myself to prayer. So they reward me evil for good, and hatred for my love. (Ps. 109:1-5)

Gossip is mean, hurtful, and destructive. Gossip is a seductive sin. Speaking about others in ways we shouldn't can make us feel important, as we have the "info." It can also feed the small part of us that might like to see others in a bad light. Sometimes it simply entertains us and we get enjoyment out of it. Now none of this may be conscious, but the seeds behind gossip are dark seeds.

There is no wonder that Paul puts gossip in a very harsh category of sins, setting it out as something the unsaved do. "They were filled with all manner of unrighteousness, evil, covetousness, malice. They are full of envy, murder, strife, deceit, maliciousness. They are gossips" (Rom. 1:29). But it isn't only the unsaved. Even the Corinthian church had gossip issues causing Paul concern: "For I fear that perhaps when I come I may find you not as I wish, and that you may find me not as you wish—that perhaps there may be quarreling, jealousy, anger, hostility, slander, gossip, conceit, and disorder" (2 Cor. 12:20). Paul taught Timothy to stop people from gossiping, "Besides that, they learn to be idlers, going about from house to house, and not only idlers, but also gossips and busybodies, saying what they should not" (1 Tim. 5:13).

All believers should guard their tongue. We need to be careful about what we say. Our words need to be meticulously honest. We need to be on guard against ever impugning someone's motives, something we can't really know. Our words should be words of love, encouragement, and life building.

At one time or another, everyone has experienced the pain of people who gossip. It is a terrible thing and an unfair thing. What should we do when people speak ill behind our backs? Jesus teaches us to find refuge in God, in prayer and love. We should pray for and love those who persecute us (Matt. 5:44). This should be our goal in tandem with our prayers for the Lord to reach out and deliver us from the consequences of gossip.

Lord, we pray for your help in two ways. First, help us to control our tongues and ears. May we not be gossips, and may we not listen to others' gossip. Also Lord, we pray for those around us who are gossiping. Help them center their lives and love on you. We bless you in the name of Jesus, Amen.

❧❧ ❧❧ ❧❧

OCTOBER 7

The LORD *says to my Lord: "Sit at my right hand, until I make your enemies your footstool."* (Ps. 110:1)

The Pharisees were frequently quizzing and testing Jesus. On one particular occasion, Jesus used today's psalm to turn the tables and quiz them! A group of Pharisees were gathered together and Jesus asked them, "What do you think about the Christ? Whose son is he?" The Pharisees answered that the Messiah would be the Son of David. Jesus then used today's passage asking, "How is it then that David, in the Spirit, calls him Lord, saying, 'The Lord said to my Lord, "Sit at my right hand, until I put your enemies under your feet"? If then David calls him Lord, how is he his son?" (Matt. 22:43-45). The Pharisees struggled to answer, eventually deciding it was best not to engage Jesus in contests over scriptural interpretations.

After these events, it is not surprising that the early church saw this as a "Messianic psalm," meaning that the psalm prophesied about Jesus, the Messiah. In Peter's sermon on Pentecost, the first sermon of the "church," Peter quoted the passage (Acts 2:34). Paul referenced it writing to the Corinthians, and the writer of Hebrews used it twice (1 Cor. 15:25; Heb. 1:13; 10:13)! This psalm was very significant to the early Jewish believers.

The idea behind the psalm, and the reason it was so important to the early church is rooted in several things. First, David was the pinnacle king for Israel. The Israelites never had another king that rivaled David. Even today, one of the very best hotels in Jerusalem is named the "King David Hotel." The Israeli insignia is a "star of David." Yet, here in the psalm, David prophesied about a day when the Lord God ("LORD" in all capitals is the translators' way of telling us that the Hebrew word is *YHWH*, the "name" of God), tells the Lord of David to sit. This is an incredible idea.

Israel had their eyes open. They were primed to understand that someone was coming who was like no one the people had ever seen. This was one who had a connection to God that was special. God was going to be working on this one's behalf to bring everything under his feet. This was Jesus.

Those with open eyes and willing hearts saw Jesus for who he was, and they put their faith in him for God's salvation. They were the early Jews who became the early church. We live thousands of years later. Our eyes should still behold the Lord, knowing that God has put all things under his feet. We rightly fall down in worship of Jesus.

Lord Jesus, we fall down before you, not as your enemies but as loyal subjects. We love and honor you as our King and Master, and we pray in your name, Amen.

※ ※ ※

OCTOBER 8

*The L*ORD *has sworn and will not change his mind, "You are a priest forever after the order of Melchizedek." (Ps. 110:4)*

Melchizedek is mentioned in only three places in the Bible: Genesis 14, here in Psalm 110, and Hebrews 5–7. In Genesis 14 we have the narrative of Abram (Abraham) returning from battle against certain tribal leaders. He met Melchizedek who was both the priest of God Most High as well as the king of Salem (likely ancient Jerusalem). After they met, Melchizedek pronounced a blessing on Abraham, they shared a meal, Abraham gave Melchizedek gifts, and Melchizedek faded into history. Other than today's one verse, Melchizedek is not found in the Bible until the book of Hebrews.

Since before the completion of the New Testament, the church has seen in Melchizedek a representation of Christ. We find in Hebrews an application of this psalm, and the underlying narrative from Genesis in the teaching on Jesus. Breaking apart this story, we see some reasons why the church saw teachings about Christ packed into these few verses:

"Melchizedek" is a significant name coming from two Hebrew words, "*melek*" meaning "king" and "*ṣedeq*" meaning "righteous." In the form used in the name, it can mean, "My king is righteous." This echoes heavily of the New Testament attributes and name of Christ, the King of kings, who was called "the Righteous One" (Acts 3:14, 7:52).

Melchizedek was the "King of Salem." The Hebrew uses *melek* again, this time tying it to the word "*salem*." The word *salem* is better known in its modernized form of "*shalom*." It means "peace." Thus we have the King of Righteousness also being the King of Peace. The church understood Isaiah 9:6 was prophetic about Christ as a child properly titled the "Prince of Peace."

Melchizedek was a "priest," a label that demands note because Christ was also a priest. Melchizedek sought God's blessing on Abraham (and through Abraham, all that would come from him), and Christ seeks God's blessings on believers.

As we read about Melchizedek, a Christ-type figure, coming out to meet Abraham, a chosen one of God, I am reminded about how God comes out to meet with us. God wants to spend time with us. He wants to bless us. He treasures our relationship. Not because we're good enough, but because he loves us. It's that simple and amazing!

Lord, we are honored and touched that you seek us out. May we never take you and your love for granted, but may we respond in love and service. In Jesus, Amen.

✺ ✺ ✺

OCTOBER 9

Praise the LORD! I will give thanks to the LORD with my whole heart, in the company of the upright, in the congregation. Great are the works of the LORD, studied by all who delight in them. Full of splendor and majesty is his work, and his righteousness endures forever. (Ps. 111:1-3)

I got a letter from an atheist who said, "Religion and science are at odds." I found *his* belief on this odd! Religion and science are two sisters that are joined closely!

Religion is our study about God and our relationship to him, Science is our study of nature and the world. As Christians, we believe that the world reflects the glory of God. Paul said that God's "power and divine nature, have been clearly perceived, ever since the creation of the world, in the things that have been made" (Rom. 1:20). If the world reflects God's power and nature, wouldn't we want to study it? As the psalmist says, the great works of the Lord are "studied by all who take delight in them."

Christianity is not a faith that finds its seat only in the word of emotions. It is not a thoughtless religion where people are urged to take of their heads as they find faith. Christians understand that God made our minds, and while our minds are not perfect, God is at work renewing our minds (Rom. 12:2). We are taught to think about God, to reflect upon his will and his law, to consider the ways in which we live, to discern right from wrong and more. All of these things require our minds.

Because God is able to work with our emotions, we often think about the many blessings that come to us emotionally in our faith. But that doesn't mean that our faith is based on emotions or feelings. Emotions and feelings are notoriously vague and somewhat fickle. Scripture teaches us that we are to let our minds overrule our emotions. So there are some times when we may not feel God's love or God's forgiveness. Those are times when our minds should engage and remind us of God's love and forgiveness. John explained this in one of his letters. "By this we shall know that we are of the truth and reassure our heart before him; for whenever our heart condemns us, God is greater than our heart, and he knows everything" (1 John 3:19-20). John speaks of what we know versus what our hearts and feelings tell us.

So as thinking Christians, we delight in contemplating the world. We delight in contemplating what God has done in our lives. The mind is a marvelous creation of God, and we are delighted at getting to use it in science as well as religion.

Lord, thank you for making us thinkers! May we use our minds to your glory as we live and grow in Jesus, Amen.

❧ ❧ ❧

OCTOBER 10

The works of his hands are faithful and just. (Ps. 111:7)

Today's passage is a blessing. The root of the blessing is knowing that we who have given our lives to Christ are the workmanship of God. He has created us in Christ Jesus and makes us into the vessels we need to be to do his will.

We don't need to worry that God is unable to form us as he needs to. We don't need to doubt that God will leave us to our own devices. We don't need to fear that we have to do it all on our own. God is working in us, and "the works of his hands are faithful and just." We can have confidence in our future. Our confidence is not based upon who we are by ourselves, but it is based upon who God is making us to be.

We can look at our past, and we can find marvelous things that happened. We can find people who have moved into our lives and blessed this helping us grow and change and wonderful ways. We can also remember people in our lives who left a wake of devastation and destruction in their path. But in the midst of everything that's happened to us—the good and the bad—we know that God is at work.

God can take the bad and use it in ways that we could never conceive. He molds us and makes us into tools that perfectly accomplish his will. One image I like is that of a woodcarver who uses tools to take a block of wood and make of it something beautiful. There is a lot of chiseling that has to happen, a lot of scrap wood that has to be removed, but in the end a beautiful bird can be carved out of the nondescript chunk of wood. God is like that. Sometimes the chiseling hurts. Sometimes he has to take off some sharp edges to make us what we ultimately need to be. But this is not something that we're doing on our own; it's something God is doing in us.

Some of the hardest times of my life, times I would wish on no one, are times that have made me uniquely fitted for tasks I could otherwise never do. I cannot think of any valley I have ever been through, where God has not used it to refine me, teach me, train me, inspire me, gift me, make me sensitive to things that I would otherwise be numb to, bring me a level of alertness I would otherwise miss, and do many other blessings to me for which I am eternally grateful.

I don't know what God has in store for me today, but I know that I am his, and I know that he is it at work in me. I know that the works of his hands are faithful and just. So I cannot wait to see what he will do in me for tomorrow.

Lord, I put myself in your faithful and just hands. Mold me after your will. In Jesus, Amen.

❧ ❧ ❧

OCTOBER 11

Praise the LORD*! Blessed is the man who fears the* LORD*, who greatly delights in his commandments!* (Ps. 112:1)

Many people believe that God's commandments are rules that must be obeyed under penalty of punishment. For them, the commandments are a burden. But this passage indicates that one who fears God will not see the commandments of God as a duty, but rather as a pleasure!

This passage sets up an interesting relationship between our fear of the Lord and our love for God. We know that God's love surrounds our lives. Because he loves us, we love him. Further, as we love him, doing his will is not a duty, it is a pleasure. But this passage speaks of the person who fears the Lord, not the person that loves God, as taking delight in following the Lord. So if we have pleasure following the will of God out of both love and fear, what does the love of God have to do with the fear of God?

I would suggest that the love of God and the fear of God are closely related. A key to understanding this relationship is knowing that the word "fear" in the Hebrew is a concept we also know of in our English word "awe." The fear of God or the awe in God both require a knowledge of God. When we know who God is, and we understand what he does, we see his greatness, his perfection, his justice, and we began to understand his mercy and his forgiveness. It is his character, his greatness, his perfection and justice that drive us in awe and fear. We know that this is a God who cannot and will not tolerate sin. It is a violation of his moral character and being.

Yet God is also a God of mercy and love. God does not give us commandments in order to condemn us. He gives us his law so that we might better understand his will for us. God's instructions for living were never meant to provide us with a way to please God by meriting his approval. His commandments work to show that we fall short of his character, which then drives us to seek his mercy and grace.

So in the commandments of God, we have the means to a better life, a better understanding of who God is, and a drive to seek God's mercy and grace. These are all delightful things. It makes sense that both our love for God as well as our awe and fear of God make following his will and commandments a pleasure not a duty.

Lord, we are in awe of you. You are a fearsome God and to fall under your wrath would be devastation. Yet even in your perfection, you have reached out to us in love and mercy giving us forgiveness in Jesus. It is an honor and a pleasure to live in your will. In Jesus, Amen!

❧ ❧ ❧

OCTOBER 12

The righteous will never be moved; he will be remembered forever. He is not afraid of bad news; his heart is firm, trusting in the LORD. His heart is steady; he will not be afraid, until he looks in triumph on his adversaries. (Ps. 112:6-8)

Most people fear bad news. Bad news means something negative is happening. It might speak of an impending doom. It might mean a crashing halt to our hopes and dreams. It could be the dreaded health news that we did not want to know. It might mean a loved one. Perhaps the bad news is the loss of the job or trouble at school. Bad news might take the form of betrayal from a person we love. There are all sorts of bad news that no sane person ever wants to hear.

Nobody likes bad news. Today's passage doesn't say that God's children never hear bad news. But when that bad news comes, the person of faith has a different reaction. The different reaction comes from a different resource. The person of faith puts their trust and reliance and the Lord God Almighty. We know that God is paying attention, and we know that God is in control. We know that however bad the news may be, it cannot change God's love for us. It cannot change God's plans for us. It cannot change our destiny in him. It cannot change our purpose in life. It cannot destroy what God is building through our sanctification.

In fact, bad news for the believer is an opportunity. Bad news is a time where we can turn to the Lord and watch the Lord perform as only he can. Bad news is a time where we can see God's hand in our life. It provides a story that in the future will enable us to give praise and glory to God. It works to draw us closer to God as we seek his refuge and protection. It can more sharply draw our focus on his will and his compassion. It can grow us in humility, as we realize how important it is to rely upon the Lord. We do not have the resources, the knowledge, or the strength to deal with most bad news. So we set aside our pride and arrogance, and we lean upon the Lord in meekness and humility.

Those who trust in the Lord, are not afraid of bad news. Bad news is just another day. We don't seek it out, and we don't laugh at its face, but we do not fear it. We set our heart as flint, ready to walk through whatever the world throws, knowing our God walks through it with us.

Lord, thank you for handling our bad news. What a joy it is to be your child, rain or shine. In Jesus' name, Amen.

❧ ❧ ❧

OCTOBER 13

Who is like the Lord *our God, who is seated on high, who looks far down on the heavens and the earth? He raises the poor from the dust and lifts the needy from the ash heap, to make them sit with princes, with the princes of his people. He gives the barren woman a home, making her the joyous mother of children.* (Ps. 113:5-9)

Most everyone loves the underdog story. In sports, if my team isn't playing, I have a strong tendency to root for the underdog. There is something satisfying about seeing the one that isn't expected to win, come out on top. In a similar vein, in America we have a respect and admiration for the rags-to-riches story. We teach our children that someone can come from nothing and become the president of the United States.

God is a proud and self-proclaimed supporter of the ones in greatest need. Over and over we read in Scripture about how God opposes the proud, those who are confident that they are special and successful because of their own drive, talents, and accomplishments. These are the people who have no need for God, or at least so they think. Their arrogance blinds them to truth, which is ironic in some cases because arrogance is a state of mind. In other words, some are proud in their own minds and thoughts, thinking they have "figured it out" and are "smarter" than those who actually believe in God. This arrogance in mind, thinking they hold the truth of the universe, is ironic because they are blind to the truth. The proud have little to no room for God. They have become their own God.

But not so the weak, the hurting, and the humble. God lifts the poor up from the "dust" and the needy from the "ash heap." The dust is where homelessness lies. The ash heap is the modern garbage dump. God takes those with nothing and gives them everything that counts. These become regal through the work of the Lord. They become daughters and sons of the King of kings! God gives offspring to the barren. A woman without child is the poetic example, but the idea applies to everyone who cannot bear fruit in life. God takes those who are unprofitable, those who work and never seem to come out on top, those who are unpopular, and more, and gives them satisfying life.

The psalmist notes the extreme irony in this. God is not someone you would expect to be in the ash heap, looking for people to help. God is seated on high, far above anything in heaven or on earth. But this is our God. He is the master at creating the rags-to-riches story, the great supporter of the underdogs of life.

Lord, may our eyes not be proud. May our hearts not beat loudly for our own achievements. May our minds not think ourselves something we're not. For Jesus' sake and in his name, may we realize our state and find your rescue and strength. Amen.

❧ ❧ ❧

OCTOBER 14

When Israel went out from Egypt, the house of Jacob from a people of strange language, Judah became his sanctuary, Israel his dominion. The sea looked and fled; Jordan turned back. The mountains skipped like rams, the hills like lambs. What ails you, O sea, that you flee? O Jordan, that you turn back? O mountains, that you skip like rams? O hills, like lambs? Tremble, O earth, at the presence of the Lord, at the presence of the God of Jacob. (Ps. 114:1-7)

Some of the most fun moments in sports for me are filled with smack talk. Yes, I appreciate good sportsmanship, and it is important, but there are some sporting events where smack talk is part of the competition. It is expected. In the NBA basketball arena, it has become an integral part of some athletes' games. Michael Jordan would tell his opponent, often in colorful language, "You can't cover me!" He would then blaze by them with some jaw-dropping move, and slam the ball into the goal in a highlight that would make the replay reels for days. Dikembe Mutombo, one of the biggest men to play the game, was a defensive genius who led the league in blocked shots. Some opponent would try to shot over Dikembe, and he would swat the ball down, followed by wagging his right index finger at his opponent, saying nonverbally, "No! No! No! Not here you don't!"

I don't know when smack talking started, but this psalm is smack talking in the name of God, so it must go back a long time! The scene is Israel leaving slavery in Egypt, with pharaoh's army in hot pursuit. Seemingly cornered by the Red Sea with the world's most potent army approaching via the only rescue route, all was hopeless. Then suddenly the sea parted, fleeing from before the Israelites. At a later time, when Israel had lost their leader Moses, and were about to go into battle under new leadership, the Jordan River also parted for the Israelites, giving them confidence that their new leader walked with the power of God as did Moses.

The psalmist smack talks the elements, asking the sea and river why they had to flee. What had them so scared they couldn't stay their course? It was God Almighty! They trembled at the presence of an awesome God. God changes the dynamics of everything. We should tremble before this God, but also be confident in him and his support! Remember the young shepherd boy David? David smack talked on his encounter with Goliath. Goliath started the smack talk with his daily taunt of the Israelites. While the Israeli army cowered in fear, David asked, "Who is the uncircumcised Philistine that he should taunt the armies of Almighty God?" (1 Sam. 17:26). David knew we can boast in our God. He is up to anything!

Lord, may we never boast in anything, except you and the cross of Jesus! In Him, Amen!

🙟 🙟 🙟

OCTOBER 15

Not to us, O LORD, not to us, but to your name give glory, for the sake of your steadfast love and your faithfulness! (Ps. 15:1)

Bragging does not become the children of God, unless we are bragging on the Lord! When I was a child, there was a television show called "The Guns of Will Sonnett." Set in the gunslinging days of the 1870s, the main character played by Walter Brennan delivered a line that became more known than the whole show. He first used it explaining that his son was an expert with guns, a quick draw, his grandson was even better than his son, and that Brennan was better than both of them. He then added the tagline, "No brag, just fact." That line was well-known and often repeated by most all of us in the fourth and fifth grade, as I was growing up.

When we consider the line from a spiritual perspective, it rings a bit shallow and maybe even hypocritical, if it is rooted in our own skills. But when we use it about our God? It is spot on. God is everything we could brag on and more. Nothing positive we say about God is puffery. It isn't made up. It isn't flattery. It is true.

God really is great. God really does care for the least of us. God really has the power to make the world or destroy the world. God really did become flesh in Jesus. Jesus really is God, so God really spent a human existence loving and serving those around him. God really did model his righteousness perfectly. God really lived a sinless life as Jesus. God really did die on a cross to satisfy divine justice. God really did conquer the grave and Jesus really was physically resurrected. He really did ascend back to heaven with a promise to come again and bring his children home. The Holy Spirit really is God, so God really did come into the lives of believers in Christ. God really set up home in our spirits. God really does care about us. God really is at work in the lives of his children. God really is set on making us more holy and changing us from creatures bound to sin, to children set free in the Spirit. God really does love us in unimaginable ways. God really does want to engage in our lives daily. God really does have the power to break down the problems in our lives. God really does walk through difficult times with us. God really does share our hurts. God really does hear our prayers. God really does console us when we hurt. God really does prepare us for when we die. God really does take us at death into his presence. God really does spend eternity with us. We can praise God for these things he really did and does.

No brag, just fact.

Lord, we praise you as a wonderful, inconceivably loving and faithful God. In Jesus, Amen.

❀ ❀ ❀

OCTOBER 16

May the LORD give you increase, you and your children! May you be blessed by the LORD, who made heaven and earth! (Ps. 115:14-15)

There is something profound about praying for God's blessings on another. It is a selfless act that shows love for the other as well as faith in God's goodness.

The Lord's Prayer gives us an excellent example of praying for others. The first three phrases lift up God in his holiness, seeking the furtherance of his kingdom and will; we have three phrases of petition. Then the prayer shifts, and each of the phrases is for "us." We ask God to give *us* our provision for the day, to forgive *us* our sins, and to keep *us* from temptation, delivering *us* from the evil one. Built into the prayer is a prayer for others as well as ourselves.

Another well-known form of biblical prayer, set out in many places as an example, is what we call an "intercessory prayer." This is where we intercede on someone else's behalf. We seek God's blessing, God's healing, God's forgiveness, God's guidance, or something else from God on behalf of another person. In Genesis 18 Abraham interceded in prayer for the people of Sodom, saving Lot and his family. In Exodus 15:25 Moses interceded on behalf of the Hebrew people, stopping God from destroying them. In Acts 12:5 Peter was in prison, the church interceded in prayer, and Peter was released by the power of God. Paul gives a marvelous intercessory prayer in Philippians 1:9-11: "And it is my prayer that your love may abound more and more, with knowledge and all discernment, so that you may approve what is excellent, and so be pure and blameless for the day of Christ, filled with the fruit of righteousness that comes through Jesus Christ, to the glory and praise of God." We read in 1 Timothy 2:1 Paul's instruction for the church to intercede in prayer: "First of all, then, I urge that supplications, prayers, intercessions, and thanksgivings be made for all people." Jesus also modeled intercessory prayer. Jesus prayed for Peter, that his faith would not fail, and that he would strengthen the other followers of Jesus (Luke 22:32). Jesus offered intercessory prayer for those responsible for the crucifixion (Luke 23:34). Jesus prayed for his disciples right before his arrest and crucifixion, and in that prayer also prayed for you and me, the believers who learn from the apostolic teachings (John 17:20-23).

It is important that we live in intercessory prayer. We need to pray for others, to be blessed by God, and have God meet their needs. It is a blessing to get to do so.

Lord, I pray for those who read these pages and ask you to bless them. May they have insight into praying for others. In Jesus' name, Amen.

❧ ❧ ❧

OCTOBER 17

O Israel, trust in the Lord*! He is their help and their shield. O house of Aaron, trust in the* Lord*! He is their help and their shield. You who fear the* Lord*, trust in the* Lord*! He is their help and their shield.* (Ps. 115:9-11)

The ideas of trust and faith run closely together. In Hebrew and in Greek, one word exists for both trust and faith. We still use the words a little bit interchangeably. We can ask someone "Don't you have faith in me?" meaning "Don't you trust me?"

Today's passage speaks of trust or faith in God, and puts it into a very important frame of reference. Those who fear the Lord should trust the Lord. The house of Aaron is singled out, and called to trust in God. God helped Aaron's house before, and they ought to trust him. The psalm then turns to show that we can use God's historical work for others as a basis for our own faith. As I read about how God worked through the priests and house of Aaron, I am motivated with reasons to put my own trust in the Lord.

Our faith and trust in God is not something Scripture urges us to give in a blind fashion. Scripture does not talk about a blind leap of faith. Those are the words of certain philosophers. Scripture talks about us having good reasons to believe. When Thomas doubted that the Jesus before him was in fact they physically resurrected Jesus, Jesus did not say close your eyes and take a leap of faith. Instead, Jesus gave rational reasons for believing. Jesus told Thomas come and put your fingers in the nail holes, touch me, feel me, and know for very good reasons that I am who I say I am.

Since the Garden of Eden, people have doubted God. Over and over again, we read in the Bible about people doubting God, even after God had done miraculous things for them. After the many miracles prompting Israel's freedom from Egypt, including dividing the Red Sea, Israel decided to make a golden calf as their god because Moses had spent a month up on Mount Sinai. It only took one month for their doubt to grow into disbelief.

Society will always try and erode our faith in God. This is the work of the devil, and it is as old as humanity. It is one reason it is important for us to see the hand of God in the lives of others as well as ourselves. When we do, we grow in our faith, and we proclaim lives that others can look to as they try to live in their own faith.

Lord open our eyes to see you. Grow us in our faith. Give us wisdom in our faith. Help us to understand the truth of who you are, the truth of what you say, and the truth of your relationship with us. Through Jesus, Amen.

❧ ❧ ❧

OCTOBER 18

I love the LORD, *because he has heard my voice and my pleas for mercy. Because he inclined his ear to me, therefore I will call on him as long as I live. The snares of death encompassed me; the pangs of Sheol laid hold on me; I suffered distress and anguish. Then I called on the name of the* LORD: *"O* LORD, *I pray, deliver my soul!" (Ps. 116:1-4)*

Today's passage is a very personal one. It is written from someone who experienced the touch of God. It is poignant and beautiful. It is a testimony to God's faithfulness. This passage resonates in my soul. I can read this passage over and over, and each time say an "Amen!"

I have found that using personal experiences with God to persuade others that God exists is usually inadequate. There are a lot of people who experience things that they interpret as God that do not match up to God as he is revealed in Scripture. So I do not like to use personal experiences to convince other people of God's reality. But that doesn't mean that we should refrain from our personal testimonies of the faithfulness of God. This is especially true when we are talking from one believer to another.

So when I see a passage like today, I relate to it. I do love the Lord. I would love to say I love him simply because of who he is, but I know that it is much more than that. I know that my love for him also grows out of great appreciation for all that is done for me. The apostle John understood this. He wrote that we love Christ because Christ first loved us and showed us his love in real demonstration (1 John 4:19).

God also showed his love to me by answering my cries for mercy. Over and over in my life I've cried out to God in dry times, in times of pain, during sleepless nights of worry, while trying to endure shame and disappointment, wracked by guilt, or paralyzed by fear. Without fail, God has come to my rescue. He has drawn me closer to him. He has helped me realize my need for him; I want to stay right by his side.

Our experience with God may not be the proof of God's reality that other people need, but it is no less valid an experience. It is one way that we grow in our knowledge of God. There is no greater use of our mind, than learning and knowing of God. Call upon his name in your hour of need. He may not give you immediate deliverance, but he will not forsake or abandon you. He did not save Daniel from going into the lions' den, but he went through the lions' den with Daniel. I love our God.

Lord, I cry out to you for your mercy, for your love, for your divine touch, for your compassion, and for your rescue. Over and over you have come to my aid. I am touched, and my heart is full of gratitude. Thank you, Lord. In Jesus' name, Amen.

❧ ❧ ❧

OCTOBER 19

Praise the LORD, all nations! Extol him, all peoples! For great is his steadfast love toward us, and the faithfulness of the LORD endures forever. Praise the LORD! (Ps. 117)

These two verses are the entire 117th Psalm. Like many psalms, it calls on God's people to praise the Lord, but this one goes a step further, it calls on the nations to praise Israel's God! This is fitting, and makes a lot of sense to us today, but at the time it was written, it was a shocking instruction.

Most tribes, peoples, countries, and nations had their own gods. The gods were generally deemed territorial. When in the hill country of Judah, it would be acceptable to praise the Lord. Many saw him as the God of the hill country of Judah. But he wasn't the god of Assyria, or Babylon, or Egypt. He wasn't even the god of the Philistines in the coastal region. While many thought territorially about gods, it was never the teaching of Scripture and how God revealed himself.

God is the God of heavens and earth, and all that are in the earth. The stars cry out in praise to God. The waters praise God. The rocks praise God. All things praise God, no person should be any different. So the psalmist calls on all the nations to praise the Lord.

This is an outward focus that all of God's children should have even today. It is too easy for us to look at our faith under a national umbrella. Here in America we often think of ourselves as God's country or one nation under God. But we err if we believe that God has a greater love for Americans than for anyone else on the earth. God would have all of us lift up our eyes and see every individual in the world as one made in the image of God. We should see every person as one for whom Jesus gave his life. Our hearts should break for anyone who is hurting. Skin color should not matter. Economic status should not matter. Level of education should not matter. And we can certainly say that their geographic location on this dirt clod in outer space we call Earth should not matter.

I want God to open my eyes to the more than 8 billion people on this planet. I want to care for them. I want to find ways to serve them. And I want God to use me and help to bring all peoples to praise him. The psalm speaks of God's great steadfast love toward "us." The US there is not the U.S. There are no periods between the U and the S in the passage. Let all peoples and all nations praise the Lord.

Lord we praise you, as a great and wonderful God who has shown steadfast love and faithfulness to all people through Jesus Christ our Lord, in whom we pray, Amen.

❧ ❧ ❧

OCTOBER 20

What shall I render to the Lord for all his benefits to me? I will lift up the cup of salvation and call on the name of the Lord, I will pay my vows to the Lord in the presence of all his people. (Ps. 116:12-14)

I make no bones about it. If I had only one band I could listen to for the rest of my life, it would be U2. Even beyond their incredible talent, we are the same age, we have walked during the same periods of earth's history, and we share a faith in the Lord. Those factors line up to make me a huge fan. One of their most played songs is "Where the Streets Have No Name." This is a song that Bono often introduces in concert by quoting today's passage. In the recording of the Boston concert on the Complete U2 CD package, while the opening chords of the song are played, Bono tells the crowd, "What can I give back to God for the blessings he poured out on me? What can I give back to God for the blessings he poured out on me? A cup of salvation, here's a toast to our Father, I follow through on a promise I made to him, to our Father." The song then proceeds in anthem fashion as Bono sings of his desires in his walk with the Lord. (By the way, I am convinced the song is rooted in the New Jerusalem with streets of gold that have no name. It is a heavenly song.)

Have you made promises to God? We often hear of people who make promises premised on God getting them out of jams. But there are more. There are promises made to God out of love and devotion. Regardless of how and why the promises were made, there is a special value in keeping them, out of love and devotion to the Lord.

Keeping our vows does not make us "Super-Christians." It is not a fear of damnation that motivates us. When they are at their best, vows are rooted in love. I made vows to my best friend and wife on our wedding day. Those vows are not a burden; they are a joyful outflowing of my love for her.

I often make vows in anticipation of New Year's Day. I also frequently make them around my birthday. Those aren't the only times, but they seem to be ones that surface most readily to me.

What vows might be appropriate for God? I remember asking the Lord for his help in making a time of daily devotion and prayer for an entire year. I have made vows to read through Scripture in a year. I have made promises to refrain from certain things, and promises to do certain things. I am not perfect in these things, but it establishes an intimate bond with the Lord, that I love.

Lord, I do love you. Grace me with the strength to fulfill my promises. May I not make rash vows, but find ways to show my love to you in what I do. In Jesus, Amen.

❧ ❧ ❧

OCTOBER 21

The Lord is on my side; I will not fear. What can man do to me? The Lord is on my side as my helper; I shall look in triumph on those who hate me. It is better to take refuge in the Lord than to trust in man. It is better to take refuge in the Lord than to trust in princes. (Ps. 118:6-9)

Fear is an interesting monster. It appears in early childhood, and it may fade, altering in intensity, but I don't think it ever flees for good in this life. Our fears vary with age. I no longer fear vampires or anything creepy under the bed (we watched horror movies a lot as a child). Funny enough. Teen fears often involve relationships, grades, being in "trouble," safety, and a huge unknown future with little economic power. Adult fears are more typically based on economics, health, work, relationships at home and work, children, aging parents, and the like.

All of these fears typically have a common thread. They are intimately linked to things over which we have little to no control. We can't dictate the future and so we often fear it. There are people we have to trust, and even the best people can be unreliable at times. We often work at the whim and fancy of others. Few are irreplaceable in their jobs. Even if they are, no one controls the economy. Everything can shift in a heartbeat. I have a good lawyer friend who frequently says, "We are all just five really bad decisions away from living under a bridge."

God is not subject to the winds of change. He is not stunned by an economic downturn. He doesn't get caught unaware by surprises. He is not numb or blind to danger, nor is he powerless to deal with it.

Of course, you and I are not God. But that doesn't make him irrelevant. He is close to his children! To the person of faith, God is a game changer. With God at our side, what should we fear? No one and nothing! God is stronger than all difficulties we may face. He has clear vision, knowing the future as easily as the past. There is no one who can separate us from his love, and no one who can overpower him to our eternal detriment.

The problem for us is the difficulty in trusting someone we can't see. If God were visible by my side, hands drawn, and ready for action, it would be easier. But this is a matter of faith. We are called to have confidence in one we can't see. We trust him with our eternity; we need to trust him with our today and tomorrow. We learn this better as we grow.

Lord, please be at our side. Please guard us, guide us, protect us. For Jesus' sake, Amen.

❧ ❧ ❧

OCTOBER 22

How can a young man keep his way pure? By guarding it according to your word. With my whole heart I seek you; let me not wander from your commandments! I have stored up your word in my heart, that I might not sin against you. (Ps. 119:9-11)

Everybody needs to learn this psalm in their preteen years! Too late? Okay, learn it today. Learn its words, and learn its meaning. The words are on the page; we simply need to repeat them enough to memorize them. The meaning? It is profound, and it will take us years to learn it through living it.

The psalm mentions the "young man," but it applies equally to a young woman. Both young and old face the challenge of keeping their lives pure before God. The key to this is living right. But living right is not so simple. It involves knowing right from wrong and being able to discern the will of God. As believers of any age, we should spend time in God's word learning his instructions for life. Many people pray and seek how God would lead them in a specific matter at a specific moment in life. It might be where to move, what to major in, what job to take, who to marry, when to have children, or any number of things. We often want to do God's will, but are uncertain what is his will.

The first step in learning God's will in a matter involves a diligent and constant understanding of his will expressed in Scripture and the life of Christ. Scripture gives us the answers for 90 percent of life's important decisions. As for those that are not found in Scripture, the more we understand and see God's word, the clearer those decisions become. This makes sense because Scripture gives us the foundation from which we build for more specific decisions. Jesus explained it this way, he summed up the "Law" of Moses in two simple commands. We should love God with all we have, our hearts, our souls, our minds, and our bodies. We should also love our neighbors as ourselves. Lest we get lost in who exactly is our neighbor, Jesus taught that our neighbor is whomever we come across in need.

These teachings are ones that give guidance in life, and from them, God teaches us to think and discern right from wrong. God works in us to help us develop into right thinking people that rightly discern his will. Part of this is storing up God's word in our hearts. We should think in terms of God's word, just as an English speaker thinks in English, or a Spanish speaker in Spanish. Our hearts should dwell on the Scriptures so much that they become our language. This will help us keep our ways pure!

Lord, help me learn your word and will and walk according to your glory and that of Jesus our Lord, through whom we pray, Amen!

❧ ❧ ❧

OCTOBER 23

*I lift up my eyes to the hills. From where does my help come? My help comes from the
LORD, who made heaven and earth. He will not let your foot be moved; he who keeps you
will not slumber. Behold, he who keeps Israel will neither slumber nor sleep. The LORD is
your keeper; the LORD is your shade on your right hand. The sun shall not strike you by
day, nor the moon by night. The LORD will keep you from all evil; he will keep your life.
The LORD will keep your going out and your coming in from this time forth and forevermore.* (Ps. 121)

Everyone needs help here and there. Sometimes I need help with problems and issues outside me. Other times I need help with problems and
issues within me. Even the most self-sufficient people need help, whether
they realize it or not! When we need help, where do we look for it?

The psalmist looked to the hills! Why the hills? That is where Jerusalem was! That was a reference to the Lord whose temple was located in
Jerusalem. The writer knew exactly where to turn for help. One in need
should turn to the Lord for help.

Why turn to the Lord? First, he wants to help! He cares about his
children and wants to meet their needs. Jesus made a point about God's
desires to give help to his children contrasting it to what poor parents on
earth might do. "If you then, who are evil, know how to give good gifts to
your children, how much more will your Father who is in heaven give good
things to those who ask him!" (Matt. 7:11).

A second reason to turn to the Lord for help is that the Lord is more
than competent at anything to which he puts his hand. God has the power
to help. He knows what help is needed. He doesn't fall asleep, but is awake
24/7 to give help. We need not worry that we have a problem too big for
God to help.

A third reason to turn to the Lord for help is his effectiveness. He
not only wants to help, is able to help, but his help makes a difference. We
can seek his wisdom, knowing he will give it. We can ask him to meet our
needs, and he will. We can ask for his strength, and he will empower us.
We have a God who is able, and any help we seek from him, that is aligned
with his will, he will provide!

Need help? Look to the Lord! He wants to help, can help, and will
help. He is the answer to our problems.

*Lord, I turn to you in my trouble. I praise you for always being there, for being my
daily help, even when I don't ask. Thank you for your constant love. In Jesus, Amen.*

❧ ❧ ❧

OCTOBER 24

I was glad when they said to me, "Let us go to the house of the LORD*!" Our feet have been standing within your gates, O Jerusalem!* (Ps. 122:1-2)

I love to go to church. Don't get me wrong, sometimes I am "not in the mood," and sometimes I get balled up in other things that distract me, but I really do love to go to church. There is a transformation that takes place when I come before the Lord in corporate worship.

Getting to sing songs of worship refocuses me, invigorates and strengthens me. It gets me out of myself, helping me remember life and the world is not about me. I love the songs that lift up the Lord. Some old hymns are still favorites, while new ones also reach deep into my soul, bringing me closer to the Lord.

Church is also a place of fellowship, something important and necessary to me. I find my brothers and sisters who, like me, want God's love and care. They are always ready to show love and support. It is amazing and empowering to be in the midst of a common group of people seeking the Lord. This becomes more and more valuable as I spend more time in church. It makes a church home important. These are the people I can call when in need. They bring meals and show love in the midst of death and illness.

One of my favorite times at church is the Lord's Supper. It is a time of focus on Jesus and what Jesus has done on the cross. I contemplate my own sins and shortcomings, I reflect prayerfully on the fact that Jesus was fully aware of my sins, and took them gladly to the cross, suffering shame, agony, and separation from God the Father. I realize that God unites me with Christ through the elements in a special way—I am taking something that Jesus infused with meaning as his body and blood. I get to thank God for his forgiveness in Jesus, and my love for him grows.

Also at church, I enjoy listening to a preacher who has worked hard to prepare a lesson based on Scripture. I occasionally disagree on a point, but I always find sermons edifying, challenging, instructive, and useful. They help me put practical tools to work to live more holy. They challenge me to dig deeper into Scripture.

Prayer time at church is another time of focusing. In prayer, I am led by others to speak with God, setting out praise and needs, expressing love, and more. It helps me grow in my walk.

I love going to church!

Lord, thank you for the church. May I never take it for granted. In Jesus' name, Amen.

❧ ❧ ❧

OCTOBER 25

Have mercy upon us, O LORD, have mercy upon us. (Ps. 123:3)

Here we have one of the oldest prayers of God's people. It has come into many languages. In Hebrew, it reads *chanenu Adonai*. (The Hebrew reads *Yhwh*, rather than *Adonai*, but an observant Jew would never try to pronounce the name of God. Rather he or she would insert the Hebrew for "Lord" or even *ha-shem*, simply meaning "the name.") In Greek we read it *Kyrie eleison*. In Latin we read, *miserere nostri, Domine*. In English it is, "Lord have mercy."

This cry was in the psalms, by one seeking God's favor in the midst of difficulty. In the New Testament, it was the cry of the blind men to Jesus: "And behold, there were two blind men sitting by the roadside, and when they heard that Jesus was passing by, they cried out, 'Lord, have mercy on us, Son of David!' The crowd rebuked them, telling them to be silent, but they cried out all the more, 'Lord, have mercy on us, Son of David!'" (Matt. 20:30-31). Even a non-Jew made the cry to Jesus, "And behold, a Canaanite woman from that region came out and was crying, 'Have mercy on me, O Lord, Son of David; my daughter is severely oppressed by a demon'" (Matt. 15:22).

It is not surprising that the early church took up the phrase and made it integral to worship and to early worship songs. Early church writings spoke of martyrs saying the *Kyrie eleison* while dying. It was a part of worship services in responsive readings. Still today in High-Church worship services, it is a refrain the people say in response to prayers of the leaders. One can hear it in Greek Orthodox, Russian Orthodox, Roman Catholic, even Slavonic churches.

What is it about the prayer that makes it so ubiquitous? Wrapped in the prayer is contrition, repentance, recognition of the saving work of Christ, and an expression of trust in that work. A heartfelt prayer for God's mercy is perhaps the most important prayer one may have.

We pray it in faith because God's people have actually received the mercy of Christ. Peter explained, "Once you were not a people, but now you are God's people; once you had not received mercy, but now you have received mercy" (1 Pet. 2:10). It is the mercy of God in Christ that makes us God's people. We didn't get that status by anything less. It is the mercy of God that sustains us day-by-day. It is the mercy of God by which we stand.

Lord have mercy upon me, a sinner. Chanenu Adonai. Kyrie eleison. In Jesus' name, and for his sake, we pray, Amen!

❧ ❧ ❧

OCTOBER 26

*If it had not been the L*ORD *who was on our side—let Israel now say—if it had not been the* L*ORD *who was on our side when people rose up against us, then they would have swallowed us up alive, when their anger was kindled against us.* (Ps. 124:1-3)

I know it's not all about me (or you!), but sometimes. . . .

It is very easy for me to get caught up in the need *du jour*. What is it right now I need from the Lord? What direction do I seek? What blessing seems necessary? What protection is vital?

It is a small step from the need *du jour* to wondering why the need isn't met. When God shows up and answers the prayer, meets the needs, satisfies the longings, then I can be thankful, and move on to the next need. But when God doesn't answer, it is easy to wonder, "Where is he? Why isn't he answering? Isn't this his job as God?"

The psalmist understood that God's hand is not simply one of moving from one need of the day to the next. God is about something much grander than our vision can capture. In the process of being God, there are countless times where God is our immediate help, even though we didn't know we had a need to pray. God gives us protection we don't ask for. God gives us health we take for granted (at least until we lose it). God gives us food, whether we thank him for it in prayer or not.

Here is where the "me" must break down. God has an enormous plan to bring the age to an end with redemption for his children and victory over the evil one. This plan entails you and me. Sometimes it entails us wallowing in blessings that make us smile deeply. But it also can (and should) entail times of suffering. Jesus told us to take up our crosses and follow him. He warned his disciples that the Christian life on this earth was not all roses. It would include persecution and pain. That is part of what we go through for *him*.

Because it really is all about him. When we are born again, we exist to do his will. His kingdom is what we seek. His name is what we proudly proclaim. We try to reflect his love in an often loveless world. We want to be what he needs, where he needs it. We walk by his guidance seeking nothing less. We walk in his Spirit, empowered for him.

So we can affirm, that if the Lord was not on our side, we would have been swallowed up alive. But with the Lord on our side, if we are swallowed up alive, it is for him. So it is an honor. Because it really isn't all about me (or you!)!

Lord, we are honored to be yours. Thank you for all you do for us. May we serve you with our lives and our deaths. Just as our Jesus did, in whom we pray an amen!

❧ ❧ ❧

OCTOBER 27

Those who trust in the LORD *are like Mount Zion, which cannot be moved, but abides forever. As the mountains surround Jerusalem, so the* LORD *surrounds his people, from this time forth and forevermore.* (Ps. 125:1-2)

This is a solid psalm. It has a great sense of weight and authority. It is what I call, "densely reassuring." Let me explain.

Anyone who has ever spent time in mountains or hills knows that even if small, they are massive. They are composed of rock found under the layer of topsoil and it doesn't matter how much it rains, snows, or sleets. You awaken the next morning, and the mountain is still there. Topsoil may wash out, but rarely the rock. It is constant.

If you want to build a significant structure, and you want that structure to be strong, you want to build it on rock. Mountains are good places to build walls and towers because you rarely have far to dig before hitting the stable bedrock. Try to take some hand tools and dig up a mountain. You will give up in futility before you make a real dent. This is the strength of mountains. They are not made up of a bunch of rocks or pebbles. They are massive rocks themselves.

Using this image, the psalmist describes people who trust in the Lord. God is likened to the mountains around Jerusalem. God is solid and weighty. God is going nowhere. God is stable enough to build upon. He doesn't shift or wash out. God's solid protection and reliable presence surround his people, protecting them and giving them stability.

God's people are likened to Mt. Zion, where Jerusalem and the temple stood, lifted above the surrounding valleys, and encompassed by the mountains. We stand as an example of his love and protection to the world around us. We project God's authority. Jesus equated God's people to a light set on a hillside. The psalmist uses a similar idea but makes the people of God the whole hill!

This picture makes me want to trust God better. I don't want to be untrusting, but trusting, surrounded by the Lord, confident in what he has planned, bravely facing anything that comes to me, knowing that nothing, NOTHING, will tear me away from God's love! Thank you God!

Lord, we do thank you for your love for us. Thank you for your protection. Thank you for your devotion to us. We live and work confident in your love. In Jesus, Amen.

❧ ❧ ❧

OCTOBER 28

*When the L*ORD *restored the fortunes of Zion, we were like those who dream. Then our mouth was filled with laughter, and our tongue with shouts of joy; then they said among the nations, "The L*ORD *has done great things for them." The L*ORD *has done great things for us; we are glad.* (Ps. 126:1-3)

Paul knew a secret that I want to know. The psalmist hints at it. Paul was blunt.

Paul had been working hard on the mission field. Churches occasionally gave him aid, but Paul took joy in working as an itinerant tent maker so that no one would ever think that Paul proclaimed the gospel for personal gain. Paul had been through a dry time when the church at Philippi sent him some aid. He was touched by their concern and love for him. He wrote a thank you note in a letter to the church and told them the secret: "I rejoiced in the Lord greatly that now at length you have revived your concern for me. You were indeed concerned for me, but you had no opportunity. Not that I am speaking of being in need, for *I have learned in whatever situation I am to be content. I know how to be brought low, and I know how to abound. In any and every circumstance, I have learned the secret of facing plenty and hunger, abundance and need. I can do all things through him who strengthens me*" (Phil. 4:10-13).

There are days of plenty and days of little. This is true in economic terms, but also in spiritual terms. The psalmist was tuned into this. The key to happiness and joy in the midst of abundance or sparsity, whether economic or spiritual is the same. Trust in God. With God, whatever we have is enough! We can do exactly what he has for us to do with what he gives us. In some cases, we can better do what God wants when we don't have abundance! Abundance can be a distraction. With a lot, you have a lot more options of what to do and when to do it. Hard choices and priorities don't always work out the same with abundance.

When we have abundance, when the days are truly "the good old days," we need to thoughtfully pause and thank God, even as we laugh, shout for joy, and brag on what God has done, just as the psalmist above. God is the reason! Conversely, when we struggle, when the days seem long, the resources scarce, the spirit dry, we need to take strength in Christ and his love. Let him define our priorities and goals, and we will find we have what we need to do his will. There is a joy we will find in that, that no money can give. It is the joy of an obedient servant to the Lord Jesus Christ.

Lord, we do thank you for plentiful bounties, and sing with joy. We also thank you for times of less, knowing we are still yours seeking to do your will in Jesus, Amen.

❧ ❧ ❧

OCTOBER 29

No one who practices deceit shall dwell in my house; no one who utters lies shall continue before my eyes. (Ps. 101:7)

Why is it that sometimes honesty can be so hard? Even though we follow Jesus, the one who is, "the way, *and the truth*, and the life" (John 14:6), it can be hard.

Jesus drew a distinction between himself and the devil when confronting some adversaries. He said, "You are of your father the devil, and your will is to do your father's desires. He was a murderer from the beginning, and does not stand in the truth, because there is no truth in him. When he lies, he speaks out of his own character, for he is a liar and the father of lies" (John 8:44).

Sometimes we lie because it seems to make things easier. We have less explaining to do. We can cover up errors or mistakes. We can pretend to be something we aren't. We don't have to be sorry about hurting someone else's feelings. We seem to more readily get what we want or need. It makes us look better. It seems to solve problems that are otherwise unsolvable.

Yet if we are honest about this, and not lying to ourselves, we see the inadequacies of each of the above reasons. In a very real sense, many of the reasons are rooted in a lack of confidence and faith in the Lord. If we think lying is the best solution to a problem, we need to think again. God's way will always be the best solution. If we think lying is necessary to protect another, we need to be careful to examine the avenues carefully.

Of course, we are always able to think of an exception that might disprove a rule. One that is often used on this issue is the World War II era family in Nazi-controlled lands who are hiding Jews in their attic. If the soldiers knock on the door and demand, "Do you have any Jews in there?" then you have two choices, tell the truth, which would deliver the Jews to a death sentence, or lie and save their lives. There is a legitimate debate about whether there are times where the choice is the lesser of two evils: contribute to wrongful killing or lie. But that is not the real circumstance most of us face day in and day out. We can have that debate, but not where it is really just simpler and easier for us to lie.

That is not to say that we speak out in ways that hurt people. Paul tells us to speak "the truth in love" (Eph. 4:15). When we do so, we will be advancing the kingdom of God as we grow in holiness.

Lord, please help me learn to be honest in heart, word, and deed. For Jesus' sake, Amen.

❧ ❧ ❧

OCTOBER 30

Blessed is everyone who fears the LORD, who walks in his ways! You shall eat the fruit of the labor of your hands; you shall be blessed, and it shall be well with you. Your wife will be like a fruitful vine within your house; your children will be like olive shoots around your table. Behold, thus shall the man be blessed who fears the LORD. (Ps. 128:1-4)

When young people ask me what they can do to find success in life, they are often looking for me to give them instructions about what careers pay the most, give them the secret roadmap to fame and fortune, or some other such thing. They might also look for my insights on majors in college, study habits, who's who, or what connections might be best to establish. My advice, however, always comes back to what I know. That is what today's psalm proclaims.

Fear the Lord. This is not an ostrich fear where we stick our heads in the sand and hope God never sees us. It is an awe that comes from a realization that God really is God, and that he is more God than we can ever imagine.

From this fear, comes a logical next step. Walk in his ways! His ways are revealed in the life of Christ and in Scripture. If we fear and hold him in awe as God, then it is only right and seemly to follow his ways. He made us to walk in them. They are what is best for us. They give us direction and fulfill our purposes before him.

Work. This comes third in the psalmist's list. As we fear God, as we walk in his ways, our hands are busy with work. Scripture does not say, "idle hands are the devil's workshop," but experience does! We are made to be workers. Adam and Eve were given jobs by God. The key is that work is third in this list. If our work trumps our fear of the Lord, we won't get it right. If our work runs contrary to walking in his ways, we need to find another job.

But those three, fear the Lord, walk in his ways, and eat the fruit of your hands (i.e., work!) makes it well. It changes the lives of those around you. Your spouse will be a better spouse. Your children will thrive. Right priorities mean a life built around God. That life transforms.

So my advice to people who want success, young or old? Easy! Love the Lord and put him first in your life. Let him teach you what to do and model your behavior after Christ. Stay busy doing God's work, not your own! Then watch life blossom!

Lord, may I grow in my awe and respect for you. Teach me your ways, and put me to work in Jesus, Amen.

❧ ❧ ❧

"Greatly have they afflicted me from my youth"—let Israel now say—"Greatly have they afflicted me from my youth, yet they have not prevailed against me. The plowers plowed upon my back; they made long their furrows." The Lord *is righteous; he has cut the cords of the wicked.* (Ps. 129:1-4)

Israel had a tough history. They had had plenty of warning. Moses told them that God set before them blessings and curses. If they walked in the ways of God, they would thrive. If they walked in the ways of the world, they would stumble and fall (Deut. 30). Each generation gets to make their own choice. And each generation often thinks they are smarter than the last. It is not surprising to read the history of Israel. Generations arose that did not experience the exodus. To read or hear about it was semi-fictional. It was easy for succeeding generations to see it as something the old-timers believed. No one in the following generations saw God part waters, much less rain down manna or quail.

So Israel followed after other nations into idolatry. They found a "better way" that was repugnant before the living and true God. God had told them what would happen. And it did. It started small enough. There were surrounding tribes and kings that marauded different parts of Israel, taking captives and subjugating the people. Then the people repented to God, cried out, and God sent judges to rescue them. Over the generations it got progressively worse. Finally, the northern ten tribes of Israel were in such rebellion that God sent prophets to warn them of an Assyrian conquest. Still walking in idolatry, the people ignored the prophets, the Assyrians came, and the ten tribes of Israel were lost. The southern kingdom lasted a bit longer, but eventually ignored their own prophets and were conquered by the Babylonians.

God spared the Jews in Babylon, and eventually brought them back to the Holy Land, restoring Jerusalem and building a second temple. But it was a long haul, and even still the Jews were not fully faithful. Finally, as he had promised thousands of years earlier, God brought the Messiah through the line of David, and many Jews believed, along with people from every nation, but many refused to believe, and still do today. Yet God has always been a redemptive God. He still is today.

I would more readily label the Israelites as foolish unbelievers, if I did not see many of the same traits in me. I have experienced the grace of God, and yet I still find myself chasing after other gods, making other priorities over those of the Lord, and doing foolish acts of rebellion. I should know better. God have mercy.

Lord, have mercy on me a sinner. For Jesus' sake and in his name, Amen.

❧ ❧ ❧

NOVEMBER 1

If you, O LORD, should mark iniquities, O Lord, who could stand? But with you there is forgiveness, that you may be feared. (Ps. 130:3-4)

If there is one thing I need on a day-in day-out basis, it is forgiveness. Sin is the stickiest substance I've ever seen! As we age, the sins change a bit, but they are still there.

Almost two months after the crucifixion, thousands of people saw their sins in a new light. We read about it in the second chapter of Acts. In Jerusalem, a lot of Jews had gathered for Pentecost when the Holy Spirit descended on the apostles. The apostles began speaking in tongues and the Spirit was unmistakable. Peter began to preach, telling those who would listen what had recently happened. The people were responsible for the death of Jesus, and Jesus was not just anyone. He was the Son of God.

Can you imagine the guilt and fear that came with realizing that you are responsible for killing the Son of God? Especially if you heard Peter's next words: Jesus came back from the dead! These people must have been terrified. They were told that they put Jesus to death, that he has come back, and that God promised to put Jesus' enemies under his feet! (Acts 2:35). Many of those listening were beside themselves. Under heavy conviction of sin, they cried out to Peter, "What shall we do?" Peter responded, "Repent and be baptized every one of you in the name of Jesus Christ for the forgiveness of your sins, and you will receive the gift of the Holy Spirit."

Notice that Peter does not speak of forgiveness of their past sins. He doesn't specify the sins of killing Jesus. Peter explains that those in Jesus have all their sins forgiven—past, present and future. This is amazing grace!

Thousands received forgiveness that day. Countless people have since. It is never dependent on how bad the sins were, because Jesus paid the price for all sins. This is the forgiveness that came to Paul, who had played a major role in the death of Stephen, the first Christian martyr. This is the forgiveness that came to Peter, who denied the Lord three times during Jesus' darkest hours. This is the forgiveness that came to John Newton, the slave trader who turned to Jesus and penned the magnificent song, "Amazing Grace." This is the forgiveness that came to me.

Anyone forgiven need not carry shame. Shame is not appropriate for one whose sin is forgiven. Remorse for sin that brings repentance is a good thing, but as we repent, fully aware of our forgiveness, our response should be one of joy and gratitude to the forgiving God.

Lord, I repent of sin. I wish I didn't do it. Thank you for the forgiveness in Christ. I will never understand the cost to you, but I am deeply appreciative in him, Amen.

❧ ❧ ❧

NOVEMBER 2

O Lord, my heart is not lifted up; my eyes are not raised too high; I do not occupy myself with things too great and too marvelous for me. But I have calmed and quieted my soul, like a weaned child with its mother; like a weaned child is my soul within me. O Israel, hope in the Lord from this time forth and forevermore. (Ps. 131)

Over three decades ago, I heard a John Michael Talbot song from this psalm. It moved me then, and still does (download it!). The mood of the song is the mood of the passage. Humble, contemplative, affirming faith.

The humility in this psalm is both physical and spiritual. The psalmist doesn't raise eyes "too high." In today's language, there is no walking about with one's nose in the air. Jesus contrasted arrogance to humility in Luke 18:9-14. The Pharisee prayed in a haughty spirit, "God, I thank you that I am not like other men, extortioners, unjust, adulterers, or even like this tax collector. I fast twice a week; I give tithes of all that I get. . . ." You get the idea. In contrast, the tax collector "would not even lift up his eyes to heaven." Like the psalmist, the tax collector lifted neither his eyes nor his heart. He knew who he was before the Almighty God. The tax collector brought his hand heavily to his chest, praying, "God, be merciful to me, a sinner!" Jesus assessed the situation clearly, "this man went down to his house justified, rather than the other. For everyone who exalts himself will be humbled, but the one who humbles himself will be exalted"

The contemplative nature of the psalm is underscored in the words, "*I have calmed and quieted my soul, like a weaned child with its mother.*" Contemplative time, quiet time, is essential in a close walk with God. We need a time of reflection, of prayer, and of one-on-one with God. It brings forth songs, instills insights, and strips the world down to bare elements. We see the Lord for who he is and we see ourselves for who we are. It is a time where we can pour our hearts out to God, and he responds.

From the humble, contemplative psalmist, we have the final sentence of faith, "*O Israel, hope in the Lord from this time forth and forevermore.*" This is affirmation of faith that comes from humble contemplation and communion with the Lord. Over and over in history God has been faithful to his people and to me. Contemplating this, I am left with the great promise of hope in the Lord.

In this moment of quiet, be reflective. In humility, see the mightiness of our God. Consider his holiness. Dwell on how he has blessed you. It will move you to trust him with any crisis today, tomorrow, or at any time.

Lord, with a humble and quiet heart, in this moment alone, I rest in my trust in you. Please take my heavy yoke and trade it for your light one. With deep gratitude in Jesus, Amen.

❧ ❧ ❧

NOVEMBER 3

How precious to me are your thoughts, O God! How vast is the sum of them! If I would count them, they are more than the sand. I awake, and I am still with you. (Ps. 139:17)

Numbers—we learn to count them when we are young. Our daughter Gracie proudly pronounced her ability to count just before kindergarten. We listened carefully. "One, two, three, four. . . ." She continued perfectly up to fifty. Then she skipped to ninety-nine. She followed that with "one hundred, one hundred and one, two hundred!" She skipped around a few various numbers till she proudly proclaimed, "One million!" She then added a few last numbers before her crescendo with "One dozen!" declared loudly as if it were the final number. We applauded.

We like to number things. We often need to number things. But our numbering ability breaks down somewhere, even for the best of us. As of the time I am writing this, the largest number with a name is a "googolplexian." Not to be confused with Google, the search engine, a googolplexian is 1 followed by a "googolplex" of zeroes. A googolplex is 1 followed by a "googol" of zeroes. The googol is 1 followed by one hundred zeroes.

Try writing that number. It will take a long time! But all of those numbers, as large as we can think of or name, cannot number God's thoughts. God does not have a mind as we humans think of minds. He is not the biological creature that we are. He is also outside of space and time, so is not caught up in the moment of thinking that we are. It is not possible for us time-bound, biological creatures, with brains that weigh about three pounds, to comprehend the "thoughts" of our God.

God knows the movements of the electrons around a nucleus of an atom in the deepest reaches of space. God knows the thoughts of all eight billion people alive today. God knows the history of time in sub-atomic detail. God knows the future. People tend to think of God as just a bit bigger than they are, when in truth, God can't be measured by people. If we ever think we have God figured out, we can rest assured, we do not have God figured out!

This is important to me. It reinforces to the greatness of our God and the stunning wonder that he cares for us on such a personal and individual level. This great God, with thoughts far beyond the googolplexian, cares about the number of hairs on my head. I can face today with courage, confidence, and love for others. The God of unlimited thoughts is in control.

Lord, thank you for the blessings of your love and care. Forgive us when we live blind to all you do. We are humbled and amazed by you. In Jesus' name, Amen.

❦ ❦ ❦

NOVEMBER 4

Behold, how good and pleasant it is when brothers dwell in unity! It is like the precious foil on the head, running down on the beard, on the beard of Aaron, running down on the collar of his robes! It is like the dew of Hermon, which falls on the mountains of Zion! For there the LORD *has commanded the blessing, life forevermore.* (Ps. 133)

I was a sophomore in high school when my spiritual mentor, a twenty-three-year-old graduate from Abilene Christian University named "Rick," sat me down and sang this song to me, playing his guitar in accompaniment. I tended to think anything Rick did was about the coolest thing anyone could do, so when he did this, I knew this was an important psalm. I quickly learned it. Unity is an important thing among brothers and sisters in the church. It is spoken of and prayed about by Jesus, emphasized and reinforced by Paul, and practiced carefully by the early church.

Right before the cross, Jesus prayed for his church saying "I do not ask for these only, but also for those who will believe in me through their word, that they may all be one, just as you, Father, are in me, and I in you, that they also may be in us, so that the world may believe that you have sent me. The glory that you have given me I have given to them, that they may be one even as we are one, I in them and you in me, that they may become perfectly one, so that the world may know that you sent me and loved them even as you loved me" (John 17:20-23). According to Jesus, the unity of believers reflects God's unity as Father, Son, and Holy Spirit. We reflect God's glory and speak to a fragmented world!

Paul wrote, "There is one body and one Spirit—just as you were called to the one hope that belongs to your call—one Lord, one faith, one baptism, one God and Father of all, who is over all and through all and in all" (Eph. 4:4-6). Because of this, Paul explained, believers are to live, "eager to maintain the unity of the Spirit in the bond of peace" (Eph. 4:3). That involved living "in a manner worthy of the calling to which you have been called, with all humility and gentleness, with patience, bearing with one another in love" (Eph. 4:1-2). Unity doesn't come easy! But it is a worthwhile goal.

The psalmist tells us that with unity come the blessings commanded by the Lord. These are blessings of life. "To life" is a Hebrew toast today, because in life we have joy, happiness, and prosperity. These are things that God has commanded would flow from unity. As we unite, while it may be difficult at times, we grow, we have support and love that bless us, we have help when needed, we have mourners in the day of grief, friends rejoicing with us in the days of blessing, and so much more. Where can I work for unity today?

Lord, help me work for unity with other believers. May we show the world your unity and bless others in your name! Amen!

❦ ❦ ❦

NOVEMBER 5

*May the L*ORD *bless you from Zion, he who made heaven and earth!* (Ps. 134:3)

During the horrific plague outbreak of 590, Pope Gregory the Great ordered the church to offer up constant prayer for God to intercede. Part of his instruction included that when someone sneezed, a frequent early plague symptom, the Christians in earshot pray a "God bless you" on the sneezing person. We still use that phrase today in response to sneezes, even though the concern is no longer a plague outbreak!

The phrase did not originate with Gregory. It had been a Christian prayer of blessing for centuries, and a Hebrew prayer of blessing even before that. The psalmist proclaims the blessing in today's passage. It is a marvelous prayer, and while it rolls off the tongue fairly easily, probably with thanks in part to Gregory the Great, we should think it through lest we say it lightly!

The Hebrew word "bless" (*baruch*) has a wide semantic range. It includes a salute or greeting with a implied blessing. (Normally people greet with *shalom*, which is often translated "peace." *Baruch* as a greeting is a bit stronger because it is not just a "hello" or "good-bye," but it is one with a blessing attached! We can think of it as the difference between telling someone "Good-bye!" or saying "Go with God!") When used with or for people, it includes the idea of being prospered by God. At its root, it conveys the image of kneeling, as was done by someone who received a blessing from a king, leader, or such. When we bless people, we are asking that the God who made heaven and earth, touch them in ways that prosper and aid them. We are asking God to work in our space and time to bring good things to that person. A blessing seeks God's power to make someone a better person with a better life.

In Numbers 6 Moses instructed the priests of Israel (Aaron and his sons) to bless the people of Israel by reciting over them, "The LORD bless you and keep you; the LORD make his face to shine upon you and be gracious to you; the LORD lift up his countenance upon you and give you peace" (Num. 6:25-26). This confirms that when we pray blessings on others, God hears our prayer and answers it. It is not idle talk, if we mean it. It is a real way we can seek to better others by praying for them.

Let this marvelous prayer of blessing readily be on our lips in a genuine way, so we seek God's blessings on others as we go through life. As we say it more and more, let's also work to bless people for God. We can be his ministers of blessing!

Lord, please bless the person reading this, and use them to bless others in Jesus, Amen.

❧ ❧ ❧

NOVEMBER 6

Come, bless the LORD, all you servants of the LORD, who stand by night in the house of the LORD! Lift up your hands to the holy place and bless the LORD! (Ps. 134:1-2)

I grew up in a marvelous church. We had superb sermons, strong singing, and the Lord's Supper every Sunday. When I moved away to college, it was important to me to find a new church home. The church I chose was one with similar strengths but with a rub. The worship was much more expressive. People were singing with their hands raised! I felt a bit uncomfortable with that because it was foreign to the way I grew up. They did what I came to call, "full-bodied worship"!

Today's passage is a "full-bodied worship" psalm from the Old Testament. Everyone was called to bless and worship the Lord with hands raised in the air. They would have felt right at home in my college church.

There is something profound about full-bodied worship. We are integrated people. Our minds are not distinct from our bodies, but are a part of our bodies. Many of us are hard-wired to use our bodies when we are into our conversations. We speak with our mouths but often our hands as well. Our faces are expressive. Our bodies convey our messages. We don't think about it, it just happens. It is because our minds are wired into our bodies. For many, then, once inhibitions are lost before the majesty and moment of experiencing God, involvement of the body is normal. It might mean bowing in prayer, looking up in prayer, holding hands with palms up, or holding hands with arms lifted high. For some it becomes hammering the sky with one hand, while others might even find themselves swaying or dancing.

How should we worship? It seems to me there are several considerations. First, whatever we do must be about worshipping the Lord, not becoming a spectacle. Second, it should flow naturally out of our worship and never be forced. Third, we should not let inhibitions preclude us from being fully responsive to the Lord in worship. Fourth, we should not sit in judgment on how other people worship the Lord.

At the root, the psalmist says it in ways that keep perspective. We are all to come bless the Lord and worship him. What we do should be a blessing to him. He is not blessed by a show that's about us. He is blessed by what we do in purity of heart and attention. So, as full-bodied people, let us come into worship in a full-bodied fashion, in whatever form that takes based upon our individuality. Not as a mark of holiness but simply to be real before God and fully before God!

Lord, may my worship always be fully about you. Help me overcome any tendency to the contrary. With worship and praise in the Lord Jesus' name, Amen!

❧❧ ❧❧ ❧❧

NOVEMBER 7

The idols of the nations are silver and gold, the work of human hands. They have mouths, but do not speak; they have eyes, but do not see; they have ears, but do not hear, nor is there any breath in their mouths. Those who make them become like them, so do all who trust in them. (Ps. 135:15-18)

I suspect every kid who enjoys a sport has a sports idol. I recall countless times, a young boy alone on my driveway, dribbling a basketball calling out to the unseen fans, "Dr. J has the ball down by one point with three seconds left." I would call out, "three, two, one . . ." and I would let the ball fly. If I made the shot, I would shout, "Dr. J wins another one in the last second!" while basking in the adulation of a pretend crowd. If I missed, I would use my announcer voice to declare, "That ends the first half!" giving me a chance to win the game again!

As we get older our idols change. If we define an idol as anything that takes the place of God in our priority chain, then we can see many idolize their cars, homes, jobs, other people, or any number of things. At the root of our idols are attitudes and values.

The psalmist teaches us a valuable lesson in today's passage: we become like the idols we value. If we idolize possessions like cars or fine clothes, we will work to get those, and the possessions will begin to take an ownership of us. If we idolize other people, we will find ourselves doing things we see in that other person. This can take on a much deeper significance than simply taking last-second shots depicting Julius Irving, or Michael Jordan, or even LeBron James.

Jesus spoke of this idea but in a more positive sense. He explained that wherever we place our treasure, we will find our heart (Matt. 6:19-21). Our heart follows what we value. This is why what we value or idolize can transform us from what we are into something quite different.

Scripture teaches us to love the Lord our God with all our heart, soul, and mind (Matt. 22:37). We are to prioritize God first, and worship no other god or thing in his stead (Exod. 20:3-6). In this way, we will find our hearts with God, we will seek to imitate God, and our lives will be the richer. It is the positive of this psalm's negative. Worship God, and grow to be more like him. Worship anything else, and grow into that. The same is true for trusting. As the psalm points out, if we trust something other than God, we will become like that, or at least enslaved or tied to it. Conversely, if we trust God, we will find ourselves growing in his image.

Lord, may we trust you and worship you above all others. Show us the idols in our lives so we can remove them from your throne and give you all praise in Jesus, Amen.

❧ ❧ ❧

NOVEMBER 8

For I know that the Lord *is great, and that our Lord is above all gods. Whatever the* Lord *pleases, he does, in heaven and on earth, in the seas and all deeps.* (Ps. 135:5-6)

What??? Did I read that right??? Does it really say, *"Whatever the* Lord *pleases, he does"*? I thought it was all about me! I thought the Lord was supposed to do whatever I please! I know there are over 8 billion people on the planet, and I know each are supposed to have free choice in life, but isn't God supposed to orchestrate this to make it all about me? After all, I gave him my life. Wasn't it kind of understood I did so with an understanding he would do what I wanted? I mean, it's okay for God to do whatever he pleases in heaven, but not on earth! This is my home!

Okay, admittedly none of us really say what I set out in the above paragraph, but I think at least I am guilty of thinking that way under the surface, even though I might not admit it even to myself.

One cannot read the Bible, certainly not the book of Revelation, without realizing that God has a cosmic plan. He has an eternity and our cosmos will fold into that eternity just as he has designed. It is like a Sudoku puzzle. All the numbers will fill out the puzzle in just the right way, but with a twist. People get to make their own choices. If someone chooses to drive while intoxicated, and hits a pedestrian killing her or him, we shouldn't expect God to have put a cork on that person's mouth to stop the drinking, or mysteriously cause the car not to work because the person was drunk. In other words, somehow God will bring his plan to fruition in spite of bad choices people make. God will work through the bad consequences from people's bad choices along the way.

This means that sometimes believers suffer. Sometimes they suffer unfairly. If an evil person chooses to strike a believer, we should not expect God to freeze that evil hand in mid-air. The evil deed happens, and we trust as believers that God will work in spite of the evil deed to fulfill his plans.

We may not be happy with all that God does or all he fails to do, but God's plans are much deeper than we can conceive. We all live on a microscopically small part of planet earth during a short vapor or wisp of time. God's plans and schemes are cosmic in scale and span from time's beginning to the final moments. How God works to achieve that is his job. How he formulates his plans and what those plans are is his responsibility. Our job is fairly simple. We are to do what *he wants*. We can modify this psalm and declare with our lives, *"Whatever the* Lord *pleases, he does, in heaven and we do on earth."*

Lord, forgive us when we make it all about us. Forgive us for our self-centeredness. Please open our hearts and minds to your plans giving us desires and strength to follow you and live according to your pleasure. In Jesus, Amen!

❧ ❧ ❧

NOVEMBER 9

Praise the LORD! Praise the name of the LORD, give praise, O servants of the LORD, who stand in the house of the LORD, in the courts of the house of our God! Praise the LORD, for the LORD is good; sing to his name, for it is pleasant! For the LORD has chosen Jacob for himself, Israel as his own possession. (Ps. 135:1-4)

When I was a child growing up, I tried to follow my parent's instructions. But there were times I was either slow to obey or maybe not so intent on obeying, and I would frequently hear, "Don't make me tell you twice!" Later as I worked to learn tools of persuasion, in both writing and speaking I was taught that saying something over, gave an emphasis that made it more understandable and memorable.

The psalmist says to "Praise the name of the LORD," and "sing to his name, for it [his name] is pleasant." "Name" is important to this passage. It is important to praise. Notice that word "LORD" is used seven times in these four short verses. English translations put the word "LORD" in large and small capitals. This indicates that they are not translating the normal Hebrew word for "Lord" (*Adonai*). When large and small capitals are used in "LORD," the Hebrew actually uses the word *Yahweh* (or the abbreviation for *Yahweh*, "*Yah*"), which is the Hebrew name for God. This is the name God used with Moses when he told Moses, "Say this to the people of Israel, 'The LORD [*Yahweh*], the God of your fathers, the God of Abraham, the God of Isaac, and the God of Jacob, has sent me to you'" (Exod. 3:15). So in four verses of this psalm, we have a total of eleven times that emphasis is drawn to the name of God.

What is so special about God's "name"? It is significant enough to merit one of the Ten Commandments! "You shall not take the name of the LORD your God in vain, for the LORD will not hold him guiltless who takes his name in vain" (Exod. 20:7). The "name" of God isn't just a label. In biblical times, your "name" stood for who you were at your core. Your name was your reputation, what you had done. It was your character. If your name didn't fit your life, then your name was changed!

God's name is special. God is a special being, unlike anything on earth or in nature. God is loving, caring, moral, upright, fair, just, interested, compassionate, forgiving, nurturing, providing, healing, whole, complex, beyond comprehension, hidden yet revealed, and more. God is worthy of our reflection and praise. He deserves our best songs. We should never take his character lightly (never "take his name in vain") for that would be not only stupid of us, but tragically wrong. God is not to be taken lightly, but to be revered and honored. Hear the emphasis of the psalm. Honor God and praise him!

Lord we praise your name, who you are, and what you've done for us in Jesus, Amen!

❊ ❊ ❊

NOVEMBER 10

To him who alone does great wonders, for his steadfast love endures forever; to him who by understanding made the heavens, for his steadfast love endures forever; to him who spread out the earth above the waters, for his steadfast love endures forever; to him who made the great lights, for his steadfast love endures forever; the sun to rule over the day, for his steadfast love endures forever; the moon and stars to rule over the night, for his steadfast love endures forever. (Ps. 136:4)

I love the creation story given in the Bible. Admittedly it is likely due to how much time I've spent reading other creation stories of the contemporaries to biblical Israel, but the uniqueness of the Bible's account speaks wonders of our God, nature, and our reality. For many ancient cultures, the gods were a part of creation. They were, in essence, the sun, the moon, or the stars. They were the waters, or a captive of the waters. They were seen in the thunder and storms. They were the earth giving crops. Gods were seen as the power or force behind things people experienced, but didn't understand. This fit with their view that the gods were fickle and moody. After all, sometimes it rained, and sometimes it didn't. Sometimes the earth gave abundant crops, other times it brought pestilence.

Not so with Israel. God was not part of nature; God existed independently of nature. Nature was God's creation. It was the reasoned and careful expression of God's understanding.

This has profound implications. It calls for us to learn more of the world, especially from a scientific perspective. We are to find the glories of nature, and give glory to the Lord who made them "by his understanding." When we see the intricacies of biology, we learn something of God's interest in life. When we see the depths of space, we learn of the magnitude of God. When we see the uniformity of cause and effect, we learn the consistency of God. When we find the marvels of modern medicine, we learn of God's tools available to fight the sicknesses and diseases of our bodies of sin.

Paul loved considering nature for what it meant about God. He wrote that God's "invisible attributes, namely, his eternal power and divine nature, have been clearly perceived, ever since the creation of the world, in the things that have been made" (Rom. 1:21). We can see God in the creation in a unique way, compared to other beliefs. Every time we learn, we have more reason to praise the Creator God. What a marvelous God we serve.

Lord, the world sings your praise by existing, may we sing your praise and draw closer to you in worship as we understand the works of your hands! In Jesus, Amen!

❊ ❊ ❊

NOVEMBER 11

Let me hear what God the Lord *will speak, for he will speak peace to his people, to his saints; but let them not turn back to folly. Surely his salvation is near to those who fear him, that glory may dwell in our land.* (Ps. 85:8-9)

We can hear lots of things in the twenty-first century. Our world is full of sounds. Horns honking with engines revving. Music and song coming from radios, computers, and hidden sources playing through nearby speakers or headphones. Televisions surround us with their noise, and we are rarely far from the chatter of people. Telephones ring and alarms sound. All of this apart from the sounds of nature—dogs barking, birds calling, wind whistling while rain patters. I frequently hear a song that is playing in my head, "earworms" some people call them. In the midst of this, we have this passage that begins, "*Let me hear what God the* Lord *will speak.*"

I want to hear God. There is no sound worth so much. It is one reason I spend daily time in his word, one reason I write devotionals, one reason I sing songs of worship.

The psalmist hears God speak "peace" to his people. Peace in Hebrew thought (*shalom*) indicates not just no turmoil, but a semantic range including "completeness," "safety," "health," "prosperity," "contentment," and "tranquility." It is a state of wholeness where one is complete. God can speak peace to his people, because God has peace to speak of! In other words, peace comes from God. He speaks it as he delivers it.

God wants to give us full peace. Of course the Bible is consistent in teaching that there are difficult times for everyone, especially the faithful. The key is that God gives peace in the midst of problems. Paul said it this way, "do not be anxious about anything, but in everything by prayer and supplication with thanksgiving let your requests be made known to God. And the peace of God, which surpasses all understanding, will guard your hearts and your minds in Christ Jesus" (Phil. 4:6-7).

This is not without some work on our part! In the psalm, God says, "don't turn to folly." He says we are to have a healthy fear or respect for him. Paul said the same, adding to the above, "Finally, brothers, whatever is true, whatever is honorable, whatever is just, whatever is pure, whatever is lovely, whatever is commendable, . . . practice these things, and the God of peace will be with you" (Phil. 4:8-9). We need to listen to God!

Lord, help me hear you above the noise of this life. Let me hear your instructions for life. Help me walk in your peace. Don't let the noise of my problems drown out the voice of your answers. May I live in your peace, and share it with others in Jesus' name, Amen.

NOVEMBER 12

Give thanks to the LORD, for he is good, for his steadfast love endures forever. Give thanks to the God of gods, for his steadfast love endures forever. Give thanks to the Lord of lords, for his steadfast love endures forever; to him who alone does great wonders, for his steadfast love endures forever. (Ps. 136:1-4)

This psalm has twenty-six verses, and each verse ends with the same phrase, "for his steadfast love endures forever." This rejoinder made the psalm a marvelous worship psalm that could be sung with a leader singing the first line in each verse followed by a congregation or group singing the refrain, "for his steadfast love endures forever." After twenty-six verses, one phrase isn't forgotten: his steadfast love endures forever.

The steadfast love of the Lord is best exemplified not by words, but by deeds. We see it in creation, in his attention to our cries, in his provision, and especially in the incarnation, ministry, death, and resurrection of the Lord Jesus Christ. God at great cost to himself, reached out to purify his people and bring us from death into life. This was not done out of obligation. God didn't owe it to us. God did this out of his steadfast love.

The psalm gives us a marvelous refrain worth remembering, "*his steadfast love endures forever.*" It would be a great earworm (one of those segments of a song that get stuck in your head). If we constantly thought about the steadfast love of God, we would see the world differently.

When trouble comes our way, we would think about the steadfast love of the Lord, and the trouble wouldn't scare us. When temptation comes our way, we would think about the steadfast love of the Lord, and temptation would lose its allure. When we feel unfairly treated, we would think about the steadfast love of the Lord and what Jesus endured, and our rights would not be our priority. When we lose direction in life, we would think about the steadfast love of the Lord, and walk in faith that he will lead us and make our ways the right ones. When we lose motivation, we would think about the steadfast love of the Lord, and his love would generate a drive to show him love in return. When we become impatient, we would think about the steadfast love of the Lord, and we would find peace in God's timing. When we get depressed or down in sprit, we would think about the steadfast love of the Lord, and we would know that joy will come in the morning. When we get worried, we would think about the steadfast love of the Lord, and peace would replace the worry. His steadfast love endures forever! Got it in your head? It is worth repeating!

Lord God, whose steadfast love endures forever, we praise you as our God. Thank you for your steadfast love that endures forever, Jesus. Amen!

❊ ❊ ❊

NOVEMBER 13

By the waters of Babylon, there we sat down and wept, when we remembered Zion. On the willows there we hung up our lyres. For there our captors required of us songs, and our tormentors, mirth, saying, "Sing us one of the songs of Zion!" How shall we sing the Lord's song in a foreign land? If I forget you, O Jerusalem, let my right hand forget its skill! Let my tongue stick to the roof of my mouth, if I do not remember you, if I do not set Jerusalem above my highest joy! . . . O daughter of Babylon, doomed to be destroyed, blessed shall he be who repays you with what you have done to us! Blessed shall he be who takes your little ones and dashes them against the rock! (Ps. 137:1-6)

This psalm is one of the saddest in the Old Testament. It is one of overwhelming pity, remorse, and a bit of surprise that the writer is proclaiming blessing upon those who might kill the infants of others.

The psalm conveys the pain and shock of the Jewish survivors exiled in Babylon in the sixth century BC. Once there, they sat by the waterways stunned and weeping. Sitting was a Hebrew posture of mourning (remember Job's friends sitting on the ground with him in mourning for seven days and nights in Job 2:13). This was what the Jewish exiles were doing as their captors asked for joyful songs of the temple. There was no joy for the exiles, however, and they put up their harps. The time for happy music was gone. They could not sing songs of the Lord with his temple and their homeland destroyed.

Even as the people were deported, they pledged themselves to remember home. One explanation for breaking the glass in a Jewish wedding is prioritizing the memory of Jerusalem's destruction (symbolized by the broken glass) above all joys, even the joy of marriage. In the psalm, the deported Jews would rather lose the ability to play and sing than to forget Jerusalem. The line about the infants smashed against the rocks stems from the events that occurred to the exiles. This is what the Babylonian had "*done to us!*" I don't know how anyone recovers from that.

This psalm also speaks to me of the misery of those who, like the Jews of that day, spurn God over and over and over again, spurning his calls for obedience, his calls for repentance, his messengers and his message, instead insisting on their own way. There comes a point, where the unheeded warnings of God bear the punishing fruit. This is not God being mean; this is the result of people insisting on poor choices over and over again. Everyone should take time to download this psalm (entitled, "By the Rivers of Babylon") as sung by Lamb, a Messianic Jewish group. It conveys the spirit and pain of those who refuse to follow the Lord, choosing instead their own way of rebellion.

Lord, I don't want to rebel against you. I want to follow your call. Help me, in Jesus, Amen.

NOVEMBER 14

The LORD will fulfill his purpose for me; your steadfast love, O LORD, endures forever. Do not forsake the work of your hands. (Ps. 138:8)

When I was a sophomore in high school, I went on a trip with an older Christian mentor of mine to Roswell, New Mexico. The purpose of the trip was to work in the community to further the outreach of a group of churches that had brought in a nightly speaker, Don Finto. I had never met Don before, but I had heard amazing things about him. His personality and attitude were enticing; his zeal for the Lord was infectious, and his t~~~~~~~~ memorable. I can still recite one fairly closely today, forty years later.

In one sermon, Don spoke of God's plans for us. Don drove home the point that God had plans for all his children, and in spite of what we have done or failed to do, God still works in us. Don explained, "Let me be clear. I have failed the Lord, and I am not on God's Plan A for my life." He continued, "I'm not on Plan B or C." He paused and then said, "Really, I may not even be on Plan Double Z! But that does not change the FACT that God has a plan for me."

Don was right. God does have a plan for all of his believers. We fail both in what we do and fail to do, but God doesn't leave us one the side of the road like an abandoned tire, blown out and left in shreds.

Think of God as the ultimate in going green! God is into major recycling. When we have made garbage in our lives, God takes that garbage and recycles it into something good for his kingdom. God has a purpose for you and a purpose for me, and not even our worst mistakes in the past can keep God from fulfilling his purpose for us today.

There is solace in this for me. I, like brother Finto, am not even on Plan ZZ at this point. I have made so many errors and failed my Lord in so many ways. I belong on a garbage heap. Yet, my recycling Lord has taken me in my sin, me in my ignorance, me in my rebellion, me in my lack of faith, and has sculpted me into a tool for his purposes. God has not forsaken me. He has sustained and rebuilt me.

Paul assured the church at Philippi, "I am sure of this, that he who began a good work in you will bring it to completion at the day of Jesus Christ" (Phil. 1:6). Paul was confident that God would not abandon his purposes for his children. We are God's work, and he will find success, in spite of all our foul ups. What an amazing God we serve!

Lord, please fulfill your purposes for me. Do not stop working in me and through me for the good of your kingdom and will. Forgive me my errors and sins, and recycle me into exactly what you need today. For Jesus' sake, Amen.

❦ ❦ ❦

NOVEMBER 15

Though the LORD is high, he regards the lowly, but the haughty he knows from afar. (Ps. 138:6-7)

In the middle of seventh grade I moved from Rochester, New York, to Lubbock, Texas. The culture shock was intense. At the middle school I attended, I was, for a considerable amount of time, an observer. At that age, most of the children had already figured out the crowd where they felt comfortable, and these cliques existed without much regard to the new kid. I noticed something that had not occurred to me before. The groups that hung out together were basically cut from the same cloth. It was a classic example of "birds of a feather flock together."

It is an interesting human social interaction that extends beyond middle school. People gravitate toward others like them. The similarity may be personality, or it may be driven by education, interests, economic levels, or even a commonality of children involved in some activity together.

In stark contrast to this human feature, we have this passage from the Psalms. The Lord God is on high. There is none higher. He has the greatest knowledge, power, presence, resources, reputation, etc. Yet God does not choose the great and powerful. God seeks out the lowly and humble.

Jesus set the earthly example of God as he is set forth in this psalm. Jesus did not walk with the rulers, the elite and the powerful. Jesus fellowshipped with the lowly and the outcasts. When the disciples were discussing who were the great people, Jesus took a child and set the child in front of them all. Jesus explained, "Whoever humbles himself like this child is the greatest in the kingdom of heaven" (Matt. 18:4). Later Jesus specified, "The greatest among you shall be your servant. Whoever exalts himself will be humbled, and whoever humbles himself will be exalted" (Matt. 23:11-12). Another time when the disciples were arguing among themselves as to which of them was the greatest, Jesus explained, "let the greatest among you become as the youngest, and the leader as one who serves. For who is the greater, one who reclines at table or one who serves? Is it not the one who reclines at table? But I am among you as the one who serves" (Luke 22:26-27). Jesus then washed the feet of his disciples (John 13:3-14).

We often see power and value very differently than God. If we want God's vision, we need to not seek out the high and mighty, but let that place be assigned only to God. We need to seek out the needy. We need servants' hearts seeking to serve those in need, even if they fail to express gratitude. This brings us into deeper fellowship with our God.

Father, help us to follow you. Teach us to serve with willing hearts, valuing the opportunities to express your love to those in need. In Jesus, Amen.

❧ ❧ ❧

NOVEMBER 16

I give you thanks, O LORD, with my whole heart; before the gods I sing your praise; I bow down toward your holy temple and give thanks to your name for your steadfast love and your faithfulness, for you have exalted above all things your name and your word. On the day I called, you answered me; my strength of soul you increased. (Ps. 138:1-3)

This is an interesting psalm in the Hebrew. The English Standard Version translators have added the words "O LORD" when in the original psalm, God is unnamed. There was a great holiness in leaving God unnamed. The Ancient Hebrews, and most devout modern Jews, do not pronounce the name of God, and usually won't write it either. Hence, the psalmist gives thanks to the Lord, "with my whole heart."

The psalmist also sings God's praises "before the gods." This can be confusing to many. It sounds like he might be referencing the polytheism that was so rampant during much of Israel's history. I think the better understanding is that "gods" were the great of Israel. Much like the "lords" of medieval society, the notable were deemed to be divine representatives. So the psalmist here sings a reverent and great praise to the Lord, before those who are great on the earth.

The psalmist directs praise to God, rather than people, bowing before God's temple and thanking him for his steadfast love and faithfulness. It is a tribute to God's steadfast love and faithfulness that well over five hundred years later, God incarnates into Jesus and redeems the world from the death of sin. God's steadfast love and faithfulness are still celebrated today as we rejoice in the salvation of Jesus, and as God continues to work in our lives.

The psalmist saw the work of God in the ways God answered prayers and "increased" the strength of the writer's soul. Every generation, believers have experienced and can testify to the hand of God answering prayer and giving strength to the weary and weak.

This faithful and steadfast work of God's love rightfully brings God glory. It shows our God to be involved in a loving, caring, long-standing way. He doesn't give up on us. He doesn't forget about us. He doesn't shun us when we are in trouble, even if the trouble is of our own making. The faithful and steadfast God stands at the ready to answer our cries for help, and to strengthen our souls as we learn and grow before him.

We should praise God for who he is and what he is doing. It is fitting that before all people, even those in high position, we direct our praise to God. God is our king.

Lord, we praise you for your steadfast love and faithfulness. We praise you for the Son of your love, Jesus, who died on our behalf reflecting your steadfast love and faithfulness. Lord, teach us to praise you more, in Jesus' name, Amen.

❧❧ ❧❧ ❧❧

NOVEMBER 17

Remember, O LORD, in David's favor, all the hardships he endured, how he swore to the LORD and vowed to the Mighty One of Jacob, "I will not enter my house or get into my bed, I will not give sleep to my eyes or slumber to my eyelids, until I find a place for the LORD, a dwelling place for the Mighty One of Jacob." (Ps 132:1-5)

I had read four or five years of Hebrew when I came across a book on the Hebrew word translated "remember" (*zacar*). Passages like this and the flood account of Noah bothered me because of the idea that God might "forget" and needed reminders! That doesn't sound like the God I worship! The book was not written as a defense of God. It was simply a scholastic treatment of the Hebrew word. The study didn't really plow new ground among scholars, but its content was important.

The Hebrew word isn't generally calling forth "recall" in the sense of "I forgot!" Rather than calling God to remember what he might have forgotten, it is asking God to take action based upon matters that are set forth. In other words, God hasn't forgotten the deeds of David, or Noah being afloat, but the psalmist calls on God to take action because of what has happened before. Similarly, when Israel was in bondage to pharaoh, and they cried out to God, then "God heard their groaning, and God remembered his covenant with Abraham, with Isaac, and with Jacob" (Exod. 2:24). The Israelites had not languished for centuries in Egypt because of a memory lapse of God. "Remember" meant God was taking action because of an earlier commitment.

In this sense, we better understand the commandment, "remember the Sabbath day, to keep it holy" (Exod. 20:8). The thrust of that command is not simply a modern, "don't forget the Sabbath!", but it is an action-based command. It is, "In thinking about the Sabbath, take the right actions to keep it holy and set apart from the other days." Seeing this helps us understand passages like Isaiah 34:25, where God says, "I, I am he who blots out your transgressions for my own sake, and I will not remember your sins." God is not simply telling us that he is able to induce sin-amnesia. God is saying that he will not take action on our sin!

What does this mean to us and our prayer life? It is a call to action! We live by God's mercy, and trust that he will act on our behalf. Similarly, we should act with minds remembering his love and devotion to us. Let our memories drive us to greater service for the Father.

Dear Lord, please bless and use me in accordance with what works best in your will, to your glory, not mine. In Jesus, Amen.

❀ ❀ ❀

NOVEMBER 18

I will praise the name of God with a song; I will magnify him with thanksgiving. This will please the LORD more than an ox or a bull with horns and hoofs. When the humble see it they will be glad; you who seek God, let your hearts revive. For the LORD hears the needy and does not despise his own people who are prisoners. (Ps. 69:30-33)

I love praise psalms. I love the psalmist calling me into a time of worship. Worship sets things aright for me. It reminds me that God sits on his throne, and that I don't. In fact, I don't even have enough personal merit to enter his presence, but he welcomes me anyway because of the purifying work of Jesus.

When I see God on his throne, I see the One who is all powerful, all caring, the destroyer of evil, supplier of needs, teacher of truth, builder of good things, planner of eternity, creator of people, hearer of prayers, dispatcher of angels, mover of hearts, all knowing, designer of things to come, and insurer of my faith. I see One who is both kind and stern, merciful and just, provider and withholder, timeless and in the moment, Alpha and Omega, beginning and end, peaceful and warring, gentle and rough, three and one. I approach the One who is unapproachable. I gaze toward the One no one can see. I touch the untouchable.

As I see God on his throne in worship, I see myself for who I am. I see myself a sinner. I have done wrong and I continue to do wrong, even when I know better. I fail to love my enemies as I should. I fail to love my neighbors as I should. I am not the husband I should be, loving my wife as Christ loved the church. I am not the parent I should be, try as I might to rear my children in the nurture and admonition of the Lord. I am not the steward of God's blessings I should be. I worry when I shouldn't. I take matters into my own hands when I should entrust them first to the Lord. I fail to trust the Lord as I should. I have no right to be before the Lord in any capacity except judgment. And yet. . . .

I have a redeemer sitting at the right hand of the Father. My God is not only judge; he is also redeemer. He knows all of my sins, past and future. He wrangled them from me and took them to the cross. He hoisted my sins on his own soul as he was hoisted onto the wood. He died with my sins, and was vanquished to hell where he didn't stay. My Redeemer God won victory over the grave and hell. He was resurrected by God in power and ascended to the right hand of the Almighty where he reigns a crucified Savior. He has cleansed me. He has not just declared me righteous; he has made me righteous. He is the reason I can be confident before the throne in praise! He is my praise! He is my God!

Lord, I PRAISE YOU!!! In spite of sin and faithlessness, I praise you in the purity of Jesus! Amen!

NOVEMBER 19

You formed my inward parts; you knitted me together in my mother's womb. I praise you, for I am fearfully and wonderfully made. Wonderful are your works; my soul knows it very well. (Ps. 139:13-14)

I was trying a case once where the issue was what happens to pioglitazone inside the cells of the human body. I had one of the world's top specialists on "PPARs" (peroxisome proliferator-activated receptors). These PPARs are smaller than we can see with a microscope, but they exist in several varieties and are capable of transporting molecules from the cytoplasm of a cell into the nucleus, where the molecule interfaces with the cell's DNA. They can alter how the DNA works.

This may not make sense to the average reader, but PPARs are working in our bodies trillions of times a day. They were first identified in frogs, and are found in cells of most higher organisms. Unknown until the 1980s, these agents are critical to human life. These are one of unknown numbers of ways our bodies are stunning to think about. Rightly the psalmist says, "I am fearfully and wonderfully made," but that is truer than even the psalmist knew. The intricacies of biology are astounding.

We do the psalmist an extreme disservice if we think he meant God takes knitting needles, somehow sneaks into a womb and knits children together. While genetics needed a few millennia to be discovered, the effect of male fertilization and growth of babies was well understood (see, e.g., Gen. 38:9). This passage is not claiming God made the psalmist by hand, but God made the psalmist nonetheless.

I like the way God makes things. My love for my sweet wife is a love from God. I rightfully say, "My marriage was made in heaven." My children are gifts from God. God works through genetics, through nature, through circumstance, through history, and through people. That is not to say that God cannot make something from nothing. He certainly can. But as the God who made the universe, he is responsible for the dynamics of the universe. He is no less my "maker" than if he fashioned me out of clay. Reproduction is an amazing process on a cellular level. God the designer, has set forth a system of life that should make us all stop in wonder.

The psalmist takes the processes, credits them to God, and teaches that God is doing this with personal awareness. As a baby grows and is birthed, it is not only nature at work, but God as well. God is at work in us. What an awesome God!

Lord, you are amazing. We cannot comprehend all that your hand has done and all you do today. As science continues to open up our minds to the intricacies of your handiwork, may we never fail to give you glory for all you have set forth. In Jesus, Amen.

❦ ❦ ❦

NOVEMBER 20

Where shall I go from your Spirit? Or where shall I flee from your presence? If I ascend to heaven, you are there! If I make my bed in Sheol, you are there! If I take the wings of the morning and dwell in the uttermost parts of the sea, even there your hand shall lead me, and your right hand shall hold me. If I say, "Surely the darkness shall cover me, and the light about me be night," even the darkness is not dark to you; the night is bright as the day, for darkness is as light with you. (Ps. 139:7-12)

In 1893 the English poet Francis Thompson published a 182-line poem, "The Hound of Heaven." The poem has influenced many, from writers like J. R. R. Tolkien and G. K. Chesterton, to painters like Ives Gammell, and even the occasional band like Daniel Amos. The poem is both a practical and a poetic interpretation of today's passage.

Let's say I wanted to flee from God. How could I do it? Where could I go? If I take an airplane to the furthest reaches of the planet or a submarine to take me to the deepest depths of the oceans, God would be there before me. If I took a rocket ship to Mars, wouldn't God be there? If I could find warp drive, and escape to the outer reaches of the galaxy, do I not realize that God holds the universe in his hand? Can the darkness of night remove me from God's sight? Of course not!

Not only can I not escape God's presence, I can't escape his care. The psalmist knew that even in our flight, God's hand leads and holds us. We can't escape the Hound of Heaven. He finds us and brings us back to him. There is a great reassurance in this. Paul wrote to the Romans and asked them if there was anything that would separate them from God's presence and love. "Shall tribulation, or distress, or persecution, or famine, or nakedness, or danger, or sword?" (Rom. 8:35). Paul's answer: "No, in all these things we are more than conquerors through him who loved us. For I am sure that neither death nor life, nor angels nor rulers, nor things present nor things to come, nor powers, nor height nor depth, nor anything else in all creation, will be able to separate us from the love of God in Christ Jesus our Lord" (Rom. 8:37-39).

I am constantly relieved that God will persist in his love for me in spite of my many faults and problems. I am reassured knowing that some dear to me who have entrusted themselves to God, later trying to flee from him intellectually or spiritually, won't succeed. They can't hide from the Hound of Heaven. He will find them, retrieve them, and forgive them.

We worship a marvelous God.

Lord, thank you for your persistent love and care. Without it, we would all be lost. We find strength, confidence, and hope in your love. In Jesus we pray, Amen!

NOVEMBER 21

O LORD, you have searched me and known me! You know when I sit down and when I rise up; you discern my thoughts from afar. You search out my path and my lying down and are acquainted with all my ways. Even before a word is on my tongue, behold, O LORD, you know it altogether. You hem me in, behind and before, and lay your hand upon me. Such knowledge is too wonderful for me; it is high; I cannot attain it. (Ps. 139:1-6)

In the 1950s two psychologists developed a model of awareness called a "Johari window." The window has four panes or compartments that look like boxes. Two of the boxes are things you know about yourself; two are things you don't know about yourself. The categories (things we recognize in ourselves and things we don't) are subdivided, producing two more windows: things others know about you and things others don't know about you. When all is said and done the four panes show: (1) an area of our lives that is open, where we know things about ourselves that others know as well; (2) an area that is almost like a façade with things we know about ourselves but keep from others; (3) an area where others see things in us that we don't see; and (4) an area of our lives unknown to us or others.

Johari Window

	Known to self	Not known to self
Known to others	Open	Blind spot
Not known to others	Façade	Unknown

The psalmist understood that God knows the whole box. The Lord knows what we know about ourselves, and he knows what we don't know. The Lord knows our actions and he knows our thoughts. God has his hand on all aspects of our being. There is nothing outside his knowledge or reach. Our blind spots are not blind to him; he knows us better than we know ourselves. We can't fool him with who we are; we can't hide who we are.

Intimacy is both scary and marvelous. There are aspects of us that we do not show others out of fear. We are afraid of what they might think or how they might handle the information. Yet as we find those who love us unconditionally, and as we open up secret places to them, it is a marvelous thing.

With God, we need not fear. He knows us, and knew us before we came to be. Knowing us fully, he loved us so greatly, that he sacrificed himself for our good. God calls us to be open and honest with him. There is nothing about us he doesn't already know. We shouldn't pretend to be anything other than what we are with him. Intimacy with God is a unique opportunity. Heaven help us if we fail to walk in it!

Lord, it is hard to believe the depths of your knowledge matched by the strength of your love. Help us walk in honesty before you. Thank you for your love in Jesus, Amen.

NOVEMBER 22

I know that the Lord *will maintain the cause of the afflicted, and will execute justice for the needy. Surely the righteous shall give thanks to your name; the upright shall dwell in your presence.* (Ps. 140:12-13)

Don't ever let the issue of timing get in the way of your faith and confidence in the Lord! God promises that he will maintain the cause of the afflicted, execute justice for the needy, and that the upright will dwell in his presence.

I have no doubt that passages like these have been relied upon by people who have subsequently been killed while never seeing justice. One need only think of Christian martyrs in parts of the world today, as well as throughout history. Many of the Jews in concentration camps surely knew the Psalms and sought refuge in them, only to find death at the end of the day. Where was God? Where was his justice? I have a friend whose father was in the Auschwitz concentration camp. My friend is an atheist, convinced if there was a God, such an atrocity could not have happened.

These are difficult issues, and my heart goes out for those involved. I find it appropriate to weep and mourn tragedy. I also find it appropriate to affirm faith, even in a psalm that declares God will maintain the cause of the afflicted and execute justice for the needy. We need to remember and affirm that this world, and our time on it, is a blur in eternity. To call our time on earth "brief" gives it too much length.

That doesn't mean our time is unimportant. It doesn't mean God isn't interested in righting the wrongs of today. He is, and we should be too. But it does mean that sometimes our timing is not God's. It means that in fights against evil and injustice, there are battles won by the enemy. But the war? The war is won by our God. That is our assurance. Many people toil over the meaning given to the book of Revelation. But in spite of all the back and forth over the significance of one thing or another, we can affirm certain truths about the vision: (1) There is a war. (2) God wins the war. (3) We can pick which side to be on. (4) We should be smart about that choice.

There are martyrs on earth. It is a sad thing, and we should not only fight against it, but should weep for those involved. The holocaust should be considered a horror-caust. But it doesn't change our faith in the God of justice who cares for the afflicted. There is a cosmic war going on, and God rescues. It just isn't always in our time or in this life. We have the assurance of the psalm that the "*upright shall dwell in God's presence.*"

Lord, help us to fight injustices, and to never lose faith over your timing. In Jesus, one who suffered such injustices, though for a greater purpose, we pray, Amen!

❧ ❧ ❧

NOVEMBER 23

O LORD, my Lord, the strength of my salvation, you have covered my head in the day of battle. (Ps. 140:7)

I pray this passage to the Lord even though I am not in the military. I still face battles daily. Some days my battles are in the courtroom, where I am fighting for truth and justice. Some days my battles are for my children, when forces of evil, immorality, and deceit seek to infiltrate their lives and take them captive. Anyone with children knows the parental concerns as those children seek their own way in the world. Some days my battles are deeply personal, as I war against sin in my life. Some days my battles are for friends who are struggling with health issues, financial issues, family issues, and more. Some days my battles are for our community and nation, as I seek to be a good private citizen. We have elected officials that need our help, or sometimes need replacing. We have community issues that call for our energy and initiative to make right.

In all of this, we should never go into battle without the Lord covering our head. The poet is using very literal terms to draw a picture. "Cover" truly speaks to covering, as one might put a blanket over a bed. "Head" means head! With those literal terms, however, the poet is drawing a picture. God becomes our helmet, protecting us and also preparing us for battle. Paul uses the same image in Ephesians when he details the Christian's armor in fighting the battles against evil. Telling the believer to "put on the whole armor of God," Paul includes the "helmet of salvation." This is part of being "strong in the Lord and in the strength of his might" (Eph. 6:10-18).

When God protects us, we no longer cower in fear. We are boldly confident. We know that following him into battle, we need not fear. While we are never assured of the specific outcome, we know that the outcome will always be used by the Father to further his purposes. We faithfully rely upon our God as we give our best in the battle, as long as our best is under his covering! Where we get into trouble is when we try to engage in these battles without the Lord's covering. We should never engage without prayer. We should never engage without being in the word, seeking God's wisdom. We should always be seeking the help of other believers, through words of encouragement, wisdom, and insight. We should never waiver in our faith as we engage. God is the strength of our salvation, the salvation we desperately seek in the battles of life.

Lord, you know the battles we face. We long to be covered with your grace and strength. We need to take you into those battles. Help us train for battle as we daily spend time growing with you. Thank you for winning the great battle on our behalf! In Jesus, Amen.

NOVEMBER 24

But my eyes are toward you, O GOD, my Lord; in you I seek refuge; leave me not defense-less! Keep me from the trap that they have laid for me and from the snares of evildoers!
(Ps. 141:8-9)

We live in a relatively safe society. When and if people "have it in for us," it rarely escalates to violence, at least once we get out of middle school! There are still occasions when we confront people who seem bent on our destruction, whether physically, economically, or socially, but they are rare, compared to the days of the Psalms.

Hopefully we are able to escape those who seek to abuse us, but not always. While the abuse can be physical, it can also be emotional. These are people who affect our psyche, some of whom can do a great deal of damage. People who hurt us may not always be doing so intentionally. Sometimes they are just dysfunctional people that leave us wounded, questioning ourselves and trying to keep it together. Others may actually intend their attacks, looking to bring us to our emotional knees. To people facing abusive others, the Psalms have given passages like today's.

The psalmist gives a key to finding God as our protection. It is to keep our eyes toward him. We keep our eyes toward God as we focus on him first and foremost. When we consider who God is, his love, his care, his attention to our lives, we are reminded of true reality. Too often emotional enemies can project an idea of reality that is not true. That can be part of the emotional trap. They can make us feel and think things that are not really valid or true. Focusing on God will always bring us back into reality. We see God for who he is, people for who they are, circumstances for what they are. We remember that we are not perfect, but we are forgiven. We are not always lovable, but we are loved. Focusing on God keeps us rooted and defended. It keeps us from the traps of emotional enemies.

What can this mean to us practically? First, I have found it important to have a committed time of daily quiet time with the Lord. This means every day, I commit to being quiet with my God, reading in his word, thinking about him and what he has to say in my life, and praying with him. From these quiet times have come this devotional book. This brings God into focus in my life every day. Another way I have found to turn my eyes to God is through song and hymns like "On Christ the Solid Rock I Stand," older Christian contemporary songs like Chuck Girard's "Slow Down," and modern songs like Hillsong's "Prince of Peace," which can all be downloaded and draw our focus to God. A key to both the quiet time and songs is prayer, where we end today.

Lord, Help me keep my eyes to you. Through Jesus, Amen.

※ ※ ※

NOVEMBER 25

Let a righteous man strike me—it is a kindness; let him rebuke me—it is oil for my head; let my head not refuse it. (Ps. 141:5)

When I was a young lawyer, I was asked to lunch by one of the leaders in our church. I was so excited. That the leader would take time out of his busy day to sit with me and get to know me was thrilling. I taught an adult class at the church, and was on a rotation system to preach every six weeks on Sunday night. This gentleman was also a teacher and was on the same rotation system. I had great esteem for him. He was one of my favorites.

Over lunch, we had an opportunity to get to know each other, but it readily became apparent that he had a special reason for our encounter. He took me to lunch to tell me that at times I came off too cavalier in my teaching and preaching. Ouch!!! I had been so excited that this man wanted to eat with me, and then I found out it was mainly to reprove and correct me. I felt I had been hit in the gut.

Taking correction and advice is a really challenging aspect of growing. For many, our natural reaction to someone giving us advice, correction, or rebuke, is self-defense. We feel as if it is an attack on who we are and how we live. We can get angry, frustrated, defensive, or we can listen to the advice, weigh it, pray about it, and if it is good advice, follow it.

This is the gist of today's passage. The psalmist was welcoming the help of the righteous in trying to become a better person. With a bit of poetic flair, the psalmist says that when the righteous corrects, rebukes, or instructs, it might feel like a blow, but it is a kindness. It might leave you feeling red-faced and embarrassed, but it is actually oil for your head (2,500 years ago that was a good thing!).

We should not refuse to learn in those situations. We can become better people by learning from others. We should not hesitate to listen, weigh, and learn. Failure to do so is often a mark of pride. We think ourselves above learning or we think that others have no place in teaching us. We would be wrong there.

I have no doubt that the gentleman I had lunch with that day had an important word for me. If my teaching was coming off to anyone as too cavalier, I needed to know that. My teaching was never supposed to be about me, it is supposed to be about the Lord. The gentleman and I became good friends over the decades since. I know he didn't relish having to talk to me at lunch. I didn't enjoy it, but I grew from it. It was a kindness and oil for my head.

Lord, please give me a teachable spirit. When others help me with instructions or even rebukes, let me not be so defensive that I fail to listen, weigh, and learn. I want to be a better person, and I thank you for all the ways you teach me. In Jesus' name, Amen.

❧ ❧ ❧

NOVEMBER 26

Set a guard, O LORD, over my mouth; keep watch over the door of my lips! Do not let my heart incline to any evil, to busy myself with wicked deeds in company with men who work iniquity, and let me not eat of their delicacies! (Ps. 141:3-4)

Sometimes, despite the best intentions, it is hard to do right. I don't mean the commands like, "Do not murder." Most of us don't have problems with those. But as my friend Tim who was reading the Sermon on the Mount for the first time told me, "I think I'm going to Hell! Before I read this, I couldn't murder. Now I can't even look!"

There are some instructions for living that aren't quite so easy to instill in our lives. Consider some of these:

- Everyone who is angry with his brother will be liable to judgment; whoever insults his brother will be liable to the council; and whoever says, 'You fool!' will be liable to the hell of fire (Matt. 5:22).
- Give to the one who begs from you, and do not refuse the one who would borrow from you (Matt. 5:42).
- Let every person be quick to hear, slow to speak, slow to anger; for the anger of man does not produce the righteousness of God (Jas. 1:19-20).
- If anyone thinks he is religious and does not bridle his tongue but deceives his heart, this person's religion is worthless (Jas. 1:26).
- For where jealousy and selfish ambition exist, there will be disorder and every vile practice (Jas. 3:16).
- Do not grumble against one another, brothers (Jas. 5:9).

How can we ever hope to live up to such admirable and important instructions? The psalmist understood the key. We need to ask the Lord for his help. The psalmist asked the Lord to set a guard "over my mouth" but it doesn't stop there. We need the Lord to work on our heart too. Sin isn't just what our physical bodies do, it is also a condition of the heart that motivates the body. We need discipline in our bodies, but also our minds. Again, we ask the Lord for that help.

A final area of prayer on this front concerns our friends and the world where we live. We live in a world filled with fallen people. While some are more virtuous than others, all have sinned and all fall short of God's holiness. The effect of this isn't always one that helps. The sins of others can rub off on us and callous our hearts to sin. After all, if others are gossiping, is it that bad to add our two cents? To borrow the psalmist's language, shall we eat of their delicacies? Let us seek God's help at cutting off that avenue of sin also.

Lord, we know we are sinful, and we are thankful for forgiveness in Jesus. While forgiven, we still need you to help us grow in righteousness. Help us control our bodies, our minds, and not be corrupted by our friends and others in our world. In Jesus, Amen.

❧ ❧ ❧

When my spirit faints within me, you know my way! In the path where I walk they have hidden a trap for me. Look to the right and see: there is none who takes notice of me; no refuge remains to me; no one cares for my soul. I cry to you, O LORD; I say, "You are my refuge, my portion in the land of the living." Attend to my cry, for I am brought very low! (Ps. 142:3-6)

There have been times of physical exhaustion where I just wanted to sit or lie down and not move. I remember running a half marathon, and afterwards, my body was in serious need of recharging. There was not a lot that was going to get me going until I was rested and rejuvenated.

This doesn't happen only with the body; it happens with the spirit too. There are times of spiritual exhaustion, where we suffer spiritual and emotional lethargy. We have trouble moving. The psalmist hit this state, bringing forth today's passage.

"When my spirit faints. . . ." This is our spiritual fatigue. It is an inner feebleness that makes it difficult for us to know what to do or how to do it. We lose the drive for figuring things out. Spiritual inertia sets in.

The psalmist was concerned because while feeling spiritually faint, one more easily falls into life's traps. With no one close to help the writer during this time of emotional malaise, the writer was concerned. To personalize it: Who can we call upon to make sure that we have secure footing when our own personal strength is lagging?

The answer is clear: The Lord! When we are brought low, when our spiritual energy is fainting, when our emotional drive seems stuck in reverse, when our zeal has flamed out, we can and should turn to the Lord. The traps of life are still there, even if we don't have the energy to be diligent. We can easily get ensnared, but for the protection and refuge of God.

So during the down times, during the times where we hit spiritual exhaustion, let us not fail to turn to God. It is a good reason for us to be in the habit of daily prayer and devotion. Having a daily quiet time brings us before the Lord in all our states. We come to him when spiritually invigorated, but we also come when we are spiritually drained. We are then in a place where God can deal with us, protect us, and deliver us. He will restore our energy, recharge our spiritual batteries, and set up back out on the road, ready to run for him. We serve an amazing God!

Lord, there are times where my spirit is faint. I confess I don't always have the spiritual energy to pray as I should. I run out of zeal for doing your good deeds, and I hit points of spiritual exhaustion. Please come to me and restore me. Bring back zeal for you and your will. Protect me while you restore my zest for living before you. In Jesus, Amen.

❧ ❧ ❧

NOVEMBER 28

With my voice I cry out to the Lord*; with my voice I plead for mercy to the* Lord*. I pour out my complaint before him; I tell my trouble before him.* (Ps. 142:1-2)

When I was young, we would frequently drive the four hours from Lubbock, Texas, to San Angelo, Texas, to spend the weekend with my grandparents. One thing that fascinated me was the way my parents, especially my mom, would sit with my grandparents for hours and talk about what was going on in life. It registered to me how important it was for my mom to have this outlet, this chance to tell her mother what was going on in her life, and get insights in return.

Everyone needs someone to listen. Everyone needs to find a sympathetic ear. Most humans are wired for wanting and needing to tell someone about their lives and problems. A good part of the job of "counselor" is simply listening. People can often come to their own conclusions as they talk through a matter. Talking about things helps us process. It forces us to think through matters when we vocalize them.

Today's passage points out that God is a listening ear. We may not think this at first blush, because God is not someone we physically see, but he is nonetheless. God pays attention when we talk. God wants us to pour out our hearts, to tell him about our lives, what is good and what is frustrating. He wants us to walk through our joys with him, and he wants to hear of our problems.

The psalmist was vocal with God: "*With my voice I cry out to the Lord.*" The psalmist talked to God in a most intimate way, speaking aloud a plea for mercy, verbally telling God all the problems in life. This is remarkable. To speak to the God of the universe about our sometimes mundane lives, to have him listen and pay attention, and to have him take action on our behalf, seems surreal. Yet it isn't. It is real.

In John 17 we read of Jesus' prayer offered right before Judas betrayed him. Jesus was praying out loud, for that is how we know what he said! Jesus was very personal and intimate with God. He poured his heart out, explaining his hopes, concerns, needs, and more. History shows God listened and honored the prayers of Christ, and we are the beneficiaries of that! (If you want confirmation, read the prayer in John 17!)

I may not be accustomed to praying to God as I might pour out my heart to a friend, but that is to my own detriment. God is there, a listening ear, ready for us to tell him what is going on and how we need his insight and help. I need to learn to do this better. Pray this prayer out loud:

Lord, I need your help in sorting out life. I want to live in ways that express your will for me and this world. Teach me, please. In Jesus' name, Amen.

❧ ❧ ❧

NOVEMBER 29

The LORD upholds all who are falling and raises up all who are bowed down. The eyes of all look to you, and you give them their food in due season. You open your hand; you satisfy the desire of every living thing. (Ps. 145:14-16)

For his children, God gives what we need when we need it. He is fully sufficient. His care is obvious in our lives, and we praise him for it.

I can give personal testimony to this passage, as can most everyone who has walked with the Lord for any extended time. Our Lord who is high and lifted up, who is exalted, reached down in my life to pick me up when I had fallen. Through sin, through times where I turned my back on God's presence, through times of ignorance, God has upheld me. I well remember identifying with the line in Amy Grant's song "Arms of Love," where she prays, "Lord, help me lift my hand so you can lift me up." There were times where I couldn't even raise my hand for God to lift me up. He had to do it all, and he did, and I am thankful. I can also testify that as often and as well as I, or anyone really, lift up our hands to the Lord, he still has to reach down all the way. He does that consistently, however, and I am blessed.

The Bible repeatedly warns us of those who don't turn to God. They think themselves something greater than they are. Some of these don't look to God because they consider themselves self-sufficient. They think they provide for their own lives and that they are doing quite well. Others don't look to God because they either think he doesn't exist or he doesn't care. These people have lives falling apart, but they do not turn to the One who cares. For those who think there is no one beyond them, I want to cry out, "There is one! Look to Him who is able to lift you up and meet your needs!"

God *is* present. He has insight into what you and I need. He has the power to meet those needs, and he desires to meet those needs. As we look to him, however feebly, he will move heaven and earth to lift us up, to give us food, to satisfy our needs, and to bring us into intimacy with him.

We live in an unreliable world. We live among unreliable people. But we serve and worship a reliable God.

Thank you, God, for your reliable love. We are needy, and we cry out for your aid. Please lift our hands, draw our focus, and feed our souls. Strengthen our wavering faith. Direct our wandering hearts. Encourage our defeated spirits. Bring peace to our warring thoughts. We look to you for our needs, trusting you and praising you in Jesus, Amen!

❧ ❧ ❧

NOVEMBER 30

For your name's sake, O LORD, preserve my life! In your righteousness bring my soul out of trouble! And in your steadfast love you will cut off my enemies, and you will destroy all the adversaries of my soul, for I am your servant. (Ps. 143:11-12)

Very few people make decisions by rolling the dice. Most of us have reasons for what we do. If I am going to eat a salad for dinner, it might be because I want to be healthy. It is less likely, but possible, that I am eating a salad because of the taste. I might even be eating it simply because I am hungry and it seems the best alternative. But there is some reason for what I am doing. It isn't random.

The psalmist gave God a reason for helping the writer in the day of trouble. The psalmist asked God "preserve my life" for the sake of God's "name." We miss out if we don't realize that "name" meant more than a label. It meant your reputation—who you were and what you had done. The psalmist called on God for rescue not based on who the psalmist was and what the psalmist had done, but based on God's character, based on who God is and what God has done.

This is a holy motivation, and it is important we recognize it in our lives today. We come to God seeking his help in ways that range from physical needs like food to salvation, with all points in between. We never do so because of who we are. We can't demand that God deliver for us because we deserve it or it is our right. We do so because of God's character. We throw ourselves upon his mercy, and ask accordingly.

Unlike the psalmist, we live on the resurrection side of the cross of Christ. We know that God loved us enough to give his Son to save us (John 3:16). We know that Jesus prepared a way to God (John 14:1-3). We know that through the blood of Jesus, we can confidently come before the holy God, finding an audience with him (Heb. 10:19). We know that we do not ever approach God based on our own merit, but by the merit of Christ.

This is why our prayers are in the name of Jesus, rather than our own. We do not pray for God to hear us based on what we've done, but rather for the sake of Jesus, and based on what he's done. In Jesus' name, we ask God to preserve our lives, to bring our souls out of trouble, to cut off our enemies, to establish us as his servants. He doesn't do this randomly or because we deserve it. He does it for the sake of Jesus. Jesus told us to ask of God in his name (John 14:13), and for good reason!

Lord, in Jesus' name we come before you in need. Please teach us your ways, meet our needs, and shower us with your love for his sake. For Jesus' sake, Amen.

❀ ❀ ❀

DECEMBER 1

Answer me quickly, O LORD! My spirit fails! Hide not your face from me, lest I be like those who go down to the pit. Let me hear in the morning of your steadfast love, for in you I trust. Make me know the way I should go, for to you I lift up my soul. (Ps. 143:7-8)

The Psalms are real and raw reflections of a godly human heart crying out in a fallen world. They serve a marvelous purpose helping us voice our own cries, but we need to be careful about using them to make our theology! Today's passage is a great example. We shouldn't let it encourage impatience, but we should see it as an authentic cry of one who impatiently wants the Lord's help! That may not be where we would like to be; after all, patience is a fruit of the spirit (Gal. 5:22), but we've all been there, and it's refreshing to know that God is alright with that! He knows us, and he loves us. We can be open and honest with him. We are humans, after all, not mini-gods.

There are times when I would love to be a paradigm of patience, but instead find myself at wits' end, desperately needing God to speak into my life and touch my soul. I need to sense his presence and experience his rescue when the world closes in; my strength is inadequate; my joy is suspended; my direction is confused; my heart hurts; and my *head hurts!* These times I echo the psalmist's plea, *"Answer me quickly!"*

I love the way the psalmist *tries* to exhibit patience. The writer wants help *now*, but he is willing to give God until the next morning! *"Let me hear in the morning of your steadfast love."* The psalmist is trusting God, but wants that trust validated in the next twenty-four hours! This is so like me. I am all for the fruit of the spirit. I want to grow in patience. I agree with the saying, "patience is a virtue," but I want that virtue right now! In reality, however, like all the fruits of the spirit, patience takes time to develop. "Fruit" is that way. God cultivates it over time in the lives of his children.

So I come to this passage and am a bit bemused. I know what it is to be hurting, and I understand deadlines all too well. But putting God on a deadline strikes me as both bold and desperate. I never pledged myself to him so he would do what I want. I pledged myself for him to do what he wants. I am touched that in Holy Scripture God reinforces our honesty before him. I want to be that honest. I know I should do so in the right spirit. God is God; I am not. Interestingly, the psalmist doesn't *demand* that God answer in twenty-four hours; the psalmist asks. There is a submissive attitude reflected in this cry of urgency. I need to learn from this.

Lord, I want to be honest and open to you. I don't want to do so in some selfish manner, but I want the intimacy of being me with you, warts and all. Thank you for encouraging that, and making my way through Jesus' blood. Amen!

❧ ❧ ❧

DECEMBER 2

The enemy has pursued my soul; he has crushed my life to the ground; he has made me sit in darkness like those long dead. Therefore my spirit faints within me; my heart within me is appalled. I remember the days of old; I meditate on all that you have done; I ponder the work of your hands. I stretch out my hands to you. (Ps. 143:3-6)

Do you ever feel overwhelmed? Do you ever feel as if there are people or powers working to bring you misery? Do you ever feel a bit desperate, wondering when or if things will get better? Do you ever feel like your prayers simply bounce off the ceiling back to you, never getting near the ear of God? The psalmist did. We all do. I like the approach of the psalmist. The psalmist gives me a "1, 2, 3, 4 list" for times like that.

First, I am going to remember the days of old. I am going to sit and work through my memory, recognizing how God has gotten me to today. I remember bad times where I was disheartened before. I remember wondering why on earth God was letting me endure some of the things going on in my life. I also remember how God brought me through those times. How he used those events to mold me into the person I am today. Without those, I couldn't be writing these devotionals! I can see how he broke me where I needed to be broken so he could reassemble me into the right vessel for his purposes.

Second, I am going to meditate on all he has done. I will think through how his hand in my life was never aimless, but moved with purpose. I will consider how God worked to my gain even in those seeking my loss. I will also meditate on his Scripture. I will consider the lives of people like Joseph, whose jealous brothers sold him into slavery, where false accusations, and false imprisonment all worked to the good of Joseph and his family.

Third, I will ponder the work of God's hands. Even as I think that my prayers are bouncing back from the ceiling, I will in faith look for the hand of God. What is it God is wanting to teach me? What lessons can I be learning? What habits is he seeking to make in my life? What godly traits can I better practice?

Fourth and finally, I will stretch out my hands to God. I will seek him in the midst of my travails with confidence he will rescue. It may not be today; it may not be tomorrow. But my Deliverer is coming, and he will find me, hands out, waiting patiently in faith.

Lord, help me remember the mighty works you've done in my life and in the lives of countless others. Show me how your hands are at work in my life right now. I wait for your deliverance. In the holy name of Jesus, Amen!

❧ ❧ ❧

DECEMBER 3

Hear my prayer, O LORD; *give ear to my pleas for mercy! In your faithfulness answer me, in your righteousness! Enter not into judgment with your servant, for no one living is righteous before you.* (Ps. 143:1-2)

Sin is nasty business. It is a snare that traps us in its clutches while it bleeds us of life. It is an enticement that hides its sharp thorns of death in deceptive little moves that seem inconsequential. It can enter through ignorance as it sneaks in to wreck our lives. It is an unfaithfulness that breeds destructive doubts. Sin is a liar, making us believe it is nothing. Sin often starts as matter of the heart, expressing itself without our minds first engaging to exercise some form of holy control.

None of us avoids sin. We sin through what we do and we sin in what we don't do (sins of "commission" as well as "omission"). We don't generally wake up and say, "Gee, I want to sin a bunch today," but it lurks and catches us unaware. This power and presence of sin puts today's passage in a certain light.

I best understand the prayer in this passage in light of Jesus Christ. This prayer is a cry for help for God's "mercy." Mercy is the help I need. It is my only hope as a sinner. The psalmist was right, "no one living is righteous" before God. I am far from it. I need God's mercy because without it, he would enter into judgment with me, and that judgment would be condemnation. It is the only just judgment. Anything else would be a fraud on God's character and goodness, a fraud on the holy. Anything else would be sin itself. It would be a sinful judgment.

I need God's mercy to be—as the psalmist prays—one that comes from God's faithfulness and in his righteousness. I need a mercy that is righteous, not false. This is the mercy that flows from the cross of Christ. The cross of Christ is the answer to this prayer for me. IT is also the answer to the psalmist's prayer, even though the psalm was written centuries before Jesus' death. Paul explained that our redemption through the blood of Jesus is one that is fully righteous and in accordance with God's justice. Yet Paul says that this was not only for the Christian believer, but for the psalmist and others who lived before Jesus, trusting God for a righteous judgment of mercy; "This [the death of Jesus] was to show God's righteousness, because in his divine forbearance he had passed over former sins" (Rom. 3:25). This prayer in the Psalms answers the cries of my own sin.

So Lord, we repeat the psalmist's prayer, asking you to give us mercy, thanking you for your faithfulness and righteousness in Jesus, allowing us to pass from judgment into life. We pray wrapped in the righteousness of Jesus, Amen!

❧ ❧ ❧

DECEMBER 4

May our granaries be full, providing all kinds of produce; may our sheep bring forth thousands and ten thousands in our fields; may our cattle be heavy with young, suffering no mishap or failure in bearing; may there be no cry of distress in our streets! Blessed are the people to whom such blessings fall! (Ps. 144:13-15)

Is it wrong to pray for bounty? Is it wrong to work for abundance? Is money evil? Is there special piety in being broke or just getting by? I think the answer to this is like the one we find in many things; it depends.

The Bible teaches a strong truth of stewardship. God owns everything. What we have are things he has entrusted to us. He doesn't give us money so we have fat bank accounts. He doesn't give us a lot of food so we have fat bellies! He gives to us as stewards so we can give to others. Paul said that we are his hands, his feet, his mouth, etc. (1 Cor. 12:27). God is going to give to others through us. God is going to nurture others through us. God doesn't give us material things so we can be collectors. He gives so we can be distributors.

One of the challenges in life is to figure out the balance between responsibly and generously giving in the name of God. We should responsibly put resources to work to generate more resources and to tend to family and other kingdom work. Scripture gives good guidance for people on this.

Tithing is a clear scriptural instruction. Starting with Abraham's giving to Melchizedek, we have an example and later an instruction to give God the first ten percent of what we have (Gen. 14:20; Deut. 14:22-24). The Hebrew word "tithe" is rooted in the word "ten." A proper tithe is ten percent. Scripture teaches that the first ten percent of what we receive is rightly considered the Lord's. On top of that, Scripture teaches us to take care of people in our path in need. In the parable of the Good Samaritan, Jesus taught those listening the importance of giving to help those we come across who need help. That may mean giving them money. It may mean time or talents, because teaching someone to fish is better than just giving them a fish. It may mean all of the above.

In the passage above, we see this attitude reflected in the psalm. The psalmist prays for God to fill the granaries, bringing in crops and livestock in abundance. But not simply for self-fulfillment. The psalmist prays for the blessings of all, seeking the good of all, *"Blessed are the people to whom such blessings fall!"*

Lord, please bless us with the proper measure of things that we can responsibly handle, giving where you want given, helping where you want help. May we see the needs of your heart and meet them in Jesus' name. Amen.

❧ ❧ ❧

DECEMBER 5

May our sons in their youth be like plants full grown, our daughters like corner pillars cut for the structure of a palace. (Ps. 144:12)

All parents have great wishes for their children. We see in children a world of possibilities. We want our children happy, contributing to the world, and developing skills and talents. We want them to be at peace, to be moral and ethical, to be law-abiding, to fit in socially, and to have aspirations and dreams. We wish them success. We fret over our children, seek to protect them from harm, try to inspire them to achieve, try to teach them right from wrong, and pour our hearts and energy into them. We love going to their activities, sports, concerts, talent shows, and more. More than one parent has found truth in 3 John, verse 4, "I have no greater joy than to hear that my children are walking in the truth."

There are lots of parenting "How To" books. There are plenty of opinions on parenting found on the Internet. Family and friends are quick to pass on their parenting expertise. For many, those books and that advice don't seem to diminish the nervousness and fear most parents feel as they bring a child into the world. Parenting is difficult, and no one is perfect. As parents, we don't have all the answers. We make lots of mistakes, and we hope and pray that the resilience of children will minimize the effects of our errors.

The concerns of parenting are not new. The psalmist prays to God for God's hand in the growth of children. *"May our sons in their youth be like plants full grown."* This picture might mean more to a gardener, but we don't have to work hard to figure out the prayer. A plant full grown is one that has developed strong roots, is well nourished, is fulfilling its potential, and bears fruit. It is a good metaphor for what I want for my son. Similarly, may *"our daughters like corner pillars cut for the structure of a palace"* is not an ordinary metaphor among most in the twenty-first century, but it makes sense nonetheless. Corner pillars are sound and solid. They give stability to the palace, a home of great importance and luxury. They are not simply adornments, but are keys to the success of the building. This echoes in different terms my prayers for my daughters. I pray their lives will be solid and well built, that they will stand fully competent to do the things God has planned for them in their lives.

We should pray for our children every day. They should be confident of our prayers. After all, ultimately our children belong to God. He entrusted them to us!

Lord, please bless our children. Bring each into the light of your truth. Help us to teach them your ways, even as we entrust them to you. In Jesus' name, Amen!

❧ ❧ ❧

DECEMBER 6

Bow your heavens, O Lord, and come down! Touch the mountains so that they smoke! Flash forth the lightning and scatter them; send out your arrows and rout them! Stretch out your hand from on high; rescue me and deliver me from the many waters, from the hand of foreigners, whose mouths speak lies and whose right hand is a right hand of falsehood. (Ps. 144:5-8)

God has revealed himself to us in different relationship terms. In the Bible, we have different expressions of God that give us different ways to relate to him. We see God as a friend in Jesus, a friend that would give his life for us (John 15:13-15). We see God as a Father who has a loving care and comfort for his children (2 Thess. 2:16). We see God as a shepherd, one who gives his own life to look out for and tends to those under his care, making sure they have what they need and are able to grow under his watchful eye (John 10:11-12). We also see God as Creator God, able to fashion the galaxies and all within them, holding the universe in his hand. Here is one who is to be feared, great and mighty.

I am thankful for God as my Father, and there are days I need him as friend. But there are days when I need the Lord God Almighty. These are the days like those prompting the psalmist to cry out, "Bow *your* heavens, O Lord, and COME DOWN! Touch the mountains so they smoke!" This is a cry not for the Father, the friend, the shepherd. This is a call for the awesome one to be feared. This is a cry for the powerful one that rightfully frightens all in his path.

What was it in the psalmist's life that called for the God of power? We don't have details, but we see that it involved the way the writer was treated by others. There were those who didn't know God ("foreigners"), who lied, deceived, and brought evil. Those people are long dead, but their type still remain! There are times when I need God to come make things right with others. There are people outside the control of anything or anyone less than the Almighty One.

There are other times when I need God in his awesomeness. These are times when the world seems fully inadequate. They are times when I am scared, uncertain, and worried. These are times when I need the miracle-working God. I need capital "G" God, and nothing less. This passage serves as my inspiration. I can and will call forth God in his greatness, not because he answers me like a genie in a bottle, but because my God hears my voice and has revealed himself as Almighty God. Sometimes nothing else will do.

Almighty God, we hold you in awe, as we pray for you to work among us. Be our Almighty God, please Lord. In Jesus' almighty name, Amen!

❧ ❧ ❧

DECEMBER 7

O LORD, what is man that you regard him, or the son of man that you think of him? Man is like a breath; his days are like a passing shadow. (Ps. 144:3-4)

We live in the era of affirmation. Social scientists have convinced us that we should encourage our children, so they grow up "winning" trophies and medals in sports simply because they compete. Our youngest children play games where the score is not kept so they don't feel like losers, but find the joy and fulfillment of playing.

We live in an era where we are taught to respect others. Everyone is valued and important, regardless of race, nationality, creed, age, ability, intelligence, social status, or education. We may not actually achieve this, but we know it is a noble goal. We want to do it.

If we don't spend real time before God, contemplating him in his majesty, then we run a real risk in our society. We risk thinking of ourselves as more than we should. Passages like today's can almost seem foreign to us. Wondering "what is a human that God regard or think of her or him," doesn't really strike us as it should. Our ingrained thought might be, "Well of course God should think well of us!" In fact, some find the idea that God might not value us the way we think we should be valued as repugnant. How often do we hear, "If God was a good God, then he wouldn't let *xyz* happen"? Or maybe we hear, "What kind of God would do that to him or her?"

People have an incredible value. God confirms that. God made people in his image, and that alone gives them inherent worth that sets them above any other creature. God becoming Christ and dying to redeem humanity is rock solid proof of the value God places on our lives. But there still is a huge chasm between the worth of anyone and the worth of God. God is high and lifted up, far beyond us. We are something he made—valuable—but still we are his creation. My sister sculptures art and pottery with clay. She has made some very special and valuable pieces. But I would never trade my sister for anything she made. She far exceeds the value of anything she made.

The psalmist in today's passage grasped the great distance between God and people. That gulf brings forth the question, "Lord, why do you even care for us? We aren't around very long, and yet you invest in us, know us by name, count the hairs on our head, and have a deep, caring love for us. Why?" The answer? It is God's nature. We have a loving and caring God who yearns for his creation in relationship. That is amazing.

Lord, let us be in awe of you and not lose sight of the wonder of your love in Jesus. Amen!

❧ ❧ ❧

DECEMBER 8

*Blessed be the L*ORD*, my rock, who trains my hands for war, and my fingers for battle; he is my steadfast love and my fortress, my stronghold and my deliverer, my shield and he in whom I take refuge, who subdues peoples under me.* (Ps. 144:1-2)

When I was a young man, I found insight from an Amy Grant song full of the angst and worries from a youth wanting to do right, but struggling, wanting to find my place in God's plan, but wondering. The song was entitled "All I Ever Have to Be."

It was a short song, one verse and a chorus. "When the weight of all my dreams is resting heavy on my head; and the thoughtful words of help and hope have all been nicely said, but I'm still hurting wondering if I'll ever be the one I think I am. Then you gently re-remind me, that you've made me from the first. And the more I try to be the best, the more I get the worst. And I realize the good in me is only there because of who you are. And all I ever have to be is what you've made me. Any more or less would be a step out of your plan. As you daily recreate me, help me always keep in mind that I only have to do is what I can find. And all I ever have to be—all I have to be—All I ever have to be is what you've made in me."

Almost forty years later, I am still amazed at the simple wisdom in that song. It fits well in today's passage from Psalm 144. We rightly bless and praise God as the one who has trained our hands for war, our fingers for battle. He has made us in Christ and prepared us for certain good works. He planned those works long ago (Eph. 2:8-10). As we struggle to understand God's plan for us, and as we get frustrated knowing the mess we can make of things, there is a simple solace we can take. God is at work in us.

God has plans for us, and he will work to see that we are able to do those plans. We might not think ourselves up to the task. Moses certainly didn't. When Moses told the Lord that he was ill equipped to lead the Israelites from Egypt, God asked him, "What is that in your hand?" (An aside, in the Old Testament, God frequently asked questions he knew the answer to so that he could make his point.) Moses answered, "A staff." God instructed Moses to throw the staff onto the ground. As it hit the ground, the stick became a snake. God told Moses to pick the snake up, and as he did so, the snake became a staff again. God was letting Moses know that in God's hands, the staff alone was enough. The stick had what it takes! If Moses didn't understand it was God who was working, then Moses didn't understand. So Moses took the staff to Egypt, and used the staff to bring plagues, part the Red Sea, bring water from a rock, and fulfill God's plans.

Lord, please work in us, through us, and even in spite of us! In Jesus, Amen!

DECEMBER 9

My mouth will speak the praise of the LORD, and let all flesh bless his holy name forever and ever. (Ps. 145:21)

I love to praise the Lord. Over and over in Scripture we learn that it is important that we praise God, and in our lives we can understand why we should do so. It isn't that we have an egotistical God who gets upset if we don't make it all about him. We can see in Jesus that God is anything but egotistical. Praise and worship are important because they place God on the throne where he belongs. As we do that, we place ourselves where we belong as well. We are God's people. We aren't God.

Importantly, while we don't worship God because his feelings get hurt if we don't make it all about him, it is, in fact, all about him! When we worship, we are living in reality. God is worthy of our worship. We are ascribing to God his rightful existence as the one with ultimate worth and value. One we respect. God is a God of love and giving. One whom we adore. He is a God of holiness and righteousness. One from whom we can learn. God has unlimited power. He is Creator and Sustainer of all things. One we hold in awe.

This passage has an important implication for our praise. As we praise God with our mouth, we lead "all flesh" to bless his holy name. In other words, with our worship, we draw others into worship. As people hear us, as people watch us, they will be drawn to the truth of what we are about. As we value God in our words and deeds, others will be drawn to value him. As we alter our lives to reflect God, others will be drawn to him. How we honor and praise God can be infectious. God can work through us to bring others into his presence and the truth that is God enthroned on high.

So I meditate on this passage and I ask myself, how can I best praise God? It is a fairly easy thing to do in church. We have magnificently blessed leaders who take us before the throne in worship and praise. In more high-church worship, we have traditions and carefully planned moments of worship and praise. In more contemporary services, we have the freshness of worship that comes from spontaneity and modernity. But beyond church, how can I best praise the Lord in ways that draw others to his throne?

When I show my trust in God in circumstances that cause most to panic, to worry, or to become angry, I praise him by actions that others see. As a worshipper of God, I know he is on the throne ruling creation. I know that my circumstances are not greater than my God, and they don't rob me of his care. In tough times, my life can praise him in ways that readily lead others to his praise.

Lord, help me praise you before a watching world, to your glory! In Jesus' name, Amen!

❧ ❧ ❧

DECEMBER 10

The Lord is near to all who call on him, to all who call on him in truth. He fulfills the desire of those who fear him; he also hears their cry and saves them. The Lord preserves all who love him, but all the wicked he will destroy. (Ps. 145:18-20)

I love the fact that we worship a God who doesn't lie. It allows me to take his promises and stake my life on them. Here is a promise I am going to take. God is near to *all who call on him in truth.* I am going to take that I am going to call on God in truth.

There is alliteration in the Hebrew of this passage that adds to the meaning. "Call," used twice, sounds like *kara* and "near" sounds like *karov.* The words themselves confirm the truth of the passage. Our crying out to God is akin to his nearness. The two sound alike because the two occur together. As we cry, he is near, closer than we know.

My cry needs to be "in truth." This is not the false temporary cry of one in trouble. It is not the "deal" of "God, get me out of this and I promise to be different!" only to be rescued and find oneself unchanged. A true cry is one that is genuine, today and tomorrow. It is one that is a wholesale abdication of one's own control over life and full offering of control to God. It is one that truly seeks God.

Of course, if we are truly seeking God, and truly giving control of our lives over to him, then we will not be surprised to see him changing our desires. Our wants in life become his wants. We see our priorities sculpted along the lines of his priorities. God's will becomes our prayer. It is not surprising then to see the first sentence in this passage married up to the second sentence. The Lord is near to those who call on him in truth, and he fulfills the desire of those who fear him. Our desires, purified by the one we have given control of our lives, are his desires. He desires the best for us.

Giving God control is an awesome thing. He is able to work his will in our lives both for our good and for the good of his kingdom. This is our preservation and his kingdom's advancement. He is preserving that within us that is righteous, as he is destroying that which is wicked in evil. God doesn't draw near to us and leave us as we were. He works on us and transforms us into the image of his Son (2 Cor. 3:18). This is the promise of a God who doesn't lie. It is a bit scary, but I am going to take him at his word, and call on him to draw near.

Lord, I call on you to draw near to me, please. I truly want your presence in my life. Save me, purify me, transform me, and use me for your good purposes. In Jesus' name, Amen!

❀ ❀ ❀

DECEMBER 11

The LORD is righteous in all his ways and kind in all his works. (Ps. 145:17)

If you think about it, as translated, this passage sets out two concepts that almost seem like opposites. God is righteous, and God is kind.

Righteousness speaks of justice, of consistency, of always doing the right thing, and of supporting the right thing. Righteousness does not countenance evil, wickedness, or unrighteousness. There is a purity associated with righteousness that purges impurity and keeps it at bay.

God is indeed a righteous God, righteous in all his ways. There is no wavering in his righteousness. He is not righteous one day, but unrighteous the next. He is not partially righteous one day. He does not step out of righteousness as it suits him (or us). There is a fearsomeness involved here. We cannot only hold a righteous God in awe, but it should genuinely stir up in us some measure of fear. For we are not righteous. If we think we are, then we are guilty of pride, and we are unrighteous even in that! So as unrighteous beings who exist before a righteous God, we have serious problems!

Yet here the opposite enters. God is also fully kind. Kindness speaks of mercy, forgiveness, of looking favorably on those who do not deserve it, and of helping those in need, regardless of merit. Kindness is not dispensed as it is earned, for then it is not kindness. It is justice.

God is a kind and merciful God, caring for the unrighteous. He ministers to those who don't deserve it. He rescues us from bondage to sin (Rom. 8:1-2). He seeks to forgive the wicked. The story of God is one of pursuing the sinner and being kind to the undeserving. Justice destroys sin; kindness forgives sinners. As contrary as these two concepts may seem, the unlikely pair coexist in our God. We see that in Jesus.

Jesus exhibited the nexus of God's righteousness and kindness. By becoming human, God was able to take on the righteous penalties of sin. God didn't need to set aside universal justice, but was fully righteous in dealing with sin. He paid sin's death penalty when humanity's sin was taken on by the human Jesus. By dying in our stead, Jesus rightly opened the door to God's kindness and forgiveness. We are not forgiven simply because God is kind. We are forgiven justly because he is righteous and kind. What an awesome God we serve!

Lord, thank you for the righteous forgiveness in Jesus. We need that and trust in that for our righteousness. You are kind to us beyond measure. In Jesus we pray, Amen!

❧ ❧ ❧

DECEMBER 12

Ascribe to the LORD, O heavenly beings, ascribe to the LORD glory and strength. Ascribe to the LORD the glory due his name; worship the LORD in the splendor of holiness. (Ps. 29:1-2)

Worship is a volitional activity. The meaning of the word "worship" helps us see this. The word comes from two old Anglo-Saxon words from which we get "worth" and "ascribe." To "worship" is to "ascribe worth" to someone or something. It is volitional in the sense that we choose to do it. The Hebrew word translated "ascribe" in this psalm means to "give," again a volitional word.

We choose to give God praise and honor, or we can choose not to. Some people are natural talkers who easily encourage, praise, uplift, and honor people with their words. My wife is this way. She can always find something good and is quick to encourage someone. Some people are not natural "praisers," however. For them it's a harder thing to do.

The psalmist doesn't limit this instruction to those who find it easy; it is also for those who find it hard. It is a common instruction for all of us. We are to join the angels themselves and call out *to God* a recounting of his glory and strength. We are to call out the glory "due his name," meaning the glory that is rightfully his because of the things he has done, the things that demonstrate his character. This instruction means I am to recount the amazing works of God, both in history and the world at large, and in my home, family, and life. I give God glory for the good things in life. For my family, for my friends, for my job, for my health, for my opportunities, for my mind and heart, for so many blessings, I give glory to God. I do not glory in my own accomplishments. Any good I have done is from the Lord, so he gets the glory.

I am also to "worship" the Lord in the "splendor of holiness." Hebrew has several words for worship, and this one means to bow down, or press one's face to the ground. It is again a volitional word, but now it includes not only ascribing God glory for what he's done, but also holding him in awe because he is like no other. As a holy God, he shines with a brilliance unlike any other. He holds perfection without sin, and he rules over anyone and everything. God is truly spectacular and unique, so much so that our appropriate and reverent response is to fall before him. This vision of God rightly comes with a vision of our shortcomings. As we place God where he belongs, we take our rightful place below him.

Lord, we ascribe you glory for your salvation, your interest in us, your touch in our lives. We bow before your holiness praying that you would wash us clean in Jesus, Amen!

❧ ❧ ❧

DECEMBER 13

Your kingdom is an everlasting kingdom, and your dominion endures throughout all generations. The LORD is faithful in all his words and kind in all his works. (Ps. 145:13)

Have you ever met anyone who bores quickly? Sometimes we are unable to stay on task and get easily distracted.

Some people are incredibly focused, but even these people find their interests and areas of focus change in life. I have been through a number of hobbies that have come and gone over the decades. For a long while, I enjoyed studying and playing chess. I spent a good decade developing and sustaining an organic garden. I played more than my fair share of guitars over the years. My baking hobby was good for at least fifteen pounds over a number of years. I still dabble in those areas; they are still interests, but I am not into them as I was in the height of my focus.

God's interests do not change. God doesn't have an interest in us this year, but get bored, or turn his interests another direction next year. We need not fear that God's desires for us fade with time. There are no golden years where God is particularly interested, followed by years of waning interest. God is one hundred percent reliable day in and day out, season after season, year after year. What's more, not only is God fully focused, God's energy and God-ness never changes. God's reign is not one that is threatened. We needn't ever worry that he might lose his strength or power. God is stronger than anything we might ever face, today and every day.

In today's passage, the psalmist reminds the reader that God's kingdom will never cease. God's ruling dominion will never cease. I can rely on it. I can teach my children and grandchildren to rely on it. I can build a future on it. What's more, God's fully reliable through the ages to complete his words and works. If God said it, we can bank on it. No one and nothing will come between God and his promises.

So in the spirit of this psalm, I contemplate the words of God. I do it with an eye toward building my life around those words and encouraging and teaching others to do the same. I do so without fear that something might change. God will not get distracted or lose his focus. He will be genuinely engaged to see matters to completion as he said.

This informs my personal choices. I make my decisions about living confident in God's decisions. As Paul told the Philippians, I can "work out" my own life as one saved, knowing God is "at work" in me, both to will and to work for the good things he has promised (Phil. 2:12-13).

Lord, help me build my life around you and your will, in Jesus' name, Amen!

❧ ❧ ❧

DECEMBER 14

All your works shall give thanks to you, O Lord, and all your saints shall bless you! They shall speak of the glory of your kingdom and tell of your power, to make known to the children of man your mighty deeds, and the glorious splendor of your kingdom. (Ps. 145:10-12)

I was trying to hail a taxi on the streets of Oxford when it started raining. (That happens a lot there!) A woman was pulling her child along on the street and I heard her mutter, "My Jesus." I don't think she was really speaking to Jesus. Part of me wanted to interrupt her bustling walk and say, "Hello, sister! He's my Jesus, too!" But thinking it better not to, I just kept silent.

We have a responsibility, and also the honor, to tell people about the mighty deeds of the Lord. We are to make known his glory, power, and the splendor of his kingdom. We are part of the "works" of God charged to bless his name.

For some reason, that is often difficult. We don't want to be seen as overbearing, and it can be uncomfortable to broach the subject of God with another person. Perhaps we don't want to spend the time. Or maybe we don't like the uncertainty of an unknown response. Maybe we fear being rejected. Perhaps our concern is being viewed as a nut.

From an intellectual standpoint, that concern makes no sense, but we do not always operate out of our intellect. Our minds tell us that God is great. We who know him, know how he has worked wonders in our lives and in the lives of others. We understand that he is worthy of our praise. He can set free those held captive to fear, addiction, worry, or any sin that binds so readily to the sinner. Yet we hesitate to speak of him, even to those in desperate need.

I need to make a resolution. I want to be different. I want to speak of our God to a world that needs him. I want God to rely on my voice as one that will tell people about Jesus Christ, crucified on their behalf.

So maybe tomorrow I will see a woman pulling her child along, taking the name of God lightly. Should God give me the opportunity, may he also give me the words to politely, without inciting anger, nudge her to recognize the Lord Jesus for who he is. Maybe next time I can smile and gently say, "He's my Jesus too, and I would love to tell you about him."

Lord, use me to spread your fame far and wide. May the world hear through me your goodness and mercy. Let my life and my words give glory to you. Let me help bring forth your kingdom. In Jesus' name, Amen!

❊ ❊ ❊

DECEMBER 15

The LORD is gracious and merciful, slow to anger and abounding in steadfast love. The LORD is good to all, and his mercy is over all that he has made. (Ps. 145:8-9)

We use human terms to understand and speak of our God. It is all we have; after all, we are human. So when we read in the Bible that God is "slow to anger," we have to be on our guard theologically. We must not let our human language turn God into a super-human, having human traits, but just in a supersized form.

This is important because the same Scriptures that note God as slow to anger do say that he gets angry! God is not an emotionally unstable God; we don't fear what side of the bed he got up from this morning. In Exodus 4:14 the anger of the Lord is "kindled against Moses" because Moses would not obey God and go to Egypt to rescue the Israelites.

Then in Exodus 32, while Moses is on Mt. Sinai receiving the Ten Commandments, God tells Moses to head back down the mountain. God's wrath (anger) "burns hot" against the Israelites because they had turned from him to a produced-on-the-spot golden calf. Moses intervenes in the narrative begging the Lord to relent, and God does. Moses then descends with the tablets, and sees what the people have done. Moses gets furious and destroys the tablets in the process. After dealing with the disobedient who were corrupting the others, Moses returns to God on the mountain and God remakes the tablets.

As God remakes the tablets, God speaks to Moses in a way that clarifies much. God's words inspired this psalm passage: "The LORD, the LORD, a God merciful and gracious, slow to anger, and abounding in steadfast love and faithfulness, keeping steadfast love for thousands, forgiving iniquity and transgression and sin, but who will by no means clear the guilty, visiting the iniquity of the fathers on the children and the children's children, to the third and the fourth generation" (Exod. 34:6-7). God's "anger" arises when the sins are those that breed. God's goodness will never tolerate the destructiveness of sin, and while all sin is destructive, some sin breeds. These are the sins that fathers pass on for generations. God will seek that sin out and work to destroy it, before it destroys the people. This we humans can call the "anger" of God.

God is slow to anger, gracious, and abounding in mercy. He desires to forgive and works to free us from our sin. But if we walk in a rebellion that threatens us and others, God will not let that threaten his plans. His "anger" will be kindled and he will do as he must.

Lord, in your graciousness and kindness have mercy on us. Keep us from sin, and when we rebel against you and choose sin anyway, please forgive us, even as you protect your plan in Jesus, through whom we pray, Amen!

✸ ✸ ✸

DECEMBER 16

I will extol you, my God and King, and bless your name forever and ever. Every day I will bless you and praise your name forever and ever. Great is the LORD, and greatly to be praised, and his greatness is unsearchable. (Ps. 145:1-3)

Our world and lives are divided into cycles. The world has days, seasons, and years. Lives also have days, seasons, and generations. The psalmist recognizes the need to praise God each day. Whether we look at the day as a Hebrew, starting as the sun goes down and extending until sunset the next day, or as westerners, beginning at midnight and running its twenty-four-hour course, not a day should pass without our praise to God.

We praise God when we affirm his marvelous care, the great wonders he has performed in our lives. Even in our most difficult days, we have reasons to be personally grateful to God. There are specific ways we can offer our personal praise for his works in our lives.

We also praise God when we call on him for help! We are praising God when we assign to him to place he deserves in our lives. God is a rescuing God who comes to our aid when we are distressed. When we call on him and trust him for rescue, we are praising him. We are attributing to him the right place in our lives. We are seeing him as our rescue, rather than putting our trust in any other.

We praise God when we tell others of his deeds. When we tell the unloved about the love of Christ, we praise God. Christ loved us enough to leave the heavens, emptying himself and taking on the form of a human. Christ humbled himself. He stooped so low, not only becoming a human, but subjugating himself to other humans. Christ then allowed ungodly and evil people who were impotent in the face of Almighty God to exercise control over his life, killing him in a most humiliating and painful way. Christ did this out of a love for us and a recognition that divine justice required such a sacrifice of divine mercy. This message is one of love, and when we tell it to the unloved, we are praising God.

We praise God when we acknowledge his presence. We live in times when people say, "My God," with no intentional meaning at all. It has become an expression. But he is my God. I am his. He is very personal to me. The God who is so great the universe sits comfortably in his hand is my Lord. He knows my name. He cares for me. He communes with me. He indwells me. He is my God, and I praise him.

I will praise you Lord, today and every day. In many ways I will lift you up in this sometimes watching, sometimes ignoring world. You are my loving and caring God and I praise you in Jesus' name, Amen!

❧ ❧ ❧

DECEMBER 17

I give thanks to you, O Lord my God, with my whole heart, and I will glorify your name forever. For great is your steadfast love toward me. (Ps. 86:12-13)

Some days I need to stop everything I am doing, turn off the music, find a place of quiet solitude, and for a time, think through the many blessings of God. I need to thank him for them one at a time, and glorify him for his great provision.

When I was young in church we would sing the song, "Count Your Blessings." I probably have not sung that in church in over thirty years, but I well remember the lyrics. The first verse: "When upon life's billows you are tempest-tossed; When you are discouraged thinking all is lost; Count your many blessings name them one by one; and it will surprise you what the Lord has done." I can personally affirm the truth of this verse. When the waves and storms of life leave me bewildered, hurting, and scared, taking the time to list off God's blessings one by one, often out loud in prayer, changes the landscape. The stormy seas seem much less threatening as I see that the wonderful God has seen to so many things in my life.

The second verse: "Are you ever burdened with a load of care? Does the cross seem heavy you are called to bear? Count your many blessings, every doubt will fly, and you will keep singing as the days go by." Again, I can testify that this verse is true as well. When I have been weighed down by responsibility, commitments, and obligations that I do not think I can meet, I have found counting aloud the blessings of God changes my load. As I count the ways God has blessed me in the past, I realize that God has put me in seats of responsibility; he has placed me with commitments and obligations, and the giving God will be there to help me meet them. I know that he will set aside my heavy yoke for the gentle yoke of the Lord.

The third verse: "When you look at others with their lands and gold; Think that Christ has promised you His wealth untold; Count your many blessings money cannot buy; Your reward in heaven, nor your home on high." This verse makes sense, doesn't it? We are not in the business of comparing blessings! We are in the business of thanking God for ours!

The final verse: "So, amid the conflict whether great or small; Do not be discouraged, God is over all; Count your many blessings, angels will attend; Help and comfort give you to your journey's end." This summarizes just a few of the benefits of thanking the Lord for the many gifts of his steadfast love.

I thank you Father for your many blessings. Thank you for [name some!]. More than all, thank you for Jesus in whom I pray, Amen!!

❧ ❧ ❧

DECEMBER 18

Put not your trust in princes, in a son of man, in whom there is no salvation. When this breath departs, he returns to the earth; on that very day his plans perish. Blessed is he whose help is the God of Jacob, whose hope is in the LORD *his God.* (Ps. 146:3-5)

My friend Louis has spent the better part of three decades counseling people. His training and calling in life involves sitting down with people and coaching them through life, up and down. He performs a lot of weddings, with the premarital counseling that is part of the preparation. He performs a lot of funerals, examining and speaking of lives that have concluded. Louis has a saying: "People are people."

Here is what he means: there is no reason to be surprised by what people do. The very nature of being a person includes imperfection, error, and doing what might seem surprising. But Louis is never surprised! After all, people are people.

Like Louis, the psalmist knew human nature. Knowing humanity brought forth the passage above. Princes are strong; they are likely heirs to a kingdom; they have resources, *but* we should not put our trust in them. They will let us down. They are human, after all, and people are people!

So what do we do? We are creatures of trust. Sometimes we trust ourselves. Sometimes we trust others. But human beings are forward-looking creatures, and this means we trust. I don't know what will happen tomorrow. I don't know how things will go at work or at home. I learned early in life that school may or may not unfold as expected. There is much that is needed today and tomorrow—food, clothing, shelter, companionship, just to name a few. Where is it going to come from? How confident can I be that it will come?

The psalmist (and Louis) knew people. They also know God. Where humans fail, God doesn't. God is able to work through people, but even if people drop the ball, God picks it up. All of the things coming up that I don't know about, God knows. Combined with God's knowledge is his caring. God is trustworthy. He has the knowledge, the resources, the love, and the availability to see to all of my cares and needs.

So we don't need to trust in ourselves for the worries of tomorrow. We don't need to trust others either. After all, people are people. They will not be there consistently. But God will. We can trust him. God is no person! He is Lord God Almighty, our Heavenly Father!

Lord, we place all of our cares, worries, concerns, hopes, fears, and needs before you. In hope and trust, we will be satisfied with your will, confident in your steadfast love. In Jesus' name, Amen!

❧ ❧ ❧

DECEMBER 19

Praise the LORD*! Praise the* LORD*, O my soul! I will praise the* LORD *as long as I live; I will sing praises to my God while I have my being.* (Ps. 146:1-2)

How much Hebrew do you know? Perhaps more than you think! If you were reading the first six words of this psalm in Hebrew, you would do quite well. You might struggle with the letters (הללו יה), but if I put those Hebrew letters along with their vowel sounds into their English letter equivalent, you would do quite well: Hallelujah! The Hebrew command to praise the LORD has been brought straight into English as Hallelujah!

The "jah" in "hallelujah" is the Hebrew abbreviation for "YHVH" or "YAHWEH" if we add the vowel sounds. (The Hebrew "y" can become an English "y" or "j.") That is the name God gave Moses at the burning bush, when he asked God what his name was (Exod. 3:14).

That leaves the "hallelu" part of the Hebrew. Of course knowing what we now know, we can see that the "hallelu" is translated "Praise!" It is in the "imperative form" because it is a command or instruction. The psalmist is ordering his soul to "praise" God. If we were to read through our Hebrew Bibles and look for various translations of the word *hallelu* in its various forms (i.e., not just the imperative), we would get a fuller sense of the semantic range. It includes to "compliment" another or even to "brag." The princes of pharaoh "praised" or bragged on Sarai's beauty to pharaoh, drawing his attention (Gen. 12:15). Absalom was complimented for his appearance more than any other in Israel during his day (2 Sam. 14:25). King Ahab answered a warring king's demand by saying the one who "brags" or "praises" himself shouldn't be the warrior who is putting on his armor, but the warrior who is still alive after the battle to take off his armor (1 Kgs. 20:11)

Here then is how our Hebrew lesson informs our reading of this passage. The psalmist is giving a self-instruction to "praise" or "compliment" the Lord. I am going to give myself that same instruction! I am going to compliment the Lord! I am going to speak of his power and glory. I am going to speak of how he uses that power and glory, how he has blessed my life, how he has loved me when I was being unlovable, how he has protected me, even from myself, how he has gently held me when I was hurting, how he has given me wisdom for living, how he has blessed me with an incredible family and friends, how he has answered my prayers, how he has forgiven me my sins, and how he has secured for me my eternity with him. Praise the Lord! Hallelujah!

Lord, in Jesus' name, I praise you. You are an awesome God, loving, and forgiving, a teaching God giving me wisdom for life. You are attentive, always listening to me in my prayers. You are worthy of my praise, and I give it with joy! Amen!

❧ ❧ ❧

DECEMBER 20

He declares his word to Jacob, his statutes and rules to Israel. He has not dealt thus with any other nation; they do not know his rules. Praise the LORD! (Ps. 147:19-20)

It's hard for us to place ourselves in the culture producing these psalms over 2,500 years ago. We live in a small world, interconnected by social media and the Internet, with cell-phone service and texting readily available worldwide. We have to make a mental effort.

Writing was not as simple as finding the nearest pen and a sheet of paper. No one was able to use a copy machine to duplicate materials. The postal service was not delivering letters as it does today. Many people could not read and write. National boundaries could be a bit fluid, with international cooperation not always present. Understanding that ancient state of affairs helps us understand the blessing referenced in this passage.

Unique to Abraham's offspring was the revelation of God through prophets. It gave the Israelites the blessing and responsibility of securing God's commands, keeping those commands, teaching them to new generations, transmitting them faithfully, and through these methods, share with a watching world as a light set on a hill.

We read an example of how important this responsibility was in Paul's letter to the Roman church. As Paul explained, Gentiles and Jews all fall short of God's perfection and all need the salvation of Christ. Paul knew that as his audience read this, there might be a question arising: "If Jews and Gentiles were/are in the same boat, then what was the historical advantage of being a Jew?" Paul said the Jews had many advantages, but then he lists only one. The one Paul listed mirrored this passage, "Then what advantage has the Jew. . . . Much in every way. To begin with, the Jews were entrusted with the oracles of God" (Rom. 3:1-2).

Many of the Jews knew their Bibles incredibly well. When the wise men came to Jerusalem to inquire of the priests where the Messiah was to be born, the priests didn't need to consult their computers. They were told. So was King Herod when he asked. Knowing Micah 5:2, the priests declared the Messiah would come from Bethlehem of Judea (Matt. 2:5-6). The stunning part is the wise men went to see Jesus. Herod sent men to have Jesus killed, and the priests *who knew where Jesus was to be born did nothing*! This is the key for me. I want to know Scripture. It is a blessing God has given us. But hand-in-hand with that, I want to know God and his will. That will let me put Scripture to work!

Lord, thank you for your word. Thank you for the ready availability of Scripture. Help me to see it for the blessing it is, and Lord, may it not be only on my shelf or even just in my mind. Help it inform my actions please Lord. In Jesus' name, Amen!

❧ ❧ ❧

DECEMBER 21

Praise the L<small>ORD</small>, *O Jerusalem! Praise your God, O Zion! For he strengthens the bars of your gates; he blesses your children within you.* (Ps. 147:12-13)

This call to worship is very personal. We have lots of reasons to praise God. We should praise him as Creator, as Designer, as Sculptor and as Transcendent Almighty God. But this passage calls us to personal praise. We should also praise God for personal reasons, for what he has done and is doing in my life.

The psalmist spoke of God strengthening the bars of "your gates." These were the gates of the city that were closed at night when threats might come. Closing the gates were key to defending the city from enemies. The weakest part of the gates are the bars. If someone was trying to force entry into closed gates, they were generally not successful as long as the bars to the gates held. The psalmist was not short on physics. This wasn't a suggestion that there was a magical infusion of strength to the gate bars. This is Hebrew poetry. God takes our weaknesses and makes them strong. God finds those areas that are danger zones, areas where the enemy might set in upon us, and he makes those areas strong.

One of my daughters was very upset one day when she called me from her work. She was assigned work that was below her talent level, and not fully within her job scope. She was upset that people were not adequately grateful for her work that she felt was a bit demeaning. In the conversation, I apologized and explained it was likely my fault. "What? Why?" she asked. I explained that I had been praying for God to teach her humility, to teach her service, and to teach her patience. I told her she *knew* those were virtues, but that doesn't mean she (and all of us) didn't need to grow in them. She laughed, but got the point. God takes our weaknesses and makes them strong. If we are only as strong as our weakest link, as my son repeatedly explained to me while he was doing his military workouts, then God's strategy becomes clear. He is strengthening us.

The personal nature of this passage's call to praise continues with the next phrasing. God blesses our children within us. This is a blessing that flows from his strengthening our gates. The stronger I am, the better I am, the stronger and better father I am, and the stronger and better my children become. God works in my children by working through me. Paul noted how God's power was made perfect in Paul's weakness (2 Cor. 12:9). This is the power and working of God. It should bring forth in us PRAISE to the Lord!

Lord, we praise you for working in our lives and in the lives of those around us. Please take our weaknesses and show your strength. Grow us into godlier servants, better able to share your love. In Jesus' name, Amen!

❧ ❧ ❧

DECEMBER 22

His delight is not in the strength of the horse, nor his pleasure in the legs of a man, but the LORD takes pleasure in those who fear him, in those who hope in his steadfast love. (Ps. 147:10-11)

Did you ever try to buy a gift for someone who has everything he or she wanted? It can be frustrating! When you give a gift, you want it to be special, you want it to be appreciated. It really doesn't do to give someone something they already have. So how do you give a gift to God, the one who has everything? The key is in this psalm passage.

The psalmist says God delights in those who fear him and hope in him, rather than the strength of a horse or human. Why?

I suspect the root of this lies in the fact that God made the horse and human. God made the muscles and set the legs in motion. No horse or human has responsibility for getting their legs. No horse decided to go to the leg market and say, "give me some legs, preferably that really strong set over there." Neither did any person. In a sense, those are "gifts God already has."

But there is a real difference in the strength of horses or people, and the decisions and volition of the heart and mind. Our fear of God or our hope in him come from our minds. Those are our decisions. We decide: shall we fear God or people? Are we awed by God and his power, his authority, his essence, or are we dismissive, being more impressed with people and things of this world? Do we trust in God, making him our hope and confidence, or do we trust in things of this world that we can see and touch?

God takes pleasure in what we are doing toward him, not what DNA does for us. If God just wanted a strong and fast horse, he could make one. God wants us to bring to him our trust, our worship, our dedication. That is something we can give him that he doesn't produce for himself. God gave us the ability to make real choices. When we choose for him, that is a precious gift we give to him.

So what am I to do with my day? I am going to think about God's greatness, and grow in awe and respect for him. I am going to let that awe and respect inform my choices of how I live and what I do. I am going to hope in him, knowing he is going to provide for me. He is going to sort through my problems, and give me direction. He is going to give me peace and patience. He is going to give me wisdom. This is my gift to God, and not surprisingly, my gift to him, blesses me the most!

Lord, I give you my heart, my respect, my trust, and my life. In Jesus' name, Amen!

❊ ❊ ❊

DECEMBER 23

Sing to the LORD with thanksgiving; make melody to our God on the lyre! He covers the heavens with clouds; he prepares rain for the earth; he makes grass grow on the hills. He gives to the beasts their food, and to the young ravens that cry. (Ps. 147:7-9)

Some cynical people might read this psalm's proclamation as "*He covers the heavens with clouds*" and say, "He doesn't do that! Ignorant psalmist!!! We know better! That is called 'condensation.' It is a natural process!" However, we should never discount the psalmist so easily!

Of course there is a natural order of things. Condensation, which the psalmist likely didn't understand, is but one example. The psalmist certainly understood that the scavenger bird ate dead carrion, but that didn't stop the psalmist from giving that credit to God. When the lion would devour the dead carcass of an antelope, the psalmist still saw that as God's work.

We have become such a science-minded society that we have divorced any working of the natural world from the hand of God. Some have unknowingly put God in a box. God is no longer allowed to work in the natural order of the world. Are we to really assume that the only thing God can do is something unnatural? I hope not!

I think that in this twenty-first century, as we have uncovered more and more the intricate workings of nature, we are seeing in greater detail the magnificent hand of God. God is responsible for the cosmos! Before time, God set the knobs of the machine we call nature. If the cosmic rays of the sun are going to cause an energy transference through the chlorophyll in plants to cause growth, place oxygen into our atmosphere, and more, then God be praised! We needn't remove those incredible processes from God and assign them to a random generator of nature. Grass is no accident! Trees didn't grow simply because atoms got together and started DNA strands that mutated. There is a God behind nature who set the processes in place. He upholds nature and made it what it needs to be in precise detail such that this world reflects his glory.

As we learn more about nature, we learn more about God. As we see how things work, we have more reasons to praise him. In the marvels of medical advances, we praise the God who built into nature those processes scientists discover. When we split the atom, we should be in awe of the power God has placed into our universe. As Christians, we understand that all of these devices are placed at our disposal to help conquer the destruction of fallen humanity, and bring some salve into our lives until the Lord replaces this universe with the perfect one to come.

Amazing Lord, may we credit you as the one gracing this world. In Jesus, Amen!

❊ ❊ ❊

DECEMBER 24

Great is our Lord, and abundant in power; his understanding is beyond measure. The LORD *lifts up the humble; he casts the wicked to the ground.* (Ps. 147:5-6)

In the twenty-first century, we know the importance of power! A hurricane put out the power in Houston, vividly reminding everyone of the need for power. People sweltered in the heat without air conditioning. There were no lights, and while that was okay during the day, nighttime became a scary adventure. Getting the power restored became priority one. Power is important in many ways. We need power in our cars when we try to pass the slow driver in front of us. We need power in our military if we wish to defend freedom. We have "power lifters" who weight train to grow powerful muscles. Power can also be used negatively. We speak of "abuse of power" in economic and political structures.

Power exists on so many different levels, and it should remind us of the Lord, who is abundant in power. God is our power source that fuels our personal power needs. Here are a few examples, I'm sure you can think of more. God has the power to overcome sin (Rom. 8:1-4). God has the power to give his people tools to build up and edify the church (1 Cor. 12:1-11). God has the power to overcome personal guilt (1 John 3:19-20). God has the power to help us overcome Satan (1 John 5:4). God has the power to raise Jesus from the dead (Rom. 1:4) and to raise us from the dead (1 Cor. 6:14). God has the power to save believers in Christ (Rom. 1:16-17). God has power over earthly leaders and power figures (Rom. 9:17). God has the power to takes life's difficulties and from them, bring good to his children (2 Cor. 4:7-12). God can destroy strongholds of darkness that bring foreboding and doom on the unsuspecting (2 Cor. 10:4). God can strengthen our thoughts, wills, emotions, when the world shakes us up (Eph. 3:16). God upholds the universe by his power (Heb. 1:3).

We need not fear in this life. We worship a powerful God. And he is using his power for our good, infusing us with power, love, and self-control (2 Tim. 1:7). God can take our weaknesses, or lack of power, and infuse them with his power (2 Cor. 12:9). He has an immeasurable power that he brings to work in our lives (Eph. 1:19). And when our lives are over, this powerful God will transform us into a glorious state for his eternity (Phil. 3:21). For God guards our lives through faith for this salvation (1 Pet. 1:5).

Lord, we worship you as the powerful God. Your power overcomes all difficulties in our lives. You overcome the enemy and his power. Please lift us when we fall. Please infuse us with strength. Forgive us for trying to live this life with our own power. We want and need yours! In Jesus' powerful name, Amen!

❧ ❧ ❧

DECEMBER 25

*The L*ORD *builds up Jerusalem; he gathers the outcasts of Israel. He heals the broken-hearted and binds up their wounds.* (Ps. 147:2-3)

The Old Testament often speaks in images and themes. These ideas are then brought into a renewed focus in the New Testament. One such image is in this passage, *"The L*ORD *builds up Jerusalem."*

In the Old Testament history, Jerusalem becomes a focal point once King David attacks and wins the city for the Israelites. He builds up its defenses, and his son Solomon follows suit. Over the centuries, many of the ruling kings of Judah would leave their mark on the city—its homes, shops, the temple and its courts—and the defensive walls and gates. Jerusalem became "the city of God," and the temple was built there. Even though people labored to build Jerusalem, God's hand was behind the construction.

There came a point where the city was destroyed by the invading Babylonians. For several generations it lay in ruins until, by the grace of God, Jews were allowed to return and the process of rebuilding the city, its temple, and the defensive walls began anew. This was again seen as the hand of God building the city.

Jesus prophesied that the city would again come to ruin (Matt. 24), something that happened toward the end of the first century and in the early second century when the Romans stomped out a Jewish rebellion. But this was not all the Bible said about Jerusalem. The theme of God building Jerusalem finds a final chorus in the vision called Revelation at the end of the Bible. Speaking of the end of days, John saw, "a new heaven and a new earth, for the first heaven and the first earth had passed away, and the sea was no more. And I saw the holy city, new Jerusalem, coming down out of heaven from God, prepared as a bride adorned for her husband" (Rev. 21:1-2). Again, God has built Jerusalem, this time as a bride adorned for her husband.

The vision is one of God's redeemed, the bride of Christ. In Revelation 19:7, just two chapters earlier, we read that, "the bride has made herself ready," yet in Revelation 21:1-2, God has prepared the bride. We are reading the same theme from the Old Testament and this psalm. Yes, we believers work to prepare ourselves for Jesus, just as the people of God built up Jerusalem of old. But it is really the hand of God at work. He is preparing his people as a bride for Jesus. God is at work in your life and mine! Get ready!!

Lord, please continue to work in us for your good pleasure and purposes. May we work through the salvation you have worked in us as we prepare for Jesus, Amen!

❧ ❧ ❧

DECEMBER 26

Praise the LORD! For it is good to sing praises to our God; For it is pleasant, and a song of praise is fitting. (Ps. 147:1)

This psalm begins with an imperative or order. It is an instruction: Praise the Lord! Why? The psalm tells us: it is good, pleasant, and fitting.

It is a good thing to praise God. When we lift him up in praise we are focusing on him. Focusing on God gives us a fresh perspective on life, including life's blessings and problems. We see our blessings flowing from his hand and this stirs up our gratitude. We see problems as opportunities for God to work in us and through us. They become our chances to grow before him in faith and understanding. It is good to praise the Lord.

It is also a pleasant thing to do! Praising God is not hard. It brings us joy and peace. As we reflect on God in praise, we reflect on all the ways he has raised us up as his people. He pours his Spirit upon us and we grow in joy, and other fruits of the Spirit (Gal. 5:22). There is no greater peace (another fruit of the Spirit) that we will enjoy than the peace that comes from praise. In the presence of God, we are reminded of his protection. We experience Paul's assurance that nothing can separate us from God's love (Rom. 8:35-39). Indeed, nothing can separate us from worship and praise of our God! Praising our God is a pleasant thing to do.

It is also fitting to praise our God. Praise is not simply heaping empty phrases or meaningless refrains. It is a proclamation of truth. God is a fitting recipient of praise. We praise people for accomplishments, but look at the accomplishments of our God! I consider them personally: He called me by name. He blessed me with a magnificent family. He forgave my rebellious sins, my stupid sins, and my unknowing sins. He brought me the fine gifts of friendships. He gave me skills and talents to use for the grand purposes of his kingdom. Life's disappointments and pains have not been wasted or destructive, but he has used them to sculpt me into the person I am today. He has rescued me from pits of my own making and from snares of others. He has taught me wisdom and instruction. He has stoked in me a love for his word. He has put a joy in my heart and a peace in my soul. All of this, and it is a drop in the ocean compared to all he's done and will continue to do in my life. Yes, it is fitting and pleasant, and good to sing praises to our God!

Lord, in Jesus' name, I lift you up in praise. You are good beyond measure. Your kind and faithful love stretches from eternity, through my life, into eternity. I am amazed at your love. There is no one like you, our God! Amen!

❧ ❧ ❧

DECEMBER 27

Praise the Lord*! Praise the* Lord *from the heavens; praise him in the heights! Praise him, all his angels; praise him, all his hosts! Praise him, sun and moon, praise him, all you shining stars! Praise him, you highest heavens, and you waters above the heavens!* (Ps. 148:1-4)

Every so often at our church, the worship pastor invites those interested to join the choir. He makes it clear, one doesn't need to know how to read music, one doesn't have to have a good voice, one just needs to make a commitment to join in with others singing as best as they can to the glory of God. I like this. Our worship leader has the perspective of the Psalms.

Psalm 148 calls us to join the heavenly chorus that is praising God. We can join with those already lifting God up as Creator and Sustainer, those who by their very existence signal the greatness of the God who planned this world, who placed the laws of nature into motion, and who is responsible for life.

Throughout the fourteen verses in this psalm, we read of many praising God: angels and the heavenly hosts, sun, moon, stars, great creatures in the oceans, fire, hail, snow, mist, storms and wind, mountains, hills, fruit trees, cedars, beasts and livestock, creeping things, birds, kings, peoples from the world over, the young, the old, men and women, all these are in choir singing praises to the Lord.

We are called to join the heavenly choir! It doesn't matter how good our voice is. We don't have to read music. There is a universe in chorus to the Lord, and we're the ones missing out should we fail to join!

The psalmist tells us reasons to praise him, using those reasons as the praise within the psalm itself. Praise the Lord because his name alone is exalted. No one has done what our God has done. No one has taken the interest in saving and helping humanity that our God has. God has "raised up a horn" for his people. The horn was not only an instrument; it was a battle cry. It was a sound for victory. God has raised the horn and played the instrument of our victory. We are now in the position to join the chorus of his praise.

This psalm has inspired a number of songs and lyrical writings, from St. Francis to T. S. Eliot. We can write our praise verses by the lives we lead. As we live to his glory, giving him the credit, we join the grander chorus. How could we pass up singing in this chorus?

Lord, we lift you up as the King of kings and Lord of lords. You have blessed us and loved us without measure. May we live to sing your praises, living in Jesus' name, Amen!

❧ ❧ ❧

DECEMBER 28

He adorns the humble with salvation. (Ps. 149:4)

Humility is an interesting virtue, in contrast to its counterpart pride. Pride is a self-adornment, where we try to show a watching world our achievements and accomplishments, taking personal credit in the process. Scripture teaches that pride puts the proud into a position that only God should occupy. No human is a self-accomplishment. If I accomplish anything worthy of praise, the one who made me, guides me, empowers me, and sustains me is the one who is to be praised. Yet in spite of this truth, pride is a lure that entices the best of people.

Humility, as the counterpart, is a godly recognition that we are not self-made. We are God's handiwork. The humble understand that if we accomplish what the world thinks are great things, then we have done only what God has enabled. If our skill set seems to be something worthy of praise, the praise should go to the Lord above who gave us those skills. If our minds are able to fathom great mysteries, then we gratefully acknowledge the one who opens mysteries to the mind.

In this psalm, we read that God "adorns" the humble with salvation. The Hebrew "adorns" conveys the idea of "beautifying" or "glorifying." God makes the humble beautiful, bringing glory to those who walk in humility. Now the contrast with pride stands out even more. The proud try to bring themselves glory, hoping others see them as something special. The humble do not try to bring themselves glory or beauty in the eyes of others, but those are the very ones that God adorns. The ones who try to make themselves something special are rarely successful, but the one who relies on God is special in that very reliance.

Peter said much the same thing writing, "Clothe yourselves, all of you, with humility toward one another, for 'God opposes the proud but gives grace to the humble.' Humble yourselves, therefore, under the mighty hand of God so that at the proper time he may exalt you" (1 Pet. 5:5-6). James 4:10 tells believers to "humble yourselves before the Lord and he will exalt you." It is an inverse rule. As we lift ourselves and try to show ourselves of special value, God will bring the proud down. "The lofty pride of men shall be humbled" (Isa. 2:11). Meanwhile those who walk in humility before God, he lifts up.

This should, of course, be genuine humility, not a fake veneer work to show oneself great. It needs to be a genuine recognition that the great God is the only reason for any greatness.

Father, may we walk in humility, joyful at bringing you all the glory for everything we accomplish or do. You are the worthy one, Lord. In Jesus' name, Amen!

❀ ❀ ❀

DECEMBER 29

The LORD takes pleasure in his people. (Ps. 149:4)

This might stun some people, but I suspect not those with children! Parents delight in their children. I remember the birth of each of our children. I remember watching them grow and develop. I took great joy in their first steps. I loved hearing them learn to talk and sing. As they got older, I reveled in their various stages of growth. Whenever I would lament the passing days that couldn't be repeated, I maintained joy in my heart because the current days were so great! Every stage that passed was a blessed memory as the days unfolding contained even more joy. Now that my children are adults (basically), I get to enjoy them in a whole new way.

I know what it is like to take pleasure in my children, and it gives me reasons to think of God's pleasure in his children. I love it when my children walk in fellowship with God. I know God takes pleasure in this as well. I love it when my children love each other and are a tight group. This is how God wants the fellowship of the saints to be. It means the world to me when my children want to spend time with me. I know God takes pleasure in my time with him. I am touched when my children honor Becky and me, and show us respect. God appreciates his children recognizing his honor and the respect that is rightfully his.

None of this is to say that God is an egoist, looking for his children to serve him, laud him, and make him feel good about himself. Far from it. God's pleasure with his children is rooted in his giving, not his taking. God has given his children life. That life is one with dignity and value, as God made it in his own image. God purchased his children with the greatest price that could be paid, becoming human and humbly dying in our stead at the hands of sinners.

God's pleasure in us is based on God's character first and foremost. Then in line with his character, as we live right before him, he takes delight in helping and experiencing our growth. He made us human beings, and enjoys our human expressions. He made us creative and enjoys our creativity. He made us with an ability to make choices, and he loves when we make wise choices. He made us able to receive gifts from him, and he loves to give us gifts we use.

So I look forward to living in ways that give him pleasure. That is right, fitting, and warmly fulfilling.

Lord, we pray that you will take pleasure and delight in what we do. May we do it to your glory in Jesus, Amen!

DECEMBER 30

Praise the LORD! *Sing to the* LORD *a new song, his praise in the assembly of the godly.*
(Ps. 149:1)

You don't have to be around Christians for long before you'll hear someone say, "Why can't we just sing the old songs?" meaning the songs they grew up with. This refrain is repeated throughout church history. Martin Luther was harangued for introducing new songs into the church, almost as much as he was for his other Reformation changes. I've heard it multiple times in my five decades. It happened in high school when we began singing a new set of songs that grew out of the Jesus movement. It happened again in adulthood when the church moved to more contemporary songs. I even heard it recently from a friend who wrote some of the contemporary songs of a few decades ago!

Christian praise is as contemporary as God. Some may think of God as an old man, after all he is called the Ancient of Days (Dan. 7:9). But we need to be careful, because we err if we think of God as old in the sense of out-of-date. God is as contemporary as tomorrow. Each generation finds a fresh God and a fresh expression of praise. My job is not to enforce worship of days gone by, but to continue to use meaningful songs of praise from the past, while encouraging and seeking out new ways of expressing praise in new songs. This reinforces the freshness of God's voice to the newer generations, and it also places responsibilities on that generation to lead forth in praise. This is a good thing.

Some get a bit nervous because the old songs are comfortable. We know the words and melodies. That's okay, but we can always learn more!

I have gone to church not always enamored with the "sound" of new songs, but I know new songs are important. God has called for them. And as I've learned those songs, God has spoken into my heart. Many of the new songs have become my soundtrack for these years of my life. For example, I have a Hillsong playlist of new songs that transform me and my worship. If you had told me in my youth that I would be singing new church songs out of an Australian Christian movement, I would have been surprised. But God uses those new songs to change me into a better image of his Son.

So let's sing a new song to the Lord! Let's get into church and find those new expressions of praise, and raise our voices. Let's learn the words, learn the music, and sing loudly. Let's not be bashful about praising our God!

Lord, please raise up a new generation of songwriters, giving us new and fresh songs for your praise. Speak to the new generations of believers, and be praised in our assemblies. In Jesus' name, Amen!

DECEMBER 31

Praise the LORD! *Praise God in his sanctuary; praise him in his mighty heavens! Praise him for his mighty deeds; praise him according to his excellent greatness! Praise him with trumpet sound; praise him with lute and harp! Praise him with tambourine and dance; praise him with strings and pipe! Praise him with sounding cymbals; praise him with loud clashing cymbals! Let everything that has breath praise the* LORD! *Praise the* LORD! (Ps. 150)*

The Psalms end fittingly with a call for a grand chorus of praise. It is an invitation, written as an instruction, to Praise the LORD! The call is to everyone. The call is for all skill sets. Every expression of praise is to be used.

I will heed the directive. As this devotional year comes to an end, my pledge is to bring God fitting praise and worship in the coming year. I want to go out on a high note of praise, and bring in the new year on an even higher note of praise, trusting God to grow me into an instrument of greater praise every day.

I will also heed the instruction to bring all I have to praise him. I don't necessarily deliver on dance with my body (at least not very well), but my spirit will dance before the Lord in joy, appreciating all he has done for me, and how he has set my spirit free. He set me free from the bondage and shame of sin. He set me free from the worries of the world. He set me free from bitterness, placing his love in my heart. He has given my soul reasons to dance in his praise.

I don't own cymbals, but I will set my hands to the work of praising God loudly! As I work in the coming year, my work will be to the glory and praise of God. I will seek to serve his kingdom next year in the ways I treat my family, my friends, and even strangers. He has prepared some things for me to do, he has empowered me to do them, and I eagerly plan to do them with joy in my heart, living in service to my king.

I have breath I can use to praise the LORD. With that breath, I will follow Psalm 150 and call others to praise God with me. I will tell others about what God has done for me, and what he has done for them. I will share the good news without fear or shame. I am not trying to bash anyone over the head with the gospel, but I will look for the doors he opens for me to call forth praise from others.

Lord, I praise you in Jesus' name, I lift up your awesome deeds, the salvation you have worked in my life. Reflecting back on this year, Father, you have blessed me, protected me, grown me, provided for me, and loved me without measure. I praise you! Amen!

❧ ❧ ❧